D1465693

CLEMENT MAROT

CLEMENT MAROT

POET OF THE
FRENCH RENAISSANCE

P. M. SMITH

BIRKBECK LIBRARY COLLEGE

UNIVERSITY OF LONDON
THE ATHLONE PRESS
1970

Published by
THE ATHLONE PRESS
UNIVERSITY OF LONDON
at 2 *Gower Street, London* WC1
Distributed by Tiptree Book Services Ltd
Tiptree, Essex

Australia and New Zealand
Melbourne University Press

U.S.A.
Oxford University Press Inc
New York

© *P. M. Smith,* 1970

0 485 11115 2

Printed in Great Britain by
WESTERN PRINTING SERVICES LTD
BRISTOL

PREFACE

It is a feature of Marot's poetry that it combines the virtues of the popular native tradition with a growing awareness of what was to be gained from a familiarity with the poets of Classical Antiquity. This dual character of his work, together with the fact that it illuminates one of the most turbulent periods in the cultural, intellectual and religious history of France, and indeed, of Europe as a whole, makes it a particularly interesting object of study from many points of view.

In spite of this, his work has been largely neglected in this country. This is not surprising when one remembers the similar neglect which has, until recent years, attended English poetry, with the exception of Shakespeare's sonnets, of the Elizabethan era. For the conventions of the latter which found little favour in the post-Romantic era are scarcely different from those within which Marot functioned. It is in fact almost a hundred years now since the first and only full length (which is not to say complete) study of Marot appeared in English when Henry Morley, Professor of English Literature at University College, London, published his *Clément Marot and Other Studies* in 1871.

The need for a new, and complete, study of Marot's life and works is not only to be justified by previous neglect however. The amount of knowledge which has recently been made available by the scholarly researches of Professor C. A. Mayer, and to a lesser extent of others, on Marot, his poetry, and the important place he occupies in the history of French poetry, is vast. The aim of the present work is to take into account all recent research on this subject, since this is something which cannot be claimed of existing studies in French,[1] and to make it generally accessible. This does not, of course, preclude its author from taking and expressing, in the last analysis, a personal standpoint.

This work is intended principally for undergraduate students of French literature, as well as for students of English, of History, and the general reader, who may have particular interest in the period of the Renaissance.

This is why, in spite of some disadvantages inherent in it, we have adopted the life and works scheme, instead of a study of the two combined under chronological headings. Our chapter headings are, as far as possible, self-explanatory. Information on any particular topic is not therefore difficult to find for the non-specialist unfamiliar with the chronology of Marot's life and works.

It is hoped that this work will provide the student with an introduction to the subject, and the notes, slightly more specialized, indications for further study.

Last but not least, my thanks are due to Professor C. A. Mayer for his kind permission to quote from his text of Marot's epigrams in the fifth volume (prior to its publication) of his critical edition of Marot, *Les Œuvres de Clément Marot*, University of London, The Athlone Press, 1958–.

P. M. S.

CONTENTS

To
My Parents

I

THE CONTEXT OF MAROT'S POETRY

THE CRITICAL PERSPECTIVE

No appreciation of the poetry of Clément Marot can be complete
without a knowledge of the context in which it was conceived, and
received. To say this much is not to deny the intrinsic literary
merit of Marot's poetry but, on the contrary, to reach an understanding and an explanation of it.

The notion fostered by Matthew Arnold in response to the plea
for historicity made by a nineteenth-century editor of Clément
Marot, Charles d'Héricault, that the 'historic estimate' of poetry
is prejudicial to the aesthetic appreciation and enjoyment of a
poem[1] is one fallacy which we may profitably discard. Perspective
is not a substitute for appreciation but a necessary prelude to it.

Another fallacy, even more tenacious since it still finds currency
among English readers nurtured from their schooldays on the
Romantic persuasion and its Victorian aftermath, is that certain
subjects, and certain subjects only, are proper to Poetry. It is
represented by the morbid contention that the only genuine
poetry is the poetry of self-expression, or 'poetry...conceived in
the soul'.[2] Of the many ideas on poetry voiced in the nineteenth
century by critics far from detached, it is difficult to recall any
which have more effectively prejudiced the wide enjoyment of
poetry—poetry, that is, conceived in other terms—or indeed, one
more unfounded. For it is impossible to prove that communion
with self and the soul is a more adequate pretext for poetry than
some external stimulus and that poetry inspired by the former
has, necessarily, greater intrinsic merit than poetry inspired by
the latter.

To judge Marot by the limited criteria of the last century then,
would be to misjudge him. To the elegant wit and humour with
which he charmed the court, and the verve and wistfulness with
which he spoke of love, he added a fervent commitment to the

ideal of Renaissance in France. Some of his greatest poetry, satirical and lyrical alike, was forged by the intensity of this moment.

THE MAN: 1496?–1544

The titles of many of Marot's poems provide the casual reader with a calendar of his progress. This is particularly so of the *Epîtres* and to a lesser extent of the *Epigrammes* which often have as their pretext, and in varying degrees their inspiration, the incidents of his life.

Marot's poetry, in fact, is often the only source of information available to the biographer. This is certainly the case for his early years. Nor is this source as complete as one would wish. The poems contain no clue to the reasons which induced Marot's father, Jean Marot, himself a poet in the *Rhétoriqueur* tradition, and who was originally from Caen in Normandy, to settle in the south, although Marot speaks of his father and his circumstances several times.[3] Nor do they contain any references to his mother or his wife.

Marot's probable date of birth and other indications are provided by the poem *L'Enfer*, written in the spring of 1526.[4] We learn that he was born in Cahors, the capital of Quercy,

> ...Au lieu que je declaire
> Le fleuve Lot coule son eaue peu claire,
> Qui maints rochiers transverse & environne,
> Pour s'aller joindre au droict fil de Garonne.
> A brief parler, c'est Cahors en Quercy,
> Que je laissay...   (*O.S.*, *L'Enfer*, vv. 391–6)

that he spent the first ten years of his life almost in this southern region speaking the *langue d'oc* and not the French which was his father's tongue, until, one day, he was taken by his father to the great royal houses of France where he has remained to the present day, some twenty years later:

> N'ayant dix ans, en France fus meiné;
> Là où depuis me suis tant pourmeiné
> Que j'oubliay ma langue maternelle,
> Et grossement aprins la paternelle,

Langue Françoyse es grands Courts estimée,
Laquelle en fin quelcque peu s'est limée,...
C'est le seul bien que j'ay acquis en France,
Depuis vingt ans...   (ibid., vv. 399–404, 407–8)

According to this information then, he would have been born in
1496.

Towards 1506 his father entered the service of Anne de
Bretagne, queen of France, as *valet de la garde-robe*.[5] He had
secured this position through the good offices of Michelle de
Saubonne, baronne de Soubise, herself a member of the queen's
household. Marot was later to reflect upon this fact when she
served the son as well as she had once served the father:

...long temps a tu fus premiere source
De bon recueil à mon pere vivant,
Quant à la court du Roy fut arrivant,
Où tu estoys adoncq la myeulx aymée
D'Anne, par tout Royne tant renommée.
                    (*Ep.*, XL, vv. 18–22)

Of Marot's boyhood we know nothing certain. The pleasures
and pursuits of a country childhood so delicately evoked in the
eclogue presented to François Ier in 1539, while they may
correspond to the reality of the poet's experience, are certainly
literary in inspiration.[6] Of his early youth at court, whether in
one of the many châteaux on the

...Loyre, qui des enfance
Fut mon sejour...   (*Ep.*, XLIV, vv. 50–51)

or in Paris, we know almost nothing. Much has been written on
the subject of Marot's education nevertheless. It seems that the
formal instruction he received at this time was very slight,[7] and
certainly, given the period, it would have been as yet untouched
by the new learning. Of this early education Marot complains
bitterly in the second *coq-à-l'âne*, written in 1535:

En effect, c'estoient de grands bestes
Que les Regents du temps jadis;
Jamais je n'entre en Paradis
S'ilz ne m'ont perdu ma jeunesse.
            (*O.S.*, VIII, *2e Coq a l'Asne*, vv. 118–21)

However, since these lines contain an unmistakable echo of humanist attitudes to medieval education as they had been epitomized the year previously in Rabelais's *Gargantua* in the caricature of the two sophist tutors Jobelin Bridé and Thubal Holoferne,[8] they belong to satirical commonplace as much as to autobiography. This fact should make us cautious in assessing the value of these lines to our knowledge of the poet's early life, although a commonplace may always correspond to a personal reality. The realization of opportunities denied to him under a system since reformed, the comparison between what was, and might have been which these lines imply, is perhaps a commonplace of this kind: a natural and entirely credible reaction on the part of a man entering middle years in circumstances compelling self-examination—for the poem was written in exile. Frequently quoted and taken in conjunction with Marot's revelation of his own attempts to improve himself culturally:

> Tu trouveras ceste langue italique
> Passablement dessus la mienne entée,
> Et la latine en moy plus augmentée...
>
> (*Ep.*, XXXVII, vv. 44–46)

in the epistle to the king on his convalescence written at virtually the same period,[9] these lines provided one basis for accounts of Marot's lack of attainments.[10] The statement of a friend and contemporary of the poet, Jean de Boysonné, in a letter written in 1547,[11] that 'Marotus latine nescivit' would appear to add weight to these accounts. By the standards of Boysonné, as also of Du Bellay and Estienne Pasquier who were later to comment on Marot's lack of letters,[12] it is true that his knowledge of Latin was not great. But it is possible to exaggerate Marot's deficiencies in this respect, and rival poets certainly did so![13] There is a certain perspective to be gained from comparing Marot's attainments with those of Shakespeare in so far as they are known.'Thou hast small Latine, and lesse Greeke'[14] would apply equally to both. Yet their suspect latinity prevented neither of them from working with Latin texts in the original when they so desired.[15] Unlike Rabelais, Marot knew no Greek at all, or Hebrew for that matter.

Marot's entry as a page into the service of Nicolas de Neufville, Seigneur de Villeroy, one of the king's secretaries, a man of considerable influence and fortune,[16] dates from the beginning of the period 1515–1519. It is difficult to be more precise than this. Such information as we have comes from a letter preceding the poem *Le Temple de Cupido* in the 1538 edition of the *Œuvres*. In this letter Marot dedicates the poem, composed between 1515 and 1520 and published for the first time during this period, although without indication of date or place,[17] to

> ...Messire Nicolas de Neufville,
> Chevalier, Seigneur de Villeroy.
> Clem. Marot.

En revoyant les escriptz de ma jeunesse, pour les remettre plus clerz, que devant, en lumiere, il m'est entré en memoire que estant encores page, & à toy, treshonoré Seigneur, te composay par ton commandement la queste de ferme Amour...C'est bien raison donques, que l'oeuvre soit à toy dediée, à toy qui la commandas, à toy mon premier maistre, & celluy seul (hors mis les Princes) que jamais je servy. Soit donques consacré ce petit Livre à ta prudence, noble Seigneur de Neufville... (*O.L.*, I, n. 1)

How long Marot remained with Nicolas de Neufville is difficult to say. Probably only a short time since he is next at work as a clerk in the law courts of Paris. A *ballade* written between 1515 and 1519 which bears the title *De soy mesme du temps qu'il apprenoit à escrire au Palais à Paris* and which alludes in passing to 'mon Maistre Jehan Grisson', a lawyer with whom Marot may have been particularly associated,[18] is the source here in the absence of any documentary evidence. Marot refers again to this period of his life in the epistle to Antoine Duprat:

> C'est pour Marot, vous le congnoissez ly...
> Et a suivy long temps Chancellerie.
>
> (*Ep.*, XIII, v. 51, v. 53)

It is worth noting that in writing to enlist the aid of this powerful figure who held the highest legal office in France,[19] Marot would naturally stress any aspect of his career which would commend him to his would-be protector. The vague allusion to his long apprenticeship to the law may conceal a tactical exaggeration. On the other hand, however, no information exists as to other employment which the poet might have pursued had there been an interval between his clerkship and the next stage of his career.[20]

Marot's father Jean had been retained in his post of *valet de la garde-robe* by François Ier whose protection he had enjoyed since the death of Anne de Bretagne in 1514, that is while François was still duc d'Angoulême.[21] Marot's own aspirations to similar status and protection seem to date approximately from this period. At least, he offered to François one of his earliest compositions, *Le Jugement de Minos*.[22] He refers to the reception which François accorded to the work when dedicating to him the first published version of the *Temple de Cupido*:

...une fille inconstante nommée Jeune hardiesse me incitoit de vous presenter ce petit traicté d'amourettes en me disant: Pourquoy differes tu? Fuz tu mal recueilly lors que luy presentas le jugement de Mynos? Adonc je respondy: Ma jeune fille, Le recueil que ce hault prince me fist alors fut de la sorte dont maintesfois l'avois souhaité. (*O.L.*, I, n. 1)

Having thus brought himself to the notice of François, Marot put his aspirations into verse in the *Petite Epistre au Roy* (I) written between 1518 and 1519:

> Si vous supply qu'à ce jeune Rimeur
> Faciez avoir ung jour par sa rime heur,
> Affin qu'on die, en prose ou en rimant:
> Ce Rimailleur, qui s'alloit enrimant,
> Tant rimassa, rima et rimonna,
> Qu'il a congneu quel bien par rime on a.
>
> (*Ep.*, I, vv. 21–26)

His petition did not go unanswered. At the instance of the king Marot was presented to Marguerite d'Angoulême his sister, duchesse d'Alençon et de Berry.[23] In 1519 he entered her service as a secretary.[24] So began the long association between Marot and Marguerite and her circle which was to exert such a profound influence on his life and on his future development as a poet.[25]

For the time being, however, Marot's life seems to have progressed without incident, other than those, of course, in which he was involved in the course of his duties. In 1521, for instance, he accompanied the duc d'Alençon on a military campaign in Flanders. The experience is described in the *Epistre du Camp d'Atigny à ma dicte Dame d'Alençon* (III). Written in the summer of that year, the epistle has a sequel in the prose letter which

Marot wrote to Marguerite on the progress of the army led by François against the troops of the emperor Charles V in Picardy in the autumn.[26] After 1521 there follows a long period in Marot's life which is almost totally undocumented.[27] Nor is it possible to state with any certainty and precision which of the poems belong to this period. Needless to say, in the absence of information, legend abounds. Such is the story of Marot's presence at the battle of Pavia in 1525 where he was supposedly not only wounded but also taken prisoner. This story may have gained some credence from the evidence quoted above of Marot's earlier presence on the military scene, even in a strictly limited and non-combatant role. Its formal basis however was in the elegy sometimes entitled *Epistre du chevallier pris et blecé devant Pavye*.[28] The legend has been convincingly demolished by recent critics.[29] For one thing, it is now known that the poem in question was written to order for an unidentified nobleman. For another, nowhere else does Marot make mention in his poems of the active service he has seen on the king's behalf. Nowhere is this omission more surprising than in the personal statement he makes to his judges in *L'Enfer* in answer to a grave accusation of heresy. In his defence Marot described his present estate, his relationships with the court, the events of his life up to 1526, protested his gratitude to Marguerite and commiserates with her on the captivity of the king her brother in Spanish hands following the disaster at Pavia. In these circumstances, one would have expected an allusion to their community of experience and subsequent hardship: an allusion which would have done more to reinforce Marot's defence than repeated protestations of loyalty.

Rather more is known of Marot's life in the period following 1525 than in the previous years. The reason is simple. Marot begins to make his appearance in the files of the civil and ecclesiastical authorities. The documents which we have, incomplete as they are, do allow us in some cases to test Marot's own accounts— sometimes imaginative and often vague—of his brushes with authority.

At the beginning of March, 1526, Marot was arrested and imprisoned by the civil authorities in the Châtelet in Paris, a circumstance which inspired him to write two epistles, *A Monsieur Bouchard* (IX) and *A son amy Lyon* (X), the poem *L'Enfer* and the *ballade, Contre celle qui fut s'Amye*.[30] What was the cause of this initial imprisonment for which no documents are available? In the first of the poems mentioned above Marot asks this question himself of his prosecutor Bouchard,[31] and answers it with a second question:

> ...Qui t'a induict à faire
> Emprisonner, depuis six jours en ça,
> Ung tien amy, qui onc ne t'offensa?
> Et vouloir mettre en luy crainte & terreur
> D'aigre justice, en disant que l'erreur
> Tiens de Luther?   (*Ep.*, IX, vv 2–7)

Lutheranism is again the charge against which Marot defends himself all too lightly in *L'Enfer*.[32] In the epistle to his friend Lyon Jamet (x) and in the *ballade, Contre celle qui fut s'Amye*, the offence is specified as a transgression of the Church's commandments on abstinence from meat:

> ...pour autant qu'il avoit
> Mangé le lard & la chair toute crue...
>   (*Ep.*, X, vv. 18–19)

The *ballade* incorporates the information in its refrain:

> Prenez le, il a mangé le Lard!
>   (*O.D.*, *Ballade* XIV, v. 8)

In addition, both the *ballade* and *L'Enfer* attribute Marot's arrest on this charge to a denunciation of the poet to the authorities by his mistress, unnamed in the *ballade*, except by allusion to another poem in which she appears as Ysabeau (*Rondeau* LXIII, *De l'inconstance de Ysabeau*):[33]

> Un jour rescrivez à m'Amye
> Son inconstance seulement;
> Mais elle ne fut endormie
> A me le rendre chauldement.
> Car des l'heure tint parlement
> A je ne sçay quel Papelard
> Et luy a dict tout bellement:
> 'Prenez le, il a mangé le Lard.'
>   (*O.D.*, *Ballade* XIV, vv. 1–8)

The passage in *L'Enfer* is a reference back to this *ballade*; the same culprit is symbolized by the name of Luna:

> Bien avez leu, sans qu'il s'en faille ung A,
> Comme je fus par l'instinct de Luna
> Mené au lieu plus mal sentant que soulphre
> Par cinq ou six ministres de ce gouffre.
>
> (*O.S.*, *L'Enfer*, vv. 21–24.)

The question must inevitably be asked: how much of Marot's account of his arrest and imprisonment can be substantiated?

A great deal, and first and foremost the charge of having broken the Lenten abstinence from meat.[34] On 13 March, Louis Guillard, the bishop of Chartres, instructed the ecclesiastical tribunal of Chartres to institute proceedings against Marot on the grounds of heresy, and on the same day issued a warrant for his arrest in those terms. Guillard was thus claiming for his own ecclesiastical jurisdiction, as he had technically the right to do since the area under his control included Paris, a prisoner held by the civil authorities. If Guillard's warrant speaks only of 'variis delictis et offensis, etiam criminibus haeresis'[35] without specifying the particular heretical offence, further documents exist which remedy this omission, documents which relate to a second attempt by the civil authorities some years later in 1532 to rearrest Marot,[36] in the company of Laurent Meigret, an extremely rich financier of the time, and five other named suspects, on a charge described in the proceedings of the higher court, that of the *Parlement* of Paris,[37] as

d'avoir mangé de la chair durant le temps de Karesme & autres jours prohibez.[38]

This second affair throws as much light on the unsavoury political and legal jiggery-pokery of the period as it does on the grounds for Marot's first imprisonment in 1526. Of the six named accused, all equally guilty according to the records, only one, Laurent Meigret, the rich financier, was seriously prosecuted and deprived of his freedom. Although some attempt was made to arrest Marot, it was soon abandoned, and the other suspects, as far as is known, were soon out of danger. Of the six accused only one, Marot, had previously been imprisoned on a charge of heresy. Meigret's indictment for heresy in the company of such a notorious offender as Marot was doubly impressive and immensely plausible. He lost not only his freedom thereby, but also his fortune. The charge of heresy was an extremely simple and effective prelude to expropriation. And since the successful perpetration of this fraud depended on the *fact* of earlier proceedings against Marot which could be conveniently and convincingly reopened, it follows that the documents of the 1532 affair both confirm and enlarge upon Marot's own accounts of the crime for which he was accused in 1526.

The potential seriousness of Marot's plight, the gravity of the charge against him in March 1526, may only be fully defined by reference to the religious history of the period. From 1520 onwards there is increasing evidence of the existence and activities in France of disciples and adherents of Luther. From this moment onwards any reluctance to observe the rites and practices prescribed by the Catholic Church acquired an unhealthy significance: omission became a sin. This, in spite of the fact that Luther in his famous *Theses* of 1517 had said not a word about the Church's commandments on fasting and abstinence in Lent. Nevertheless, the sermons delivered in 1524 at Lyons and Grenoble by the dominican Aimé Meigret, doctor of the Sorbonne, contained, among other propositions which read like a breviary for intending heretics, a defence of Luther and a condemnation, on the grounds that it constituted a negation of Christian free will, of the Church's commandment on abstinence from meat at certain times on pain of eternal damnation.[39] Such was the scandal provoked by these sermons which outraged not only certain dignitaries of the Church in France but also the Queen-Regent, Louise de Savoie, that Aimé Meigret, in spite of the protection afforded him by Marguerite d'Alençon, was arrested and thrown into prison. Catholic reaction in other respects was equally swift, both from the Sorbonne—the Faculty of Theology of Paris and an official organ of the Catholic Church—whose members pledged themselves in a solemn oath to root out by their collective efforts the Lutheran heresy in France,[40] and from the *Parlement* of Paris whose immediate concern it was to set up a special commission which would be empowered to proceed against all suspected heretics, including if need be the highest dignitaries of the Church. Hence their petition to Louise de Savoie to obtain an authorization from the Pope to this effect.[41] The Pope's reply indicated that all those suspected of the Lutheran heresy should be pursued with no right of appeal, that they should be punished with the full severity of the law including the ultimate sanction. The text of the Papal bull describes the errors of the sect with particular reference to their contempt for the Church's commandments on the Lenten abstinence and their failure to observe them.[42] The Papal bull dates from 17 May 1525. On 10 June Louise de Savoie commanded that the Pope's instructions be put into effect.

It is in the context of a situation where breaking the Lenten fast was regarded as conclusive evidence of Lutheran sympathies that Marot's offence must be seen.[43] It is in this context that it assumes the proportions, not of a misdemeanour or of a prank, but of a highly charged act consciously and deliberately committed. For it cannot seriously be argued that Marot, in his capacity of secretary to Marguerite d'Alençon whose sympathies for the new ideas were manifestly shared by many of her entourage, was either ignorant of the implications of his act, or that he intended it to be seen as anything but an act of commitment, perhaps more emotional than intellectual, but an act of commitment nonetheless, to the new ideas.

If Marot's account of his first offence can be substantiated, his story of his denunciation to the authorities by a mistress is pure legend, a legend inspired moreover by literary tradition. Marot would find his precedent in Villon whose influence is perceptible in Marot's early work,[44] notably *L'Enfer*, and whose poems he was later to edit. Villon, after breaking into and robbing the Collège de Navarre, hurriedly left Paris when he was denounced by an accomplice. In the *Lais*, however, he attributes his departure to an unhappy love affair with an unfaithful mistress. In the *Testament* the mistress, Catherine de Vaucelles, who was almost certainly fictitious, is alleged once again to be the source of the poet's misfortunes and the cause of the punishment he now suffers. Although there are many circumstances of Villon's life which Marot cannot possibly have known, there are others which his familiarity with the work of the poet might have led him to suspect, notably the fictitious nature of the mistress and hence of her role.

Marot's fictitious mistress Ysabeau does not appear under this name in any version of the poems in which she is involved until the publication of the 1538 edition of the *Œuvres*.[45] In *L'Enfer*, the same woman, cold and distant, is represented by the name Luna. Luna is no less a product of literary reminiscence being the name given by Chariteo, the Italian Petrarchist poet by whom Marot was much influenced in his poetry at this moment, to his mistress, the archetypal cold and distant woman, in the sequence of poems entitled *Endimione*.

The legend with which Marot thus embellished the account of his arrest and its attendant consequences in 1526 is not at all uncharacteristic. On many subsequent occasions when Marot falls foul of authority an element of fantasy creeps into the narrative for reasons more or less easy to discern. And on this particular occasion? The most plausible hypothesis is that suggested by C. A. Mayer who, noting that Marot delayed until 1534 before publishing the poems relating to this affair, suggests that it had been the poet's concern to attenuate in the public mind the gravity of the charge which had been made against him eight years previously by attributing his accusation to the vindictive action of a woman following a lovers' quarrel.[46]

Many aspects of this episode in Marot's life remain obscure, particularly those relating to his transfer to Chartres and his eventual release. Guillard's intervention in claiming Marot from the *Prévôté* in Paris[47] as a prisoner under the Church's jurisdiction, highlights the fact that Marot's case had not been dealt with at all by the specially constituted commission concerned with suspected heretics. Why we cannot say. No documents exist on Marot's translation to Chartres or on his imprisonment there. It would seem therefore that no further proceedings were taken against him on arrival. The conditions of his detention, unlike those of the Châtelet, were certainly far from severe. His 'prison' was in all probability a hostelry in which Marot was able to write *L'Enfer* and apparently to receive visits from friends, visits alluded to in this same poem.[48]

The net result of Guillard's intervention had been to rescue Marot from a potentially dangerous position. Did he intend this, and if so why? There appears to have been no previous connection between the two men and in any case Louis Guillard was soon to

become one of the most hated and feared enemies of the reformists in France. In all this, what was the role of Marot's friend
Lyon Jamet whose aid the poet ostensibly sought in the epistle
A son amy Lyon (x)?[49] Many other questions of this kind remain
unanswered.

Marot was finally released from captivity on 1 May 1526. The
event is commemorated in the *Rondeau parfaict à ses Amys, apres
sa delivrance*.[50] François had at that moment just returned to
France from his captivity in Madrid. There is possibly more than a
coincidence between the two events. Marot may have owed his
freedom to the king's intervention.

It was to be short-lived in any case. In the following year Marot
was again arrested and imprisoned, this time for having rescued a
prisoner, unidentified, from the hands of the Watch. Nothing
more is known of the circumstances of this affair apart from the
extremely vague account which Marot gave of it to the king in
the epistle in which he petitioned him for his release, *Marot,
Prisonnier, escript au Roy pour sa delivrance* (xi). The king duly
intervened on Marot's behalf in a letter dated 1 November 1527.
The poet had been in prison it seems for only a short time before
he was released.[51]

In the course of the previous year Marot's father Jean had died,
leaving vacant the position he had held in the king's service.
Marot immediately sought leave to succeed his father in his post
of *valet de la garde-robe*. His request was more than granted for
he was given the somewhat higher position of *valet de chambre* to
the king, only to find however at the end of that year that since
his name had been omitted by some oversight from the roll of
persons attached to the king's household, his wages had not been
paid. By numerous petitions in verse Marot then sought to obtain
the money that was due to him, and to have his name placed on
the roll for the following year.[52]

It was in the years 1528–1534 that Marot's position at court
and in the royal favour was most firmly established. It fell to him
to give expression to the hopes and joys occasioned by such events
as a royal marriage, which he did in 1528 in his first epithalamium,
the *Chant nuptial du Mariage de Madame Renée, Fille de France,
& du Duc de Ferrare*;[53] a peace treaty signed at Cambrai in the
summer of 1529 which was to put an end to hostilities between

France and the Holy Roman Empire in the *rondeau*, *De la Paix traictée à Cambray par trois Princesses*;[54] the return from captivity in 1530 of the young French princes, hostages in Spanish hands since 1526, in a *chant de joye* (*Ballade* XVI);[55] the arrival in France and her subsequent marriage at Bordeaux to François Ier of Queen Eléonore who had accompanied the princes from Spain in the epistle *A la Royne Elienor* (XXI).

The royal favour which Marot enjoyed at this time certainly alleviated the double misfortune which overtook him in the year 1531 when he suffered a robbery at the hands of his thieving valet and a grave attack of the plague. He was treated for the latter by three of the king's physicians and was reimbursed by his majesty with the sum of one hundred gold crowns to the extent of the theft. The gift was the outcome of a plea from Marot for a 'loan' in the justly famous epistle traditionally known by the title *Au Roy, pour avoir esté desrobé* (XXV). Yet a third possible calamity was averted when an attempt by the *Parlement* of Paris to have the poet rearrested on an earlier charge of breaking Lent was foiled. This attempt coincided with Marot's convalescence and the absence of the king from Paris in the spring of 1532:

> ...mesmes ung jour ilz vindrent
> A moy mallade, & prisonnier me tindrent,
> Faisant arrest sus ung homme arresté
> Au lict de mort, & m'eussent pis traicté
> Si ce ne fust ta grand' bonté, qui à ce
> Donna bon ordre avant que t'en priasse.
>
> (*Ep.*, XXXVI, vv. 31–36)

In spite of Marot's allusion to the king's intervention on his behalf on this occasion, the documents suggest that it was in fact Marguerite de Navarre, acting through one of her secretaries, Estienne Clavier, who was responsible for the poet's deliverance.[56]

The anxiety which Marot's serious illness had occasioned, the messages of sympathy in verse which he received, both in Latin and in French from fellow poets,[57] many of whom considered him to be their most illustrious representative, as shown by the following lines:

> Il fut un bruit, o Marot, qu'estois mort...
> Morte donq' est Françoise Poésie![58]

are clear indications of Marot's standing at the time and the extent of his fame, which was widespread beyond the confines of the court.

There were, too, other less welcome signs. One was the growing tendency to attribute to Marot the authorship of dubious pieces of verse, scurrilous, satirical, or subversive. This had already happened to Marot once, in 1529, when a scandalous poem attacking the honour of several ladies of the Paris bourgeoisie, *Les Gracieux Adieux Faitz aux Dames de Paris*, had been widely believed to be by him.[59] In vain did he reply with an *Epistre des excuses* protesting his innocence, and that for a very good reason:

> Et ne sortit onc de ma forge
> Ung Ouvrage si mal lymé;
> Et ne sera mien estimé
> Par ceulx qui congnoissent ma veine;
> Il est ung petit mal rimé,
> Et la raison en est bien vaine. (*O.S.*, II, vv. 11–16)

A second denial was necessary, the epistle *Aux Dames de Paris qui ne vouloient prendre les precedentes excuses en payement*. This was more in the nature of a warning for the poet promised to demonstrate

> Combien mieulx picque ung Poete de Roy
> Que les Rimeurs qui ont faict le desroy.
> (*O.S.*, III, vv. 27–28)

Much more serious for the poet's peace of mind, however, was the appearance in 1531 or thereabouts of the first pirated edition of his poems, *Les Opuscules et petitz Traictez de Clement Marot*, printed in Lyons, which was followed by a second pirated edition printed in Paris a year later, in 1532.[60] The potential threat which such editions posed to the poet's security can well be imagined. Apart from the incorrect attribution of possibly subversive poems, even the premature publication of nearly authentic texts unpurged by the poet of the indiscretions or provocations they might contain, and which for this reason he had not yet judged it prudent to commit to print, could have had grave consequences for a man who had already suffered imprisonment for heresy. Realizing this, Marot authorized an expurgated edition of some of his poems which was printed and published in

Paris on 12 August 1532, under the title of the *Adolescence Clementine*. It was a great success and was reprinted at least three times in the years 1532 and 1533.[61] Towards the end of this period, or at the beginning of 1534, a second volume of poems was published under the title *Suite de l'Adolescence Clementine*.[62] In the same year, indeed, very shortly after the appearance of the second volume, a third work by Marot appeared, *Le Premier Livre de la Metamorphose d'Ovide*, a translation he had completed and presented in manuscript form in 1530 or 1531 to Antoine, duc de Guise.[63] A second edition of this work published in 1534 contains additional poems, all those, in fact, inspired by his first imprisonment, with the exception of *L'Enfer*, and here published for the first time.[64] A third consequence of Marot's growing favour at court, and his increasing stature as a poet, was the rivalry he inevitably incurred from poets less inspired and less in favour. Such a one was François Sagon, an obscure poet of the *Rhétoriqueur* tradition.

The year 1534 marks a turning-point in Marot's career. The decision to publish poems relating to his arrest and imprisonment in 1526 at all, indicates a new boldness on Marot's part, even though he retained the subterfuge of the fictitious mistress which he had evolved earlier. The text of the epistle *A Monsieur Bouchard* (IX), contains a statement which is nothing if not compromising:

> ...Point ne suis Lutheriste
> Ne Zuinglien, encores moins Papiste
> (*Ep.*, IX, vv. 7–8, *var.*)

and which, significantly, Marot saw fit to emend in 1538.[65] One may attribute this new mood to two things: confidence and trust in his protectors and a belief, widespread among humanists and many sections of the court, that the long sought after reformation of the Church was imminent. Marot's boldness and optimism may have been at the origin of his quarrel with Sagon whose religious sensibilities he outraged when both were present in August 1534 at the wedding of Isabeau d'Albret to the Vicomte de Rohan.[66] It is believed that on this occasion Marot attempted to convert Sagon, a bigoted Catholic, to the cause of evangelism, thereby transforming poetic rivalry into a far more dangerous enmity.

But it was a circumstance outside Marot's control which was finally to change the course of his life dramatically at this point. This was the *affaire des Placards*.[67] On the night of the 17–18 October 1534, posters denouncing the Catholic mass in the most violent terms were put up in the streets of Paris and other large towns including Amboise where the king was staying at that moment. A poster appeared on the very door of the king's bedchamber. This wanton act by Protestant fanatics which the king was only too easily persuaded by extremists of the Sorbonne and the *Parlement* of Paris constituted a threat not only to religious orthodoxy but also to political stability, to the person and authority of the monarch himself, resulted in the most immediate and atrocious acts of repression, sanctioned by the king in his fury. Arrests, executions, mutilations, of the innocent in the absence of the guilty, followed on a large scale.

Marot's reaction to the furore caused by the *placards* was immediate. He had been in Blois on the night they appeared and without waiting to justify himself in the eyes of the king, or to throw himself on the king's protection, which, if we may believe the account he afterwards gave, had been his first thought:

> ...pour me justifier,
> En ta bonté je m'osay fier
> Que hors de Bloys partys pour à toy, Syre,
> Me presenter. Mais quelcqu'ung me vint dire:
> Si tu y vas, amy, tu n'es pas saige;
> Car tu pourroys avoir maulvais visaige
> De ton seigneur...   (*Ep.*, XXXVI, vv. 163–9)

he took flight. The wisdom of this course of action was only too clearly demonstrated by subsequent developments. Marot was one of the first targets of the *Parlement* of Paris and its officers took immediate action against him as is revealed by a passage from the epistle *Au Roy du temps de son exil à Ferrare*:

> Le Juge doncq' affecté se monstra
> En mon endroict, quand des premiers oultra
> Moy qui estoys absent & loing des villes
> Où certains folz feirent choses trop viles...
>   (ibid., vv. 157–60)

Thwarted by his absence, the magistrates ordered his house to be

searched and all his possessions confiscated. These included books
and manuscripts of work in hand. The same epistle describes the
seizure:

> Rhadamanthus avecques ses suppostz
> Dedans Paris, combien que fusse à Bloys,
> Encontre moy faict ses premiers exploicts,
> En saisyssant de ses mains violentes
> Toutes mes grandz richesses excellentes
> Et beaulx tresors d'avarice delivres,
> C'est assçavoir mes papiers & mes livres
> Et mes labeurs.   (ibid., vv. 124-31)

Two other contemporary accounts confirm these details. Both are
contained in poems written by enemies of Marot, namely Sagon's
Coup d'Essay,[68] and the *Epistre du general Chambor* by an
unknown poet whose pseudonym appears in the title.[69] Written
in reply to Marot's epistle *Au Roy du temps de son exil à Ferrare*,
the latter gives important indications as to the nature of the
manuscripts seized, and their fate. It is clear that a translation of
biblical texts was found:

> De tes papiers que tu nomme sacrez
> Du doy de dieu, que on a tant massacrez,
> Sacrez n'estoyent, mais dampnez & mauldictz,
> Veu les erreurs comprins en leurs tradictz
> Soubz la couleur de l'escripture saincte.
> On a bien sceu d'eux & leur letre faincte
> Feu allumer & les reduyre en cendre,
> Car trop de maulx en eussent peu descendre.[70]

The Sorbonne had formally condemned the translation of the
Bible into the vernacular as an heretical activity. A translation
into French of the sixth Psalm, together with the daily prayers
from the liturgy, by Marot, had already appeared in 1533 in an
edition of Marguerite de Navarre's first work, *Le Miroir de l'Ame
Pécheresse*,[71] a work which the Sorbonne had tried in vain to
suppress. The evidence which the search of Marot's house had
yielded would reveal the full extent of his activities in this
field.

Not content with these measures, however, the authorities

issued a warrant for his arrest, wherever he might be found. Marot had made his way south and west, presumably to seek refuge at the court of Marguerite de Navarre. At the end of November 1534, he was arrested at Bordeaux. The proceedings of the *Parlement* of Bordeaux contain a record of the arrest and of the subsequent interrogation in which Marot declared his identity and his official position as *valet de chambre* to the king and secretary to the Queen of Navarre.[72] Marot's account of the same proceedings in his third *coq-à-l'âne* (vv. 139–62) belongs to the realm of literary fantasy rather than of fact. However, when he goes on to say that he managed to escape and put a safe distance between himself and his would-be captors, we can only assume that this was indeed so, although in exactly what circumstances must remain unknown. The Bordeaux authorities had acted in the first place at the instance of the Paris authorities and were not free to release the prisoner on any lesser authority, but Marot arrived safely at his destination in Navarre, where he placed himself under the protection of Marguerite, in December 1534.

On 25 January 1535 Marot's name appeared on a list of suspected Lutherans who had successfully evaded capture by flight and self-imposed exile, and who, in the event of their failure to appear before the authorities, were to be sentenced in their absence to banishment, forfeiture of their possessions, and death at the stake.[73] Marot's name was high on the list which was issued by public proclamation in the streets of Paris. Four days later, the king published an edict which, by the severity of its terms and the violence of its language, demonstrated his increasing intolerance and renewed determination to root out the Lutheran heresy, to exterminate the sect in France. It was forbidden henceforth, on pain of death, to give asylum to Lutheran fugitives.[74]

These circumstances may explain Marot's departure from Navarre in March 1535, on Marguerite's advice.[75] She obviously felt herself unable, for one reason or another, to guarantee the poet's future security even in her own domains. This did not, however, indicate any withdrawal of her sympathy, or indeed, support, for the poet, for it was almost certainly on her advice that Marot acted once again in choosing for his second place of refuge the court of Renée de France at Ferrara.[76] Indeed, in the epistle written later to Marguerite from Venice, Marot alludes to the

correspondence which passed between Renée de France, duchesse
de Ferrare, and Marguerite on his account:

> Passa ton serf torrentz et montz et vaulz;
> Puis se saulva en la terre italique,
> Dedans le fort d'une dame galique
> Qui le receut, dont la remercias
> Bien tost apres.   (*Ep.*, XLVI, vv. 56–60)

Marguerite therefore continued to work in Marot's interests,
albeit from a distance.

The choice of Ferrara would have been an obvious one for a man
in Marot's position, even without the promptings of Marguerite
de Navarre. For at the court of Ferrara Marot could continue in
the service of a member of the French royal family, his loyalty
unimpeached. This thought was certainly uppermost in his mind
when he later wrote to the king the epistle *Du temps de son exil à
Ferrare* (XXXVI) justifying his actions:

> Et vins entrer aux Lombardes campaignes;
> Puis en l'Itale...
> ...au lieu où residoit
> De ton clair sang une Princesse humaine,
> Ta belle soeur & cousine germaine...
> Parquoy, ô Syre, estant avecques elle,
> Conclure puys d'ung franc cueur & vray zelle
> Qu'à moy, ton serf, ne peult estre donné
> Reproche aulcun que t'aye abandonné.
>   (*Ep.*, XXXVI, vv. 198–202, 209–12)

In addition, Renée's personal entourage was exclusively French,
she herself insisted on speaking nothing but French, and she had
thereby succeeded in creating for herself what might almost be
regarded as a French enclave on Ferrarese soil. She was, too, an
intelligent and cultured woman, appreciating culture and artistic
achievement in others, and she had surrounded herself with
retainers who shared her tastes and attainments. Chief among
these was Michelle de Saubonne, baronne de Soubise whose
protection Marot could count upon—had she not previously
extended her patronage to his father, Jean Marot?[77] In such
circumstances, Marot could look forward to the further development of his poetic gifts fostered by enlightened encouragement:

> Toy et les tiens aymez litterature,
> Sçavoir exquis, vertus qui le ciel percent,
> Artz liberaulx, et ceulx qui s'y exercent;
> Cela (pour vray) fait que tresgrandement
> Je te revere en mon entendement.
>
> (*Ep.*, XL, vv. 28–32)

Last, and by no means least, Renée's Protestant leanings, even more pronounced than those of Marguerite de Navarre, were well known. In this respect, too, her entourage was like-minded.

Marot arrived in Ferrara in April 1535. In an epistle to the duchess (XXXIV) he offered her his services,[78] an offer which was immediately accepted since Renée ordered that Marot was to receive payment for the three quarters of the year from 1 April to the last day of December. In the following year Marot is listed as poet and secretary in the accounts of Renée's entourage.[79] Marot's arrival in Ferrara was followed shortly afterwards by that of two other French Lutheran fugitives, his friend Lyon Jamet, and Jehannet de Bouchefort, who joined a growing contingent.

It is quite clear that Marot's arrival at the court of Ferrara was an event warmly welcomed by the duchess and her entourage, and that Marot's own response was immediate and appreciative. The poems he composed during his stay there bear witness to his involvement in the day-to-day life of the household and of his personal contacts with members of the duchess's suite. One thinks of the epistles addressed to Madame de Pons (XXXVIII), the eldest daughter of Michelle de Saubonne, and, in a more serious vein— for it contains veiled allusions to the circumstances of her departure from Ferrara—to Michelle de Saubonne herself (XL), and finally, to her youngest daughter Renée de Parthenay before she left for France (XLI). And yet it would be a mistake to think that Marot, once in Ferrara, was content to let his links with the king remain severed. Moreover, there were many in France who would seek to damn him irretrievably in the king's sight on the principle that 'les absents ont toujours tort'. Of these dangers Marot was acutely aware. Hence the vigorous self-justification and the outspoken attack on his enemies wherever they might be found, in the epistle *Au Roy, du temps de son exil à Ferrare* (XXXVI). A second epistle in November 1535, welcoming the news of the

king's recovery from illness (XXXVII) betrays the same preoccupations but in a different tone. Marot hopes

> Que je ne perde au moins ta bonne grace
>
> (*Ep.*, XXXVII, V. 28)

and that the king will continue his wages and allow their transfer
to Ferrara, until such time as it please him to recall his loyal servant (vv. 38–39, 42–43). Nor did Marot forget his fellow poets in
France, or they him, for the flood of imitations which greeted his
epigram *Du Beau Tetin* (LXXVII)—known in France almost as soon
as it was written in Ferrara—and which led to the competition
for the best descriptive poem in praise of a portion of the human
anatomy, organized by Marot and judged by Renée de France,[80]
is the clearest possible evidence that his following and his standing
among them remained undiminished.

Marot's stay in Ferrara was abruptly curtailed and the exact
circumstances of his departure on 10 June 1536 are still somewhat
obscure.[81] It is certain however that Renée's husband, Ercole II
d'Este figured prominently in the whole affair. His marriage to
Renée de France in 1528 had been dictated by purely political
considerations: his father sought thus to seal the alliance recently
concluded between France and the duchy of Ferrara. Ercole had
little sympathy for his wife or her beliefs, he himself being a
Catholic of the most rigid and uncompromising kind, and he had
even less for her entourage. In addition, when the French
position in Italy appeared seriously prejudiced, his sympathy was
correspondingly diminished. He had no further use for the alliance.
Worse still, on his father's death, he sought an alliance with the
emperor Charles V whom he met in Naples in the autumn of
1535. The French presence in Ferrara was now a considerable
embarrassment to him. Furious to learn of a projected visit by his
wife, on the advice of Michelle de Saubonne, to Lyons to see the
French king and Marguerite de Navarre, he returned to Ferrara
in January 1536 in time to frustrate his wife's plans and to order
the immediate expulsion of Michelle de Saubonne, Renée's
closest friend and chief support. This was a separation which he
had tried many times previously to bring about. Michelle de
Saubonne left Ferrara on 20 March 1536.

To the political motives which Ercole had for seeking to dismiss

Renée's French entourage must be added religious ones. Ercole had an alliance with the Pope. He had had negotiations with the Pontiff in September 1535, immediately before his meeting with Charles V. Could he really tolerate the presence of Lutheran fugitives from France at his court? He was left in no doubt on this point by the reports reaching Ferrara from his diplomats. Giacomo Tebaldi in a letter to the duke from Venice describes a recent conversation he has had with the legate and former rector of the University of Paris, the arch enemy of Luther, Girolamo Aleandro, who had warned him specifically against the presence in Ferrara of Clément Marot, a man capable of spreading the plague of Lutheranism wherever he went.[82] And this warning came only five months after the poet's arrival in Ferrara. Six months later, in March 1536, the duke's ambassador in Rome wrote to advise him on the seriousness with which the presence of French Lutheran fugitives was regarded by the Pope and certain Cardinals.[83] The word excommunication had been heard in the context of their august concern. Pressure on the duke was increasing. Only a pretext for action remained to be found.

This, in the event, proved to be a simple exercise. On Good Friday, Jehannet de Bouchefort, attending a church service, was observed to leave the church before the adoration of the cross, for reasons known only to himself. He was immediately arrested and the machinery of the Inquisition moved into action seeking the other 'conspirators' in the 'plot'. Jehannet was tortured, with no apparent result, and witnesses were summoned. One of these, a French franciscan, questioned particularly about Clément Marot, replied that he was known to all as a Lutheran and had been banished from France for this reason.[84] Marot's case was investigated but whether he was arrested and detained is not known. The other members of Renée's entourage were summoned to appear before the Inquisitor and on their refusal to comply, on the grounds that the Ferrarese authorities had no jurisdiction over them, the Inquisitor ordered Renée herself to hand them over to him. Renée's protests to Marguerite de Navarre[85] and to the French ambassador to Venice resulted in a protest lodged by the latter with the duke: to no effect. Renée's next tactic, to write to the Pope requesting his protection and intervention in the affair had more success. The Pope ordered the Inquisitor to surrender the prisoner Jehannet de Bouchefort to the jurisdiction of the governor of Bologna. The duke of Ferrara, however, not only refused to comply with this request, but intensified his persecution of his wife's entourage, imprisoning her personal secretary Jean Cornillan, and writing to his ambassador in Paris to obtain a complete legal dossier on Cornillan, Marot, and Bouchefort. It required eventually the massive intervention of François Ier, Montmorency and the Cardinal de Tournon, who saw in the persecutions not their religious implications but a political affront by an ally, and who acted uniquely to safeguard the French presence in Ferrara, to secure the release, with the Pope's authorization, of the prisoners Bouchefort and Cornillan in August 1536.

Marot, in the meantime, had succeeded in evading the Inquisition by escaping from Ferrara to Venice on 10 June 1536 with the connivance of the French ambassador, Georges de Selve. These, at any rate, are the implications to be drawn from the correspondence which passed between the duke and Filippo Rodi, his ambassador in Rome, concerning an unidentified person, recently fled from Ferrara, and from whom the Inquisition had hoped to extract a testimony which would further their prosecution of the two prisoners.[86] A letter from Rodi on 30 June to the duke,[87] gives credence to the proposed identification of the unknown person with Clément Marot, by relating the details of a conversation in which the Cardinal of Capua describes the person as having recently fled from Paris and being well known to Aleandro, the man who had already warned Ferrara through Giacomo Tebaldi against Clément Marot. It is from this reported conversation that we learn of the part played by the French ambassador in helping the 'prisoner' to escape. The extent of the annoyance felt by the Ferrarese authorities at the escape of their prey which is reflected in correspondence, is also confirmed by Marot's own fear that even in Venice he was not entirely safe from the fury of his pursuers. Such is the sense of these lines from the epistle *A la Royne de Navarre:*

> ...crains que ma destinée
> Suive son train, tant est acheminée;
> Car chiens du Pau de relais & renfort
> Sont ja venus eslanser de son fort

> Ton povre serf qui en l'estang sallé
> Venitien jecter s'en est allé,
> Où les mastins ne le laisront longtemps,
> Car clabauder d'icy je les entens.
>
> (*Ep.*, XLVI, vv. 77–84)

An interesting postscript to this whole affair is provided by the text of two epistles written after the flight from Ferrara, *Au Roy* (XLIV) and *A Madame de Ferrare* (XLII). In the former Marot, concerned lest any hint of the true nature of the persecution which forced him to flee from Ferrara should prejudice his possible return to France, insists, in a way that could only reinforce the king's conviction that France had suffered a political affront at the hands of an ally, the duke of Ferrara, that his only crime was in being French:

> ...je n'y ay fait oultrance,
> N'aucun forfait, fors que je suis de France.
> Mais quant je y vins, certes je ne pensoys
> Que ce fust cryme illec d'estre Françoys.
> Voila le mal; voila la forfaicture
> Qui m'a fait prendre ailleurs mon adventure.
>
> (*Ep.*, XLIV, vv. 11–16)

The farewell epistle written ostensibly for Renée de France is equally silent on the subject of the religious persecution of which Marot had been one of the targets. Marot again insists, although in suitably evangelical terms,[88] that his reason for leaving was the anti-French feeling in Ferrara which had culminated in an armed attack against his person one night:

> ...Penses tu que l'oultraige
> Que Ferraroys mal nobles de couraige
> M'ont fait de nuyct, armez couardement,
> Ne soit à moy ung admonestement
> Du seigneur Dieu pour desloger d'icy?
> ....
> Parquoy, Princesse, ouvre moy de ta grace
> De mon congé le chemin et la trace,
> Affin que voyse en ville ou en pays
> Où les Françoys ne sont ainsi hays,
> Et ou meschantz, si aucuns y en a,
> Sont chastiez.   (*Ep.*, XLII, vv. 13–17, 29–34)

No other source of information on the attack against Marot exists
by which it might be confirmed, although Marot's remark in the
last two lines of the passage quoted above, with its hint that the
affair was officially condoned and even mounted, seems to silence
any objections on that score. What is more surprising though, is
that Marot should have maintained his story about the night
attack in an epistle to Renée de France who was certainly not
unaware of the true circumstances of his departure from Ferrara.
Again, the lengthy consideration (vv. 17–29) which Marot affects
to have given to the question of his departure would have been
scarcely possible in the true circumstances of the affair as far as
they are known. It is however doubtful that the epistle in the
form—the only form—in which it is known to us, was written
solely for Renée's eyes, or that it represented Marot's leave-taking.
The epistle appears in only one sixteenth-century manuscript, the
presentation manuscript offered by Marot to Montmorency,
Grand-Maître de France and rigorous defender of orthodoxy, in
1538. It is almost certain that this epistle was composed, or at
least extensively revised, some time after the event to which it
relates took place, perhaps at the time when Montmorency's
manuscript was being prepared. Since the poems in this collection
relate the events of Marot's exile, the omission of one concerning
his departure from Ferrara and his formal leave-taking from the
duchess would have been perhaps too conspicuous. Such a poem,
in addition, offered the poet a further opportunity to consolidate
his story. That the text of it should have been tailored to fit the
requirements of Montmorency's orthodoxy is not at all surprising.
It is a characteristic of all the poems in this collection.[89]

Marot's stay in Venice is known to us only through the poems
he composed there, none of which were published by the poet
during his lifetime.[90] Unlike the poems composed in Ferrara,
these give no indication of the poet's material situation, of any
resources he might have had, of any post he might have held or of
any contacts he might have enjoyed. Having cast a disenchanted
eye on the Venetian scene, Marot's one preoccupation was to
obtain leave to return to France at the earliest possible opportunity. With this end in mind he wrote three epistles, *Au Roy*
(XLIV), *Au tresvertueux prince, Françoys, Daulphin de France*
(XLV) and *A la Royne de Navarre* (XLVI). The first was written in

July very soon after Marot's arrival in Venice and the second before Marot had learnt of the dauphin's tragic death on 10 August 1536. Both contain a specific request for a safe conduct for a six months' stay in France:

> Te plaise, Roy, à ton humble Clement,
> A ton Marot, pour six moys seulement,
> La France ouvrir...   (*Ep.*, XLIV, vv. 187–9)

> A me donner le petit saufconduict
> De demy an...   (*Ep.*, XLV, vv. 22–23)

and the latter hints that Marot would be pleased to extend his stay if the king chose to retain his services.[91] The epistle to Marguerite de Navarre, less precise on the possible terms of a return to France by the poet, seems to have elicited in reply an immediate promise of help to which Marot alludes warmly in the *cantique* addressed to her from Venice:

> ...suis icy en angoisseux esmoy,
> En actendant secours promis de toy
> Par tes beaulx vers, cela je ramentoy
> Avecques gloire.

> Et bien souvent, à part moy, ne puis croire
> Que ta main noble ayt eu de moy memoire
> Jusque à daigner me estre consolatoire
> Par ses escriptz.   (*O.L.*, *Cantique* I, vv. 121–8)

Marot had to wait considerably longer for his answer from the king. His reasons for seeking a special authorization at all must remain a subject for conjecture[92] for since July 1535 François had issued two edicts pardoning banished Lutherans and allowing them to return to France on certain conditions. The first of these, the edict of Coucy of 16 July 1535, which promised the cessation of all legal action against the Lutheran fugitives and allowed them to enter France on condition that they renounced their errors against the Catholic faith on oath within six months of the date of promulgation of the edict, was greeted with a certain scepticism by the majority of those whom it was intended to safeguard. Only a very few availed themselves of its terms which, moreover, did not extend to all classes of heretics.[93] Subsequent events, in addition, confirmed that it would take more than one royal edict to restrain zealous authorities from their holy task: the

executions, by fire and water, continued. Hence no doubt the full
and unrestricted amnesty which the king granted on 31 May 1536
to all those who were not covered by the terms of the previous
edict. The abjuration clause, however, was to remain in effect.[94]
There was therefore no reason, as far as one can see, why Marot
should not have returned to France without special permission. It
has been suggested that Marot was hoping to be spared the indig-
nity, moral and physical, of the abjuration ceremony.[95] This is
made all the more plausible by Marot's specific plea to be allowed
to return for just six months, followed by the hint 'unless the king
chose'...etc. Presumably Marot's thought was that if the king
chose to retain him longer, it would be at his own discretion and
that Marot himself could not therefore be held to the abjuration
clause. On the other hand, the insistence by the poet on a 'safe-
conduct' signed by the king's own hand, and the anxieties this
betrays, might be taken to indicate that the poet considered his
own case to be extremely serious, particularly in view of his recent
experiences in Ferrara, the true nature of which—in spite of the
poet's attempts at concealment—might at any time reach un-
friendly ears in France with the most undesirable results. Marot,
in short, was seeking to guarantee his personal security against
all eventualities.

It is difficult to ascribe a precise date for Marot's departure
from Venice on his return to France. Both late October and late
November have been suggested.[96] But that he set out with the
king's special authorization is clear from the text of the epistle to
Monseigneur le Cardinal de Tournon estant à Lyon (XLVII):

> Puis que du Roy la bonté merveilleuse
> En France veult ne m'estre perilleuse;
> Puis que je suis de retourner mandé,
> Puis qu'il luy plaist, puis qu'il a commandé,
> Et que ce bien procedde de sa grace,
> Ne t'esbahys si j'ay suivy la trace,
> Noble Seigneur, pour en France tyrer.
>
> (*Ep.*, XLVII, vv. 1–7)

although no documentary evidence of the king's pardon is extant.
One thing is certain however. There was to be no exemption for
Marot from the formal condition of abjuration set out in the
general amnesty.

Marot's route from Venice took him through the Alps and there are grounds for believing, on the evidence available, that before entering Lyons Marot passed through Geneva, perhaps even stopping there for some time.[97] However this may be, it was in the early part of December that Marot arrived in Lyons. His disposition clearly impressed the Cardinal de Tournon who wrote to Montmorency, the *Grand-Maître*, in the following terms, on 14 December:

Mons[r.] Clement Marot est depuis plusieurs jours en ceste ville, qui est venu en bonne volonté, ce me semble, de vivre aultrement qu'il n'a vescu, deliberé de faire abjuration solempnelle en ceste ville devant moy et devant les vicaires de Mons[r.] de Lyon. Et vous prometz, Mons[r.] qu'il a grand repentance de ce qu'il a faict pour le passé et bonne envye de vivre en bon chrestien pour l'advenir.[98]

The ceremony itself, during the course of which the repentant heretic was beaten with rods, took place sometime between 14 and 31 December. This is confirmed by a poem addressed to Marot on 1 January by a fellow poet, Eustorg de Beaulieu:

> ...Que ne salues tu
> A ce jour Marot qu'a batu
> Rigueur, Rage & Fureur ague?
> Or, dis je, O homme de Vertu
> Treshumblement je te salue.[99]

It seems that Marot did not immediately leave Lyons to rejoin the court. The end of the letter which the Cardinal de Tournon wrote to Montmorency after seeing Marot soon after his arrival in Lyons may hold some clue to the poet's hesitations on this score:

mais sans doubte, Mons[r.], je le vois en bon chemin: parquoy, s'il vous plaist, vous luy ferez escripre par le Roy que, apres l'abjuration faicte, il puisse venir en seuretté devers luy et aller en son royaume, et je vous en supplie.[100]

It would seem from this that the Cardinal was not entirely impressed by the assurances which Marot had received already and which had encouraged him to leave Venice for Lyons, assurances which were not perhaps as complete as has been assumed.[101] Was Marot then awaiting further guarantees as a result of the Cardinal's intervention on his behalf? It was

probably not until the end of January, or the beginning of
February at the latest, that Marot left Lyons, having previously
paid his farewell tribute to the city in the *Adieux de Marot à la
ville de Lyon*.[102]

Marot's abjuration did not lessen the esteem and admiration in
which he was held by his friends and fellow poets. In Lyons his
arrival had been greeted with enthusiasm by Beaulieu as we have
already seen, and in addition by Des Périers, Estienne Dolet and
Jean Visagier.[103] They did not reproach him with inconsistency
on the surrender of his Protestant beliefs, not even the most
ardently reformist among them, and yet it is Marot's abjuration
which has provoked many unfavourable comments on his character and personality from later critics. If Marot considered the
symbolic ceremony as a disagreeable but unavoidable formality to
which he would submit his public self but not his private convictions then he would have acted no differently from the many
Protestants returning at this time.[104] And if he returned thinking
that the two edicts of toleration, combined with the projected
discussions on a possible reform of the Church which were to be
attended by the German reformer Melanchthon, heralded a return
to the climate of opinion which existed at the French court before
the *affaire des Placards*, many returning fugitives thought likewise. Such indeed had been Calvin's hope, a hope expressed in the
dedication to the king of his *Institutio Christiana* of 1536.[105] How
could Marot know, how could any of them know, that the king
was never again to be won over to the support of their cause?

Marot's destination after leaving Lyons was Paris.[106] Towards
the end of February he was present at the dinner given there to
celebrate the release from prison of Estienne Dolet who had been
arrested in connection with the murder of a painter, Compaing,
in Lyons at the end of December. The occasion saw an impressive
gathering of Dolet's friends who represented the cream of the
humanist intellectual and literary elite of Renaissance France.
Among them were Budé, Toussaint and Danès—two of the holders
of the first chairs of Greek established by the king—the neo-Latin
poets Salmon Macrin, Nicolas Bourbon, Jean Visagier, and not
least François Rabelais. Marot's friendship with Dolet, a man of
immense erudition and complex attitudes[107] was to last until the
middle of 1538.

It is not until 8 March 1537 that Marot's presence at the French court, which was at that moment in Compiègne, is formally attested.[108] He celebrated his return in the *Dieu Gard de Marot à la Court de France*.[109] He immediately resumed his functions as court poet and *valet de chambre* to the king, although his formal reinstatement on the household list and the recovery of the back pay due to him from the years of exile necessitated a campaign of epigrams addressed to the king. This was successfully concluded at the beginning of 1538.[110] Marot continued in his post of secretary to Marguerite de Navarre—since 1527, in fact, he had combined his functions in the two royal households, and shortly after rejoining the French court in 1537, he accompanied the Queen of Navarre and her husband on their journey through south-west France.[111]

Marot had announced in his *Dieu Gard à la Court de France* his intention to extend to all his enemies, on his return, his complete forgiveness:

> Je dy Dieu gard à tous mes ennemys
> D'aussy bon cueur qu'à mes plus chers amys.
>
> (*O.L.*, *Cantique* III, vv. 73–74)

There is no doubt at all that he was thinking principally of Sagon who during his absence in exile had published a collection of violent diatribes against Marot under the title of *Le Coup d'Essay* which were intended to establish beyond doubt, by commentary and analysis, the heretical nature of passages in two epistles written by Marot in Ferrara, *Au Roy* (XXXVI) and *A deux sœurs savoisiennes* (XXXV).[112] True, two other poets, Jean Leblond and the unidentifiable Général Chambor, had published in the same year (1536) and with the same intention their replies to Marot's epistle to the king[113] in the *Printemps de l'humble esperant*, likewise a collection of pamphlets, but Sagon had been the only one to incur a counterblast from the exiled poet, then in Venice, in the third *coq-à-l'âne* (vv. 110–39).[114] The spirit of forgiveness which Marot showed on his return did nothing to mollify his old adversary, however, who had signally failed in his campaign to usurp from him Marot's position in the king's service. The quarrel flared up anew, in circumstances somewhat obscure, when the two men met in June 1537 at Saint-Cloud where Marguerite de

Navarre was then staying.[115] On this occasion Marot seems to have prudently reserved his defence while his friend and fellow poet Bonaventure des Périers valiantly championed his cause. Marot's reply when it came was considered and definitive, and took the dispute from possibly dangerous ground to concentrate the attack on Sagon's sorry personality and inept verse. The *Epître de Frippelippes* provoked the inevitable counter-attack in the *Rabais du caquet de Fripelippes*, a conclusive demonstration of Sagon's inability to match the style and conception of the model he had foolishly tried to copy. Marot's abstention from the tedious warfare which ensued when the poets of France rushed to their pens and took up their respective positions of attack and defence was well judged. His poetic superiority was unassailable.

Perhaps it was the consciousness of this fact that led him, in March 1538, to present to Anne de Montmorency, Constable of France, a manuscript containing a carefully edited selection of the poems he had composed during his exile and to authorize his friend Estienne Dolet to publish under his directions an edition of his works, which was to include two books of epigrams never previously published as such.[116] *Les Œuvres de Clement Marot* appeared in Lyons in July 1538.[117] It was some time after this that the friendship which had existed between Marot and Dolet was ended in mysterious circumstances.[118]

Official poetry seems to have occupied Marot to a considerable extent after his return from exile, particularly official poetry of a political nature. Such are the various poems, starting with the *Cantique* (v), *La Chrestienté à Charles Empereur et à Françoys roy de France S.* of 1538 commemorating the discussions which took place between the two sovereigns, the understandings ostensibly arrived at, and the results thereof: the visit of the Queen of Hungary, sister to Charles V, to France in October 1538 (*Cantique* VI), and a further visit of Charles himself at the end of 1539 at the head of an army crossing France on its way to put down the revolt of the citizens of Ghent (*Cantique* VIII). An exception to this general political trend is the *Eglogue...au Roy soubz les noms de Pan & Robin* (*Eglogue* III) written soon after July 1539 to thank François Ier for the gift of a house in the *rue du Clos Bruneau* in Paris.[119]

Apart from his official poetry Marot's main concern after his return in 1537 was the completion of his translation of the Psalms which he had undertaken as early as 1532, most probably at the instance of Marguerite and doubtless also with the encouragement of the king, for it is worth noting that during the years 1532–34 François Vatable, one of the Readers appointed by the king in what was later known as the Collège de France, was lecturing on the Psalms in the original Hebrew,[120] much to the fury of the Sorbonne. During his exile Marot had occasion to think back to his uncompleted *Psautier*, remembering Marguerite's encouragement

> Autour de toy, Royne tres honorée,
> Comme souloye, en ta chambre paree,
> ...me faiz chanter en divers sons
> Pseaulmes divins, car ce sont tes chansons
>   (*Ep.*, XLVI, vv. 117–20)

and, in another epistle, *A Madame de Ferrare* (XLII), he tells how his gratitude

> A proposé en pseaulmes et cantiques
> Rememorer les nouveaux et antiques
> Dons du Seigneur, ses graces et bienfaictz,
> Et mesmement ceulx que par toy m'a faictz.
>   (*Ep.*, XLII, vv. 45–48)

Shortly after his return in 1537 it appears that Marot's Psalm translations were circulating in manuscript form at the court and in 1539 the translation of the *Trente Pseaumes de David* was completed. It was not unfavourably viewed by the king who ordered Marot to present a copy to Charles V. He did so and received from him a gift of money.[121] It would appear therefore that these two pillars of the orthodox Catholic Church were authorizing a translation which could not please the Sorbonne. From 1539 onwards editions of the translations were published in various centres abroad, Geneva, Strasburg, Antwerp and in these last two cases at least, without the poet's consent.[122] It was not until late in 1541 that Marot's translation was published with his consent, prefaced by a dedicatory epistle to the king, in France.[123] The edition, for which Marot had obtained two *privilèges d'imprimer* in spite of considerable official opposition from the Sorbonne, appeared in Paris.

Little is known of the circumstances of Marot's life in the

months preceding his flight to Geneva which marks the beginning of his second period of exile in the latter part of 1542.[124] Although this second flight may be explained to some extent by reference to the circumstances of the period, it is not, unlike the first in 1534, directly attributable to any one cataclysmic event. If the promulgation of the two edicts of toleration in 1535 and 1536 had been forced upon François Ier by the political pressure of the German Lutheran princes and those Swiss cantons whose continued alliance was essential to the foreign policy he then sought to pursue, it is equally true that his meeting with Charles V at Aigues Mortes in the summer of 1538 which caused him to abandon his former policy and Protestant alliances, signalled a return to intolerance at home. Between December 1538 and June 1540 François issued four edicts against the Lutherans.[125] There is clear evidence to suggest, however, that these edicts were not rigorously implemented at the time by the judicial authorities, although why this should have been so is not at all clear. What is more, the summer of 1540 was to see yet another reversal of François's foreign policy which was accompanied by a relaxation in his attitude to the Protestants. No further edicts were issued by him until the end of August 1542.[126] This relaxation brought with it a renewal of Protestant propaganda against Catholic dogma and practices. It was presumably this new climate of opinion which enabled Marot to publish his translation of thirty Psalms at the end of 1541, as indeed it seems to have encouraged the spate of evangelical publications from Dolet's presses in Lyons.[127] A final attempt was being made in these years to win back François's support to the evangelical cause for a reformation of the Church in France. It failed, and with predictable consequences. A wave of persecutions swept through France, initiated by the regional *Parlements* and consecrated by the two edicts issued by the king on 29 and 30 August 1542. These referred back to the earlier edicts of 1539 and 1540 and ordered their vigorous implementation. If this return to intolerance gave Marot cause for concern, so must also the fate of his Psalm translations. Their publication in the Protestant centres outside France was merely the prelude to their adoption by the Protestants, to their incorporation into a Protestant liturgy. They acquired in the process a distinctly heretical taint which allowed the Sorbonne to act against Marot once more. The Paris edition of the *Trente Pseaumes de David* was second on a list of prohibited books drawn up by the Faculty between Christmas 1542 and the beginning of March 1543.[128] Even before this, however, it appears that Marot had had word of a warrant issued by the *Parlement* of Paris for his arrest. By the beginning of December 1542, he was already in Geneva. A letter from Calvin to Pierre Viret, dated 8 December, gives the news of Marot's presence in the city.[129]

To Calvin Marot's arrival in Geneva promised much: the completion of the translation of the Psalms into French, a task to which Calvin had attached the utmost importance since the time of his installation in Geneva in 1537.[130] Accordingly, Calvin set out to obtain from the city a pension for the poet to enable him to devote himself to this task. In this he was unsuccessful, and the poet's lack of resources must be considered as one at least of the reasons which led him to leave Geneva after a stay of barely a year in December 1543. He had, however, completed the translation of another nineteen Psalms which, added to the original thirty were prepared for publication in two different editions, one under the aegis of Calvin for the use of the Protestant church. It is the second, though, which is the more interesting as recent criticism has shown.[131] Containing not the preface by Calvin but the dedicatory epistle to François Ier of the 1541 Paris edition, and, in addition, a new *huitain* dated 1 March 1543 addressed to the king

> Puis que voulez que je poursuive, ô Sire,
> L'oeuvre royal du Psautier commencé...[132]

together with an epistle *Aux Dames de France* written in Geneva and dated 1 August 1543, plus, most surprisingly of all, the *Ave Maria*, this edition was clearly intended for the French court and betrays Marot's hope of an eventual return to favour.[133]

The same may be said of the epigram 'Lors que la paour aux talons met des esles' (CCXXIX) which Marot addressed to the king after his departure from Geneva for Savoy at the end of 1543. In this poem he compares the Protestant citadel to Hell and asks to be allowed to continue his service to the king from the safety of Savoy. Presumably he was thinking of his functions as court poet since at the beginning of 1544 he wrote an eclogue to commemorate the birth of a son to the dauphin.[134]

Marot's stay in Savoy was considerably happier than that in Geneva. For one thing, it inspired two of his most delightful poems in the personal vein: the visit to Geneva inspired little but unease. Marot went first to stay with Pétremande de la Balme, the sister-in-law of François Bonivard with whom he had been friendly in Geneva. The epigram 'Adieu, ce bel oeil tant humain' (CCXXVIII) is his tribute and farewell to her. From the Château de Longefan, near Annecy, Marot went to the Château de Bellegarde near Chambéry, the home of François de Bellegarde. His life in this pleasantly cultured milieu which he was not slow to appreciate and to which he had again been introduced by Bonivard, is described in one of his last epistles, A ung sien Amy (LVI).

It seems that Marot may have lived next in Chambéry for some time and that the arrival of the French army in Piedmont under its commander François de Bourbon, whose victory at Ceresole inspired the poet's last epistle (LVII) may have encouraged him to hope that he could secure his return to France by winning the duke's protection.[135] The date of this epistle was July 1544. How it was received is unknown as also is the sequence of events which took Marot to Turin some time afterwards. There he died, probably in September, and was buried by his friend Lyon Jamet at San Giovanni Battista in Turin.[136]

To one aspect of his life Marot's poetry gives few clues: his marriage. Although it is known that he was indeed married, and that the event must have taken place before 1529,[137] Marot makes no reference in his poems to his wife. This fact alone has been sufficient to discredit the man and his works in the eyes of some nineteenth-century orientated, and moralizing critics. This omission appears all the more conspicuous and unpardonable since Luna, Ysabeau, and Anne especially, all have their place in the poems. Pastor Pannier writes thus:

Sa jeunesse est dissipée; plus tard, le nombre de ses 'amies' est incalculable, qu'elles soient de la plus basse espèce ou d'une condition très élevée. Il finit par se marier; mais lui qui adresse des vers à tant d'autres femmes, n'en consacre pas un seul à son épouse légitime.[138]

The comment is ill-advised in more ways than one, but primarily because of its uncritical assumption of the strictly biographical nature of Marot's love poetry. In this it is not supported by the facts. Only Anne's existence has been proved, and even with Anne d'Alençon Marot's alliance was a purely platonic one.[139] In many respects Anne is a pretext for poetry, rather than herself a living inspiration.

Finally, Marot's moral qualities and his character, often assailed by those who have seen only the apparent inconsistencies of his conduct in love or faith, are more than vindicated by his poetry. This is his monument for he never sought to abdicate the responsibilities which his mission as a poet laid upon him.

THE MOMENT: RENAISSANCE AND REFORMATION

Marot, like Rabelais, belongs to the generation of writers who took their collective inspiration from the French Renaissance. Their formative and most productive years coincide with the reign of François Ier, 1515–47.

The Renaissance in France[140] is easier to describe than to define although it may be limited historically from its beginnings in the last third of the fifteenth century, to its apogee in the years 1530–60, and its gradual transformation in the last decades of the sixteenth century. Promoted and ensured to a large extent by repeated and reciprocal contacts between the two countries sustained over a period of many years, the French Renaissance differs from that of Italy in emphasis and outcome. Less artistic, or less powerful in artistic expression, the French Renaissance is characterized by a revival of literature, a refinement of taste and a flowering of social life inspired by Italianism; by intellectual activity and ethical values redirected and renewed by a fuller awareness and a more profound appreciation of Classical Antiquity than had hitherto been possible. In Italy humanism, the second of these developments, was conceived of as an embellishment of the mind and spirit, in France as a liberation of it; from being an adjunct of elegant living in Italy, it became in France an instrument of Reformation. The term Renaissance applied to France therefore embraces Italianism, humanism and Reformation, three aspects of a single reality.

Italianism in France as a largely aristocratic phenomenon dates from the opening of the French military campaigns in Italy under

Charles VIII in 1494, campaigns which were continued intermittently by successive French monarchs, Louis XII, François Ier and Henri II, until France renounced her territorial ambitions in Italy under the treaty of Cateau-Cambrésis in 1559. Of little consequence politically, the Italian wars introduced the flower of the French nobility who led the invading armies to a splendid and elegant civilization, to a refined and sumptuous way of life as yet undreamt-of in a France slowly emerging from the Middle Ages.[141] Little wonder that the victors should seek to emulate the example of the vanquished in this respect: the process is a classic one in history. Relentless in their pursuit of splendour they returned with priceless *objects d'art*, they commissioned from Italian architects, artists, sculptors, craftsmen of all kinds, magnificent châteaux, stately houses, galleries hung with paintings and decorated with bronzes, ornamental gardens inhabited by statues and enlivened by fountains. All this is confirmed by contemporary observers, admiring or censorious. There were many of the latter among those who had stayed at home. Jean Bouchet is of this kind:

(ils) font les maisons de plaisance à colonnes de marbre, représentations d'images et symulachres si bien faicts, qu'il semble à les veoir qu'on les ayt dérobés à la nature. Le dedans est tout d'or et d'azur, les jardins semblent villes, tant sont les galeries bien couvertes, et pour la multitude de tonnelles et cabinets, tout pleins de lascivie et volupté, que mieulx semblent habitations de gens vénérés que marciaulx, et de gens lascivieulx que de gens de vertus.[142]

Fashions of dress and personal ornament, entertainments, pageants and masquerades all showed the same influence at work. But in all this the nobility assiduously followed the style and example set by the monarch and the great dignitaries of church and state. Louis XII, the Cardinal d'Amboise and Florimond Robertet, the treasurer of France, were all greatly impressed by the art treasures of Milan, and particularly by the work of Leonardo da Vinci who at one time was working both for the king and Robertet. François Ier employed both Leonardo and Andreø del Sarto for a short time in the first years of his reign. He engaged the painters Rosso and Primaticcio to work on the apartments of the royal palace at Fontainebleau. Here it was that Cellini was to display his powers as a sculptor in the great statue of Mars and the Nymph of Fontainebleau. Benvenuto Cellini was certainly the most notorious of all the Italians to work for François Ier, and his autobiography provides an account of the French court and the king's generous but erratic patronage of the arts which is not to be neglected.

Italianism in more important respects than the purely artistic was, too, enshrined at the French court. As a result of the trend towards absolutism in the French monarchy which the Italian wars and the end of feudalism confirmed and accentuated by hastening the economic and political destitution of the nobility and their consequent dependence on the sovereign, this institution was already undergoing a profound transformation. Gradually at first under Louis XII and Anne de Bretagne, on the pattern of the brilliant ducal courts of the peninsula—and Milan in particular, perceptibly under François Ier and significantly in the second half of his reign when Castiglione's book of the courtier's art, *Il Cortegiano* was the influence at work, the court became the highest expression of French society, a society in which women, learning and literature were accorded increasing acceptance and respect.[143] The civilizing influence of women at the French court, their role as arbiters of taste and guardians of urbanity was not only a reflection of their situation described in the third and fourth books of the *Cortegiano* where late Petrarchan and neo-Platonist concepts place women on a pedestal; it had been consecrated earlier by French imitations of Petrarchist love poetry. Jean Marot seems to have been one of the first poets to introduce into French literature the influence of Serafino dall' Aquila in particular with his *rondeau* 'S'il est ainsi que ce corps t'abandonne'.[144]

The invading armies of Charles VIII had been preceded into Italy by a peaceful infiltration of scholars and teachers attracted by the progress of Italian humanism, a century in advance of the movement in France. It had enjoyed the stimulus provided by the frequent contacts which Italy maintained with Byzantium and the Greek world in the fifteenth century in the attempt to heal the schism between the eastern and western branches of the church. An outstanding example of such stimulus was the visit to Florence of the patriarch Bessarion and of Gemistos Plethon, to name only two of very many, for the Council of 1438; the one remained in Italy to give direction to the study of Greek, the other with a book comparing the systems of Aristotle and Plato commissioned by Cosimo de Medici, founder of the Florentine Academy, launched the famous dispute between adherents and disciples of the two philosophers which was itself to inspire much of the subsequent work of critical exegesis in this field. Thus, in the context of Italian humanism and its development, the fall of Constantinople in 1453 (for long regarded as one of the great dates in the history of the Renaissance) was dramatic rather than primordially significant. It represented the final spurt, as it were, of a movement of men, manuscripts and ideas already under way. Italian Renaissance humanism, however, as a philological discipline in its critical study of the works of Classical and more particularly Greek Antiquity, as a feeling for their literary elegance, and even more as a belief in perfectibility and progress through the new sources of knowledge is quite distinct from the superficial cult of Roman Antiquity, inspired by patriotism and glorying uniquely in the past, which was the tendency of medieval 'humanism'.

The teachers and scholars who made the journey to Italy[145] came to study at the universities of Padua and Bologna; they visited Florence and the Academy devoted to the study of Plato; they worked at the great libraries there and in Venice and Rome; they were impressed by the labours of the Italian printers, humanists in their own right and men of enormous erudition whose workshops, like that of Aldus Manutius in Venice for instance were to become power houses of the humanist movement. They included, over the years, Guillaume Fichet, a doctor of the Sorbonne whose mission to Milan in 1467–90 was in the first instance a diplomatic one, his pupil Robert Gaguin, Jacques Lefèvre d'Etaples who went specifically to study philosophy, Christophe de Longueil and Erasmus among many others. They made repeated visits: Gaguin in 1465, 1471, 1483 and 1486; Lefèvre in 1492, 1500 and 1507; and so on. Fichet and Longueil (for whom Marot wrote an epitaph)[146] died there, the one shortly after his return there in 1472 and the other in 1522.

The results of this intellectual commerce were soon felt in France. On his return to Paris in 1470, Fichet obtained permission to install the capital's first printing press in the precincts of the

Sorbonne. He and his pupil Gaguin were concerned to establish in France a standard of elegance in Latin studies which had previously been lacking. Fichet published a treatise on style and texts of Cicero and Sallust, Gaguin a treatise on Latin versification. Their efforts were reinforced by the lectures on the poetry of Virgil and Lucain given at the University of Paris by the Italian scholars Fausto Andrelini, Girolamo Balbi and Beroaldo.[147] In other words, the whole emphasis and nature of the curriculum changed. These new literary courses, based on the direct study of the text, came to be called *disciplinae* or *literae humaniores* as opposed to the study of divine writings in the discipline of Theology: hence the derivation, and partial explanation of the later terms *humanism* and *humanists*.

These developments, however, represent only the initial impetus of humanism at the dawn of the Renaissance in France. Gradually, as humanism extended its appeal to the aristocracy on their contact with, and their enthusiasm for, all things Italian after 1494, its progress was furthered by its new public. Appreciating the personal prestige which the rulers of Italian principalities derived from their patronage and protection of the humanists, perhaps also dimly aware of the potential force of the movement, successive French monarchs sought to enhance their reputations in a similar way. Thus Charles VIII extended an invitation to Janus Lascaris who eventually came to France to enter his service in 1496 and remained to serve his successor Louis XII. Although Lascaris himself was too busy following the court to found a school himself in Paris,[148] other humanists, observing the slackening demand for their talents in Italy since the trickle of grammars and reliable editions from the presses had become a flood and made self-instruction increasingly feasible, turned their attentions to France, aware of the opportunities for teaching which awaited them there, and of the fees which they could command from wealthy *amateurs*, often illustrious personages, for private lessons in the Greek language. Such was François Tisserand, a French-born hellenist who, on the completion of his studies in Italy, had translated three tragedies of Euripides into Latin and dedicated them to François d'Angoulême who was then accompanying the army of Louis XII in Italy. Tisserand returned to Paris in 1507, published the first Greek books in France, a

Greek grammar followed by various *moralia* previously published by Aldus in Venice in 1495, an edition of the burlesque poem *Batrachomyomachia* and of Hesiod's *Works and Days*, and finally, started lecturing at the Collège de Boncour. These were public lectures attended by humanists and scholars. He gave in addition private lessons. Tisserand's arrival was followed by that of Girolamo Aleandro in 1508. He arrived with the encouragement and exhortations of Erasmus to establish the teaching of Greek and Hebrew on a regular basis in Paris. However, until 1509 he gave nothing but private lessons, to the detriment of Tisserand from whom he took most of his pupils. His public lectures, while not regular—they were interrupted by frequent bouts of illness and his absences from Paris—drew large and distinguished audiences.[149]

Both Tisserand and Aleandro had been preceded by George Heronymus,[150] a Spartan who arrived in Paris in 1476 and started giving private lessons. However, he placed a higher value on his own confused learning than either Erasmus or Guillaume Budé who had occasion to hear him, and seems to have won the approbation only of his friend Lefèvre d'Etaples. These three men were the pioneers of Hellenism in France.[151] Guillaume Budé, perhaps a more distinguished Greek scholar than Erasmus in quality was very largely self-taught and later encouraged others, notably Rabelais, to follow his example in this respect. He was constantly active in exploiting the advantages which his position and his rank in court circles conferred upon him to maintain the interest of aristocratic *amateurs* and to gain their support for the movement. Erasmus and Lefèvre were to a large extent self-taught as well, and the latter doubtless had the opportunity to improve his Greek on his visits to Italy, although he remained, it is true, less competent in this respect than the other two. Erasmus certainly improved his Greek in Italy: he went there with this express intention. All of them realized that it was only by the study of Greek, almost totally unknown at the University of Paris in the Middle Ages, that humanism in France could be definitively established and the Renaissance, in the fullest sense of the word, with its moral, intellectual and spiritual implications, assured. In the meantime, since humanism in practice was seen to involve a rejection of everything—or most things—medieval, modes of thought and education embodied in scholasticism and authorized by the Sorbonne which, as the most senior of the four Paris faculties (Theology, Canon Law, Medicine, Arts) exercised a right of control over the instruction given in the other three, it was to incur the implacable opposition of this obscurantist body.

It is in the dispute between humanism and scholasticism that the characteristics of the former emerge most clearly. The philological revolution proposed by Budé to renew the study of jurisprudence, by Lefèvre to renew the study of philosophy and by Erasmus that of theology challenged the dogmatic authority and pronouncements of the scholastics and the Sorbonne by substituting as the sole authority the Classical authors or the scriptures studied at first hand in texts critically established by humanist scholarship. Philology challenged the primacy in the scholastic system of a sterile dialectic, a compounding of syllogisms in a travesty of Aristotelian logic; it scorned the glosses which generations of medieval commentators had elaborated on texts of little authenticity transmitted through unreliable sources; it rejected those aspects of medieval scholasticism which had perverted science and confined knowledge within areas ceaselessly defined and constantly revisited, as an intolerable obstacle to intellectual progress. Erasmus was perhaps the most articulate in his criticisms. He writes in the *Adagia* of 1515 on two proverbs which

are to be used of those who rush into an undertaking either recklessly, or else without sufficient knowledge of the important facts...as if an attempt to interpret Divine scripture were made by one who was unschooled and ignorant of Greek, Latin and Hebrew, and of the whole of antiquity—things without which it is not only stupid but impious, to take on oneself to treat the mysteries of Theology. And yet—terrible to relate—this is done everywhere by numbers of people, who have learnt some trivial syllogisms and childish sophistries and then, heavens above, what will they not dare? What will they not teach? What will they not decide...Plenty of people judge rightly without knowing the rules of logic, to say nothing of the quibbles of the schoolmen. There were wise people on earth before Aristotle (the god of those people) was born. No one ever understood any other person's opinion without knowing the language in which that opinion was expressed. And so what did Saint Jerome do, when he had decided to expound Holy scripture, and did not wish to set about it with unwashed hands as they say? Did he fill his head with nonsensical sophistries? Or with the rules of Aristotle? Or with nonsense even more frivolous than this? Not he. What then did he do? With incalculable toil, he made himself master of the three tongues...[152]

In 1526 he again pilloried the system which accepted

a youth as a student in Philosophy, Law, Medicine or Theology, who can understand nothing in the ancient authors owing to his ignorance of the language they speak...[153]

and which excluded

from the Holy of Holies of Theology anyone who has not sweated for years over Averroes and Aristotle...any arguments which are brought from the sources of Holy Scripture, and only accept those which are taken from Aristotle, from the Decretals, from the determinations of the Schoolmen, from the glosses of the professors of papal law, or from precedents (inane for the most part) distorted from Roman law.[154]

In its values too, humanism was no less aware of the distance which separated it from scholasticism. It delighted in antitheses which pointed the contrast between the old and the new. And although such antitheses inevitably tended to oversimplify, they contained a large element of truth. Medievalism and scholasticism, ascetic and metaphysical, deferred hope to the Hereafter, scorned as vanity all earthly endeavours, preached the wickedness of man and stifled the individual conscience with considerable success under a monolithic Catholicism. Humanism, conscious of the progress already achieved by intellectual effort in the distant past, gloried in the present, was confident in a future assured by the perfectibility of man through the humanities, preached the freedom of man to be good and therefore claimed for the individual freedom of thought and conscience. In general terms, it moved from the metaphysical to the ethical, from the transcendental to the human values in its desire to relate all things to man, without, however, being necessarily anti-Christian. The notion of the essential dignity of man, of the human spirit and the human reason adds another dimension to humanism originally defined as the study of the humanities.

Humanism was triumphant in France when, in 1529, François Ier, after earnest and prolonged entreaties from Budé and others, created the Collège des Lecteurs Royaux, the first institution of its kind to be completely independent of the authority and control of the Sorbonne. There he established chairs of Latin, Greek and Hebrew.[155] The event was welcomed by humanists and partisans of humanism everywhere. It was saluted by Rabelais in this passage from his *Pantagruel* (1532) which fittingly reflects the magnificent achievement of Renaissance humanists as well as their awareness of the historical moment to which they belonged:

...comme tu peulx bien entendre, le temps n'estoit tant idoine ne commode es lettres comme est de present, et n'avoys copie de telz precepteurs comme tu as eu. Le temps estoit encores tenebreux et sentant l'infelicité et calamité des Gothz, qui avoient mis à destruction toute bonne litterature. Mais, par la bonté divine, la lumiere et dignité a esté de mon eage rendue es lettres...

Maintenant toutes disciplines sont restituées, les langues instaurées: Grecque, sans laquelle c'est honte que une personne se die sçavant, Hebraïcque, Chaldaïque, Latine. Les impressions tant elegantes et correctes en usance, qui ont esté inventées de mon eage par inspiration divine, comme, à contrefil, l'artillerie par suggestion diabolicque. Tout le monde est plein de gens sçavans, de precepteurs très doctes, de librairies très amples, et m'est advis que, ny au temps de Platon, ny de Ciceron, ny de Papinian, n'estoit telle commodité d'estude qu'on y veoit maintenant...Je voy les brigans, les bourreaux, les avanturiers, les palefreniers de maintenant, plus doctes que les docteurs et prescheurs de mon temps.

Que diray-je? Les femmes et les filles ont aspiré à ceste louange et manne celeste de bonne doctrine. Tant y a qu'en l'eage où je suis, j'ay esté contrainct de apprendre les lettres Grecques.[156]

Founded in defiance of the Sorbonne's bid to ban the teaching of Greek and Hebrew, the college was soon known as the Anti-Sorbonne.

Humanism and Reformation had initially much in common: both Erasmus whom we have already quoted, and Lefèvre, saw in the linguistic and critical discipline of humanism an essential ancillary science to theology, a means of restoring authority and exactitude to the sacred texts just as they had to the Classical ones. Nor did they stop there. They applied the principles of humanism to theology: the text in the original Greek or Hebrew as the sole authority, and autonomy of conscience in evaluating it. The critical examination and exegesis of the sacred scripts which followed in spite of the fulminations of the Sorbonne, exposed the divorce which existed between Christianity divinely revealed and the subsequent doctrinal accretions of divines accredited to the Catholic Church. It was found that many of the abuses rampant in the Roman Church had their origins in these *doctrines humaines*. Thus the enormous increase in the sale of Indulgences, designed to raise money for the Church, as well as the superstitious observance of certain practices, fasting, the mumbling of ritualistic prayers, pilgrimages, the veneration of dubious relics and the worship of Saints were justified, if that is the word, by the doctrine of salvation through good works. Basing himself upon St. Paul, Lefèvre concluded that good works without faith were as nothing and could not alone guarantee salvation which depended upon God's grace.[157] He therefore condemned the superstitious performance of such observances.[158] Erasmus, with his desire to rationalize religion, to demystify it and above all to bring it within the grasp of the layman, went further than Lefèvre. He scorned asceticism and monasticism. He was forthright in his condemnation of formalism and in his attacks on certain of the traditional observances in themselves. Making adroit transpositions from the satirical works of the Greek writer Lucian, whom incidentally Lefèvre considered to be a most pernicious sceptic, Erasmus attacked the cult of saints in its many manifestations: pilgrimages to their shrines, votive offerings, veneration of their statues and supposed relics, their power to effect miraculous cures.[159] Erasmus sought a Christianity based on faith and charity, a dialogue between man and Christ through the Gospels and in direct prayer. In short therefore, it was proposed to sweep away those practices and dogmas of the Church for which there was no scriptural justification: hence the name *evangelism* sometimes given to this movement to return to the authority of the Evangel and to reform the Church in accordance with its teachings. The fear of the Sorbonne, guardian of orthodoxy, that the spread of humanism and Greek scholarship in particular would subvert her authority becomes explicable in this light.

Not all the humanists wished to leave the Church however. Erasmus and Lefèvre wanted a reform within the Church. Erasmus made repeated declarations in his correspondence of his intention never to break with Rome. Yet he continued to hope that the Church might be changed into something it was not, a

naive hope in the context of Catholicism, and certainly not a sign
of orthodoxy. In addition, the fact that many of the tenets of the
French reformers bore a resemblance to the outlawed doctrines of
Luther, which in many respects they had anticipated, did nothing
to appease the wrath of the Sorbonne. Copies of Lefèvre's French
translation of the Bible were seized and burnt, Briçonnet, bishop
of Meaux and a follower of Lefèvre was forced to speak out
formally against Luther and Louis Berquin, who had translated
works of both Luther and Erasmus, was sent to his death at the
stake.[160] The writings of Erasmus were placed on the index of
prohibited books. In the face of rigid intolerance and indiscrimi-
nate repression directed against liberals and extremists alike,
humanists and advocates of humanism, French reformers and
Lutherans made common cause. There is hardly a writer of the
period whose works do not bear witness in some way to the
struggle. Many, who closely identified the movement of Reformation with the humanist desire for intellectual enlightenment
and moral progress, and in this sense willingly associated themselves with it, found their careers interrupted by persecution,
imprisonment, banishment or self-exile. Rabelais and Marot are
typical in this respect.

After the *affaire des Placards* in 1534 and the violent reaction
of François Ier against the new ideas, a realignment of forces
began to take place however. The divergence of humanism and
Reformation in France became inevitable when Calvin, who in
1536 published the first edition of his *Institutio Christiana*, took
the initiative on the death of Erasmus and Lefèvre that same year,
and constituted outside the Catholic Church a dogmatism more
repressive than that which the humanists had originally sought
to overthrow within it. The essential incompatibility between
humanism and Calvinism had an earlier parallel in the dissension
which had set Erasmus and the non-German humanists against
Luther, particularly on the question of free will. Neither Lefèvre
d'Etaples who attempted to reconcile his belief in the necessity of
God's grace for salvation with a belief in the autonomy of the
human will,[161] nor Erasmus whose belief in the freedom of man
to be good left less scope for the action of grace, could accept
Luther's concept of the enslaved will.[162] Calvinism, which
developed Luther's arguments against free will to their logical

conclusion, was even more fiercely deterministic.[163] Far from
exalting man's potential as humanism did, it presented him as a
helpless creature predestined to be saved or damned by an omni-
potent God. Nor was there any place in Calvin's philosophy for
tolerance, for the individual's right to freedom of thought and
conscience. Faced with a choice between Calvinism and Catholicism, few humanists opted for the former, many tried to reconcile
themselves to the latter. Rabelais, Des Périers and Dolet rejected
both dogmatisms. And towards the middle of the century, the
traditional principle of authority which the humanists, paradoxically, had strengthened rather than undermined when they sub-
stituted for the discredited authority of Aristotle and the Schoolmen
that of the restored Classical or sacred texts, was swept away by
those who believed on the one hand, in the primacy of reason and
experience, and on the other in the honesty of doubt. With
rationalism,[164] the dawn of empiricism, and scepticism, the
emancipation of the Renaissance mind was complete.

THE MILIEU: THE FRENCH COURT

Under François Ier the French court became one of the principal
centres, and a powerful agent, of the Renaissance in France. The
interests of the king (Italianism and humanism) and of his sister
Marguerite d'Angoulême (humanism and reform) were in a
sense complementary, and the direction which they combined to
impart to the Renaissance—Marguerite's influence on her brother
was often considerable in this respect—gave to the movement
much of its initial cohesion.[165]

Conscious of the hopes which rested upon him at the beginning
of his reign to promote the Renaissance of learning and of literature
at the French court,[166] no doubt flattered by them too, François
Ier worked hard to fulfil them. The tributes which greeted his
efforts during his own lifetime and the veneration in which his
memory was held by subsequent generations of writers and
scholars are some indication of his considerable success in this
respect.[167] The supremacy of Italian culture, which he acknowledged in his patronage of writers, humanists and artists especially,
constituted at the same time a challenge which his temperament
could not resist. Hence his intelligent patronage of indigenous

talent. Aware, for instance, of the disparity of achievement between Italian vernacular literature—whose revival had been championed in the previous century by the humanist Leon Alberti—and the vernacular literature of his own country, François Ier conceived the idea of demonstrating the capacity of the French language, and of extending it, by commissioning the publication of French translations[168] of the classics of Greek and later, Italian literature. This enterprise was placed in the hands of Jacques Colin,[169] *lecteur du roi*, who published first of all the translations of the humanist Claude de Seyssel (1455?–1520), historiographer to Louis XII and bishop of Turin, which had so far remained in manuscript. These included a translation of Thucydides (1527), of Xenophon, of Diodorus of Sicily, Eusebius, Appian and a partial translation of Plutarch's *Lives* (1530). Colin himself translated an episode of Ovid's *Metamorphoses* and, more importantly, Castiglione's *Cortegiano* (1537), although in his case it would be more proper to speak of adaptation or paraphrase of the original works. The translation of the *Cortegiano* was in fact revised and corrected by Estienne Dolet and Mellin de Saint-Gelais in an edition published the following year. From Hugues Salel the king commissioned a translation of Homer's *Iliad* which appeared in 1545 and from Amyot the now famous translation of Plutarch which was not, however, to be published in François's lifetime. By this policy of vulgarization, the enrichment of the vernacular and the wider diffusion of Renaissance humanism were simultaneously ensured and mutually promoted. At the same time, on a rather higher level, the king encouraged the work of French scholars by making freely available to them the resources of the royal library at Fontainebleau which was constantly being enriched by the acquisition of manuscripts procured all over Europe by his agents, while the successful endowment of the Collège des Lecteurs Royaux is the abiding monument (now the Collège de France) to his encouragement of humanism.

Humanists and reformers gravitated even more willingly perhaps to the entourage of Marguerite de Navarre.[170] Not only was she more intelligent than her brother, more reserved and cultured too, she was also more deeply and personally committed to their cause. A reliable ally therefore, since her protection was not subject, like her brother's, to the fluctuations of foreign policy demands, she was also a valuable intermediary between them and the king, pleading their cause, communicating to him their works and ideas, enlisting his support and protection when their activities were curtailed and their liberty threatened. This applies particularly of course to the reformers: to Briçonnet with whom she exchanged an abstruse and deeply mystical correspondence between the years 1521–4, to Louis Berquin whom she was ultimately unable to save, to Gérard Roussel her chaplain and one of three reformers she called upon to preach the Gospels before the assembled court at the Louvre in Lent 1533, to Lefèvre d'Etaples and to Calvin, both of whom—the former definitively after 1531—found a much-needed refuge at her court in Nérac in her own domains. She was largely instrumental too, in securing the king's approval in 1535 for a proposed visit to Paris of the German humanist Melanchthon for discussions on a reform of the Church.

No less than her brother, whom she influenced in this respect too,[171] did Marguerite stimulate and direct the work of vulgarization. In this sphere again her particular intellectual sympathies are clearly illustrated. She was not content merely to receive the translations of Luther's works which her cousin S. de Hohenlohen sent to her from Strasburg as soon as they were published. Berquin her protégé had translated several of his works and a certain Papillon (who may or may not be the poet Almanque Papillon, it is not known) was commissioned by her to translate Luther's *De Votis Monasticis* into French.[172] Her encouragement to Marot to translate the Psalms has already been alluded to. Later, she was largely responsible for the diffusion of Platonism in French literature.[173] The discussion of neo-Platonic concepts in her entourage which is reflected in the pages of her *Heptaméron*, was reinforced by translations and then by original works. For instance, in 1536 Antoine Héroet, a poet who had been a member of Marguerite's entourage at least since 1524, presented to the king at her instigation *L'Androgyne*, a free translation of those pages of Plato's *Symposium* relative to this myth. In 1542 this translation appeared together with an original composition by the poet, *La Parfaicte Amye* which was deeply imbued with many of the neo-Platonic concepts of spiritual love. Jean de la Haye was responsible at her suggestion for a translation of Ficino's commentary on the *Symposium* which appeared in 1546. In the meantime, a manuscript of Jean de Luxembourg's French translation of the *Phaedo*, completed before 1540, had been in circulation at the court. One can only wonder whether the same was true of its companion dialogue, the *Ion* (so important to the poetic theory of the *Pléaide*), of which Richard Le Blanc, another protégé, published a French translation in 1546. Des Périers translated the *Lysis* (1544), Estienne Dolet the *Hipparchus* and the *Axiochus*— the latter with disastrous personal consequences,[174] and Pierre du Val the *Crito*. It is difficult to judge, on the other hand, to what extent the elaboration of Marguerite's ideas in her own works contributed to the diffusion of evangelism and Platonism during her own lifetime. The greater part of her work was published posthumously and the extent to which it circulated among her entourage is largely a matter for conjecture.

In the patronage of poets and humanists, the example of the king and his sister was followed by the great officers of state, notably Anne de Montmorency, and by the dignitaries of the Church. The Cardinals François de Tournon, Jean de Lorraine and Jean du Bellay were considerable patrons in their own right.

The constant interchange of ideas which this milieu promoted in a less formal way, in conversation and discussion, can obviously never be measured. But there is no shortage of contemporary accounts which describe the king's table almost in the terms of an Academy. This one is from the poet Claude Chappuys:

> Et c'est tascher d'espuiser la grand mer
> De vouloir tous les illustres nommer
> Et mesmement les doctes personnaiges
> En Grec, Hebrieu, Latin & tous langaiges
> Dont sort tousjours quelque propos notable
> En toutes artz quand le roy est à table.[175]

And the household of Marguerite de Navarre was no less esteemed.[176]

CONDITIONS OF CREATIVITY: POETRY FOR PATRONAGE

> Mais puis qu'avons ung vray Mecenas ores,
> Quelcque Maro nous pourrons veoir encores.
>
> (*O.S.*, *L'Enfer*, vv. 365–6)

Patronage of poets by the rich and powerful was no new development as Marot's allusive pun reminds us. Nor was the system,
sanctified by this Classical precedent, considered as anything but
prestigious to the patron and favourable to the poet. Hence the
distinctly optimistic and congratulatory note of this couplet and of
similar verses. And yet the full implications which the relationship between writer and patron held for the work of literature are
not always appreciated by a later age which, if it has not forgotten
altogether the system of patronage as it was formerly practised,
remembers it with scorn[177] and dismisses it with repugnance.

It is a fact that social and material factors impinged deeply on
many French poets of the fifteenth and sixteenth centuries.[178] To
Marot, on his own admission

> Bas de sçavoir, en bas degré nourry,
> Et bas de biens...   (*Ep.*, xv, vv. 3–4)

as to his father and the majority of the *Grands Rhétoriqueurs*,
patronage was an essential condition of creativity. In the early age
of printing when author's rights were unprotected and royalties
non-existent, and when publication in the first instance still con-
sisted very often in the reading of the newly composed works in
the intimacy of the court circle in which they were produced, or
in the passing from hand to hand of manuscripts which might be
freely copied, the writer had no other means of assuring his livelihood and his creative effort than by securing a position in the
household of a noble:

> Ce qu'il attend en ceste Court gist là;
> Et ce pendant pour tous Tresors il a,
> Non Revenu, Banque, ne grand Practique,
> Mais seulement sa Plume Poëtique.
>
> (ibid., vv. 17–20)

Thus at the court of the dukes of Burgundy, of Bourbon, of

Luxemburg, of the duchesses of Savoy and Brittany, of the kings
of France, *Rhétoriqueurs* such as Pierre Michault, Georges
Chastelain, Jean Molinet, Jean Lemaire de Belges, Jean Meschinot, Jean Marot and Guillaume Cretin[179] held posts as *valets de
chambre* (a title which clearly differentiated them from the nobles
who waited upon the person of the duke or king and who were
known as *gentilshommes de la chambre*), as secretaries, treasury
clerks and official chroniclers for which they received, at intervals
of widely varying duration, an annual emolument which might
or might not be supplemented by honoraria for poems which had
found especial favour, or for those executed to command for
lesser or occasional patrons. But the vagaries of such employment
were many and are well illustrated by the career of Jean Lemaire
de Belges who found himself repeatedly deprived of his livelihood
on the demise of his patrons and the dissolution of their households;[180] he served in succession, Pierre de Bourbon, Antoine de
Lorraine, Philibert le Beau, his wife Marguerite d'Autriche,
Anne de Bretagne and finally Louis XII. The precariousness of the
poet's situation is tellingly described in these lines in which
Marot made his plea to François Ier to be allowed to fill his
father's position:

> Je quiers, sans plus, Roy de los eternel,
> Estre Heritier du seul bien Paternel:
> Seul bien je dy, d'aultre n'en eut mon Pere,
> Ains s'en tenoit si content & prospere,
> Qu'aultre oraison ne faisoit icelluy,
> Fors que peussiez vivre par dessus luy;
> Car, vous vivant, tousjours se sentoit riche,
> Et, vous mourant, sa Terre estoit en frische.
>
> (*Ep.*, XII, vv. 31–38)

If the poet was able to secure his livelihood in this fashion, it
was not, of course, without contracting certain obligations to the
milieu which had assimilated him. His dependent condition therefore imposed a certain direction upon his creative effort, for it was
necessary to satisfy the known tastes and immediate requirements
of a predetermined public. This direction is most apparent in
those works which belong to the category of official court poetry.
Thus the court poet would be required to evoke in eulogies the
'bruit resplendissant' of his prince and of his exploits, to chronicle

in verse the significant events both political and domestic (the two were often inseparable) of the reign, to celebrate the births and marriages, to commemorate the dead, all in the time-honoured fashion. For just as custom decreed the form of ceremonial which should solemnify court occasions, so convention prescribed the level of expression and the literary form which the poet should give to the collective joy or sorrow. On a less formal level the professional poet might be commissioned by individual members of the court circle to execute for them epistles or love poems after a certain style. On his own account too, the poet would exchange courtesies in verse with the illustrious and less illustrious among his friends at court: seeking assistance, rendering thanks, recounting his experiences and on occasion his misfortunes, but in a way which should engage the attention, not only of the recipient, but also of the intimate court community.

One cannot reproach the court poets of the fifteenth and sixteenth centuries with the conditions in which they exercised their talents although one may regret them. It is easy to regard with suspicion, if not horror, a system which seems to restrict the creative imagination rather than to promote it, and even to compromise the moral integrity of the writer. But are such objections invariably justified? Much of the output—there is no better word in this case—of the *Grands Rhétoriqueurs* illustrates the pitfalls to be avoided in executing official poetry: undiscerning and immoderate in their praises, their homage tainted with false humility, in their political poems servile propagandists, in their commemoration of events rarely rising above the functional, communicating but not communing, above all banal, it was almost as if they had capitulated to their task. Yet they can hardly be said to be more successful in their 'personal' poetry. Their general mediocrity is not therefore an indictment of poetry for patronage. In very similar circumstances in the Ancient world Pindar produced the greatest lyric poetry of Greece in odes devoted to the praises of victors in the Games; Virgil's *Aeneid* was conceived in obedience to the Augustan desire to rekindle Roman pride in Rome's origins; Horace's official odes celebrating the glories of the Augustan age, its military victories, its secular festivals, represent the very real level of excellence which it is possible to attain in this kind of poetry. And which has been attained since.

Even the much-maligned office of poet-laureate, a survival of patronage in its old form, has commanded memorable talents to not unnotable effect. Tennyson's great funeral ode on the death of Wellington is a much-admired poem.

Marot, while conscious of the demands of his task, was not inhibited by them. He recognized its hazards—to the point of attempting a parody of the bombastic flatteries of some of his kind in the epistle *Au Roy* (XXV)

> Voila le poinct principal de ma Lettre;
> Vous sçavez tout, il n'y fault plus rien mettre.
> Rien mettre? Las! Certes, & si feray,
> Et ce faisant, mon stile j'enfleray,
> Disant; O Roy amoureux des neufz Muses,
> Roy en qui sont leurs sciences infuses,
> Roy plus que Mars d'honneur environné,
> Roy le plus Roy qui fut oncq couronné...
>
> (*Ep.*, XXV, vv. 119–26)

and was largely successful in avoiding them. The dignity of his conception of the poet capable of conferring immortality, a legitimate pride in his reputation which, notwithstanding his material dependence, gives him princely standing

> Et mon renom en aultant de provinces
> Est despendu comme celluy des princes.
> S'ilz vainquent gens en faict d'armes divers,
> Je les surmonte en beaulx escriptz et vers;
> S'ilz ont tresor, j'ay en tresor des choses
> Qui ne sont point en leurs coffres encloses;
> S'ilz sont puyssantz, j'ay la puyssance telle
> Que fere puys ma maistresse immortelle...
>
> (*O.L.*, *Elégie* XXIV, vv. 65–72)

leaves little room for servility, and his personal convictions, even in the face of royal opposition, were courageously maintained (*Epître* XXXVI). Aesthetically his work, unlike that of most *Rhétoriqueurs* but not to the same extent as Ronsard's perhaps, represents the possibilities of court poetry rather than its limitations. It reveals the distinction vital to this kind of poetry between pretext on the one hand, and themes and inspiration on the other. Thus in his second eclogue, the *Avant-naissance du troiziesme enffant de madame Renée, duchesse de Ferrare,* Marot's inspiration rises above the customary felicitations to dwell on the theme of Renaissance, on the progress achieved in this world and the hope of eternal life in the next. Similarly in the *Eglogue au roy soubz les noms de Pan & Robin* written by the poet to thank the king for his gift of a house, Marot evokes the delights of youth and the fears of old age with lyrical intensity. Thus conceived his poetry satisfies not only the requirements of the circumstance or event which called it into being, not only the demands of his immediate public, but those too of posterity.

Marot reconciled himself to his conditions of creativity more completely than did either of his immediate successors Ronsard and Du Bellay whose resentment at the need to canvass beneficiaries and whose disparagement of the culture and tastes of their public at court are themes frequently encountered in their poetry.[181] Marot is a striking example of a writer whose sensibility and whose gifts were completely in accord with his circumstances.

II

FORMATION AND EVOLUTION

Not the least interesting aspect of Marot's poetry is the problem
it presents to the literary historian concerned to trace the evolution of the poet's work and to establish thereby the place he
occupies in the history of French poetry. This is no easy matter
as the wide divergence of critical opinion on the subject shows.
Marot has been variously proclaimed the last of the *Rhétoriqueurs*;[1]
a transitional figure; a precursor of the *Pléiade*, of Ronsard and
Du Bellay in particular, and as such the first of the modern
French poets.

THE ELEMENTS OF THE PROBLEM

Some of this divergence of opinion may be explained historically
by reference to the material difficulties, difficulties of transmission for instance, which have for so long hampered later critics in
their study of Marot's poetry.[2] The poems of Marot's youth were
those most completely represented in the editions published
during his lifetime. Of the important poems of his maturity some,
like the *Avant-naissance*, were published only in posthumous
editions.[3] The value of the texts they offered, and in some cases
their authenticity, had to be carefully scrutinized before they
could be accepted. Many more of the important poems from
Ferrara and Venice (*Ep.* XXXV, XXXVII, XLI, XLII, XLIII, XLIV, XLVI),
however, although known to a limited public at the time of their
composition or just afterwards, were consigned to manuscripts and
incidentally to obscurity, an obscurity from which the majority
were retrieved as late as 1898.[4] And the process has continued in
this century. Only in the last few years has Marot criticism been
based on a critically established chronology in a critical edition
offering a complete range of the poems.[5]

It is in this light that we must examine some of the critical judgements of the past. Thomas Sebillet, Marot's contemporary and the author of the *Art Poétique Françoys* of 1548 and Jacques Peletier, another contemporary though slightly later theoretician, were not handicapped in their assessment of the poems by material difficulties to the same extent as later critics. They were, after all, closer to their subject. The latter, however, were limited in their knowledge of the poet's work to the early editions and hence mainly the poems of his youth, and to anthologies which reproduced selections from them. Thus, while Sebillet and Peletier[6] saw that Marot's poetry represented a complete break with that of his predecessors, Brunetière, among others, concluded that Marot had always remained unswervingly faithful to the traditions of the *Rhétoriqueurs* and even reproached him with having delayed the renaissance of French poetry.[7]

But the impression of a Marot *rhétoriqueur* persists still in the minds of some critics in spite of the advances made by recent scholarship. For this difficulties of transmission cannot be held to account. The arguments advanced in support of this impression are, however, based on serious misapprehensions; in fact, on the failure to appreciate the effect of the poet's conditions of creativity on his work. Without such an appreciation all aesthetic and interpretative judgements of the poems are rendered suspect. The unacceptable conclusion that Marot was a *rhétoriqueur* all his life because like the *Rhétoriqueurs* he wrote official poetry at intervals throughout his career is one such instance. Marot was required by his circumstances to do so, but so too was Ronsard who has never, to my knowledge, been accused of being a *rhétoriqueur*. Such a conclusion, in addition, ignores the innovations which Marot, as the influence of the Renaissance made itself increasingly felt on some sections of court taste, ventured to introduce into the writing of official poetry. Again, it is pointed out by Jourda, for one, that unmistakable echoes of the *rhétoriqueur* style are found in Marot's poetry at all the stages of his development and not only during his early years. He cites the case of the eclogue composed in 1531 to commemorate the death of Louise de Savoie and, even more significantly since it was composed in 1543 at the end of his life, that of the *Complainte du Général Preudhomme*.[8] This is indeed so, except that the eclogue, while faithful to the stylistic idiosyncrasies of the *Rhétoriqueurs*, was an innovation from the point of view of genre and the direct imitation in part of a Greek model.[9] The *complainte*, though, was archaic in both form and style and certainly in the use of the device of prosopopoeia.[10] One might also mention in this context the epistle *Au Chancellier du Prat* (XIII) of 1528 with its long closing passage in *rimes équivoquées*[11] which the poet had not used to such an extent for ten years. In these cases it is obvious that Marot, as a professional poet, was consciously, and conscientiously, reverting to the style of verse he considered to be most in accordance with the tastes and wishes of the persons addressed or commemorated. All three belonged to an older generation (Louise de Savoie was born in 1476, Du Prat in 1463, and so on)[12] which was precisely that of his father and of the last of the *Rhétoriqueurs*. And any innovations in the poem commemorating Louise de Savoie may easily be explained by the need to satisfy in part at the same time the tastes of François Ier, her son and Marguerite d'Angoulême, her daughter, both of whom Marot served. This apart, the three poems represent an exercise in conscious archaism[13] rather like (to take an example from another field) Mozart's *Clemenza di Tito*, a commission hastily written in a style the musician no longer cared for.

There are other examples of conscious archaism in Marot's poetry unconnected with the conditions in which he exercised his *métier* of professional poet. They serve other designs. Conscious archaism appears for instance when the poet, dwelling on an aspect of life in the past, wished to relate his style closely to his subject-matter.[14] This he did in 1527 in the epistle *Au roy, pour succéder en l'estat de son père* (XII) when he introduced the voice of his dead father and his advice on the writing of poetry according to the precepts of his own generation. Later still, in 1538, Marot returned to the style and a genre of his youth when he wrote a *rondeau* on the subject of *L'Amour du Siècle Antique* (*Rondeau* LX). This genre was by far and away the most practised by the love poets of the fourteenth and fifteenth centuries as they are represented in such anthologies as the *Jardin de Plaisance*.[15] Thirdly, it has been shown that Marot was equally adept at pastiching the style of his predecessors in order to obtain a comic or satirical effect, as in the *Petite Epistre au Roy* (I) and the *coqs-à-l'âne*.[16] That

Marot was able so successfully to adapt his style to meet his artistic intentions is not only a tribute to his qualities, it also demonstrates unequivocally his own awareness of the differences between himself and his predecessors, and his willingness to exploit them. In so doing he confirmed the break he had brought about from previous poetic traditions.

Another factor which has delayed recognition of Marot's true position in the history of French poetry is that the poet left no explicit statement of his aims and intentions in the form of a manifesto. Unlike the poets of the *Pléiade* Marot did not trumpet abroad his proposed or accomplished innovations, neither did he proclaim explicitly any rupture from the past. This omission undoubtedly explains the readiness of many critics to bestow upon the poet the label of *poète traditionaliste* or *poète de transition*. One may quote either Villey[17]

Encore une fois il n'y a pas rupture avec le passé: jamais Marot n'a condamné explicitement aucune des formes poétiques dont il tend à s'écarter...

or Plattard[18]

à aucun moment, il n'a rompu avec ses maîtres, ni renié ses 'coups d'essais'. Ni théoricien, ni critique, il ne s'est pas piqué de substituer un idéal nouveau à un idéal ancien...Il s'est soucié seulement de ne pas laisser sa poésie trop à l'écart...de la restauration des bonnes lettres...Pour le reste, il a été un poète traditionaliste...

in support of this. In this view, the undeniable progress which Marot's poetry represents over that of his predecessors is only grudgingly admitted ('tend à s'écarter' and 'il s'est soucié seulement...') and then attributed to the *ambiance* in which the poet functioned and to which he half-consciously responded. The difference between Marot and his predecessors, according to another critic, is simply the nature of their experience, rather than any new conception of poetry.[19] This will not stand up to examination however. The few statements on his art which Marot did make, together with his own hesitations in the establishment of poetical genres and his frequent revision of their nomenclature and classification, point to a conscious design to renew French poetry and a full awareness of the influences which could best serve this intention.

Marot's failure to leave a manifesto of his intentions was made far more damaging, in terms of his reputation, by the subsequent utterances of the *Pléiade*. They claimed for themselves the credit for Marot's earlier reforms while at the same time damning their predecessor with faint praise. For a long time after Sainte-Beuve's reassessment of the *Pléiade*, critics tended to take at their face value the assertions and innuendoes contained in Du Bellay's *Deffence et Illustration de la langue françoyse*. The work was, however, part of an ill-tempered polemic inspired by the appearance in 1548 of Sebillet's *Art Poétique* which had anticipated most of the cherished projects of the rising young poets.[20] And Sebillet's theories and recommendations were based almost exclusively on Marot's poetry.

Finally, any discussion of Marot's place in the history of French poetry must take into account the value of the terms used to describe the poet and his achievement. For instance, such labels as transitional poet and precursor of the *Pléiade* may in a sense be useful retrospectively since it is true that Marot, as indeed any writer does, took up where his predecessors left off, and further, left behind him many innovations for which the *Pléiade* later claimed responsibility. But they both have serious shortcomings. Accurate in one respect, they attribute at the same time to the poet a prescience which he could never have had. Or, in order to escape this implication, they must acquire another and equally untenable one, namely that of the poet's unconscious creation of his own work. The problem is most readily solved as one critic has already found[21] by the use of the simple term innovator to describe Marot and his role.

MAROT'S EARLY YEARS

That Marot began his career as a disciple of the *Rhétoriqueurs* is beyond dispute. Nor should this surprise us. In addition to the considerable influence upon the poet of his father,[22] Marot also received some instruction from Jean Lemaire de Belges. He was one of the most highly regarded, and justly so, of the *Rhétoriqueurs*, who was at one moment attached to the entourage of Anne de Bretagne at the same time as Marot's father.[23] To this instruction and its precise nature Marot alludes briefly in the preface to the *Adolescence Clementine* of 12 August 1532. He spoke of:

les couppes femenines, que je n'observoys encor alors, dont Jehan le Maire de Belges (en les m'aprenant) me reprint.[24]

It is probable too that at the court of François Ier Marot was acquainted with Guillaume Cretin whose reputation among the poets of his day was considerable. Marot composed an epitaph of homage to Cretin on his death in 1525 which shows a flattering imitation of the latter's expertise and virtuosity in matters of versification.[25]

To delimit the stages of a writer's development with any precision is a hazardous enterprise. However, in this case the works which bear the imprint of Marot's apprenticeship are designated by the poet himself as those which appear in the *Adolescence* proper. They are followed by, and carefully distinguished from, certain other poems which appear under the heading of *Aultres œuvres faictes depuis l'eage de son Adolescence* and to which Marot alludes when he expresses the hope:

...de brief vous faire offre de mieulx, & pour arres de ce mieulx, desja je vous mectz en veue (à la fin de l'Adolescence) Ouvraiges de meilleure trempe & de plus polie estoffe, mais l'Adolescence ira devant, & la commancerons par la premiere Eglogue des Buccoliques Virgilanes, translatée (certes) en grande jeunesse...[26]

All the poems in the *Adolescence* proper would appear to have been composed before 1527.[27] They represent a pattern of activity typical of the *Grands Rhétoriqueurs*.[28]

They include several translations. The success of Octovien de Saint-Gelais's translations of Ovid's *Heroides* (1497) and of Virgil's *Aeneid* had been an intimation to other *Rhétoriqueurs* to follow his suite. With this thought in mind Jean Marot allegedly encouraged his son:

> Tu en pourras traduire les Volumes
> Jadis escriptz par les divines Plumes
> Des vieulx Latins, dont tant est mention...
>
> (*Ep.*, XII, vv. 57–59)

Clément, as if in obedience to such advice, started his career with the translation, or paraphrase—depending upon the degree of one's indulgence—of Virgil's first eclogue, followed by attempts on such oddly assorted works as the *Jugement de Minos* (Marot's task in this instance being merely to transcribe into verse an existing French prose translation of Aurispa's Latin version of one of Lucian's dialogues!) and the devotional *Carmen lugubre de die dominicae passionis* by Beroaldo which appears as *Les Tristes Vers de Béroalde*.

They include the *Temple de Cupido*,[29] belonging to a genre which has never been strictly named, the long semi-lyrical moralizing allegory which has as its prototype the *Roman de la Rose* and counts among its other predecessors the *Hospital damour* attributed to Chartier, Molinet's *Temple de Mars* and Jean Lemaire's *Temple de Venus*.

The verse epistle is another genre of the *Rhétoriqueurs* to be found, in various forms, in the *Adolescence* proper. The *épître artificielle* for instance, conceived on the model of the imaginary letters written by Ovid's heroines of mythology to their departed husbands or lovers, and which enjoyed a tremendous vogue at the beginning of the sixteenth century in France following upon Octovien de Saint-Gelais's translation, is represented in Marot's *juvenilia* by the *Epistre de Maguelonne*.[30] The only difference is that the two protagonists, the heroine Maguelonne and her lover Pierre are taken from a little-known medieval romance *Pierre de Provence et la Belle Maguelonne*. In conception however it is in every respect true to the genre, and in execution no less, even to the great strain placed upon plausibility by the epistolary convention. Thus Maguelonne's letter is sent to a lover whose whereabouts are at the time completely unknown. Worse still, the heroine is made to recount a scene which takes place while she is fast asleep and unaware of what is happening. Perhaps in the absurdity of its development Marot's epistle outdoes those of Ovid who was not entirely without a respect for credibility even in his fictions![31] In addition to this *épître artificielle*, all the forms of the *épître naturelle*, so called to distinguish it from the former, have their equivalents in the *Adolescence*. The *épître équivoquée*, much practised by Guillaume Cretin, is represented by the *Petite Epistre au Roy* (I),[32] the allegorical epistle by the *Epistre du despourveu* (II), the descriptive by the *Epistre du Camp d'Atigny* (III). Although intended to be a personal composition, the *épître naturelle* of the *Rhétoriqueurs* owes nothing to the tradition of such poetry created by Horace's example, nor do those of Marot.

The *complainte*, of which there are two examples in the *Adolescence*, the *Complainte du Baron de Malleville*[33] and the *Complainte d'une Niepce sur sa tante*,[34] is similarly an established genre of medieval poetry, devoted to the lamentation of the dead. Marot has preserved the almost statutory features, the invocation against death and the praise of the deceased in the form of an apostrophe to Nature or to one of its personified elements.[35]

Marot in his youth was a prolific exponent of the *chanson*, including three-quarters of all such compositions dating from before 1527, in the *Adolescence*. They represent the survival not of the *chanson* of the fifteenth century as it is found in the works of Charles d'Orléans where it is not a distinct literary genre but may be any poem set to music be it *rondeau* or *ballade*, but chiefly of popular lyricism with which poets of standing did not concern themselves. Without destroying its essential simplicity Marot transformed this form of popular lyricism into a literary genre with a unity of its own.[36]

Of the fixed form genres of the Middle Ages the *rondeau*, the *ballade* and the *chant-royal* are represented in the *Adolescence*.[37] It is in the *rondeau* that the influence of Marot's father upon him is most discernible. The *rondeau* of medieval poetry was for a long time distinguished as such only by the presence of a refrain but received its definitive form at the hands of Jean Marot. In the *Adolescence* the *rondeau simple* consists of a first quatrain rhyming ABBA, thus:

Au feu qui mon cueur a choisy,	A
Jectez y, ma seule Deesse,	B
De l'eau de grace & de lyesse!	B
Car il est consommé quasi.	A

followed by a distich plus the refrain—AB R thus:

Amours l'a de si pres saisy	A
Que force est qu'il crie sans cesse:	B
Au feu!	R

closing with a second quatrain which repeats the rhyme scheme of the first and the refrain, ABBA R

Si par vous en est dessaisy,   A
Amours luy doint plus grand destresse   B
Si jamais sert aultre maistresse.   B
Doncques ma Dame courez y,   A
    Au feu!   R

(O.D., Rondeau v)

The majority of Marot's *rondeaux* in the *Adolescence* however belong to the category of the *rondeau double* constructed of a first verse of five lines rhyming AABBA, followed by a tercet plus the refrain AAB R and the final verse of five lines plus refrain AABBA R. There is in addition one example of the *rondeau parfait* (*A ses amys apres sa delivrance*, LXIV) consisting of six quatrains, the last followed by a refrain with a rhyme scheme thus: ABAB BABA ABAB BABA ABAB BABA R. The *ballade* was originally distinguished not only by its fixed form but also by the character of its subject-matter, as Sebillet remarked:

La Balade est Poéme plus grave...pour ce que de son origine s'adressoit aus Princes, et ne traitoit que matiéres graves et dignes de l'aureille d'un roy. Avec le temps empireur de toutes choses, lés Poétes François l'ont adaptée a matiéres plus légéres et facécieuses, en sorte qu'aujourd'huy la matiére de la Balade est toute téle qu'il plaist a celuy qui en est autheur...[38]

If Marot is included among those poets who thus enlarged the scope of the *ballade* he introduced no innovations to its formal structure to judge from the thirteen which appear in the *Adolescence*. Each is composed of three verses of identical rhyme schemes, followed by an *envoi* which reproduces some of these rhymes. The length of the verses varies from eight to twelve lines from poem to poem, and that of the *envoi* from four to seven usually in proportion to the length of the main stanzas. The sole *chant-royal* of the *Adolescence* properly so called, *Chant Royal de la Conception* written in 1521 for the verse competition, the *Puys de Palinod* at Rouen, to a set theme, conforms in every respect to the established pattern of this genre, consisting of five stanzas of eleven lines in length with a scheme of five rhymes repeated in each stanza, followed by an *envoi* reproducing some of these rhymes.

The sources exploited by Marot in his early works are, too, an important indication of his allegiances. Thus the *Roman de la*

Rose, Ovid's *Heroides* and *Ars Amatoria*, the sources upon which
Marot's *Temple de Cupido* and *Epistre de Maguelonne* lean most
heavily, were also those most constantly plundered by the
Rhétoriqueurs.[39] Similarly, Marot inherited the attitude of his
predecessors to Chartier, referring to him with traditional
reverence as Maistre Alain, and taking inspiration from a work
attributed to him in the *Temple de Cupido*, as well as from some
of his love poetry in his *chansons* and *rondeaux*.[40] In addition,
Marot imitated the works of the *Rhétoriqueurs* themselves:
Molinet's *Temple de Mars*, Lemaire's *Concorde des deux
Langages* in the *Temple de Cupido* and an *héroide* by André de la
Vigne in the *Epistre de Maguelonne*. These were often combined
with reinforcements from the works of poets *hors-série*. Martial
d'Auvergne's *Arrêts d'Amour* and Coquillart's *Droitz nouveaulx*
are remembered in the *Temple de Cupido*, Villon's *Ballade des
Pendus* in the *complainte* for Semblançay. Most interesting,
however, is the use which Marot makes in his *rondeaux*, of the
conceits of Petrarchist love poetry, taking his inspiration from
Serafino, Sassoferrato and Chariteo.[41] The influence of the
strambottistes and their neo-Latin counterparts also brings early
traces of the *Greek Anthology* to the *huitains*, *dizains*, *blasons*,
envois etc., of the *Adolescence*.[42]

In treatment and in style, no less than in the choice of genres
and some sources, Marot's early poetry shows the unmistakable
influence of the *Grands Rhétoriqueurs*. It reflects firstly their
predilection for allegory often pursued to absurdity and nowhere
better demonstrated perhaps than in Jean Meschinot's *Lunettes
des Princes*. Here, the political wisdom urged upon the ruler by
the poet is contained in the pages of a book called *Conscience*
which may only be read with spectacles whose particular proper-
ties lie in lenses inscribed *Prudence* and *Justice* respectively.[43]
The *Temple de Cupido*, allegorical in conception and execution, is
not so prosaically absurd. It's theme is that of the *Rose*. The poet,
hitherto immune from Cupid's law, is wounded at last by one of
the god's shafts. He sets out, as many have done before him, on
the quest for *Ferme Amour*:

> la Dame pure et munde,
> Qui, long temps a, ne fut veue en ce Monde.
>
> (*O.L.*, I, vv. 65–66)

For long unsuccessful in his search he decides at last on a pilgrimage to the *Temple cupidique* which he believes may be the refuge of True Love. In common with other symbolical sanctuaries gardens, orchards, palaces etc., of medieval poetry, its approaches are guarded by personified abstractions. Thus the poet is welcomed on arrival at

> Le premier huys de toutes fleurs vermeilles
>
> (ibid., v. 183)

by *Bel Accueil* while *Faulx Dangier* lies in wait at the gate of thorns and thistles. After initial discouragement in his exploration of the *Temple* where he has found only *une Amour venerique* and *une Amour legiere* both of which he rejects, he moves on from the nave to the choir to which he is admitted by *Bel Accueil*. There it is that he finds *Ferme Amour*, the object of his quest, presiding over a happy royal couple, none other than the king of France and his queen, François Ier and Claude. The moral which convention demanded at the end of an allegory is predictable both in content and in its play on the two senses of the word *cueur* (choir: heart) in these lines:

> Parquoy concludz en mon invention,
> Que Ferme Amour est au cueur esprouvée.
> Dire le puis, car je l'y ay trouvée. (ibid., vv. 536–8)

The parent narrative allegory is interrupted in the middle of the poem by the allegorical description of the *Temple* itself which turns out to be a 'clos flory Verger'. This initial statement is minutely elaborated. Thus the high altar of the temple is a large rock, its canopy a fragrant cedar, and its supporting pillars two cypresses; the roof of the temple is a trellis of vine leaves, the choir stalls the overhanging branches of near-by trees and, inevitably, Matins is sung by the birds, nightingales chant the responses. One could go on, but this is not all. As Marot knew from his reading, the allegorical conception of a temple of love (or of war etc.) allowed of an endless substitution and interplay of the rites of love or war with those of the church. Lovers are therefore pilgrims who pray and lay offerings at the shrine of their love, the bells which summon the faithful to worship are harps, lutes and other instruments associated with profane music, mass is an *aubade*, the missals and psalters and lessons are similarly profane:

> Ovidius, maistre Alain Charretier,
> Petrarche, aussi le Rommant de la Rose,
> Sont les Messelz, Breviaire & Psaultier,
> Qu'en ce sainct Temple on list en Rime & Prose;
> Et les Leçons que chanter on y ose,
> Ce sont Rondeaulx, Ballades, Virelais,
> Motz à plaisir, Rimes & Triolletz,
> Lesquelz Venus aprend à retenir
> A ung grant tas d'amoureux nouveletz,
> Pour mieulx savoir dames entretenir.   (ibid., vv. 323–32)

and the Saints to be implored are personifications of those qualities which lovers need if they are to be successful in their suit, *Beau parler*, *Bien celer*, *Bon rapport*, *Grace*, *Mercy*, *Bien servir*, *Bien aymer*. So far so good perhaps, but it is difficult not to regard as incongruously comic the visual impression offered by the poet of ladies bathing in the baptismal fonts, which happen to be

> une Fontaine,
> Où decouroit ung Ruisseau argentin...
>
>   (ibid., vv. 303–4)

attended by their lovers equipped with combs and sponges and even with fronds of greenery with which to protect them from the implacable sun. But such incongruities abound in the poetry of his predecessors.

Allegory, and the personification of abstractions essential to its elaboration is again a characteristic, as indeed the title leads one to expect, of the *Epistre du despourveu*. *Le despourveu* is the poet who addresses himself to Marguerite d'Alençon at the bidding of the god Mercury. However, just as the poet found himself inspired to write in 'ung souverain style' he was confronted by

> une Vielle hideuse,
> Maigre de corps et de face blemie,
> Qui se disoit de Fortune ennemye.
> Le cueur avoit plus froid que glace ou marbre,
> Le corps tremblant comme la feuille en l'arbre,
> Les yeux baissez comme de paour estraincte,
> Et s'appelloit par son propre nom Crainte
>
>   (*Ep.*, ii, vv. 53–59)

who upbraids him for his audacity and presumption in thinking to present his verses to the duchess. Fortunately the poet is rescued from *Crainte, Doute* and *Souci*—the last two her attendants, by *Bon Espoir*

> Ung bon Viellard, portant chere joyeuse (ibid., v. 99)

who speedily puts them to flight, and whom the poet then thanks for sustaining him in the

> ...Forest nommée longue Attente   (ibid., v. 165)

from which may it please the duchess herself to release him by acceding to his request. The allegory here is not essentially narrative or descriptive. Its purpose is the poeticization of a state of mind and of the contending forces which produce it. Allegory used to such an end is a substitute for sustained simile which is an ornament strangely absent in *rhétoriqueur* poetry. It was a convention dictated by an impoverished art. Hence its predictability and, thereby, its principal weakness.

Paradoxical as it may seem, a concern for verisimilitude often accompanied the elaboration of allegorical inventions. Even more paradoxically perhaps, the device chosen to safeguard verisimilitude was the dream.[44] By such means cohorts of personified abstractions, invariably escorted by more august personalities drawn from Classical mythology could be conveniently introduced into natural surroundings in which the reader of sound mind would hardly expect to find them. In a dream, however, no possibility could be discounted, fantasy took on the substance of reality. By this simple expedient the vast development of the *Roman de la Rose* was initiated, and, although on a considerably reduced scale, that of Marot's *Epistre du despourveu* to the duchesse d'Alençon.

Another aspect of the presentation of their works which Marot copies at this stage of his career from the *Rhétoriqueurs*, is the tiresome pretence of humility. This is again demonstrated by the *Epistre du despourveu*[45] where the whole allegory subserves this convention, presenting in poetic form (a small mercy) a synthetic debate on a pseudo-dilemma, that is, whether the poet should presume to submit his verses 'si mal bastiz' to the attention of one who 'de sçavoir toutes aultres precelle'.

This false humility appeared in conjunction with a determination to cast poetry in the learned mould, to impress by weight of erudition. The pedantic and recondite litanies of Classical and historical allusions which characterize much *rhétoriqueur* poetry are evidence of this. They certainly do not demonstrate, as one might hope, an awareness of the plasticity of myth and a concern to impart the same to their own creations. Jean d'Auton was probably one of the worst offenders of all and his poem *Les Alarmes de Mars*[46] lists, *à propos* Louis XII's expedition to Milan, the following conquerors: Nemrod, Ninus, Balthazar, Xerxès, Cyrus, Minos, Thésée, Atlas, Cadmus, Josué, Samson, David, Etéocle, Polynice, Hercule, Epaminondas, Jason, Hector, Alexandre, Enée,...Cila, Fabricius, Minucius etc., etc., with a nice impartiality for provenance and chronology before remembering the heroes of Arthurian romance and of French expeditions to the crusades. By comparison, Marot's use of Classical and literary allusion in his early works is almost niggardly although whether this is due to his having escaped the full rigours of a scholastic education or to a nascent sense of moderation is difficult to tell. In the *Temple de Cupido* for instance Zephirus, Tityrus and the great god Pan are plausibly invoked in a pastoral setting.[47] Similarly discreet are the poet's references to Cupid's victims, whether their passions had been extinguished by his actions, as in the case of Apollo and Daphne, or inflamed as were those of Dido, Biblis and Helen of Greece.[48] Such moderation commends itself to modern taste far more than the exhaustive catalogues of the *Rhétoriqueurs*.

It was by means of a ludicrously latinized vocabulary that these poets sought to confirm the exceptional brilliance of their utterances. This is especially true of Molinet and of Jean Robertet.[49] For a very short time only Marot, too, was tempted by this ploy. Thus in the earliest published version of his *Temple de Cupido*[50] Marot preferred the word *Ver* to the more usual *printemps* (v. 1); he spoke of the *altitonens dieux* (v. 15); described a *trousse* as a *pharette* (v. 28); evoked the coming of daylight by the flight of the *tenebre nocturne* before the *essence diuturne* (vv. 97–98); imagined sermons which exhorted the *conjunction de creatures* (v. 302), in obedience to love's laws.

The elaboration of purely formal stylistic effects was, however, the prime concern of the *Rhétoriqueurs* in their pursuit of poetic excellence. They practised alliterative enumeration and assembled whole convoys of adjectives.[51] Marot did likewise, for the space of seven whole lines, in the *Epistre du despourveu*:

> Ces motz finiz, demeure mon semblant
> Triste, transi, tout terny, tout tremblant,
> Sombre, songeant, sans seure soustenance,
> Dur d'esperit, desnué d'esperance,
> Melencolic, morne, marry, musant,
> Pasle, perplex, paoureux, pensif, pesant,
> Foible, failly, foulé, fasché, forclus,
> Confus, courcé. Croyre Crainte concluz
> Bien congnoissant que verité disoit...'
>
> (*Ep.*, II, vv. 81–89)

Such superficial virtuosity—for it has no melodic significance—was only achieved at the expense of spontaneity of expression and very often of sense and meaning too. This is the price Marot has paid to maintain alliteration in the penultimate line quoted above, the last half of which defies analysis and interpretation.

Word play and punning are scarcely less obtrusive effects admired by this school to reappear in the works of Marot's *Adolescence*. Typical of them is the one incorporated in his poetic device 'la Mort n'y mord' and recurring in this line from the second *complainte*[52]

> O Mort mordant, o impropre impropere
> (*O.L.*, *Complainte* II, v. 27)

Such effects were even more striking when consistently allied to patterns of versification.

It was in this last respect that novelty was most assiduously cultivated. Not content to exhibit the virtuosity which the fixed form *genres* already demanded of the versifier, and to intercalate wherever possible these fixed form poems into the structure of non-strophic *genres* such as the epistle—to which practice Marot's second epistle containing two *rondeaux* and a *ballade* conforms—the *Rhétoriqueurs* introduced further taxing refinements. In short, technical complexity was held to be the highest manifestation of poetic excellence. The multiple rhymes[53] so laboriously effected by them are often present in the works of Marot's youth.

Such are the rhymes called *rimes annexées, couronnées,* and *enchaînées* which Marot employed successively in the three stanzas of his *Chanson* III. The first of these rhymes is produced by repeating the last syllable of a line at the beginning of the following line. For example:

> Dieu gard ma Maistresse et Re*gente*,
> *Gente* de corps et de façon!
> *Son* cueur tient le mien en sa *tente*
> *Tant* et plus d'ung ardant fris*son.*
> *S'on* m'oyt poulser sur ma chan*son*
> *Son* de voix ou Harpes doul*cettes*,
> *C'est* Espoir qui sans marris*son*
> *Song*er me faict en amourettes.
>
> *(O.L., Chanson* III, vv. 1–8)

A normal terminal rhyme scheme, ABABBCBC, is simultaneously maintained. The second, the *rime couronnée,* involves the repetition of syllables which rhyme within the same line of verse. Thus:

> La blanche Colom*belle belle*,
> Souvent je voys *priant*, c*riant*,
> Mais dessoubz la cor*delle d'elle*
> Me gette ung oeil f*riant, riant*,
> En me con*sommant* et *sommant*
> A douleur qui ma *face efface.*
> Dont suis le rec*lamant amant*,
> Qui pour l'oul*trepasse trespasse.*
>
> (ibid., vv. 9–16)

If this instance calls forth enthusiasm for the way in which the poet has skilfully exploited the richness of the internal rhymes for onomatopoeic effect, how much greater this enthusiasm becomes when Marot's verses are compared with these of Molinet on the evils of war:

> Guerre a fait maint chaste*let let*
> Et mainte bonne *ville vile*,
> Et gasté maint jardi*net net.*
> Je ne sçay à qui son *plaid plaist...*[54]

or these from a *complainte* by the same author where these artifices are in no way allied to the subject-matter treated:

Quant tu tuas joye, doeul suscitas;
Tué tu as mon coeur pul*ente lente*;
R*egente gente*, ne la pre*sente sente*,
N'*attente attente*, or n'ay je en ta morsure,
Par ta lai*dure*, qu'ar*dure dure*, *dure*...[55]

The *rime enchaînée* which appears in the final stanza of Marot's third *chanson* is in effect very similar to the *rime annexée*. It consists in the repetition at the beginning of each line of the last word (normally), or of a word radically and syntactically related to the last word of the previous line. Thus—with a slight variation in the position of the 'catch word' in the second, third and fourth lines:

> Dieu des Amans, de mort *me garde*;
> *Me gardant donne* moy bon heur;
> *En le me donnant, prens* ta Darde;
> *En la prenant, navre* son cueur;
> *En le navrant*, me tiendras *seur*;
> *En seurté*, suyvray l'*accointance*;
> *En l'accoinctant*, ton *Serviteur*
> *En servant* aura jouyssance.
>
> (*O.L.*, *Chanson* III, vv. 17–24)

Another formal effect, the *rime concatenée*, so called because it forms a link between one stanza and the next, is obtained simply by repeating the whole of the last line of a stanza at the beginning of the succeeding one. Marot's second *complainte* demonstrates this device throughout (ex: vv. 11–12, 22–23, 33–34, 44–45, 55–56).

Slightly more conventional since they are all terminal rhymes are the *rime léonine*, the *rime équivoquée*, the *rime en écho* and the *rime rauque*. The *rime léonine* which is an extension of the *rime riche* is achieved when the last two syllables of each line of a couplet are identical. Thus:

> Trouva moyen & maniere & *matiere*,
> D'ongles & dentz, de rompre la *ratiere*
> Dont maistre Rat eschappe vis*tement*,
> Puis mist à terre ung genoul gen*tement*...
>
> (*Ep.*, x, vv. 21–24)

Epistles IX, x, from which these lines come, and XI are composed almost entirely in *rimes léonines*. The *rime équivoquée*, perhaps the most highly esteemed of all by both poets and theoreticians, is one which results in a play on words. The following examples are taken from the *Epistre du despourveu* II:

> En me incitant d'avoir hardy *courage*,
> De besongner & faire à ce *coup rage*...
>
> (vv. 107–8)

and

> Si me souvint tout à coup de *mon songe*,
> Dont la pluspart n'est fable ne *mensonge*;
> A tout le moins pas ne fut *mensonger*
> Le bon Espoir qui vint à *mon songer*   (vv. 152–5)

The *rime en écho* of which there are conflicting definitions[56] is really a complication of the *rime équivoquée*, and far more demanding since the rhymes and puns are all dependent upon the repetition of the same basic word. Thus Marot's *Petite Epistre au Roy* is constructed entirely around the word *rime*.

> En m'esbatant je faiz Rondeaux *en rime*,
> Et en rimant bien souvent je *m'enrime*;
> Brief, c'est pitié d'entre nous *Rimailleurs*,
> Car vous trouvez assez de *rime ailleurs*,
> Et quand vous plaist, mieulx que moy *rimassez*,
> Des biens avez et de la *rime assez*.   (*Ep.*, I, vv. 1–6)

This virtuosity is sustained for twenty-six lines. In the elaboration of the *rime rauque* the versifier eschews harmony for cacophony restricting himself to consonantal rhymes. There is only one example of this phenomenon in the work of Marot. This is the *ballade* XI, *Du Jour de Noel*, where each stanza is built on the rhymes *ac, ec, ic, oc, uc*. This is the first stanza:

> Or est Noel venu son petit tr*ac*,
> Sus donc, aux champs, Bergieres, de resp*ec*!
> Prenons chascun Panetiere et Biss*ac*,
> Fluste, Flageol, Cornemuse et Reb*ec*!
> Ores n'est pas temps de clorre le b*ec*.
> Chantons, saultons et dansons ric à r*ic*,
> Puis allons veoir l'Enfant au pauvre n*ic*,
> Tant exalté d'Helye, aussi d'En*oc*,

Et adoré de maint grant Roy et D*uc*!
S'on nous dit nac, il fauldra dire n*oc*.
Chantons Noel, tant au soir qu'au desj*ucq*.

(O.D., Ballade XI, vv. 1–11)

Earlier examples of this device are to be found in the works of Jean Molinet and Jean d'Auton.[57]

It has not been difficult to demonstrate by means of examples the attachment which Marot maintained in his early works to the traditions of his predecessors. Yet even here the poet left his own mark, not merely by virtue of superior talent, but also by conscious intent. Evidence of this can be seen in the *Petite Epistre au Roy* (I). Versification elaborated with all seriousness by his predecessors is here used by Marot with comic intent as a device calculated to amuse and divert the king. And in this we know that he fully succeeded. That Marot was prepared to make a joke of a form of rhyme regarded as quintessentially poetical by previous writers is a clear indication of his departure in spirit from their poetic traditions and aesthetic values.

There is a further category of poems which reflects similarly on Marot's intention and ability to transform in certain respects the legacy he had received from the past. These are the poems relating to the poet's arrest and imprisonment in 1526. They remained in manuscript[58] until after the publication of the *Adolescence* to which, nevertheless, by their date of composition they form a tail-piece. One of the most noticeable transformations effected by Marot here concerns the use of the pun on a proper name, a device which was a perennial favourite with his predecessors. A few examples will make this point clear. In *L'Enfer*, a burlesque play on Marot's christian name Clément with that of a contemporary Pope is used for satirical purposes. It serves in fact to preface an attack on Papal dogma as presented by the mendicant orders.[59] In the same poem a play on Virgil's surname Maro and Marot's own inspires the poet quite naturally to make an implicit comparison between the Augustan age and the French Renaissance of letters which is the occasion for a hymn of praise to the latter.[60] In Marot's tenth epistle a pun on the name of his friend Lyon Jamet:

Mais ce Lyon (qui jamais ne fut Grue)

is the key upon which turns the whole animal allegory. It is exploited for the economy of exposition which it confers and which is so essential to any fable.[61] In the epistles of the *Rhétoriqueurs* on the other hand puns on proper names justified themselves without reference to artistic design. They might stand as signature or passing salutation

> Ces jours passés du gentil *Honorat*,
> Tendant à fin que ma plume *honorast*
> Son Charbonnier...[62]

but they were in any deeper sense gratuitous. This may be amply demonstrated by further recourse to the voluminous works of Cretin, and of Jean Molinet, who probably considered themselves fortunate in having names which lent themselves so well to this exercise:

> Molinet n'est sans bruyt ne sans nom non...
> Car souvent vent vient au Molinet net... [63]

It is a strange thought.

Marot's use of allegory in the *Epître à Lyon Jamet* and in *L'Enfer* offers another point of comparison with the usage of the *Rhétoriqueurs*. Although the subject of allegory will be examined at greater length in the chapters relevant to these two works,[64] the nature of the transformation effected by Marot can be expressed quite briefly here. Firstly, his starting-point is the reality of his own experience. The dreams and apparitions which were an inescapable prelude to allegory, and a justification of it in the earlier poetic tradition and in the works of Marot's first youth, are therefore unnecessary. The prolixity which accompanied the elaboration of allegory is thereby eliminated. In positive terms allegory ceases to be merely a pretext *for* something else and becomes an instrument *of* to a greater degree than before. To this extent also the diffuseness so inimical to poetry and to satirical poetry in particular is removed and density achieved. The animal allegory of Marot's tenth epistle is thus an instrument of concision and internal economy. In *L'Enfer* the allegory, an extended satirical analogy, is an instrument of polemic.

The tendencies revealed so far in the works Marot composed before he was thirty are significantly confirmed and accentuated in the postscript to the *Adolescence* proper. This section is composed of works written, as far as can be ascertained, between the years 1527–32.[65] It includes a *dizain* and an *huitain*,[66] a *ballade*,[67] two *chants-royaux*,[68] the *complainte* known as the *Deploration de Florimont Robertet* (*Complainte* IV) four epistles (that is, XI, XIII, XV, XXV), the first *coq-à-l'âne* and finally the eclogue on the death of Louise de Savoie (*Eglogue* I). Marot presented them to the public with the consciousness that they constituted an advance on his earlier manner and were in some sense a guarantee of further development. Literary history endorses the poet's own view. The *Aultres œuvres* reveal clearly the limits of his adherence to the *Rhétoriqueur* tradition which he attempted to renew before discarding. But before examining Marot's evolution after 1527, it will be useful to consider the influences at work on the poet and their precise effect.

POST-'ADOLESCENCE' AND MATURITY

Marot made few explicit statements which have a bearing on the conditions of his own development as a poet but those he did make are very instructive indeed. They concern the indebtedness he felt to the court and which he acknowledged on at least three separate occasions. The first of these acknowledgements is an indirect one. Writing as the editor of Villon's poems in 1533 Marot made this statement:

ne foy doubte qu'il n'eust emporté le chappeau de laurier devant touts les poetes de son temps, s'il eust été nourry en la court des roys & des princes, là où les jugements se amendent & les langages se polissent...[69]

which is clearly dictated by his own personal experience. Three years later, in the epistle to the dauphin (XLV), he referred to the French court as his 'maistresse d'escolle'.[70] He was no less sensible of the advantages he had derived from his period of exile at the court of Ferrara and in particular of the instruction he had received

> Soubz Celius, de qui tant on aprent...
>
> (*Ep.*, XXXVII, v. 41)

which had improved his competence 'en l'art de poésie' as in

other spheres of activity. These statements would appear to con-
tradict the notion cherished by some critics of a poet absorbing
passively and without awareness the influences of his milieux; a
notion which thereby minimizes such influences as a factor in any
conscious design to renew French poetry.

Another impression contradicted by recent research concerns
the nature and extent of these influences. Thus it has been
asserted by one critic that Italian influence on Marot was negligible;[71] by others that Italian influence on the poet dated from
the period of Marot's exile in Ferrara and was consequently
confined to the poems of his maturity.[72] This is now known to be
false. It was at the court of France that Marot was initiated in
Italianism.[73] This influence is most precisely discernible in those
rondeaux of the *Adolescence* which display many of the Petrarchist
concetti. To these poems may be added at least seventeen others
appearing either in the *Adolescence* or the *Suite de l'Adolescence*
(1533) as *huitains*, *dizains* or *blasons* and later to be described by
the author as epigrams, as well as the *Chant-Royal dont le Roy
bailla le Refrain* appearing in the postscript to the *Adolescence*,
and the *Ballade* (XVII) 'Amour me voyant sans tristesse' first
published in the *Suite*. Of the epigrams published for the first
time in 1538 and composed between 1533–8 in all probability
fourteen are inspired by Petrarchism. Of the hundred or so
epigrams attributed to Marot after his death only five could be so
described. It follows therefore that the poet's exile was not the
decisive factor in his introduction to Petrarchism that has sometimes been assumed, although he did bring back with him the
form of the sonnet. Its importance, paradoxically, may well be
the negative one suggested by Mayer.[74] Namely that Marot found
on arrival in Italy that the poets of the *quattrocento* were no
longer in favour among cultured people and that noting this fact,
he accordingly abandoned them more or less completely as models
or sources of inspiration.

Italianism has also been judged a factor in Marot's concern for
polished language and for a refinement of discrimination,
qualities he associated with the court as we know and which he
esteemed of such importance to the poet. This is very probable.
There is certainly a conjunction between Italianism and increasing refinement and ease in Marot's art before 1534. In this he

reflects the trend of French society in general. But cause and effect is always more difficult to establish.

Marot's commerce with humanism was also the result of his presence at the French court and the contacts which this ensured. The effects of this commerce are visible in his poetry from 1527 onwards both in his sources of inspiration, and the genres he cultivated. But it is especially from the period of his exile in Ferrara where he was fortunate to enjoy the instruction of the humanist Celio Calcagnini, the friend of Erasmus, editor of Aristotle and translator of Lucian, that humanism becomes a more precise factor, perhaps also a more potent one, in Marot's development and in the orientation of his poetry. From this period dates his awareness of the importance of sustained imagery and his attempt to endow his own style with the intensity which such ornament conferred upon Latin epic and elegiac poetry.[75]

Evangelism too, is a source of Marot's inspiration, more noticeably so at certain periods than at others. In 1527 for instance, when he came under the influence of the dominican Mathieu Malingre[76] who had delivered evangelist sermons in public at Blois that year, and again in 1536 when he was a member of Renée de Ferrare's essentially Protestant entourage.[77]

The events of Marot's own life, finally, and in particular the personal support he lent to humanism and evangelism as forces of moral and intellectual enlightenment, gave to his poetry a gravity of purpose and an intensity of spirit which also helped to lift it far above the vapid outpourings of many of his predecessors.

Marot's evolution after 1527 represents a break with the medieval poetic tradition and is marked by experimentation and innovation. Sources, treatment, style, genres, all confirm the break with the past.

He discarded the sources he had favoured in his youth—apart from the Petrarchists and the Italian neo-Latins in which respect he was already something of an innovator[78]—with two exceptions. Many of the commonplaces of medieval love poetry, including those inspired by Ovid's *Ars Amatoria* and *Heroides*, persist in Marot's elegies.[79] Secondly, Marot drew with increasing felicity upon the works of Jean Lemaire de Belges until late in his career. The most outstanding example of this is to be seen in the *Eglogue de Marot au Roy* (III) of 1539.[80] It is significant however that of all the *Rhétoriqueurs*, Jean Lemaire was hailed by Marot's generation as the one who most anticipated their own, and even the *Pléiade* did not disdain to recognize in him one of their immediate precursors.[81] During the period of his middle years, 1527–34, Marot's new sources are Classical: Catullus (*Epithalame* I), Ovid, *Metamorphoses*[82] (*Eglogue* I), Virgil, *Bucolics* (*Eglogue* I), Tibullus and Propertius (*Elégies*), Theocritus and the pseudo-Moschus presumably via a Latin translation (*Eglogue* I); neo-Latin, Erasmus's colloquy *Proci e Puellae* providing some part of *Epithalame* I; scriptural and reformist, St. Paul's epistles to the Hebrews and Romans (*Deploration de Florimont Robertet*), and Luther's treatise *De Votis Monasticis* (*Le Second Chant d'Amour fugitif*). In the period of his maturity, 1535–44, Marot has less recourse to Catullus and to Ovid's *Metamorphoses* (*Epithalame* II), but draws increasingly on Virgil's *Bucolics* in his own *Eglogues* (II, III, IV). New to this period is his use of Ovid's *Tristia* and *Epistulae ex Ponto* in his epistles from exile, and his imitations of Martial in the *Epigrammes*. His neo-Latin sources are the Italian-born poets Marc Antonio Flaminio (*Cantique* IV) and probably, too, Battista Spagnuoli of Mantua (*Eglogue* III). From the Bible Marot draws occasionally on Proverbs (*Epithalame* II) but more often on the Psalms, and in two poems particularly (*Epithalame* II and *Cantique* VII). It is not only the increasing sophistication of his sources which is noticeable at this stage, but also the increasingly sophisticated use he makes of them by skilful transposition.[83] In general, then, Marot's sources after 1527 are not those of the *Rhétoriqueurs*. For even though his predecessors invoked the *Metamorphoses*, Proverbs, and the Psalms in their avid pursuit of moral truisms, the edification which was the concern of the *Rhétoriqueurs* is far removed from Marot's appreciation of the poetry, and above all, the plasticity, of these same works.

In treatment, the poetry of Marot's post-*Adolescence* and maturity, with the exception of certain of the elegies, is characterized by an absence of didacticism and abstraction. This is partly explained by the greater extent to which his personal experience provides a point of departure for his epistles, some epigrams and his satirical works. The trend towards more sophisticated sources is in no way incompatible with this, so well are they chosen or adapted to suit the poet's own situation. The rest of the explanation lies in the fact that Marot has shed certain *Rhétoriqueur* mannerisms, the false humility and the pretentious latinisms. It is in this last respect that a study of the later versions of *Le Temple de Cupido* is so instructive. The latinisms of the original *plaquette* edition had by 1532 been reduced to one (*essence diuturne* becoming *clartez diuturnes*, v. 97) with an addition which resulted from the substitution in 1532 of *fulgente* for *tresgente* in (v. 96). In the 1538 edition of the *Œuvres* all the latinisms had been ruthlessly expunged from the poem at a cost very often of the complete recasting of the lines in which they had appeared.[84] Ornaments of style suffered the same fate as Marot's youthful pedantries. The ponderous allegory of the *Rhétoriqueurs* makes its last appearance in the *Deploration de Florimont Robertet*[85] of 1527. It was replaced, when this was appropriate, by mythology or by Classical imagery and extended simile.[86] The complicated patterns of versification demanded by his predecessors proved equally irrelevant to Marot's new design. They were resurrected only by request, or in jest, or to serve some conscious artistic intent.[87]

Nowhere, however, is Marot's rupture with the medieval poetic tradition more completely consummated than in his abandonment of the fixed form genres of the *Rhétoriqueurs*. This represents a movement towards simplicity of execution quite in keeping with the similar trend already noted in treatment and style. This rupture was largely completed by 1527 and in some cases it was preceded by an attempt on the poet's part to renew the genres he later abandoned. This is so, for instance, with the *rondeau*[88] to which Marot attempted to impart a certain ease and elasticity and which he enriched with themes of Petrarchan inspiration. Here, by imitating the poets of the late fifteenth century, he followed initially in the footsteps of his father, but was more original in his imitation of the later poet Bembo, author of the *Azolani*. Nevertheless, Marot composed only six *rondeaux*, out of a total of sixty-four, after 1527. Three of the remainder were composed before 1533 and the date of the others is impossible to determine. One of these last, however, is the result of conscious archaism and so may be discounted. The contemporary theoretician Thomas Sebillet confirms that the *rondeau* was a genre peculiar to Marot's youth:

sont plus exercices de jeunesse fondés sur l'imitation de son pere, qu'oeuvres de téle estofe que sont ceus de son plus grand eage: par la maturité duquel tu trouveras peu de rondeaus creus dedans son jardin.[89]

The case of the *ballade* is similar.[90] Fourteen of Marot's nineteen *ballades* were written before 1527. Three appeared later in the *Suite de l'Adolescence clementine* (1533) and the last two in the *Œuvres* of 1538. What is interesting is the distinction of manner which can be drawn between the *Adolescence ballades* and the last five which show a clear attempt on Marot's part to transform the *ballade* into a lyrical genre *par excellence*. These are the *Chant de joye au retour d'Espagne de Messeigneurs les enfans*, the *Chant pastoral à Monseigneur le cardinal de Lorraine*, both in the vein of official lyricism, *De s'amye bien belle*, the *Chant de May* and the *Chant de May & de Vertu*. Most interesting of all is the fact that at one stage the poet included the third of these *ballades*, *De s'amye bien belle*, among his elegies. Marot wrote only four *chants-royaux* as far as is known and abandoned the genre before 1531 without in any way attempting to rejuvenate it.

The *complainte*,[91] not a fixed form genre, although requiring a preordained treatment, is largely absent from Marot's work after 1527 when he composed the *Deploration de Florimont Robertet* and tried to renew the genre by means of evangelical sources and reformist sentiments. True, two *complaintes* were composed after this date but one was classified among the elegies (*De Jehan Chauvin, Menestrier*) in 1538, as indeed were two of the early ones, and the second (*De Monsieur le Général Guillaume Preudhomme*) is another conscious archaism. Three-quarters of all Marot's *chansons*, like the *complainte* a genre with no fixed form, belong to the period before 1527. Only ten are found in the *Œuvres* of 1538 and none are found after this date.[92] Even so, it may be that the great strophic variety which Marot introduced into the popular genre, its resulting ease and grace, ensured its survival to this extent.[93]

Other genres inherited from his predecessors Marot continued to cultivate throughout his life, but not without transforming them, often beyond recognition. The only apparent exception to this is the *épitaphe* where continuity may be the result of social convention. At any rate it is conceivable that the poet received instructions, as well as *honoraria*, when executing them.[94] On the other hand, it has been said with some justification of the *épître* that this genre demonstrates Marot's greatest reaction against the poetry of the *Rhétoriqueurs* since it is here that Marot achieves as nearly as possible the purely colloquial poem.[95] This is only half the truth; it represents only half the transformation. The rest lies in the intelligent classicism of the later epistles. Even Marot's translations are undertaken in the period from 1527 onwards in a different spirit and with another intention than that which directed his first attempts. These are in a sense Marot's own contribution to the vulgarization which furthered the movement of Renaissance in France. The poet's preface to his translation of *Le Premier Livre de la Metamorphose* (1534) is fairly explicit on this point. His intention was, he says, to

mieulx faire entendre & sçavoir à ceulx qui n'ont la langue latine, de quelle sorte il (Ovide) escrivoit: & quelle difference peult estre entre les Anciens & les Modernes. Oultre plus, tel lit en maint passage les noms d'Apollo, Daphné, Pyramus, & Tisbée, qui a l'Hystoire aussi loing de l'esprit, que les noms pres de la bouche: ce qui pas ainsi ne iroit, si en facile vulgaire estoit mise ceste belle Metamorphose: laquelle aux Poetes vulgaires & aux Painctres serait tres proufitable & aussi decoration grande en nostre langue...[96]

This translation, part of which Marot read to the king at Amboise, may have been started as early as the second half of 1526 and was completed by 1530.[97] Others include *Le Chant d'amour fugitif* (before 1533), a translation of a poem by Moschus via a Latin version. Significantly, Marot believed the work he was translating to be that of the Greek satirist Lucian, the idol of the humanists, and the Latin version that of the great Italian humanist Poliziano. This pedigree, as it were, would certainly have convinced Marot that his translation was suited to the times and assured of a welcome. In addition Marot undertook to translate six sonnets of Petrarch, *Les Visions de Petrarque* at the king's bidding at approximately the same period.[98] Whatever may have been Marot's main concern when he undertook his translation of the *Psalms* at the instigation of Marguerite de Navarre in the early 1530s, and the problem is a complex one, the work eventually presented to the king, and to the French court, was offered too as an exercise in vulgarization.[99]

For the rest, Marot's intention was clearly to replace the genres of his predecessors with those of Classical Antiquity.[100] This design was accomplished not without hesitations here and there for Marot was in the van of this movement to reorientate French poetry. In this respect he was not merely responding to the tastes of his milieu, he was in advance of them very often. Thus he was the first poet to introduce the elegy into French literature.[101] In the *Suite de l'Adolescence clementine* of 1533 Marot published a collection of twenty-one poems under this heading. Six more were added in the *Œuvres* of 1538 of which two had been previously published as *complaintes* and another, of the four as yet unpublished, could be so considered. This was the poem on the death of Jehan Chauvin. Two facts emerge from a consideration of these poems. The first is that Marot thought of the elegy as chiefly a long love poem. This was certainly so initially. And by this criterion the elegies of *La Suite* constitute a unity in themselves. In addition, after 1527 no love poem by Marot longer than a *chanson* or an *épigramme* was called by any other title than that of *élégie*. One possible anomaly here was quickly removed when Marot changed the nomenclature of the *Ballade d'une dame et de sa beaulté par le nouveau serviteur* (XVII) to that of *Elegie en forme de ballade* in the *Œuvres* of 1538. This would seem to indicate a conscious policy on his part. It was at this stage however that Marot sought not merely to confirm his conception of the elegy as predominantly a love poem, but also, in three instances, to enlarge it to include the funeral lament. Secondly, as the *ballade* instance shows us, Marot had no hard and fast notions as to the form which an elegy should assume. To one of them he gave strophic form (*Elégie* XVIII). In practice though, the vast majority of his elegies are formally indistinguishable from his epistles. This is attested by some of their titles and explained by their origin in the *héroide* and the *épître amoureuse*. It is interesting to note that Sebillet found a formula which recognized and expressed the two characteristics of the Marotic elegy when he called them *epistre*(s) *amoureuse*(s). He insisted only that the decasyllabic line was proper to the genre and should be rigorously maintained.[102] This was not of course necessary in the epistle itself.

Chant nuptial was Marot's translation of the Latin *epithalamium,* a genre which he imitated from Catullus in particular.[103]

A vehicle of official lyricism, the epithalamium first appeared in Marot's repertoire to celebrate the wedding of Renée de France to Ercole II d'Este in June 1528. Marot's second and only other epithalamium was written at the beginning of 1537 on the occasion of the wedding of James V of Scotland and Madeleine of France.[104]

Marot was considered to be the first poet to introduce the *églogue* into French literature when he composed his poem on the death of Louise de Savoie in 1531.[105] Although Marot had already translated one of Virgil's eclogues, the second, into French in his youth, he drew upon the example of Theocritus, the creator of the genre, for his first original *églogue*. His second followed in July 1535 on the occasion of the pregnancy of Renée de Ferrare. It took its title *Avant-naissance* from the word *genethliacum* which was the heading under which Virgil, in his fourth eclogue, commemorated the birth of a son to Asinius Pollio. His third was the *Eglogue au Roy soubz les noms de Pan & Robin* of 1539 and his last, in 1544 the *Eglogue sur la Naissance du filz de Monseigneur le Daulphin*. Like the epithalamium therefore, the eclogue belongs to the realm of official lyricism. It takes over the function of the medieval *pastourelle*. In addition, Marot's first eclogue fulfils the same function as his *complaintes* had done.

The *cantique*, not the least interesting of Marot's innovations, belongs to his post-exile period. It poses problems of definition which do not occur with the epithalamium or the eclogue.[106] Its function does not appear to have been so clearly delimited as theirs. Marot's first work to bear the title *cantique* was that addressed to the *Deesse Santé pour le Roy malade* in 1537 and published in the *Œuvres* of 1538. However, the same poem reproduced earlier in the year 1538 in the manuscript presented to Montmorency was headed *Hyme à la Deesse Santé*. Again, the poem known by the incipit 'Plaigne les mortz qui plaindre les vouldra' appears under the title of *complainte* in the Chantilly manuscript, and under the title *cantique* in two others. Yet another poem, Marot's *Dieu gard à la Court* which the poet himself did not classify in any of the editions supervised by him, contains a line

Doy je finir l'elegie presente   (v. 69)

which might have placed it among the elegies had it been a love poem. The poet's intentions become clearer, however, with the publication in 1540 of four occasional poems which he called *Les Cantiques de la Paix*.[107] These are *La Chrestienté à Charles empereur et à Françoys roy de France S.*, *Clement Marot à la royne de Hongrie venue en France S.*, *Clement Marot sur la venue de l'empereur en France,* and *Le cantique de la Royne sur la maladie et convalescence du Roy par Marot.* These, together with the earlier *Cantique à la Deese Santé* suggest a genre devoted to official lyricism. But the *Cantique sur la maladie de s'Amye* published in Dolet's 1542 edition of the *Œuvres* rules out such a description.[108] Nor is there any homogeneity of form which might help definition. Of the five poems above classified by the author as *cantiques,* three have the form of the epistle and two are strophic. In these circumstances the *cantique* appears to be simply a lyrical poem in serious vein and so may include the three poems not classified by the author himself, namely, *Plaigne les mortz qui plaindre les vouldra,* the *Adieux à la ville de Lyon* and the *Dieu gard à la Court.*[109] It takes the place of the *rondeaux* and *ballades* in which similar subjects were treated by the *Rhétoriqueurs,* and formally, by Marot himself. The origin of the *cantique* lies not in the official odes of Horace of which Marot had no direct knowledge, but more probably in the *Carmina* or *Odae* of the neo-Latin poets. As a result of his stay in Ferrara Marot had discovered, and imitated in one *cantique* the work of Flaminio.[110]

The *épigramme,* another genre from Antiquity, has an interesting history in the early stages of its introduction into French literature. The first collection of French epigrams was those for which Michel d'Amboise obtained a privilege in 1532 and published shortly afterwards under the title *Les Cent Epigrammes.*[111] They are, however, mostly translations from the neo-Latin poet Angeriano.[112] After Amboise both Jean Bouchet and Marot used the title epigram very closely upon each other,[113] Marot in the 1538 edition of his *Œuvres.* This is not to say however that all the poems so called were here published for the first time. On the contrary. Of one hundred and fifty-one epigrams forty-four had previously been published among the *petits genres* of the *Adolescence* or *La Suite de l'Adolescence.*[114] Marot was thus assimilating these genres of his youth into the Classical one with which he became acquainted through the works of the neo-Latin poets and through those of Martial. It is generally thought that this latter development was one of the results of his stay in Italy. The epigram has a definite evolution of its own in Marot's work. Sebillet held that it was the natural successor to the *rondeau* in the works of Marot and his contemporaries.[115] In fact, the epigram covers the same variety of subject-matter as the Marotic *rondeau* and has as many different levels of expression being in turn lyrical, satirical, and often purely conversational. In this last respect it is distinguished from some of the shorter epistles which may have identical pretexts, by even greater brevity and a more pointed conclusion, the hallmark of many Classical epigrams. In addition, the passage from a fairly rigid fixed form structure to a simple non-strophic one which would occur in the substitution of the epigram for the *rondeau*, is a characteristic trend of Marot's evolution.

This fact itself may explain Marot's failure to recognize the full aesthetic potential of the sonnet,[116] which is a fixed form genre, or his inability or reluctance to develop it. Of three sonnets which can with certainty be attributed to Marot only one, *Pour le May Planté par les Imprimeurs de Lyon*, was published by the poet himself. This was in the *Œuvres* of 1538, in the section entitled *Le Second Livre des Epigrammes*, and under the heading *épigramme*. The other two, of earlier date, the *Sonnet à Madame de Ferrare*, composed during the poet's stay in Italy and probably during the course of the summer of 1536, and the *Sonnet de la difference du Roy et de l'empereur*, written between December 1536 and March 1538, both clearly bore the title *Sonnet* in the Chantilly manuscript. Marot lacked the confidence in this genre which he undoubtedly had in the epigram. The rhyme scheme adopted by him, ABBA ABBA CCD CCD, was destined to become the regular pattern of the French sonnet. It is different from that adopted by Jean Bouchet in a collection of poems headed *Epigrammes*, although in fact sonnets, and which may well predate those of Marot. Bouchet's scheme was ABAA BBCC DDE DDE.[117]

The *Estreines de Clement Marot*, published separately in 1541,[118] discharged one of the court poet's traditional social obligations at the time of the New Year. For these are the poems in which the poet conveyed his seasonal greetings and good wishes to members of the court.[119] The custom was a well-established one. The manuscript collections of the fifteenth century contain numerous *étrennes*. The title, however, does not as yet relate to a specific genre. Medieval *étrennes* were variously *rondeaux* or *ballades* etc.[120] Marot's *Etrennes* of 1541, addressed to the *Dames de la Court*, are also to be distinguished from the compositions described as *estrennes* in the *Adolescence* and later included in the *épigrammes*. The *Etrennes aux Dames de la Court* form a homogeneous group,[121] not only by reason of content and function, but also by their form. Each poem consists of five lines of which the first, third, and fourth are of seven syllables, and the second and fifth of three with a rhyme scheme AABBA which was invariable. The adoption of a genre with a fixed form, although very light in construction and entirely of Marot's invention, would seem to indicate that at this late stage of his career the poet was returning to the manner of his youth. What is more significant perhaps is that Marot should have returned to the elegant and easy witty style for which the court had first applauded him in some of his early epistles at a time when his main concern was the completion of his translation of the Psalms and the elaboration of his political *cantiques*, both exercises in lyricism in the grand and lofty manner. This would strengthen the impression that in the *Etrennes* the poet was offering an indulgent encore to a faithful public.

Marot's satirical poetry does not show the same pursuit of the genres of Classical Antiquity which marked his lyrical poetry. True, he imitated the epigrams of Martial, but he did not cultivate the epigram as a purely satirical genre. This difference may be explained quite simply. The works of the Roman satirists, of Horace, of Juvenal and Persius, remained to a very large extent unknown before the middle of the sixteenth century in France.[122] As a result Marot's *Œuvres Satiriques* reveals initially the indigenous genres of his predecessors of which some are more indeterminate than others. Thus *L'Enfer* is a long poem satirical in tone and inspiration. The two poems relating to the *Dames de Paris* belong to the genre of the *épître artificielle*. The following two, *Le Second Chant d'Amour fugitif* and the *Chant de Folie, De l'Origine de Villemanoche* have no strictly formal characteristics and were originally classified under the vague heading *Chants Divers* which included lyrical poems, satirical poems and even translations.[123] The *Epître de Frippelippes* of 1537 is another *épître artificielle* although far superior in conception and execution to anything the genre had yet known in France; in this respect it bears the marks of its author's maturity.

Marot's greatest contribution to the evolution of French satirical poetry, however, lies in his creation of a new genre from indigenous stock. This was the *coq-à-l'âne* or *épître du coq-à-l'âne*.[124] Marot's first *coq-à-l'âne* was written probably in the spring of 1531 and addressed to his friend Lyon Jamet. It ended with an invitation to his friend to try his hand at a similar composition. During the period of his exile Marot composed three more of these poems. His friends and disciples were quick to imitate his example, just as they were to follow the fashion launched by him for *blasons anatomiques*. The *coq-à-l'âne* is a parody of the normal Marotic epistle.[125] The salutations and genialities exchanged as well as the dating are inspired by the intention to parody; they have no other connection with reality. The purpose of these pseudo-epistles, as they have been described, is not to give information to a far-distant correspondent, but to comment satirically on a variety of seemingly unrelated topics. The impression of incoherent fantasy which results is of the essence of the genre. It is indicated in the curious title which comes from the proverb *sauter du coq en l'âne* which means to talk inconsequentially, to jump about from subject to subject as a person with a grasshopper mind would do. Such incoherence is itself a clue to the most probable origin of Marot's invention. This is the *sottie*, a popular dramatic genre of the fifteenth and early sixteenth centuries in which a handful at the most of characters, attired as fools (*sots*), would exchange in rhyming couplets a commentary on current issues or abuses well seasoned with the lunatic fantasy which their role demanded. In the intervals of lucidity a degree of political, social and moral satire was achieved.[126] Marot's *coq-à-l'âne* is a *sottie* without the *dramatis personae* and with a stricter control of the incoherent fantasy which pervaded the latter. As with the *chanson*, Marot had here shown himself capable of creating a new *literary* genre from the elements of a popular native tradition. The dignity and status of the new genre were recognized by mid-century theoreticians who did not hesitate to describe the *coq-à-l'âne* as the truly French equivalent of Latin satire.[127] Sebillet writes thus:

Car a la vérité lés Satyres de Juvénal, Perse, et Horace, sont Coqs a l'asne Latins: ou a mieus dire, lés Coqs a l'asne de Marot sont pures Satyres Francoises.[128]

Peletier, in his *Art Poétique*, described the genre as 'vręę especę de Satirę'.[129] Although not cultivated by the poets of the *Pléiade*, *coqs-à-l'âne* continued to be written until the first quarter of the seventeenth century. From the beginning of the religious wars however they became essentially an instrument of party polemic and lapsed into the realms of semi-literature.

In terms of Marot's own evolution the *coq-à-l'âne* represents as great a reaction to the characteristics of *rhétoriqueur* satire— visible to some extent in his own *Enfer*—as his colloquial epistles had represented to the stylized, allegorical ones of the earlier tradition to which he had conformed in his youth. And it is a reaction of the same kind as well as of the same extent.

For Marot the gradual discovery of the poetry of Antiquity was a revelation to him of the direction in which his own efforts should tend. Comparisons between 'les Anciens & les Modernes' were never far from his mind as his preface to the *Le Premier Livre de la Metamorphose* showed. This fact is vital to an understanding and an explanation of his intention to renew French poetry by intelligent classicism. An assessment of his achievement in this respect must logically await a detailed examination of his work. To this we shall turn now.

III

MAROT IN THE EPISTLES

In the verse epistle Marot was supreme. It is to a large extent on his achievements in this genre that his reputation rests to this day. The isolated attempts of later poets and later of their own admirers to disparage the epistle as practised by Marot[1] may be attributed to the extraordinary success which he enjoyed and the dominance he had established in this field. Significantly enough neither Ronsard nor Du Bellay attempted to challenge Marot on his own ground. None of their compositions bore the title of epistle. They declined to offer such a direct comparison with their predecessor.

Many attempts have been made to define the character of Marot's epistles. Most have erred by omission. This is particularly so where critics have sought to impose a specious unity upon the poems. They have a purely functional unity as communications addressed by one living person to another or others. And if one disregards those few epistles in which Marot is writing on behalf of someone else, then the remainder have a certain unity in the record they provide of their author's career and its vicissitudes. But this is as far as one can safely go. The range of the epistles cannot be adequately encompassed in any one succinct formula. They are poems of wit and pathos, of firm ideals and courageous protest, of bitter satire and intense lyricism. They have for the most part a diversity of content and theme, manner and style which makes any classification of them,[2] apart from the chronological, extremely difficult and, at best, approximate.

It would be too much to claim for Marot that he succeeded in creating in his epistles the taste by which they were relished. It is far more probable that the reason for his success lay on the one hand in his ability to gauge the taste of his public, and on the other, in his ability to satisfy it. A task easily stipulated but less easily performed. And nowhere perhaps was a literary genre more

perfectly accommodated, both by its own nature and the writer's
art, to the requirements of a court poet's situation and his milieu
than in Marot's epistles, particularly in those of lighter mood
which he composed for the most part at the French court before
his exile in 1534, and again on his return there early in 1537.

THE LIGHTER EPISTLES

Marot's lighter epistles were written with two publics in mind:
their immediate recipient and the wider, but still intimate, circle
of the court. It was essential that the interests of both should be
simultaneously engaged. This Marot achieved by applying to the
literary genre the techniques of elegant conversation, itself increasingly practised and much admired at the Renaissance court.
There is in this development of the literary (verse) epistle under
Marot's pen evidence of that correlation between a society and
the literature it gives rise to which prompted Madame de Stael
to observe later that all literature is the expression of a given
society.[3] A similar correlation in the next century, when Voiture
frequented the *Chambre bleue* of Madame de Rambouillet, gave
to the world his prose letters which are still admired as models of
the genre.

The natural affinities between polite society conversation and
the literary epistle are clear enough. They may both be initiated
by the same pretexts and cover the same topics. Often the letter
is a continuation of a conversation in more considered terms, or
simply a refinement of it. Thus, in many of his lighter epistles
Marot gives literary expression, with that additional elegance
supplied by art, to a conversational exchange of courtesies, compliments and best wishes. The pretext is often of the slightest.
Thus *Epître* XVI was born of a lost game of cards in which the poet
had offered a new composition as his stake against the Colours of a
lady-in-waiting. *Epître* L is presented to a sick child with the poet's
good wishes for her recovery. In *Epître* LI writing on behalf of the
young princess of Navarre, the poet sends greetings, news and
obeisance to her cousin Madame Marguerite, the young daughter
of the king of France. The measure of the poet's talent is that he
could engage the interest of a public not immediately concerned
in these poems, and still commands respect for his ability to do so.

In the first instance, Marot alludes with mock severity to all those of her friends who took the part of the lady-in-waiting against him and who disturbed his concentration. The simple, conversational repetition of the formula *Prenez vous en* designates these unscrupulous culprits and invites a censorious reaction from all who may read the poem

> Je l'ay perdue: il fault que je m'acquitte;
> En la payant, au fort, me voyla quitte;
> Prenez la donc, l'Epistre que sçavez,
> Et si dedans peu d'elocquence avez,
> Si elle est sotte, ou aspre, ou à reprendre,
> Au Composeur ne vous en vueillez prendre.
> Prenez vous en aux fascheuses qui prindrent
> Vostre party & qui lors entreprindrent
> De haultement leurs caquetz redoubler
> Durant le jeu, affin de me troubler;
> Prenez vous en à ceulz qui me trompoient,
> Et qui mon jeu à tous coups me rompoient;
> Prenez vous en à quatre pour le moins,
> Qui contre moy furent tous faulx tesmoings;
> Prenes vous en à vous mesmes aussi,
> Qui bien vouliez qu'ilz feissent tous ainsi.
>
> (*Ep.*, XVI, vv. 1–16) XXXI

In the second instance the means employed are less direct but no less effective. For this *causerie* as Villey has so aptly termed it, the poet adopts a direct, simple, childish style and a shortened three-syllable line:

> Ma Mignonne,
> Je vous donne
> Le bon jour.
> Le sejour
> C'est prison;
> Guerison
> Recouvrez,
> Puis ouvrez
> Vostre porte,
> Et qu'on sorte
> Vistement,
> Car Clement
> Le vous mande.   (*Ep.*, L, vv. 1–13)

admirably suited to the cajolery which accompanies his encouragement to her for her recovery. By these same formal and stylistic
means which reproduce the staccato rhythms of a child's delivery,
Marot evokes the personality of a sick child, suggests her presence
to the reader in an almost tangible way, but without having
recourse to a cloying accumulation of diminutives. With an
economy of means which is the product of great art an impression
of intimacy is created by the writer and shared by all his
readers. In the epistle *Pour la petite Princesse de Navarre* (LI)
there is a change of emphasis. It is the personality of the young
writer, assumed temporarily by the poet, which is evoked in a
description of the delights of a long-awaited visit from her mother
and the journey by river from Blois to Tours. With an insight into
the mind of a child which was only rivalled in that century by
Rabelais's,[4] Marot accords pride of place in the letter to the pets
which accompanied the little girl and her mother on the exciting
journey:

> Par eau jusque icy l'ay suyvie,
> Avecques mon bon Perroquet
> Vestu de Vert, comme ung Bouquet
> De Marjolaine. Et audict lieu
> M'a suyvie mon Escurieu,
> Lequel tout le long de l'année
> Ne porte que robbe Tanée.
>   J'ay aussi, pour faire le tiers,
> Amené Bure en ces Quartiers,
> Qui monstre bien à son visage
> Que des trois n'est pas la plus sage.
>   (*Ep.*, LI, vv. 18–28)

and whose welfare was a more overriding concern than even the
presence of her mother. A note of childish fantasy is introduced
into the description of the great river, observed, as if through the
child's eyes, with mingled apprehension and delight, and the
fantasy allows an ingenuously made compliment:

> Loyre est belle & bonne Riviere,
> Qui de nous revoir est si fiere
> Qu'elle en est enflée & grossie,
> Et en bruyant nous remercie.

> Si vous l'eussiez donc abordée,
> Je croy qu'elle fust desbordée:
> Car plus fiere seroit de vous
> Qu'elle n'a pas esté de nous;
>
> (ibid., vv. 37–44)

There is a childish worldly wisdom at times:

> Joye entiere on ne peult avoir
> Tandis que l'on est en ce Monde   (ibid., vv. 50–51)

and a solicitude for her young friend's feelings which is none the less typical for being an afterthought. Thus, the account of the joy provoked by the arrival of her mother is interrupted momentarily:

> Si vous n'en sçavez rien, j'espere,
> Qu'au retour du Roy, vostre Pere,
> Semblable joye sentirez,
> Puis des nouvelles m'en direz.
>   Or, selon que j'avoys envie
> Par eau jusque icy l'ay suyvie...
>
> (ibid., vv. 13–17)

The impression is completed by stylistic means. There is throughout a certain brusqueness in the transitions of the epistle:

> Ce sont là des nouvelles nostres;
> Mandez nous, s'il vous plaist, des vostres.
>
> (ibid., vv. 29–30)

which is quite in keeping with a child's manner of writing. The form, too, of the epistle is again adapted to the personality it helps to present. Restored now to full health and spirits Jeanne de Navarre commands a vigorous and not too ample eight-syllable line.

In addition to these poems which one might term, purely and simply, courtesy epistles, there are others in which Marot's immediate purpose in writing was to solicit of his correspondent some precise service or favour for himself. With such a particular end in view Marot's adeptness at establishing immediately a complicity between himself and his recipient into which a wider public might be drawn was more than ever essential. And incidentally furthered his demands too. Nowhere is this adeptness better illustrated than in the opening lines of the epistle to his friend Lyon Jamet (x). Not only are these couplets an elegant negative definition of the proposed subject-matter of the poem, they also define Marot's relationship with Jamet. Not only do they reveal his friend's personality in a way which is of the essence of the genre, they suggest his presence almost as if he were, temporarily, the silent party in an oral exchange:

> Je ne t'escry de l'amour vaine & folle,
> Tu voys assez s'elle sert ou affolle;
> Je ne t'escry ne d'Armes ne de Guerre,
> Tu voys qui peult bien ou mal y acquerre;
> Je ne t'escry de Fortune puissante,
> Tu voys assez s'elle est ferme ou glissante;
> Je ne t'escry d'abus trop abusant,
> Tu en sçais prou & si n'en vas usant;
> Je ne t'escry de Dieu ne sa puissance,
> C'est à luy seul t'en donner congnoissance;
> Je ne t'escry des Dames de Paris,
> Tu en sçais plus que leurs propres Maris;
> Je ne t'escry qui est rude ou affable,
> Mais je te veulx dire une belle Fable.
>
> (*Ep.*, x, vv. 1–14)

Every second line invites either sympathetic agreement from his friend on the hazards of love, war, or fortune, or pretends to an intimate knowledge of Jamet's reactions in certain areas of experience. In general terms the hazards Marot enumerates would not be unfamiliar either to the court; the vagueness of the allusions assures a universal relevance. The knowledgeable at court, however, might relate them to specific incidents such as Marot's alleged denunciation by his mistress, the disaster which overtook the French army at Pavia, the vagaries of fortune which had seen Marot imprisoned and had, in different circumstances and for other reasons led to the captivity of François Ier in Madrid. All those would have been recent talking points at the court. Similarly, the affirmation of belief in a direct dialogue between God and man and the consequent intimation of the reformist sympathies shared by Marot and Jamet (vv. 9–10) would evoke a warm response in Marot's circle. And the jocular, bantering reference to his friend's acquaintance with the prostitutes of Paris which follows incongruously upon it, would have been none the less appreciated by those who knew Jamet had this penchant been real or only imagined! The same *causerie* and the same technique, although obviously more limited in the particular circumstances, appears in Marot's epistle to the king on the occasion of the poet's illness and the theft he suffered (XXV). Without ignoring the gulf which separates him from his sovereign Marot can still establish a bond: they are companions in adversity:

> On dit bien vray, la maulvaise Fortune
> Ne vient jamais, qu'elle n'en apporte une
> Ou deux ou trois avecques elle (Sire).
> Vostre cueur noble en sçauroit bien que dire;
> Et moy, chetif, qui ne suis Roy ne rien,
> L'ay esprouvé.　　　　　　　　　(*Ep.*, XXV, vv. 1–6)

Again the allusion is transparent. Had not the king, at the head of his army been defeated at Pavia, and captured? The poet invites the co-operation of his readers in completing it. And the proverb which introduces this allusion with such economy is itself an indirect appeal to the experience of a still wider public. In his epistle to the dauphin (XLV) Marot creates a *rapport* not by means of allusions to shared experiences—that possibility did not arise—but more obliquely, by addressing the young prince in his own idiom as it were and on his own level before invoking his assistance. The epistle abounds with puns (v. 16, v. 38, v. 44)—the last of which is borrowed from the game of real tennis, the overriding and fatal passion of the dauphin.[5] It is full too of other pleasantries which refer back to earlier epistles (v. 16 to epistle X; v. 25 to epistle XXV) assuming a familiarity on the part of the prince with them and hence perhaps a lively enthusiasm for them. Such a *rapport* is communicated to the reader, as in the courtesy epistles, but it is not shared to quite the same extent perhaps as in the epistles to Jamet and the king.

The anecdote is as essential a feature of Marot's lighter epistles as it is of many a memorable conversation. It is very often by such a means that he sustains the interest he has already engaged in the opening exchanges whether he writes for himself (X, XXV) or for another (VI, XX). Alternatively, the anecdote itself may give rise to a further discussion on topics more or less related to it (XI, XXV) and is invariably the justification for a specific request. For

the anecdotes recount the poet's misfortunes, or those of others
when he was writing on their behalf. Artistically, Marot was as
adroit at exploiting his personal experiences as he was shared ones.
This time, however, his object is to amuse and divert. In this he
was supreme.

Marot's anecdotes acquired in the telling an immediacy which
has never faded. This is a measure of his narrative art which
selects and transmits to the reader a wealth of concrete and
picturesque detail imagined or observed. Always Marot has at his
command the image which captures in close-up a scene, a person,
now distant in time or space. Here for instance is the sight which
would, more often than not, greet the eyes of a weary courtier at
the end of a day's royal progress from one sleepy hamlet to
another:

> (peult estre) ce jour
> Prendrons d'assault quelcque rural sejour,
> Où les plus grands logeront en Greniers
> De toutes pars percez comme Paniers.
>
> (*Ep.*, xx, vv. 35–38)

This vivid simile has long since become proverbial. Marot himself
may have done little more—we can never know for certain,
obviously—than to confer literary status on a colloquial expression
current in his own day. But how judiciously he exploited these
resources. And the same remark applies elsewhere. To the simile,
for instance, which completes in visual terms the moral portrait of
Marot's thieving valet as, with effrontery undiminished, he
disappears

> ...monté comme ung sainct George
>
> (*Ep.*, xxv, v. 38)

But such descriptive felicities as those which Marot applied to his
own weakened and emaciated state after the illness which left him
with

> ...la cuisse heronniere,
> L'estomac sec, le Ventre plat & vague
>
> (ibid., vv. 60–61)

or the physical precision with which he implied the criminality of
his valet

> ...chastoilleux de la gorge   (ibid., v. 37)

and his ripeness for the hangman's rope may well be original, if not in their coining then almost certainly in their application.

There is a burlesque quality in Marot's determined application of precise or realistic detail to scenes of fantasy. And this must include to some extent the account of the theft in epistle XXV, and the departure of the thief, witnessed and described by the sleeping victim! The same quality enlivens two of the lesser-known epistles where it accompanies the account of a treatment for syphilis in *Pour le Capitaine Raisin* (VI) or the erotic dreams of a peripatetic courtier and their subsequent interpretation by a friar under a full moon in the epistle *Pour ung gentilhomme de la Court* (VI). But the prime example is provided by the fable of the lion and the rat which constitutes the greater part of epistle X. Here the burlesque realism with which Marot depicts the thoroughly human actions and reactions of animal characters is even more striking and otherwise significant for it accommodates the two levels of allegory. As the lion turns a scornful glance on the rat and his offer of assistance, it is a visual detail suggesting close observation of the animal world—the lowering of the lion's heavy, indolent, lids—which indicates the physical manifestation of a (human) attitude of mind:

> Lors le Lyon ses deux grands yeux vestit,
> Et vers le Rat les tourna ung petit   (vv. 47–48)

In the case of the rat his deferential attitude before his saviour and superior the lion is graphically portrayed in two lines. Maistre Rat:

> ...mist à terre ung genoul gentement,
> ...ostant son bonnet de la teste.   (vv. 24–25)

Like those of any inferior being, his expressions of gratitude are profuse and unnecessarily reiterated. Briefly, and comically, his animal identity is reasserted in an interplay of realism and fantasy:

> A mercié mille foys la grand Beste,
> Jurant le Dieu des Souriz et des Ratz
> Qu'il luy rendroit.   (vv. 26–28)

Later in the anecdote when the rat has an opportunity of repaying his debt there is a delightful return to this vein when, without

the intervention of the author—or so it seems—the gallant rat
ceases to be just plain *maistre* ('filz de Souriz') and becomes *sire*
for services rendered to the king of beasts! It is perhaps worth
noting, in passing, that even the two adverbs forged by Marot's
comic genius and attributed to the rat:

> Secouru m'as fort Lyonneusement;
> Ors secouru seras Rateusement.
>
> <div align="right">(<i>Ep.</i>, x, vv. 45–46)</div>

are burlesquely realistic in their fantasy context.

Marot's talent is not merely for pictorial representation, whether
burlesque or otherwise, but also for dramatic effects achieved by
the combined resources of language, style and versification and
thereby eliminating unnecessary intervention on the author's
part. The authentic voices of the participants in the dramas
Marot presents are clearly heard. The gruff majesty and empty
pomposity of the lion reveals itself in his answer to the rat's offer
of assistance:

> ô pauvre vermyniere,
> Tu n'as sur toy instrument ne maniere,
> Tu n'as cousteau, serpe ne serpillon
> Qui sceust coupper corde ne cordillon,
> Pour me getter de ceste estroicte voye.
>
> (ibid., vv. 49–53)

The *rime léonine* beloved of the *Rhétoriqueurs* is rich to the point
of heaviness. And the useless pedantic precision of *serpe ne
serpillon, corde ne cordillon* which fashions the rhyme, also slows
the rhythm and inflates the pleonastic rhetoric of this regal
utterance. For the irrepressible rat on the other hand the rhythm
is chirpy and this effect is reinforced by intermittent alliteration:

> Adonc le Rat, sans serpe ne cousteau,
> Y arriva joyeulx & esbaudy…
> Pour secourir le Lyon secourable,
> Auquel a dit: tays toy, Lyon lié,
> Par moy seras maintenant deslié:
> Tu le vaulx bien, car le cueur joly as;
> Bien y parut, quand tu me deslias
>
> (ibid., vv. 34–35, 40–44)

The police too, are given a language all their own when they
arrive to arrest the poet. It is the style of their warrants

> Nous vous faisons Prisonnier par le Roy
>
> (*Ep.*, XI, v. 10)

in which they declaim, the tone of officialdom in which they
question:

> Vous souvient il...
> Que vous estiez l'aultre jour là dehors,
> Qu'on recourut ung certain Prisonnier
> Entre noz mains?   (ibid., vv. 17–20)

Marot's conduct of the narrative adds to the impression of
immediacy which visual detail, verbal felicity and dramatic
effects in their elaboration confer on his anecdotes. In exposition
there is an economy achieved or at least suggested by concise
narrative formulae. Such is the

> J'avois ung jour ung Valet de Gascongne,   (v. 8)

the justly celebrated opening to the first anecdote in epistle XXV.
Or the poet may simply plunge *in medias res* stating his immediate dilemma and reserving a minimum of explanatory comment
for later. This is very much the case in epistle XI, *Marot, Prisonnier, escript au Roy pour sa delivrance*:

> Roy des Françoys, plein de toutes bontez,
> Quinze jours a (je les ay bien comptez),
> Et des demain seront justement seize,
> Que je fuz faict Confrere au Diocese
> De sainct Marry, en l'Eglise sainct Pris;   (vv. 1–5)

in spite of the badinage and word play which accompanies this
announcement of the poet's continuing imprisonment. In epistle
X no explicit expository statement from the author explains the
significance of the allegorical fable, nor is one necessary. The true
identity of the animal protagonists, and hence the key to the
whole allegory, is contained in the double pun of line 20:

> Mais ce *Lyon* (qui *jamais* ne fut Grue)

and the earlier allusion to the circumstances which led to the rat's
detention:

> ...pour autant qu'il avoit
> Mangé le lard & la chair toute crue   (vv. 18–19)

Overall, the narrative is conducted within a strong framework which minimizes any passing exuberance and the use of conversational formulae to introduce, underline and conclude each successive stage of the action furthers the impression of immediacy and directness. Such formulae punctuate the account of the robbery in epistle xxv, and might almost be accompanied by gestures in the telling of it. The celebrated exposition is followed after exuberant elaboration by the ironical demonstrative:

Ce venerable Hillot...   (v. 15)

which spotlights the malefactor as he proceeds to commit his crime.

Brief, le Villain...   (v. 24)

leads into the final stages of the operation and

Finablement...   (v. 31)

preludes the thief's imminent departure. The whole is rounded off by the author's interjection

...Pour abreger le compte,   (v. 34)

and the almost valedictory

Ainsi s'en va...   (v. 37)

Sometimes the directness of the narrator's interjections may be expressly emphasized by their clever disposition in the line of verse. Hence Marot's

...Maintenant tu verras
Le bon du compte   (*Ep.*, x, vv. 28–29)

with the *rejet*, as a stimulus to the reader's curiosity, of the vital part of the phrase in the second line. Both the intervention and its emphasis is ironical here since the point of the story, as indeed the whole fable, was well known to everybody.

Apart from these narrative formulae which provide the framework and structure of the anecdote Marot maintains immediacy with an oral style the chief features of which are the raconteur's parentheses:

...(ce me dirent ilz lors)
...Et moy de le nyer   (*Ep.*, xi, v. 17, v. 20)

and the superfluous insertion of personal pronouns:

> Puis la vous mist tresbien soubz son Esselle
> Et vous laissa Monsieur dormir son saoul
>
> (*Ep.*, XXV, v. 20, v. 39)

The use of the present tense to achieve directness in the narrative merits comment in its own right:

> Finablement, de ma chambre il s'en va
> Droit à l'Estable, où deux Chevaulx trouva;
> Laisse le pire, & sur le meilleur monte,
> Picque & s'en va. (idid., vv. 31–34)

It is not, in French, confined to the oral style as it tends to be in English.

The immediacy with which Marot variously endowed his anecdotes did not exclude a certain reticence, a necessary reserve, in the presentation in the epistles of his own misfortunes and his supplications. While this may have corresponded with something in his character, it was also in the nature of a professional requirement. Poetry designed to amuse and divert might with advantage be personal, but it could not be obsessively so. Marot achieved a nice balance by a combination of formal means, stylistic devices, and his unique command of wit and pathos which is often characterized by the expression 'élégant badinage'.

Marot's adoption of the fable within the framework of epistle X is of the first category. It allows him to conduct a vivid narrative but on an allegorical level which removes the reader one step from too direct an involvement in the poet's dilemma. The fable is a more elaborate and sustained version of a similar distancing effect obtained by stylistic means, namely, Marot's habit—intermittent in the earlier epistles—of referring to himself in the third person. The distance is achieved not merely by the poet's ability to detach himself from the plight in which he found himself and to look at himself through the eyes of another, but also from the comedy which attends any apparently serious statement of the obvious and absurd. This is how he interrupts the account of his arrest in epistle XI:

> Incontinent, qui fut bien estonné?
> Ce fut Marot, plus que s'il eust tonné. (vv. 11–12)

There is another such comment, occasioned by the activities of the thieving valet, in epistle XXV. It is another pseudo-explanation:

> Et vous laissa Monsieur dormir son saoul,
> Qui au resveil n'eust sceu finer d'un soul,
> Ce Monsieur là (Sire) c'estoit moymesme.
>
> (vv. 39–41)

This is a device consistently exploited by comic writers and by none to such great effect perhaps as Mark Twain.[6] The comic element in the two examples from Marot is what distinguishes them from other examples of his habit of speaking of himself in the third person elsewhere in the epistles. In the epistle to Duprat (XIII, vv. 51–54), in the epistle to the Cardinal de Lorraine (XV, vv. 11–14) and in the more lengthy passage from the later epistle to the dauphin, the third person lends a necessary, but momentary and feigned detachment to Marot's purpose of soliciting intervention on his behalf:

> En mon vivant n'apres ma mort avec,
> Prince royal, je n'entrouvry le bec
> Pour vous prier: or devinez qui est ce
> Qui maintenant en prent la hardiesse?
> Marot bany, Marot mis à requoy,
> C'est luy sans autre; et sçavez vous pourquoy
> Ce qu'il demande a voulu vous escrire?
> C'est pour autant qu'il ne l'ose aller dire.
> Voyla le poinct; il ne fault point mentir
> Que l'air de France il n'ose aller sentir,
> Mais s'il avoit sa demande impetrée,
> Jambe ne teste il n'a si empestrée,
> Qu'il n'y volast!   (Ep., XLV, vv. 1–13)

In addition, in all of these three passages, the device is used out of a narrative context which undoubtedly added to its piquancy in epistles XI and XXV. Nevertheless, distance is still achieved even without the insulating effects of laughter.

More generally, wit and humour were Marot's principal and most efficient weapons in warding off obsessive self-concern and sentiment. In fact, it is noticeable that Marot made only brief excursions into lyricism of any kind in his lighter epistles.[7] When writing to the king for leave to succeed to his father's position in the royal household, the poet applied to his own condition of supplicant an image often associated with Petrarchist love poetry:[8]

> L'Estat est faict, les Personnes rengées,
> Le Parc est clos, et les Brebis logées
> Toutes, fors moy, le moindre du Trouppeau,
> Qui n'a Toyson ne Laine sur la peau.
> Si ne peult pas grand los Fortune acquerre
> Quand elle meine aux plus foybles la Guerre.
>
> (*Ep.*, XII, vv. 13–18)

Marot returned to this image in his next epistle, *Au Chancellier du Prat* (XIII, vv. 7–12). Another Petrarchist conceit drew attention to the poet's condition in the epistle *Au reverendissime Cardinal de Lorraine* (XV) in which he referred to himself as:

> ...ce gentil Salueur,
> Qui ose ainsi approcher sa lueur
> Du cler Soleil qui la peult effacer?
>
> (*Ep.*, XV, vv. 11–13)

It was not, therefore, any lack of feeling or inspiration which caused Marot to eschew lyricism and lyrical imagery in the lighter epistles of this period. For the time being at any rate Marot seems to have recognized that humour was more appropriate to his condition and his public. Later he would give restrained expression to a lyrical theme in concluding his jocular epistle to the Dauphin (XLV) when, with unforeseen poignancy, he promised him immortality.[9] It is precisely in this preponderance of humour over lyricism that Marot's lighter epistles differ, as Villey has so judiciously observed, from Villon's personal poetry. There the proportions are reversed.[10]

Nevertheless, Marot shared with Villon that type of humour which allowed both of them to deride misfortune and near calamity. Marot, however, was rarely as macabre or as grotesque in his indulgence in this vein as his predecessor. The witty, but morbid pun which introduces the account of his severe and prolonged illness is an exception in this respect:

> Bien tost apres ceste fortune là,
> Une aultre pire encores se mesla
> De m'assaillir, & chascun jour me assault,

> Me menassant de me donner le sault,
> Et de ce sault m'envoyer à l'envers
> Rymer soubz terre & y faire des Vers.
>
> (*Ep.*, XXV, vv. 49–54)

The comparison which he makes between his emaciated body and the proverbially scraggy and joyless Paris prostitutes is altogether more light-hearted:

> Et si m'a faict la cuisse heronniere,
> L'estomac sec, le Ventre plat & vague;
> Quand tout est dit, aussi maulvaise bague
> (Ou peu s'en fault) que femme de Paris,
> Saulve l'honneur d'elles & leures Maris.
>
> (ibid., vv. 60–64)

And elsewhere Marot's compounding of wit and pathos in his refusal to take himself seriously produces a feigned naivety unknown to Villon. His account of his brush with the police in epistle XI is very much in this vein. Hurt surprise and a suggestion of innocence overwhelmed by superior forces is manifest in the lines:

> Trois grands Pendars vindrent à l'estourdie,
> En ce Palais, me dire en desarroy:
> Nous vous faisons Prisonnier par le Roy.
> Incontinent, qui fut bien estonné?
> Ce fut Marot, plus que s'il eust tonné.
>
> (*Ep.*, XI, vv. 8–12)

To make matters worse the innocent victim of the law's tyranny is pathetically unable to understand its official terminology, or even to repeat it correctly:

> Puis m'ont monstré ung Parchemin escrit,
> Où n'y avoit seul mot de Jesuchrist;
> Il ne parloit tout que de playderie,
> De Conseilliers & d'emprisonnerie...   (ibid., vv. 13–16)

as the last word of the quotation, a particularly happy invention of the poet's own, shows. The eloquent but specious attempts at self-justification introduced with every initial semblance of rigorous logic, the strenuously flimsy denials of guilt which are tantamount to admissions of it are another expression of this feigned naivety and badinage:

> ...Et moy de le nyer,
> Car soyez seur, si j'eusse dict ouy,
> Que le plus sourd d'entre eulx m'eust bien ouy.
> Et d'aultre part, j'eusse publicquement
> Esté menteur. Car pourquoy & comment
> Eussé je peu ung aultre recourir,
> Quand je n'ay sceu moymesmes secourir?
>
> (*Ep.*, XI, vv. 20–26)

So too is the specious precision with which Marot scrupulously endows the obvious:

> Quinze jours a (je les ay bien comptez),
> Et des demain seront justement seize,
> Que je fuz faict Confrere au Diocese
> De sainct Marry, en l'Eglise sainct Pris.
>
> (ibid., vv. 2–5)

The painstaking reckoning of time served lends realism here as well as waggish humour to this opening. A variation on this technique occurs when Marot affects to take seriously a humorous parenthesis which stresses a self-evident fact. Thus his valet walked off with his purse:

> Argent & tout (cela se doit entendre).
> Et ne croy point que ce fust pour la rendre,
> Car oncques puis n'en ay ouy parler,
>
> (*Ep.*, XXV, vv. 21–23)

and:

> N'oublya rien, fors à me dire Adieu.   (ibid., v. 36)

Sometimes a similar effect is achieved when the poet takes an amusing simile almost literally and corrects it with incongruous precision. These lines describe how he was led away between the 'trois grands Pendars':

> Et m'ont mené ainsi que une Espousée;
> Non pas ainsi, mais plus roide ung petit.
>
> (*Ep.*, XI, vv. 30–31)

Simple understatement of the type:

> Sur mes deux bras ilz ont la main posée   (ibid., v. 29)

which reduces physical and forcible arrest to a gentle laying-on of hands, or understatement and visual antithesis comically accentuated by the parenthesis in which it occurs as in:

> Mais ce Lyon (qui jamais ne fut Grue)
>
> *(Ep.*, x, v. 20)

and antithesis and antiphrasis as in this character portrait of the *valet de Gascongne*:

> Gourmant, Yvroigne, & asseuré Menteur,
> Pipeur, Larron, Jureur, Blasphemateur,
> Sentant la Hart de cent pas à la ronde,
> Au demeurant, le meilleur filz du Monde
>
> *(Ep.*, xxv, vv. 9–12)

all these, not to speak of the innumerable puns, are further marks of Marot's humour in adversity.

Similar procedures accompanied Marot's requests for help. None knew better than he how to present his case, whether by specious attenuation and apparent compromise in this plea for a safe-conduct:

> De demy an, qui la bride me lasche,
> Ou de six moys, si demy an luy fasche
>
> *(Ep.*, xlv, vv. 23–24)

or by amiable man-to-man give and take (in Marot's favour) since he admits a hypothetical guilt in return for a hypothetical fine to be paid by the king:

> Vous n'entendez Proces non plus que moy;
> Ne plaidons point; ce n'est que tout esmoy.
> Je vous en croy si je vous ay mesfaict.
> Encor posé le cas que l'eusse faict,
> Au pis aller n'escherroit que une Amende.
> Prenez le cas que je la vous demande;
> Je prens le cas que vous me la donnez;
> Et si Plaideurs furent onc estonnez
> Mieulx que ceulx cy, je veulx qu'on me delivre,
> Et que soubdain en ma place on les livre.
>
> *(Ep.*, xi, vv. 49–58)

Sincere apologies to the king for the impudence and facetiousness of this request are merely the prelude to a final, inimitable shaft of wit, a delicate and tactful reminder of the poet's detention:

Treshumblement requerant vostre grace
De pardonner à ma trop grand audace
D'avoir empris ce sot Escript vous faire;
Et m'excusez si pour le mien affaire
Je ne suis point vers vous allé parler:
Je n'ay pas eu le loysir d'y aller.

(Ep., XI, vv. 63–68)

This is not far removed from the apparent sincerity and impressive reluctance which Marot displays in epistle XXV to ask for anything, any financial help whatsoever, in marked contrast to certain persons whom he refrains from naming on this occasion:

Ce neantmoins, ce que je vous en mande,
N'est pour vous faire ou requeste ou demande:
Je ne veulx point tant de gens ressembler
Qui n'ont soucy aultre que d'assembler;
Tant qu'ilz vivront, ilz demanderont, eulx;
Mais je commence à devenir honteux,
Et ne veulx plus à voz dons m'arrester.

(Ep., XXV, vv. 83–89)

However, this touching protestation does not prevent Marot from advising the king that he would, if pressed, accept a 'loan'. This airy impertinence is reinforced by a popular proverb and increasing effrontery:

Je ne dy pas, si voulez rien prester,
Que ne le preigne. Il n'est point de Presteur
(S'il veult prester) qui ne fasse ung Debteur.
Et sçavez vous (Sire) comment je paye?
Nul ne le sçait, si premier ne l'essaye.

(ibid., vv. 90–94)

It becomes clear beyond doubt in the lines that follow that the arrangement Marot has in mind to give the king some security for his money, I.O.U.s guarantors, and promises to pay, are purely hypothetical, that the loan he confidently envisages is an outright gift. How better to suggest this than with discreet flattery at the same time redeeming impudence with a saving grace and an inimitable tact which consists in knowing how far to go too far:

> Vous me debvrez (si je puis) de retour,
> Et vous feray encores ung bon tour;
> A celle fin qu'il n'y ayt faulte nulle,
> Je vous feray une belle Cedulle,
> A vous payer (sans usure il s'entend)
> Quand on verra tout le Monde content:
> Ou (si voulez) à payer ce sera,
> Quand vostre Loz & Renom cessera.
>
> *(Ep.*, XXV, vv. 95–102)

Never were elegance and badinage more perfectly allied.

The qualities of mind which Marot employed with such advantage in his narratives and supplications, his wit and his fantasy, served equally his satirical intent. How sharply, for instance, Marot's feigned naivety throws into relief the corruption and bad faith of his attorney who, according to the custom of the day, has accepted all the bribes offered him, and would doubtless have accepted even more, but with no advantage to the prisoner:

> Il a bien prins de moy une Becasse,
> Une Perdrix, et ung Levrault aussi:
> Et toutesfoys je suis encor icy.
> Encor je croy, si j'en envoioys plus,
> Qu'il le prendroit.   *(Ep.*, XI, vv. 36–40)

Next a play on the word *chanté* with its additional meaning of *bought off* and *partie* in its legal acceptation in these lines:

> Mais pour venir au poinct de ma sortie:
> Tant doulcement j'ai chanté ma partie,
> Que nous avons bien accordé ensemble,
> Si que n'ay plus affaire, ce me semble,
> Sinon à vous   (ibid., vv. 43–46)

introduces a sly dig at another abuse which allowed the men of the Watch to sue the individuals in their charge for blows received—and more often than not, expressly invited—when they effected an arrest. Both Rabelais and Racine were later to extract great comedy from this situation created by this abuse.[11] Later it is his sense of fantasy which allows Marot to support the urgency of his supplication for royal munificence by reference to the cost of upkeeping his two new residences in his adjoining domains at Clement and at Marot:

Advisez donc si vous avez desir
De rien prester: vous me ferez plaisir,
Car puis ung peu j'ay basti à Clement,
Là où j'ay faict ung grand desboursement,
Et à Marot, qui est ung peu plus loing:
Tout tumbera, qui n'en aura le soing.

(Ep., xxv, vv. 113–18)

This excursion into fantasy is not only villonesque in its humour, but far more important, it is satirical in its application to a real contemporary abuse: the mania of courtiers to construct splendid châteaux which they could ill afford and which were often only completed after large subsidies had been extracted from the royal coffers.[12]

There remain the criticisms which have been levelled at Marot's lighter epistles (although their authors rarely trouble to make the distinction explicit). The charge is one of prosaism. With a weary scorn normally reserved for English poets of the Augustan age, they belittle Marot's facile verse and the platitude into which octo-syllabic or decasyllabic rhyming couplets allegedly deteriorate.[13] In this they are less than fair to Marot's skill as a technician, acknowledged even by Sainte-Beuve,[14] and more than misguided in isolating style and versification in their comments from the conception of the society epistle and the conditions of its develop-ment. Marot succeeded in establishing a literary genre in a con-versational idiom which style and verse reflect and to which, as we have seen, they were both necessarily, and often brilliantly, accommodated.

THE ELEGIAC EPISTLES FROM EXILE

Marot's manner in the epistles was to change in keeping with his personal circumstances during the two periods he spent in exile. His poetry became more deeply personal not only in the themes to which it gave expression but also in its intended destination. For in a sense Marot was now writing for a changed public and, with the most notable exception of the great epistle to the king from Ferrara (XXXVI) which has many of the characteristics of an open letter of self-justification and as such was widely known in France and published soon after its composition, for a more *immediately* limited one. The qualification is important. Marot had little inclination, it seems, to make widely accessible during his own lifetime the thoughts engendered by exile, or at least, not as they were originally expressed. In many cases they were deliberately, and more significantly, successfully withheld from the printers of the day even after they found their way, sometimes after careful emendation, into the rare manuscript or two.[15] Hence, on the one hand, the epistles from exile were conceived increasingly as a personal correspondence but, on the other hand —an apparent contradiction—they were written with an increasing consciousness of posterity. In execution they acquired a greater nobility of tone and a distinctly more literary emphasis. For this Marot's own increasing maturity as a poet is partly responsible, a maturity which affects both his conception of his art and his execution of his art. This needs, perhaps, some explanation which is best provided by an illustration. Two of Marot's epistles, one in his lighter manner (XVI) composed before 1533 and one from exile (XXXVIII) have identical pretexts. They were both forfeited by Marot as his stake at a game of cards. But here the resemblance ends. We have already quoted from the earlier of the two.[16] Here is a passage from the later:

> Reçoy le doncq en gré, je te supplye;
> Et l'ayant leu, ne le perds, mais le plie
> Pour le garder; au moins quant ce viendra
> Que seray mort, de moy te souviendra.
> Et si d'icy à grant temps et long aage
> Du tien Clement se tient aucun langaige
> Là où seras, par maniere de rire,
> Aux assistans pourras compter & dire
> (Qui ne sera pour moy ung petit heur)
> Comment jadis fuz bien ton serviteur;
> Et pour tesmoing de se que leur diras,
> Ce myen escript sur l'heure produiras,
> En leur disant: Quant Marot m'escrivoit
> Ces vers icy, à Ferrare il vivoit,
> Là où j'estoys. Et lors à grant oultrance
> Le povre gars estoit banny de France,...
>   Mille autres cas, mille autres bons propos,
> Quant seras vieille, et chez toy en repos,
> Dire pourras de moy à l'advenir,

S'il t'en souvient; et pour t'en souvenir,
De bon cueur laisse à la tienne excellence
Ceste escripture, où je impose silence.

(*Ep.*, XXXVIII, vv. 51–66, 75–80)

Both the theme to which this epistle for Madame de Pons gives
expression, that of celebrity and immortality through poetry, and
the mood of nostalgia so delicately evoked in a way which Ronsard
scarcely bettered in his *Sonnets pour Hélène*, even in the most
famous of them 'Quand vous serez bien vieille, le soir à la chandelle' (XLIII) which is so obviously reminiscent of Marot's lines,
are evidence of the poet's changing manner and maturity.

Only the intrinsic requirements of the genre remain the same.
Accordingly, the style of each epistle reflects the personality or
preoccupations of its recipient, or Marot's relationship with him or
her. For Rénee de Ferrare Marot adopts an ample cadence, a
biblical rhetoric and, on occasion, a tone of fervent exhortation
reminiscent of an evangelical sermon (XLIII). Increased fervour
and the expression of reformist sentiments appropriate to it
characterize the epistle to the *Deux Sœurs Savoisiennes* (XXXV).
Old Testament allusions and a religious tone enter too into the
epistle to Marguerite de Navarre (XLVI) but it is throughout the
expression of a close but courtly relationship which predominates.

We may look for the immediate inspiration of Marot's lyricism
and satire lyrical in its intensity which distinguishes these
epistles,[17] in the bitter aftermath of persecution, the apparent
defeat of cherished ideals, the anguish of indefinite exile. In
addition, the parallels between his own situation and that of Ovid
banished to the Black sea by the emperor Augustus sent him to the
elegiac epistles of that poet, the *Tristia* and *Ex Ponto*, for further
inspiration and ornament.

The circumstances we have outlined give a clear enough indication of the themes of the epistles from exile, for Marot's
lyricism is the expression of the fears and aspirations, feelings and
emotions aroused by them. Essentially personal therefore, it
nevertheless transcends the personal in so far as Marot's reactions
faithfully reflect the reactions of others of his time to the moment
they were experiencing. Such is the celebrated passage of the
epistle *Au Roy, de Ferrare* in praise of the Renaissance and the
enlightenment consequent upon it. Combative, as well as lyrical,

this development and others similar to it in the same epistle will be considered in another chapter.[18]

Far more interesting than a detailed catalogue of themes in themselves is a study of the ways in which they are expressed, and how, in their expression, the problems attendant upon such highly subjective poetry are avoided. As we shall see the two exercises are in fact one. The charge against Ovid's poetry of exile, and hence one reason for its comparatively restricted popularity among this author's works, was that it was monotonous in its index of the tribulations of exile, plaintive in tone and abject in its repeated appeals for clemency and intercession on his behalf. For all that, Marot was inspired, and happily so, by this poetry which was somewhat of an object lesson to him. The comparison provided by the poems of exile of the two men is highly instructive. Ovid's suffer inevitably as a collection. The poet himself was the first to admit this.[19] Marot's epistles from exile form only a small part of his total production in this genre and within this group offer accidental diversity. Individually, Marot's poems exemplify personal dignity unrelinquished in the most wretched of circumstances and artistic discipline and moderation to which, even here in his most personal compositions, he was conditioned perhaps not only by his own temperament, but also by the *métier* he had learnt. These two factors, personal and artistic, inevitably influenced him to be selective in his borrowings from the work of his predecessor in exile. In this way, Marot avoided the defects already alluded to in Ovid's poems and in addition his diffuseness. What he learnt from the Latin writer was a range of literary artifice hitherto absent on such a scale from French poetry: namely, the power of sustained imagery and symbolism to confer universality on subjective emotions by allowing the reader to identify himself with the poet, and to relive his experience through such imagery and symbolism.

Marot learnt to express his state of mind in an image, and his successive reactions in a series of images. Here, for instance, is how he describes the prudence which guided him away from the court and peril:

> Lors, comme le nocher
> Qui pour fuyr le peril d'ung rocher
> En pleine mer se destourne tout court,

Ainsi, pour vray, m'escartay de la court,
Craignant trouver le peril de durté
Où je n'euz oncq fors doulceur & seurté
                              (*Ep.*, XXXVI, vv. 169–74)

The image of the stag in the epistle *A la Royne de Navarre* in
feverish flight from its pursuers similarly combines in an account
of the hunted man's progress, an evocation of anguished fear
underlined by the internal structure of the verse:

Lors comme ung cerf eschappé des dentées
Qu'il a des chiens ja experimentées,
Puis les sentant de bien loing aboyer,
Se mect encor à courre et tournoyer
En si grant peur que desja il pense estre
Saisi aux flans, à dextre et à senestre,
Par quoy ne cesse à transouer marestz,
Saulter buissons, circuir grans forestz,
Tant qu'en lieu soit où nul chien ne l'offense,
Ainsy passay Languedoc et Prouvence:
En telles peurs et semblables travaulx
Passa ton serf torrentz et montz et vaulx;
Puis se saulva en la terre italique.
                              (*Ep.*, XLVI, vv. 45–57)

Both of these extended similes are Virgilian in character if not in
immediate origin.[20] It is from Ovid though that Marot takes the
images which crystallize the exaggerated fears and the constant
mistrust with which the persecuted man views every overture,[21]
albeit of assistance, which may be made to him:

ces espoventables
Doubtes et peurs, non encores tollues,
M'en ont causé tout plain de superflues,
Qui me font craindre où craindre je ne doy.
Donq trop de peur m'excusera vers toy.
L'homme subgect à nauffrages terribles
Crainct toutes eaues, fussent elles paisibles;
Souvent aux champs la brebis apperçoit
Ung chien de loing, et cuyde que ce soit
Ung loup cruel; si se prend à courir
Et fuyt celluy qui la peult secourir.

> Ainsy actainct de calamitez toutes,
> Je ne conçoy en moy que peurs et doubtes,
> Tant qu'advis m'est que ceulx là qui ont soing
> De mon prouffit me faillent au besoing.
>
> (Ep., XLVI, vv. 62–76)

Like every exile he is beset by the wish to return, and the wish is father to the thought, expressed in concrete terms after Ovid:[22]

> Regarderoys la maison desolée
> De mon petit et povre parentage
> Qui sustenté estoyt de l'advantage
> Que j'euz de toy. Mais pourquoy metz je avant,
> Sot que je suis, tous ces souhaictz d'enfant
> Qui viennent moins quant plus on les desire.
>
> (Ep., XLIV, vv. 54–59)

The most famous wanderer of them all, Ulysses, who forsook Calypso's island paradise and spurned her offer of immortality so strong was his own desire to return home, is taken by Marot as the symbol of all who languish far from their homelands in this celebrated passage which presages Du Bellay's famous sonnet in *Les Regretz*:[23]

> ung chascun pour tout seur
> Trouve tousjours ne sçay quelle doulceur
> En son pays, qui ne luy veult permectre
> De le povoir en oubliance mectre.
> Ulixes sage…
> Fit bien jadis refuz d'estre immortel
> Pour retourner en sa maison petite,
> Et du regret de mort se disoit quitte
> Si l'air eust pu de son pays humer
> Et veu de loing son vilage fumer!
>
> (Ep., XLVI, vv. 153–62)

Meanwhile, Marot sustains himself with the hope of better fortune to come. This idea too is expressed by reference to Ovid's *Tristia*:[24]

> J'espere veoir ma liberté premiere:
> Apres noyr temps vient souvent la lumiere;
> Tel arbre fut de fouldre endommagé,
> Qu'on voit de fruict encores tout chargé.
>
> (Ep., XLIV, vv. 157–60)

He remains touchingly loyal to his friends at court: that they should withdraw their favour as soon as the king withdrew his support from Marot seems to him as natural a phenomenon as the progressive collapse of an old building:[25]

> A ce courroux soudain pour moy print cesse
> Maincte faveur de prince et de princesse;
> Et en ta court chascun (selon l'usaige)
> Sagement sceut en suyvre ton visaige.
> Quant la maison caduque et ancienne
> Commence à tendre à la ruine sienne,
> On voit tousjours que tout le fais d'icelle
> Se vient jecter du costé qui chancelle.
> J'ay fait l'essay de la comparaison,
> Et d'ainsy faire ilz ont tous eu raison.
>
> (ibid., vv. 137–46)

When at last he is invited to return from exile, he may liken his absence enforced by a hostile climate of opinion to the delays experienced by other travellers during intemperate weather:

> Le marinier qui prent terre et s'arreste
> Pour la fureur de l'orage et tempeste
> Desancre alors que les cieulx sont amys.
> Le chevaucheur qui à couvert s'est mis,
> Laissant passer ou la gresle, ou la pluye,
> Des que de loing voit qu'Aquilon essuye
> Le ciel moillé, il entre en grant plaisir,
> Desloge et tire au lieu de son desir.
>
> (*Ep.*, XLVII, vv. 9–16

While the poet's state of mind, his reactions and his thoughts are precisely indicated by the imagery and symbolism of Latin epic and elegiac poetry, more general expressions of feeling are conveyed by the time-honoured formulae of lyrical poetry and by the movement and rhythm imparted to the verse. Such a formula is the apostrophe which translates a spontaneous outpouring of emotion, be it of despair at the unattainable as in this passage of the epistle to the king from Venice (XLIV) where the exclamatory O is the literary expression of a sigh breaking on the poet's lips:

> O que je n'ay le cheval Pegasus,
> Plus hault volant que le mont Pernasus,

> Ou les dragons avec lesquelz Medée
> Est de la tour de Corinthe evadée.
> De Dedalus ou Perseus les esles
> Vouldroys avoir,...
> Bien tost vers la France alors voleteroys
> Et sur les lieux plaisans m'arresteroys
>
> (*Ep.*, XLIV, vv. 39–46)

or of religious fervour, worthy in its intensity of the Hebrew Psalmists as in the prayer which Marot intercalated into his epistle *Au Roy, de Ferrare*:

> O Seigneur dieu, permettez moy de croire
> Que reservé m'avez à vostre gloire.
>
> (*Ep.*, XXXVI, vv. 103–4)

Often the apostrophe is not only the indication of a passage of heightened emotion and corresponding lyrical movement which is to follow, it may also conclude such a development, breaking into the writer's consciousness disrupting intensity of thought and movement, transferring the reader to another plane, preparing a new development. This, for instance, is how Marot's prayer to God comes to a close before a resumption of the narrative:

> Que dys je? où suys je? O noble Roy Françoys
> Pardonne moy, car ailleurs je pensoys.
>
> (ibid., vv. 121–2)

In quite another vein is the irrepressible enthusiasm with which Marot announces his return to the Cardinal de Tournon (XLVII). This is suggested in lines of marked rhythm itself reinforced by the repetition of an introductory formula at the beginning of successive lines, and even in one case at the hemistich after the caesura:

> Puis que du Roy la bonté merveilleuse
> En France veult ne m'estre perilleuse;
> Puis que je suis de retourner mandé,
> Puis qu'il luy plaist, puis qu'il a commandé,
> Et que ce bien procedde de sa grace,
> Ne t'esbahys si j'ay suivy la trace,
> Noble Seigneur, pour en France tyrer.
>
> (*Ep.*, XLVII, vv. 1–7)

The same lively movement marks the greetings which the poet

extends to the Cardinal and the city of Lyon in concluding his epistle:

> Humblement donq, sur ce je te salue
> Hoir de Turnus, plain de haulte value.
> Dieu gard aussy d'infecte adversité
> L'air amoureux de la noble cité;
> Dieu soubz son Roy la maintienne eternelle,
> Dieu gard tous ceulx qui habitent en elle.
> Dieu gard la Saulne au port bien fructueux
> Et son mary, le Rosne impetueux,
> Qui puis ung peu se demonstra si fier,
> Que l'ennemy ne s'i osa fier;
> Et dont naguere, en dilligence prompte,
> S'est retyré Cesar avecques honte.
> Si vous supplie, o Fleuves Immortelz,
> Et toy, Prelat, dont il est peu de telz,
> Et toy, cité fameuse et de hault pris,
> De ne vouloir contemner par mespris,
> Ains recevoir tous amyablement
> L'humble dieu gard de vostre humble Clement.
>
> (ibid., vv. 51–68)

The effect of the figures and formulae which we have seen is not merely to translate or suggest the lyrical state or impulse though. It has been argued that the genre practised by Marot, the *épître familière*, was inappropriate to the expression of lyrical sentiments.[26] Precise criticisms have been directed against its undisciplined form. It has been described as 'shapeless'[27] by a recent anthologist and Ronsard, for reasons which can too easily be surmised, implied that the same defect fatally compromised the lyrical intensity of Marot's last epistle *A Monsieur d'Anguyen* (LVII) when he 'rewrote' it in strophic form. His comment on this occasion is interesting as he first damns Marot's work with faint praise before extolling his own expertise in the more appropriate genre, the Pindaric ode:

> Je confesse bien qu'à l'heure
> Sa plume étoit la meilleure
> A desseiner simplement
> Les premiers trais seulement,
> Attendant la main parfaite

D'un ouvrier ingenieus,
Par qui elle seroit faite
Jusque au comble de son mieus.

Ores moi qui tien au poin
L'arc des Muses bien peignées,
J'envoirai le los plus loin
De tes couronnes gaignées,
Faisant bruire ta victoire
Dessus ma Lire d'ivoire.[28]

But one cannot help feeling that criticisms of the form employed
by Marot are somewhat facile. For if, like Ovid's moreover which
the *Pléiade* signalled out as models of their kind,[29] Marot's
epistles have no formal structure, they have a rhetorical one. For
another notable effect of the imagery in simile and metaphor
which Marot, following Ovid, employs to contain and exemplify
the abstract is to impose upon the development of the epistle a
series of divisions—quasi-strophic—but in which a metrical
pattern is replaced by a rhetorical figure or a repeated formula of
invocation, salutation or negation.[30]

Marot's imitation of Ovid is often extensive. Hence the epistle
to the king from Venice (XLIV) is inspired very largely by the
great elegy which Ovid addressed to Augustus and which forms
the second book of the *Tristia*. But it is also varied. He may com-
bine passages drawn from multiple sources in any one of his
epistles.[31] Thus the epistle to the king, has a secondary source in
Tristia III. 8. The epistle to Marguerite de Navarre (XLVI) draws
on passages from *Pontics*, I. 2 and 3, II. 2 and 8, from *Tristia*,
v. 7 and 12 and includes a reminiscence of Virgil in the stag
simile. This does not mean, however, that in seeking to confer
upon his own poetry the universality which posterity had recognized in Ovid's, Marot was prepared to sacrifice its particular
significance and strict relevance to his personal situation—or even,
having due regard to the circumstances in which such a concept
might be applied to sixteenth-century poetry—its originality.[32]
In fact, by safeguarding the former he promoted the latter and
his imitations, while close, are never slavish. Choice was the first
step to creativity in imitation, and skilful adaptation of the chosen
source was the next. How well this is illustrated by Marot's haunting
evocation of the trauma and hallucinations experienced by a

fugitive in exile in his epistle to Marguerite de Navarre (XLVI).
First of all, his choice has rested most successfully upon a passage
of his model whose psychological realism—while obviously offering an eternal relevance—does so without prejudice to its immediacy and its personal validity. Sleep, welcomed here as a release
from the harshness of reality, has its own tortures to inflict,
whether they be nightmare recollections or sweet dreams which
cruelly revive the exile's longing to return home and which, just
as cruelly, fade away again:

> Aucunesfoys je dy: la nuict viendra,
> Je dormiray, lors ne m'en souviendra;
> ....
> Mais en dormant viennent m'espovanter
> Songes divers et me representer
> Aupres du vif de mon malheur l'ymaige,
> Et mes espritz veillent à mon dommaige,
> Si qu'advis m'est ou que huissiers ou sergens
> De me chercher sont promptz et diligens,
> Ou qu'enserré suis en murs et barreaux,
> Ou qu'on me livre innocent aux bourreaux.
>   Quelque foys suis trompé d'un plus beau songe,
> Et m'est advis que me voy, sans mensonge,
> Autour de toy, Royne tres honorée,
> Comme souloye, en ta chambre parée,
> Ou que me faiz chanter en divers sons
> Pseaulmes divins, car ce sont tes chansons,
> Ou qu'avec vous, mes amys singuliers,
> Je me consolle en propos familiers.
> Ainsy ayant senty à la legere
> Ceste lyesse et joye mensongere,
> Pis que devant je me trouve empiré
> Du souvenir de mon bien desiré;
> Et en ce point, soit que le cler jour luyse,
> Soit que la nuict à repos nous induise,
> Je vy en peine;   (*Ep.*, XLVI, vv. 103–4, 107–29)

Secondly, with what skill the too particular detail of the Latin
original has been transposed. Ovid's tormentors are the barbarian
Sarmatians whose raining arrows he vainly seeks to elude:

> aut ego Sarmaticas videor vitare sagittas
>   (*Ex Ponto*, I, 2, 45)

but Marot flees before the *huissiers*, *sergens* and *bourreaux*, agents
of the persecution instituted jointly by the Church and the state.
Ovid imagines his own surrender to a captive's bonds:

> aut dare captivas ad fera vincla manus
>
> *(Ex Ponto*, ibid., 46)

and Marot his imprisonment and execution. To the dream
sequence Marot brings greater precision than Ovid who evokes
the buildings of his native city, the conversation of his friends, his
dear wife in the lines:

> aspicio patriae tecta relicta meae.
> et modo vobiscum, quos sum veneratus, amici,
> et modo cum cara coniuge multa loquor.
>
> *(Ex Ponto*, ibid., 48–50)

Marot remembers the pleasures afforded by the company of
Marguerite de Navarre, the room in which her intimates gathered
around her, the Psalms she loved to hear. Similarly, in the earlier
epistle to the king (XLIV), it is by the addition of precise personal
allusions that Marot transposes Ovid's vision of home which he
thought to glimpse had his wish for the wings of Daedalus been
granted:

> Bien tost vers France alors voleteroys
> Et sur les lieux plaisans m'arresteroys,
> Pendant en l'air, planant comme ung gerfault;
> Si te verroys peult estre de là hault
> Chassant aux boys; contempleroys la France,
> Contempleroys Loyre, qui des enfance
> Fut mon sejour, et verroys mes amys.
>
> *(Ep.*, XLIV, vv. 45–51)

But these are not the only instances, nor are they the only means,
of skilful assimilation into his own compositions of the elements
Marot had borrowed from his predecessor in exile. How poignantly
in concluding his epistle to Marguerite de Navarre he echoes
Ovid's own fear that prolonged exile had corrupted his native
tongue and robbed him of that facility in its use which to a poet
was his most precious gift. And how typical of Marot is the final
twist which he imparts to this excuse and which allows him one
last appeal:

Aussy ayant cest escript visité,
Si quelque mot s'y trouve inusité,
Pardonne moy: c'est mon stile qui change
Par trop oyr parler langage estrange,
Et ne fera que tousjours empirer,
S'il ne te plaist d'icy me retirer. (*Ep.*, XLVI, vv. 191–6)

The fear itself was by no means an empty one, a purely literary reminiscence, at a time when the French language was experiencing a massive influx of Italian words to which expatriots in Italy, like Marot, contributed their share. And his own syntax at this time showed some hint of foreign influence.[33] Nor was such concern for the state of his native language unusual in Marot's work.[34] Again, the repeated affirmations made by Ovid in his *Tristia* of the power of poetry, not only to confer immortality but also to console (partially for this reason) the poet for the tribulations experienced in his daily life, have their parallels in the poetry of Marot's exile. So personal however is his adaptation of Ovid's conclusion to the autobiographical poem in *Tristia*, IV, 10, combined perhaps with a reminiscence of one to his wife in *Tristia* V, 14, 5 in this very moving conclusion to the epistle *A ung sien Amy* (LVI), that its source has escaped notice:

Ne voy-tu pas, encore qu'on me voye
Privé des biens & estatz que j'avoye,
Des vieulx amys, du païs, de leur chere,
De ceste Royne & maistresse tant chere
Qui m'a nourry, & si, sans rien me rendre,
On m'ayt tollu tout ce qui se peut prendre,
Ce neantmoins, par mont & par campaigne,
Le mien esprit me suyt & m'acompaigne?
Malgré fascheux, j'en jouyz & en use;
Abandonné jamais ne m'a la Muse.
Aulcun n'a sceu avoir puissance là;
Le Roy portoit mon bon droict en cela.
Et tant qu'ouy & nenny se dira
Par l'univers, le monde me lira.
Toy donc aussi, qui as savoir & veine
De la liqueur d'Helicon toute pleine,
Ecry, & faictz que mort, la faulse lisse,
Rien que le corps de toy n'ensevelisse.

(*Ep.*, LVI, vv. 71–88)

In these lines Marot has made his own Ovid's expression of
gratitude to the Muse:

> ergo quod vivo durisque laboribus obsto,
>   nec me sollicitae taedia lucis habent,
> gratia, Musa, tibi: nam tu solacia praebes,
>   tu curae requies, tu medicina venis.
> tu dux et comes es, tu nos abducis ab Histro,
>   in medioque mihi das Helicone locum
>
> (*Tristia*, IV, x. 115–19)

his legitimately proud boast:

> non fuit ingenio fama maligna meo,
> cumque ego praeponam multos mihi, non minor illis
>   dicor et in toto plurimus orbe legor
>
> (*Tristia*, ibid., 126–8)

and his defiant conclusion:

> protinus ut moriar, non ero, terra, tuus.
>
> (*Tristia*, ibid., 130)

The most conspicuously successful feature of such adaptation is
that it is so inconspicuous. The feelings expressed by Marot here
are no less personal to him for being confirmed by the experience
and the writings of another.

Marot's circumstances and his felicitous encounter with the
elegiac epistles of Ovid encouraged him to confer upon the *épître
familière* the right of expression in a major key. The result was
some of the most moving poetry in French Renaissance literature.

IV

MAROT'S LYRICAL POETRY

By inclination, as well as from circumstance[1] Marot devoted the greater part of his literary activity to lyrical poetry. It was in this sphere that he concentrated his efforts to rehabilitate French poetry and in this sphere too that Classical authors, providing both a model and a stimulus, became more abundantly accessible to him. Until recently however critics afforded his efforts scant sympathy or acclaim. There are a variety of explanations for this, some of which we have already examined in a broader context.[2] Even when critics have conceded the importance of Marot's lyrical works as a matter of literary history, they have most often confined themselves to his technical innovations, finding in the enormous metrical variety of the *chansons* and the Psalm translations a prelude to Ronsard's achievements in the *Odes* and *Odelettes*.[3] For the fact is that Marot, as a lyrical poet of the French Renaissance, has been overshadowed by Ronsard and the *Pléiade*. Although his poetry was more widely popular in the sixteenth century, and he was much preferred to Ronsard in the seventeenth,[4] and certainly in the eighteenth too when the *Pléiade* poets were virtually unknown until the latter part of the century,[5] he suffered an eclipse in the nineteenth from the moment that the fortunes of the *Pléiade* were restored by Sainte-Beuve.[6] In addition, many modern critics, basing themselves on the most dubious assessments of the poet's character and temperament, citing his inconstancy and frivolity, have doubted his capacity for lyricism. Even his qualities, wit, humour and elegant facility have been held to militate against it.[7] Yet these critics would doubtless have hesitated to draw the same conclusion about another poet equally well endowed. Wit, humour and elegant facility were never an impediment to the lyrical vein of Horace!

Marot's lyrical poetry is that which is to be found in the genres proper to lyricism, that is, the *complainte*, the *chanson*, the *élégie*, the *cantique*, the *épithalame* and the *églogue*. It is also found outside of these genres, for instance in the elegiac epistles we have already examined,[8] and may be distinguished by its tone and inspiration. Its functions or intentions are to commend, lament, deprecate, celebrate, plead with and persuade. It is sometimes, but not always or even necessarily, subjective for the poet may be required to give expression to the collective mood as well as exploring his own state of mind on other occasions. Marot's lyricism is extremely varied ranging from the personal to the universal, from the political and secular to the religious and in tone and manner from light to grand and lofty. The criterion adopted, explicitly or implicitly by some critics for determining the lyrical character or otherwise of Marot's poems, namely their capacity for being set to music,[9] often bears little relation to the poet's intention for the classification of his work. Nor does the practice of the period give any confidence in such a criterion.[10] We may therefore reject it without hesitation. Only in the case of the Psalms and two of the *chansons*[11] did Marot give musical directions. Some of the *chansons* in fact were never set to music at all during the poet's lifetime, whereas other poems which were so treated happened to be satirical or simply obscene.[12]

LIGHT LYRICISM: LOVE POETRY

The most obvious theme of lyrical poetry is love. What is not always so obvious however is the extent to which this theme may be inspired by convention, whether it be popular or literary, rather than necessarily by the poet's own direct and particular experience. Or to what extent convention and experience may coincide and reinforce each other. For whatever its provenance or inspiration the sum of a perfect love poem, for reader and critic alike, will be the suggestion, the amplification, the refinement or the confirmation of an eternal and recognizable human experience. In the case of Marot's love poetry there is no single answer. His inspiration varies from genre to genre and even sometimes within a genre.

His *chansons* belong to the vein of light popular lyricism. Like many poems belonging to this vein they are impersonal. They do

not reflect a specific personal experience. They are not addressed
to any one individual. Indeed, they do not even purport to come
from the same individual. While the majority are expressive of a
lover's plight, some (*Chansons* IV, XXXVI and XXXVII) are given
over to the woman's voice. The inspiration of this group of poems,
all but two of which are concerned with love (the exceptions are a
Chanson de Noel, XXV and a *Chanson bachique*, XXXII) is largely
medieval. The amorous sentiment which Marot portrays ranges
from the ethereal to the delicately realistic and the distinctly
earthy while the *Chanson bachique* is in fact a rejection of love and
its unpleasant effects in favour of the vine and its cultivation.[13] Its
brisk opening lines:

> Changeons propos, c'est trop chanté d'amours;
> Ce sont clamours;   (*O.L.*, ibid., vv. 1–2)

are an additional indication of the conventional element in the
love poems. It is the concepts of fourteenth- and fifteenth-century
French love poetry which predominate in the *chansons*. These
reached Marot in all probability from two main sources. On the
one hand from the early sixteenth-century anthologies of the type
best represented by the *Jardin de Plaisance et Fleur de Rethorique*
containing works essentially popular in appeal but often more
literary in origin.[14] With the exception of Chartier's *Belle Dame
Sans Mercy* to which the *chansons* make some allusion, Marot
himself can have had no direct knowledge of the works of the
courtly love poets of the fourteenth and fifteenth centuries, of
Machaut and Chartier himself, of Garancières, Grandson and
Charles d'Orléans except in so far as they and others unknown
were represented in works such as the *Jardin de Plaisance* and the
Chasse et Depart Damours.[15] The former in particular must be
considered as an influence upon Marot's *chansons*.[16] In addition,
it is certain that the motifs of the courtly tradition were adopted
and perpetuated, perhaps in a slightly simplified form, by the
anonymous writers of the numerous popular songs which enjoyed
such enormous vogue in the fifteenth century.[17] These songs were
certainly present in Marot's mind when he was writing the
chansons for he often took as his starting-point the incipit or
refrain of one or more of them.[18] In addition to providing a
second and less direct source of the courtly tradition, the popular

song as Marot knew it, with its great variety, inspired him to
diversify his treatment of the love theme in his own *chansons*.[19]

It is perhaps too much to speak of themes within the range of
love poems which present themselves in the *chansons*. Frequently
Marot does no more than introduce a given situation and the
mood or intention which accompanies it. Thus some poems depict
the start of an alliance and the lover's hopes and fears for its
future course (*Chansons* V, VIII); others his admiring contemplation of his lady's beauty and his dream of eventual satisfaction
(*Chansons* III, XI); yet others the acceptance of his suit and his
joyful reaction (*Chansons* IV, X, XII). Rather more however are
appeals to the loved one in a situation of hope long deferred and
relief impatiently awaited (*Chansons* II and XVII). The more
desperate the situation the more inspired is the poet. *Chansons*
XV, XVI, XIX, XXII and XXXVIII owe their existence to the discovery
of the loved one's disloyalty and *Chansons* I, VI, XIII, XIV, XXXI,
XXXIV, XLII to the separation of the lover from his lady. This will
be of varying degrees of finality, according to its cause; the cool-
ness of the lady herself (XIII, XIV); the activities of rumour-
mongers which make it imperative to safeguard the lady's honour
(XXXI, XLII); the lover's decision to sever the relationship (XXXIV);
and the most tragic of all, separation through death (I, VI). These
basic situations are possible in both the courtly and the more
popular vein but the moods they induce and their presentation
may be more characteristic of the one than the other. Thus the
courtly lover is distinctly more dolorous in adversity[20] being by
turns melancholy (XX), plaintive (IX), suppliant (II), menacing
with piteous irony (XX) and despairing (XXIII) while his more
realistic fellow is resourceful and masterful in supplication
(XVIII), cynical in his disillusionment (XXII), vengeful in his raillery
(XV) but at times resigned and philosophical in his disappointment
(XIX and XXXVIII). There are *chansons* which assume a given
situation as their pretext and present advice—on how to choose a
mistress (XXIV) or the necessity to avoid an alliance in which one's
advances are not returned (XXI)—or protestations of fidelity and
worth XXVI, *Pour la Brune* and XXXVII, *Pour la Blanche*, as if in
response to inquiry or doubt.

Whatever their content, these love poems are remarkable for
the ease of their development. Sometimes both situation and mood

will be introduced with directness and clarity in the very first line of the poem. This is so in *Chanson* VI, 'Amour et Mort m'ont faict oultrage', *Chanson* X, 'Je suis aymé de la plus belle', *Chanson* XIII, 'Languir me fais sans t'avoir offensée', and 'D'amours me va tout au rebours' in *Chanson* XXVII. The point is made and the remainder of the poem simply reiterates and supports the initial statement. At other times there may be a simple but visible progression, from the particular to the general in giving advice (XXI), from the object of his love to the imaginary realization of his passion in a lover's fantasy (II). This progression is of course most obvious and direct in the narration of incidents and the dramatization of mental conflict as for example in *Chansons* VII, XXIII, XXVI and XXXVIII. In the case of the more deliberative *chansons* ease of development is facilitated by the use of rhetorical conventions such as allegory and antithesis. But more of these later.

The commonplaces of courtly lyricism, easily apprehended, swiftly assimilated, recalling in a moment the reactions of a moment and offering in varying degrees the poignancy so often inseparable from the familiar, are invoked by Marot in many of the *chansons*. They are the commonplaces of a heightened and spiritualized lyricism whose mode of expression is hyperbole. Thus the beloved is described as the 'belle sans sy', perfect in every point[21] (*Chanson* IX) and the lover is a slave, both to his passion (*Chanson* VI):

> Amour me retient en servage (v. 2)

and to his beloved (*Chanson* IX):

> Des que mon oeil apperceut vostre face,
> Ma liberté du tout m'abandonna (vv. 9–10)

who has power of life and death over him (*Chanson* V):

> Car s'elle veult, ma vie perira; (v. 7)

life, when she chooses to grant him 'mercy', and death when she refuses:

> Vostre rigueur veult doncques que je meure.
> (*Chanson* IX, v. 17)

Her beauty alone may prove mortal to the lover (*Chanson* XVII):

> Vostre beaulté, qu'on voit flourir,
> Me faict mourir; (vv. 8–9)

and when it is accompanied by great cruelty (*Chansons* IX, XXIX) often synonymous with virtue, the lover experiences acute distress. *Chanson* XXX which rejects 'Amytié desmesurée' in favour of a more modest passion, describes the symptoms of this distress as 'clamours', 'follye', and 'melancolye'. The lover himself will speak of his 'tourment' (*Chanson* IX), his 'Dueil' and 'Ennuy' (*Chanson* VIII) and, *in extremis* his 'Martyre' (*Chansons* XX and XLII) which he is resolved upon occasions to flee. For while the lover may regard the 'don d'Amoureuse liesse' as his legitimate recompense and boldly prescribe in *Chanson* II:

> Jouyssance est ma medecine expresse (v. 21)

his beloved is inclined to withhold it and to impose her own more spiritualized conception upon the consummation of their love:

> Ne faictes plus ceste demande.
> Il est assez maistre du corps
> Qui a le cueur à sa commande.
> (*Chanson* VII, vv. 14–16)

The hyperbole of the courtly love commonplaces is greatly reinforced by the traditional conceits, images which visualize the abstract. Thus love may be described as a wound inflicted by the shaft of the god of love (*Chanson* XVIII):

> D'un nouveau dard je suis frappé. (v. 1)

The lover may invoke the god's help in inflicting such a wound upon the object of his passion—'Dieu des Amans...prens ta Darde' (*Chanson* III). The presence of the mistress and her implied beauty will also wound the lover, through his eyes.[22]

In *Chanson* IX the lover declares himself paralysed, enslaved

> Des que mon oeil apperceut vostre face. (v. 9)

The gift of one's affections is expressed by a conceit so conventional that it is scarcely retained as such by the reader. The lover will protest that the beloved is mistress of his heart (*Chanson* II)

and he for his part will be sent into a state of exaltation by such a
token as this:

> Puis m'a donné son noble cueur,
> Dont il m'est advis que je volle.
>
> (Chanson VII, vv. 7–8)

The conceit of the migratory heart is at one and the same time an
attempt to depict the movement of the passions and to spiritualize
them. It is briefly expressed in this line from *Chanson* III:[23]

> Son cueur tient le mien en sa tente   (v. 3)

and more fully developed in *Chanson* IX:

> Car mon las cueur esperant vostre grace
> De moy partit et à vous se donna.
> Or s'est il voulu retirer
> En lieu dont ne se peult tirer.   (vv. 11–14)

The personified abstractions which abound in many of Marot's
chansons inform, analyse and dramatize without the visual
quality of the conceits. They offer a concise system of notation.
*Bel Acueil, Envie Decevante, Danger faulx blasonneur, Faulx
Rapport, Espoir, Mort* are, in addition, as familiar as the tradition from which they are descended.[24] But they are bereft of any
independent vitality, any too particular reality. Strictly controlled
by the poet's intention and the requirements of a minor genre,
they function without arresting or impeding the lyric. They are
the terms of courtly psychology. The following lines are from
Chanson II of Marot's *Œuvres Lyriques*:

> Vostre rigueur me feit plusieurs destours,
> Quand au premier je vous vins requerir.
> Mais Bel Acueil m'a faict d'assez bons tours,
> En me laissant maint baiser conquerir.   (vv. 15–18)

Chanson XXIII consists entirely of an allegorical representation in
interior monologue of a lover's despair:

> Long temps y a que je vys en espoir,
> Et que Rigueur a dessus moy pouvoir;
> Mais si jamais je rencontre Allegeance,
> Je luy diray: ma Dame venez veoir;
> Rigueur me bat, faictes m'en la vengeance!

Si je ne puis Allegeance esmouvoir,
Je le feray ay Dieu d'Amours sçavoir,
En luy disant: o Mondaine plaisance,
Si d'aultre bien ne me voulez pourveoir,
A tout le moins ne m'ostez Esperance!

While allegory may codify and analyse in these *chansons*, anti-thesis hints with economy at the indefinable and the incomprehensible in the phenomenon of love which can produce such conflicting responses as these, in *Chanson* VIII:

Et vostre amour me semble tant heureuse,
Que je languis; ainsi voyla comment
Ce qui me plaist m'est chose doloreuse[25]

(vv. 14–16)

and these again in *Chanson* XVII:

Ainsi j'ayme ce qui me blesse;
C'est grand simplesse;
Mais grand sagesse,
Pourveu que m'en vueillez guerir.   (vv. 10–13)

Physical descriptions are conspicuously absent from the *chansons*. In only two of them is reference made to the setting in which an encounter takes place between the lovers. Even this is of the most meagre. The erotic dialogue between Guillot Martin and Helene in *Chanson* XXVI occurs 'en ung Jardin'. *Chanson* VII offers another dialogue and another garden:

Où tous arbres sont en vigueur   (v. 4)

in direct contrast to the attitude of the languishing lover. The physical beauty of the beloved is more often stated than described (*Chanson* X) although a certain use is made of affective epithets, of which the most frequent are 'noble' (*Chanson* VI, 'son noble corsage') and 'beaulx' (*Chanson* VIII, 'voz beaulx yeux'). The most extensive description is this brief enumeration in the second verse of *Chanson* XXXIV:

Adieu Amours, adieu gentil corsage,
Adieu ce tainct, adieu ces frians yeux.   (vv. 5–6)

Metaphor, where it occurs in this connection, is of the most restrained. The mistress may be apostrophized thus, in *Chanson* II, 'O noble fleur' and in *Chanson* XVII the lover speaks again of

> Vostre beaulté, qu'on voit flourir.   (v. 8)

The most exuberant, and developed of the physical metaphors is that of the *Colombelle* in *Chanson* III:

> La blanche Colombelle belle,
> Souvent je voys priant, criant,
> Mais dessoubz la cordelle d'elle
> Me gette ung oeil friant riant,
> En me consommant et sommant   (vv. 9–13)

but the impression here is one of *mignardise* rather than of precision. Restraint in physical detail is not something which is confined to the more ethereal expressions of love in the *chansons*. The 'plaisant Gibier amoureux' which Marot envisages as worthy of pursuit in *Chanson* XXIV is simply described in the following terms:

> Quand vous vouldrez faire une Amye,
> Prenez la de belle grandeur,
> En son Esprit non endormye,
> En son Tetin bonne rondeur,
> Doulceur,
> En cueur,
> Langage
> Bien sage,
> Dansant, chantant par bons accords,
> Et ferme de Cueur et de Corps   (vv. 1–10)

Nor are the sensations of passion any more vividly conveyed. In fact they are only once described in physical terms (*Chanson* II):

> Las, vos baisers ne me sçavent guerir,
> Mais vont croissant l'ardant feu qui me presse.
>
> (vv. 19–20)

In physical description, as in other aspects of the *chansons* we have considered, the too particular is not pursued. This was a lesson to be learnt from the popular song.

So, too, was its converse. The general statement of a popular truth in axiomatic terms was often used to give finality to the conclusion of a lyric. Marot was reminded of such a procedure in his fourth *chanson*[26] where it preserves a conversational realism and is not without a certain piquancy. A woman is comforting her love with vague promises:

> Mais s'il vous griefve d'estre ainsi,
> Appaisez vostre cueur transi.
> Tout vient à point qui peult attendre.   (vv. 10–12)

Self-evident, if not yet proverbial truths, are used to conclude *Chansons* IX and XXVI. And they are given the characteristic symmetry of expression associated with the same: 'Trop est rude à son Ennemy / Qui est cruel à son Amy' (IX); 'Car par trop grand appetit / Vient souvent la pance pleine' (XXVI)—this last, both witty and obscene, capable of double interpretation. Proverb-images illustrate the fate of the lover in *Chanson* XXXVIII which is almost a fable in reverse. There are four such images compressed into eight lines and the last, which is neither an exhortation nor a prediction but a statement of fact in the past, is for this reason the most pointed and conclusive:

> J'ay trouvé moien & loisir
> D'envoier Monsieur à la chasse,
> Mais un aultre prend le plaisir
> Qu'envers ma Dame je pourchasse.
> Ainsi pour vous, gros Boeufz puissans,
> Ne trainez Charrue en la Plaine;
> Ainsi pour vous, Moutons paissans,
> Ne portez sur le dos la Laine.
>
> Ainsi pour vous, Oyseaux du Ciel,
> Ne sçauriez faire une couvée;
> Ainsi pour vous, Mousches à miel,
> Vous n'avez la Cire trouvée.

Just as it was common to conclude a lyric with a moral truism, so it was not unusual to open by recalling or quoting a well-known line from earlier poems. One of Marot's most celebrated *chansons* —and justly so—artfully combines these two procedures of popular lyricism in a composition of light and elegant concision. *Chanson* XXXVI, *Pour la Brune*, opens with the retort of a woman which echoes the famous line—probably even better known then than now—from the *Song of Solomon*, I.5: 'I am black, but I am comely'. It continues and concludes with the woman claiming the superior virtues proverbially associated with this colour, in contrast to white, in the popular symbolism of the period:

> Pourtant, si je suis Brunette,
> Amy, n'en prenez esmoy,
> Aultant suis ferme & jeunette
> Qu'une plus blanche que moy;
> Le Blanc effacer je voy,
>
> Couleur Noire est tousjours une;
> J'ayme mieulx donc estre Brune
> Avecques ma fermeté,
> Que Blanche comme la Lune
> Tenant de legiereté.

With the addition of the unexpected and the element of surprise—with or without a note of humour—to the concision and finality demonstrated by some of the *chansons*, an epigrammatic composition is achieved. Such is *Chanson* XXXIII which opens with a covert allusion to the judgement of Paris in the very first line which is only progressively, and delicately, revealed in the second verse:

> La plus belle des troys sera
> Celle qui mourir me fera,
> Ou qui me fera du tout vivre,
> Car de mon mal seray delivre,
> Quand à sa puissance plaira.
>
> Pallas point ne m'aidera;
> Juno point ne s'en meslera;
> Mais Venus, que j'ay voulu suivre,
> Me dira bien: tien, je te livre
> Celle qui ravy ton cueur a.

This poem rivals and indeed surpasses in its transparent grace some of the best epigrams of Sannazaro and Pontano.[27] *Chanson* XVIII consists of two *huitains* which could each stand separately as epigrams. They are in fact of the type which Marot was composing almost simultaneously with the *chansons* under the title of *dizains*, *huitains* etc., and which he was only later to call by the Classical name. Here is the first verse:

> D'un nouveau dard je suis frappé,
> Par Cupido cruel de soy;
> De luy pensoys estre eschappé,
> Mais cuydant fuyr, me deçoy,
> Et remede je n'apperçoy
> A ma douleur secrette,
> Fors de crier: allegez moy,
> Doulce plaisant Brunette.

The last line could stand as the parting shaft. But the two stanzas are linked, if not in effect, then by their source to which this line, and the last of the next, allude. The second *huitain* concludes on a note of humorous reticence surprising for its context but concise in its wealth of implication:

> Si au Monde ne fussiez point,
> Belle, jamais je n'aymerois;
> Vous seulle avez gaigné le poinct
> Que si bien garder j'esperois;
> Mais quand à mon gre vous aurois
> En ma chambre seullette,
> Pour me venger, je vous feroys
> La couleur vermeillette.

Chanson XXXIV closes with an ironical *trait* which is all the more unexpected for the contrast of mood which it introduces into the last quatrain:

> Puis que de vous je n'ay aultre visage,
> Je m'en vois rendre Hermite en ung desert,
> Pour prier Dieu, si ung aultre vous sert,
> Qu'aultant que moy en vostre honneur soit sage.
>
> Adieu Amours, adieu gentil corsage,
> Adieu ce tainct, adieu ces frians yeux;
> Je n'ay pas heu de vous grand adventage;
> Ung moins aymant aura, peult estre, mieulx.

It is by their rhythm and movement that Marot's *chansons* demonstrate most clearly their affinities to light popular lyricism. Together with his Psalm translations Marot's *chansons* offer the most flexible verse forms of all his poetry.[28] The majority of his stanzas are isometric but within the strophe versatility and marked rhythms are introduced by juxtaposing and combining lines of

differing length. Long and shorter lines may alternate as in
Chanson XXXI where hexasyllabic lines follow octosyllabic ones; a
series of eight tetrasyllabic lines may be capped by four lines twice
their length rather as a longer musical phrase will round off two
shorter ones (*Chanson* XVI): or yet again, very short lines may be
enclosed between sets of longer lines as in *Chansons* XXIV and XXV
where four disyllabic lines are preceded by four octosyllabic lines
and rounded off by a further two in each strophe. There may be as
many as three different metres to a strophe. *Chanson* XII has two
strophes of six decasyllabic lines, six tetrasyllabic and one octosyllabic line. This variety in metre is matched, if not surpassed, by
the enormous variety of rhyme schemes. Of the seven *chansons*
consisting of five-lined strophes, four follow the scheme AABBA,
one has rhymes AABAB and two have four rhymes, ABABB introducing yet another pattern into the *quintil* and CCDCD in the second
strophe. There is variety too in the *quatrain* and its compound the
huitain. These may be constructed on three rhymes, that is two
quatrains in *rimes croisées* ABABBCBC or on four in which case one
quatrain will have *rimes croisées* and the second *rimes plates* thus:
ABABCCDD. In the six *chansons* composed in *septains* there are
three different schemes: ABABBCC; AABBBAA; ABABABA. And so on.

Rhythm and movement is not merely a matter of metre and
rhyme scheme though, however important these may be. In
lyrical poetry, and even more particularly in light popular lyricism, certain features of language or rhetoric may be regularly
invoked to confirm or emphasize rhythm and movement. These
may be merely traditional formulae of invocation—'Dieu gard
ma Maistresse et Regente' (*Chanson* III) or of Adieu (*Chanson*
XXXIV) which impart some of their own *élan* to the verse. More
frequently, movement and rhythm is derived from enumeration
and repetition. The following example incorporates both of these
as well as the adieu:[29]

> Adieu amours, adieu gentil corsage,
> Adieu ce tainct, adieu ces frians yeux.
> > (*O.L., Chanson* XXXIV, vv. 5–6)

Both these lines are of equal length: they are not animated by any
metrical variation. But they are broken and enlivened by the
rhetorical grouping, the first phrase of each corresponding with,

and strongly marking the natural break of the decasyllabic line
which falls after the fourth syllable. Other examples will show
how strong a cadence may be induced into lines of verse simply by
the regular repetition of 'catch-words' within the line. I say
induced, since ultimately, both the voice and the ear come to
expect and anticipate the cause and its effect. These lines are from
Chanson VIII:

> Si de nouveau j'ay nouvelles couleurs,
> Il n'en fault ja prendre esbahissement,
> Car de nouveau j'ay nouvelles douleurs,
> Nouvelle amour & nouveau pensement.   (vv. 1–4)

A simple reversal of the two repeated adjectives is sufficient to
break the cadence to coincide with the natural break in the sense
and the eight-lined stanza (v. 4). The refrains so common in light
lyricism are merely an extension of the principle of repetition.
Thus the whole of the incipit of *Chanson* XVII, 'Je ne fais rien que
requerir' is repeated at the end of each of its stanzas to produce a
haunting effect, a dying cadence. A similar effect may be produced within a stanza, as well as from one to the next, by diminishing progressively the extent of the repetition in the repeated
line. Here are a few lines from *Chanson* XL which show this:

> Amour aultre nom deust avoir;
> Nommer le fault Fleur ou Verdure
> Qui peu de temps se laisse veoir.
>
> Nommer le donc Fleur ou Verdure
> Au cueur de mon legier Amant;
> Mais en mon cueur, qui trop endure
> Nommer le Roc ou Dyamant.   (vv. 5–11)

There is a risk inherent in the use of such effects that metrical
variation may be nothing but an abstract and arithmetical disposition of syllables and that rhetorical conventions such as
repetition and enumeration will degenerate into facile mechanical
procedures, prolonged for their own sake, often to the detriment
of sense and logical progression. Light popular lyricism is especially prone to gratuitous repetition, or perhaps not so gratuitous,
since this is often the only way of developing a nonsense. In the
case of the *chansons* one can only speak of the skill with which

Marot has accommodated the resources of metre, versification and
rhetoric, separately and in combination, to the primary intention
of communicating mood and meaning. This in *Chanson* XVI, the
choice of a short metre in the first eight lines of each strophe is
determined by the intention to suggest thereby the flighty,
changeable nature of the mistress who has disappointed her
admirer. Equally, the choice of the longer line to conclude each
strophe is justified by the content of these closing verses, respectively self-admonitory and exhortatory with a touch of the sen-
tentious. Here is the second of the two stanzas in its entirety:

> Cueur affeté,
> Moins arresté
> Qu'ung seul moment,
> Ta lascheté
> M'a dejecté
> Fascheusement.
> Prens hardiment
> Amandement.
> Et vous, Dames de grand beaulté,
> Si l'honneur aymez cherement,
> Vous n'ensuyvrez aulcunement
> Celle qui est sans loyaulté.

Several of the rhyme schemes of the *Rhétoriqueurs* involving
repetition Marot adapted to the *chanson* where these were appropriate to his purpose. The *rime annexée* in *Chanson* I becomes a
vehicle for the expression of the writer's grief with its heavy
insistence on the same syllable at the end of one line and the
beginning of the next:

> Fort suis dolent & regret me remord,
> Mort m'a osté ma Dame de valeur,
> L'heur que j'avoys est tourné en malheur,
> Malheureux est qui n'a aulcun confort.   (vv. 5–8)

The *rime couronnée* of the second stanza of *Chanson* III achieves
with economy the auditive effects necessary to complete the
metaphor of

> La blanche Colombelle belle,
> Souvent je voys priant, criant,
> Mais dessoubz la cordelle d'elle

> Me gette ung oeil friant riant,
> En me consommant et sommant
> A douleur qui ma face efface.
> Dont suis le reclamant amant,
> Qui pour l'oultrepasse trepasse.   (vv. 9–16)

The *rime enchaînée* of the third stanza is aptly named and aptly invoked. It facilitates the communication of a chain of desired events, underlines and directs their progression towards an inescapable conclusion by the inexorable repetition:

> Dieu des Amans, de mort *me garde*;
> *Me gardant donne* moy bon heur;
> *En le me donnant, prens ta Darde*;
> *En la prenant, navre son* cueur;
> *En le navrant*, me tiendras *seur*;
> *En seurté*, suyvray *l'accointance*;
> *En l'accoinctant*, ton *Serviteur*
> *En servant* aura jouyssance.   (vv. 17–24)

There is nothing forced or experimental in any of these intricate combinations. So perfectly are they accommodated to the poet's lyrical intention that virtuosity and spontaneity are inseparable. And we touch here upon the paradox of the *chansons* as a whole. They bear witness to the facility so essential to light lyricism be it that of a Catullus, a Campion or a Burns, but for which Marot himself was so often criticized in his verse; a facility so seldom easily achieved, being won by labour, restraint and the highest art. The triumph of the *chansons* is the triumph of art concealing art.

The *rondeaux* which have love for their subject are on the whole more elevated in tone and more stylized in execution than the *chansons* with which they are largely contemporaneous. To this extent the difference is one of kind since some degree of stylization is inherent in the fixed form of the *rondeau* which is not so inherent in the free form of the *chanson*. And needless to say the more stylized form may accommodate a more stylized treatment even of an identical theme. From this point it would be easy, though unwise, to exaggerate the differences between the two. Against the inherent fixed form of the *rondeau* one must set the fact that its evolution, throughout the fifteenth century, and

most noticeably in the sixteenth in the works of the two Marot,
was towards increasing lightness and simplicity, particularly in
the use of the refrain.[30] One need not be surprised therefore to
find some of the love *rondeaux* to which these qualities have been
communicated, in form and thence in execution, which match the
chansons in these respects. *Rondeau* XXXVII, *De sa grand Amye*
(*O.D.*, XXXVII) is one example:

> Dedans Paris, Ville jolye,
> Ung jour, passant melancolie,
> Je prins alliance nouvelle
> A la plus gaye Damoyselle
> Qui soit d'icy en Italie.
>
> D'honnesteté elle est saisie,
> Et croy (selon ma fantaisie)
> Qu'il n'en est gueres de plus belle
>> Dedans Paris.
>
> Je ne la vous nommeray mye,
> Si non que c'est ma grand Amye;
> Car l'alliance se feit telle
> Par ung doulx baiser que j'eus d'elle,
> Sans penser aulcune infamie,
>> Dedans Paris.

De l'Amoureux ardant (*Rondeau* V) and *D'ung soy deffiant de sa
Dame* (*Rondeau* XLII) are other examples among several.

Both the *chansons* and the *rondeaux* are brief and impersonal
in their treatment of love. Both maintain an attachment to certain of the commonplaces of fifteenth-century French lyricism.
There is an additional influence present in the *rondeaux* however,
that of Petrarch and his Italian imitators of the late fifteenth and
early sixteenth centuries.[31] In one sense this is a novelty which
distinguishes the *rondeaux* from the *chansons*. But in effect, this
new source of inspiration did not greatly alter the treatment of an
identical theme in the two genres. Nor is this surprising in view
of the features common to fifteenth-century French lyricism and
to Petrarchism independently of each other and through their
common origin in the work of the *trouvères*.[32] This is undoubtedly
one of the reasons why the Petrarchist sources of some of the
rondeaux have for so long escaped notice and identification. There
are other reasons for this too though. The first is the eclectic

nature of Marot's imitations—one might almost speak of an infusion of reminiscences. The second is that these were drawn from the relatively little-known works of such imitators as Olimpo di Sassoferrato and Chariteo as much as from the better-known Serafino imitated already in a previous generation by Jean Picart and by Marot's father. Olimpo's *Strambotti d'amore* had been published in 1518 but success came to him in measurable degree only in the second half of the century. Chariteo's works had only two editions in the whole of the first half of the century, the first in 1509 and the second probably in 1515. How these little-read authors came to be known in France at the period at which Marot was writing must remain a matter for conjecture. Our knowledge of the reciprocal contacts between France and Italy which flourished at this time is not such as to enable us to trace the precise manner of their diffusion. Suffice it to say that it would not have been at all improbable. At this stage in his career Marot chose from Petrarch and his imitators those motifs which complement those of the native lyrical tradition as it is reflected in his own *chansons*. Inspired by the Petrarchists Marot brings to the *rondeaux* a preciosity and a refinement in analysis, together with a certain sensuality which the native tradition had not conferred in the same degree upon the *chansons*. The *rondeaux* however show little more attention to vivid and colourful imagery in the description and praise of physical beauty than did the *chansons*. This aspect of Petrarchism was to belong to the *épigrammes*.[33]

Of the themes which occupy Marot in the love *rondeaux*, the following are executed in the manner of Petrarch or more frequently his imitators: the lover tortured by content and content to be so tortured (*Rondeau* XXVI), the melancholy solitude of the lover separated from his beloved (*Rondeau* XLVI), the physical and moral perfection of the lady (*Rondeaux* XL and L), the transience of physical charms and the necessity to enjoy them before they are wasted by time (*Rondeau* LI), the obsession with the image of the beloved (*Rondeau* XLIII) and the *baiser* (*Rondeau* LV). In addition, the two *rondeaux* (XXXVI and XXXVII) whose refrains specify the occasion upon which an *alliance* began (dansant en une Salle / Ung Mardy gras—XXXVI) and (Dedans Paris—XXXVII) may be an attempt to follow Petrarchist precedents in this respect.

The *concetti* of the Petrarchists are much in evidence too. The conceit of the migratory heart, only briefly encountered in the *chansons*, receives considerable development in the *rondeaux* under the Petrarchist influence. It finds its most poetic expression in the *Rondeau* XLII, *D'ung soy deffiant de sa Dame*. Following Petrarch Marot likens his heart to a bird, in this case a swallow, which flies on the wings of prayer and entreaty to the beloved. Exaltation and despair are the moods respectively symbolized as it soars upwards before, rejected, it plunges to its death:

> Plus qu'en aultre lieu de la ronde
> Mon cueur volle comme l'Aronde
> Vers toy en prieres et dictz;
> Mais si asprement l'escondis
> Que noyer le fais en claire unde.
>
> (*O.D.*, *Rondeau* XLII, vv. 1–5)

In *Rondeau* LII, *A une Dame pour luy offrir cueur & service*, the conceit is greatly extended. The lover envisages the exchange of his heart with that of his lady:

> Tant seullement ton Amour je demande,
> Te suppliant que ta beaulté commande
> Au cueur de moy comme à ton serviteur,
> Quoy que jamais il ne desservit heur
> Qui procedast d'une grace si grande.
>
> Croy que ce cueur de te congnoistre amande,
> Et vouluntiers se rendroit de ta bande
> S'il te plaisoit luy faire cest honneur
>   Tant seullement.
> Si tu le veulx, metz le soubz ta commande!
> Si tu le prendz, las, je te recommande
> Le triste Corps! ne le laisse sans Cueur!
> Mais loges y le tien, qui est vainqueur
> De l'humble Serf qui son vouloir te mande
>   Tant seullement.

This particular conceit was much invoked by the poet Serafino Aquilano from whom Marot's father had once imitated it. In this case Marot's *rondeau* seems to be partly inspired by one of the Italian's *strambotti*, 'El cor te dedi, non chel tormentasti' and partly by Bembo's *Azolani*, a source which in fact reflects more closely the development with which Marot has concluded his *rondeau* than does Serafino's *strambotto*.[34] This same conceit reappears in the *rondeau*, *Pour ung qui est allé loing de s'Amye* (LVI) under the influence of Sassoferrato's *Capitolo di partenza ala sua signora*. Greater relief is given, and poignancy, to the idea of the separation of the two lovers which the conceit dramatizes, by the juxtaposition of heart and body as well as by occasional antithesis of detail in the development of the *rondeau*:

> Loing de tes yeux t'amour me vient poursuivre
> Aultant ou plus qu'elle me souloit suivre
> Aupres de toy; car tu as (pour tout seur)
> Si bien gravé dedans moy ta doulceur
> Que mieulx graver ne se pourroit en cuivre.
>
> Le corps est loing; plus à toy ne se livre
> Touchant le cueur, ta beaulté m'en delivre.
> Ainsi je suis (long temps a) sans mon cueur[35]
>   Loing de tes yeux.
> Or l'homme est mort qui n'a son cueur delivre;
> Mais endroit moy ne s'en peult mort ensuyvre,
> Car, si tu as le mien plein de langueur,
> J'ay avec moy le tien plein de vigueur,
> Lequel aultant que le mien me faict vivre
>   Loing de tes yeux.

This conceit in another guise, that is the separation of the heart and body of the beloved, is encountered in *Rondeau* XLIII, *De celluy qui ne pense qu'en s'Amye* but its striking development, entirely foreign to the tradition of Petrarch, deserves comment elsewhere.[36]

In two of his *rondeaux* Marot introduces the conceit of the lover wounded by the piercing glance of the beloved. This is explicit in *Rondeau* XI, *De l'Amant doloreux*:

> Avant mes jours mort me fault encourir
> Par ung regard dont m'as voulu ferir,
> Et ne te chault de ma griefve tristesse.   (vv. 1-3)

The same conceit is implied in the opening lines of a *rondeau* from which we have already had occasion to quote, *Pour ung qui est allé loing de s'Amye* (LVI). The beloved's qualities shining forth in her eyes have been lastingly engraved by them upon his soul:

> Loing de tes yeux t'amour me vient poursuivre
> Aultant ou plus qu'elle me souloit suivre
> Aupres de toy; car tu as (pour tout seur)
> Si bien gravé dedans moy ta doulceur
> Que mieulx graver ne se pourroit en cuivre.   (vv. 1–5)

To this must be added the related conceit of the lover wounded by his beloved's kiss which appears in *Rondeau* XLIX, *D'alliance de Sœur*:

> Las, elle m'a navré de grand vigueur,
> Non d'ung cousteau, ne par haine ou rigueur,
> Mais d'ung baiser de sa bouche vermeille   (vv. 6–8)

Marot was to devote a whole *rondeau* to the *baiser de s'Amye* (LV). Like Petrarch's imitators he evokes the sweet breath of the beloved and this is combined with a conceit whose original intention was probably to spiritualize an erotic experience: the lover's soul is drawn from his body by his mistress's kiss and hovers upon her lips. Marot's *rondeau* is probably a free imitation of a *strambotto* by Serafino Aquilano:[37]

> Incolpa, donna, amor se troppo io volsi
> Aggiungendo alla tua la bocca mia:
> Se pur punir mi voi di quel ch'io tolsi,
> Fa che concesso replicar mi sia,
> Che tal dolceza in quelli labri accolsi,
> Che'l spirto mio fu per fugirsi via,
> Sì che al secondo tocco uscirà fora:
> Bastar ti dé, che per tal fallo io mora

and offers in addition certain similarities with a *capitolo* of Olimpo di Sassoferrato of which the text is as follows:[38]

> E poi con la mia bocca li donava
> Un bacio tanto dolze e saporito
> Che per dolceza l'alma milassava
> Ascese el spirto per infino al sito
> Della mia bocca per quel bacio ameno
> Che dal cuor per dolceza era partito
> Ma se spirava nel suo bianco seno
> Lo spirto viveria lieto e contento
> Che cosí stando sempre io arde e peno
> Perché e svoi sguardi m'hanno a morte spento.

A comparison between these two texts and Marot's poem reveals the latter's originality in the development of this conceit. Marot has dramatized the whole encounter and, opening with the words of the beloved followed by the reactions of the lover, has situated it within a psychological context. The *baiser* itself, momentarily suspended by the initial conversation, is prolonged throughout the rest of the *rondeau* and highlighted by the refrain. The reference to the soul, far from mitigating the poem's sensuality actually increases it so intimately is it associated with the climax of the physical experience described at the culmination of the *rondeau*. The whole drama is perfectly accommodated to the structure of the genre which underlines and perpetuates the completeness of a moment, a moment nicely poised between satisfaction promised and satisfaction ultimately achieved:

> En la baisant m'a dit: Amy sans blasme,
> Ce seul baiser qui deux bouches embasme
> Les arres sont du bien tant esperé.
> Ce mot elle a doulcement proferé,
> Pensant du tout appaiser ma grand flamme.
>
> Mais le mien cueur adonc plus elle enflamme,
> Car son alaine odorant plus que basme
> Souffloit le feu qu'Amour m'a preparé
> En la baisant.
> Brief mon esprit, sans congnoissance d'ame,
> Vivoit alors sur la bouche à ma Dame;
> Dont se mouroit le corps enamouré;
> Et si sa Levre eust gueres demouré
> Contre la mienne, elle m'eust sucé l'ame
> En la baisant.

French lyricism of the fifteenth century had nothing to offer which could compare with the sensuality of Marot's *rondeau* outside the works of the poetess Christine de Pisan. But even her attempt to immortalize the *baiser* of her lover is discreet in comparison:

> Doulz ami, mon cuer se pasme
> En tes bras, t'alaine entiere
> Me flaire plus doulz que basme,
> Baisiez moy, doulce amour chiere.[39]

Marot's *rondeau*, perhaps his finest love poem, may have been surpassed in sensuality and eroticism by Ronsard's celebrations of the *baisers de Cassandre* but it concedes nothing to the later poet in the delicate perfection of its execution.

In the tradition of Petrarchist poetry Marot was to establish a correspondence between the mood and emotions of the lover and the changing aspects of the natural universe. This pathetic fallacy accommodates the conceit of the mistress likened to the sun although whether Marot was here following Petrarch's habit of referring to Laura as 'il mio sole' or borrowing from Charles d'Orléans the phrase 'le doulx soleil gracieux' which he applied in one of his *ballades* to the beauty of his mistress is a nice point.[40] All this occurs in *Rondeau* XLVI, *De celluy qui est demeuré et s'Amye s'en est allée*:

> Tout à part soy est melancolieux
> Le tien Servant, qui s'esloigne des lieux
> Là où l'on veult chanter, dancer et rire.
> Seul en sa chambre, il va ses pleurs escrire,
> Et n'est possible à luy de faire mieulx.
>
> Car, quand il pleut, et le Soleil des Cieulx
> Ne reluist point, tout homme est soucieux,
> Et toute Beste en son creux se retire
>   Tout à part soy.
> Or maintenant pleut larmes de mes yeux.
> Et toy qui es mon Soleil gracieux
> M'as delaissé en l'ombre de martyre.
> Pour ces raisons loing des aultres me tire,
> Que mon ennuy ne leur soit ennuyeux,
>   Tout à part soy.

Metaphors of the changing seasons representing the transience of physical beauty are found in another *rondeau*, *A la jeune Dame melancolique et solitaire* (LI) for which sources in the works of several Petrarchist poets, namely Tebaldeo, Serafino and Chariteo have been suggested:[41]

> Par seulle amour qui a tout surmonté
> On trouve grace en divine bonté,
> Et ne la fault par aultre chemin querre.
> Mais tu la veulx par cruaulté conquerre,
> Qui est contraire à bonne voulunté.

Certes, c'est bien à toy grand cruaulté
De user en dueil la jeunesse & beaulté
Que t'a donné Nature sur la terre
    Par seulle amour.
En sa verdeur se resjouist l'Esté,
Et sur l'Yver laisse joyeuseté;
En ta verdeur plaisir doncques asserre;
Puis, tu diras (si vieillesse te serre):
A dieu le temps qui si bon a esté
    Par seulle amour.

Perhaps Marot's most striking debt to Petrarchism in the *rondeaux* is to be found in his use of rhetorical antithesis to give stylized expression to the force of love, and his attempt by the association and the juxtaposition of opposites to approach a definition of the indefinable. Marot's aptly named *Rondeau par Contradictions* (XXVI) develops an antithesis in every line which communicates to the reader, not only by language but also by the movement it confers upon the verse, the lover's extreme fluctuations between hope and despair:

En esperant, espoir me desespere
Tant que la mort m'est vie tres prospere;
Me tourmentant de ce qui me contente,
Me contentant de ce qui me tourmente
Pour la douleur du soulas que j'espere.

Amour hayneuse en aigreur me tempere;
Puis temperance aspre comme Vipere
Me refroidist soubz chaleur vehemente
    En esperant.
L'enfant aussi, qui surmonte le pere,
Bande ses yeulx pour veoir mon improbere;
De moy s'enfuyt & jamais ne s'absente,
Mais, sans bouger, va en obscure sente
Cacher mon dueil affin que mieulx appere
    En esperant.   (*O.D.*, *Rondeau* XXVI)

Several of these antitheses are common in the poetry of Petrarch himself but in this case Marot's most immediate source of inspiration was probably two sonnets of Chariteo, 'Poi che saper volete in quale stato' (XVIII) and 'Io seguo chi mi fugge e si nasconde' (XIII) while v. 7 of his *rondeau* is a reminiscence of Olimpo di Sasso-ferrato's *Gloria d'Amore* and in particular of the following:[42]

> Chi non te fosse a tutte l'or fidele
> Dimonstra un tigre, un serpe aspro e mordace.

Although antithesis was an essential part of French lyricism of the fifteenth century, and was discreetly present in Marot's *chansons*, there seems to be no example in the native tradition which could have inspired Marot to so systematic a deployment of this feature as the Italian sources already mentioned.

Metaphorical antithesis takes its place in the *rondeaux* beside its rhetorical counterpart. It is by its nature more concisely, and for this reason more discreetly elaborated than the latter, though it is scarcely less *précieux* in effect. Marot's most consistently invoked motif is that of fire and water, or fire and balm. This last appears in the incipit of *Rondeau* IV, *De celluy qui incite une jeune Dame à faire Amy*:

> A mon plaisir vous faictes feu et basme.

The former is developed at greater length in the *Rondeau De l'amoureux ardant* (V):

> Au feu qui mon cueur a choisy,
> Jectez y, ma seule Deesse,
> De l'eau de grace & de lyesse!
> Car il est consommé quasi. (vv.1–4)

and reappears very briefly in *Rondeau* LIV, *A la fille d'ung Painctre d'Orléans belle entre les autres*. Her painted image

> I mect le feu & a dequoy l'estaindre. (v. 13)

This metaphorical antithesis conveys the eternal paradox of love which is killed by the assuagement which it incessantly demands as its remedy.

In some of the *rondeaux* a fusion of old and new, French and Italian sources of inspiration is achieved by the poet. This is noticeably so in the *Rondeau De l'Amant doloreux* (XI) whose lines:

> Aupres de l'eau me fault de soif perir;
> Je me voy jeune & en aage fleurir,
> Et se me monstre estre plein de vieillesse
> Avant mes jours.

Or si je meurs je veulx Dieu requerir
Prendre mon Ame, & sans plus enquerir,
Je donne aux vers mon Corps plein de foiblesse;
Quant est du Cueur du tout je le te laisse,
Ce nonobstant que me fasses mourir
Avant mes jours   (vv. 6–15)

are inspired partly by one of the most famous themes of fifteenth-
century French lyricism 'Je meurs de soif auprès de la fontaine'
around which Charles d'Orléans organized his celebrated *concours*,
and partly by these lines of Olimpo di Sassoferrato in which the
Italian poet affected to draw up his will before taking final leave
of his beloved:

Il cuor ti lasso, donna di valore:
Di lui fa quel che voi, quel che te piace,
Ch'obedir deve il servo il suo signore.
Gli ossi alla terra lasso, doue iace
Ogni fidele amante. Pien di fede
Arsi d'un'amorosa e dolce face.[43]

The two developments complement each other perfectly. An even
more intimate fusion of sources is discernible in the *Rondeau* v, *De
l'amoureux ardant*, here in its entirety:

Au feu qui mon cueur a choisy,
Jectez y, ma seule Deesse,
De l'eau de grace & de lyesse!
Car il est consommé quasi.

Amours l'a de si pres saisy
Que force est qu'il crie sans cesse:
Au feu!
Si par vous en est dessaisy,
Amours luy doint plus grand destresse
Si jamais sert aultre maistresse.
Doncques ma Dame courez y,
Au feu!

This poem reflects the vogue enjoyed by the so-called 'style
flamboyant' in the fifteenth-century French tradition and seems
to be directly inspired, in part, by a poem of Alain Chartier,
Chançon Nouvele:[44]

Au feu! au feu! au feu! qui mon cuer art
Par ung brandon tiré d'un doulz regart
Tout enflambé d'ardent desir d'Amours.
Grace, mercy, confort et bon secours,
Ne me laissez bruler, se Dieu vous gart.

Flambe, chaleur, ardeur par tout s'espart,
Estincelles et fumee s'en part.
Embrasé sui du feu qui croit tousjours.

Tirez, boutez, chacez tout à l'escart
Ce dur dangier, getez de toutes part
Eaue de pitié, de larmes et de plours.
A l'aide, helas! je n'ay confort d'aillours.
Avancez vous ou vous vendrez trop tart!

Chartier's poem offered to Marot the dramatic appeal for assistance which the latter has preserved and accentuated by its position as the refrain to the *rondeau*. The remedy which Chartier demands (getez de toutes part / Eaue de pitié, de larmes et de plours) is essentially similar to that imagined by Marot. Chartier, however, does not address himself directly to his lady but to the qualities which, ideally, she might be expected to possess and to employ in his favour (Grace, mercy, confort et bon secours). The direct appeal to the lady is however a feature of the second source of Marot's *rondeau*, a *strambotto* by Serafino Aquilano which also stresses the constant cries of the distressed heart:

De picola favilla è nato un foco
Dentro al mio cor che'l mio consuma e struge,
Tal che non trova pace in alcun loco
E qual fiero leon per doglia ruge.
E io mi sforzo invano a poco a poco
De retenir la mia vita che fuge:
Però madonna, extingue il foco acceso
Del cor che m'hai sí gravamente offeso.[45]

In both cases Marot has consistently simplified the developments given to this theme by his predecessors. And to excellent effect. His own poem has nothing of the excessive and lachrymose enumerations of Chartier's and avoids the too particular, and somewhat *déplacé* image (qual fiero leon per doglia ruge) of Serafino's. It is capped, in addition, by a development of his own, an urgent protestation of undying fidelity offered with commendable presence of mind!

> Si par vous en est dessaisy,
> Amours luy doint plus grand destresse
> Si jamais sert aultre maistresse.

The melancholy lover of *Rondeau* XLVI who withdraws from the society of his fellows:

> Tout à part soy est melancolieux
> Le tien Servant, qui s'esloigne des lieux
> Là où l'on veult chanter, dancer et rire.
> Seul en sa chambre, il va ses pleurs escrire,   (vv. 1–4)

is probably closer to Chartier who likewise insists on the antithesis between society and the lover in his *Complainte contre la Mort*:[46]

> J'oy les autres chanter et je me plains,
> Ilz vont dansant et je destors mes mains,
> Ils festoient et je tout seul remains;

than to Petrarch, who describes himself in sonnet XXXV:[47]

> Solo e pensoso i piu deserti campi
> Vo mesurando a passi tardi e lenti

although, as we have seen, the pathetic fallacy invoked later in the poem by Marot is a Petrarchist development. *Rondeau* XLIV, *De celluy qui entra de Nuict chez s'Amye*, on the other hand, shows a certain disparity in manner rather than an artistic fusion of two trends of inspiration. It opens with the concern felt by the lover for his lady's honour which might be attacked by the activities of the 'Langars dangereux', in fact the descendants of *Malebouche, Faulx Rapport,* and *Envie Decevante* who figure so often in medieval French lyricism and have a place in Marot's own *chansons*. This is followed by, rather than combined with, a development which appears Petrarchist in its preciosity and its conceits:

> De nuict & jour fault estre adventureux
> Qui d'amours veult avoir biens plantureux.
> Quant est de moy, je n'euz onc crainte d'ame,
> Fors seulement, en entrant chez ma Dame,
> D'estre aperceu des Langars dangereux.

Ung soir, bien tard, me feirent si paoureux
Qu'advis m'estoit qu'il estoit jour pour eulx;
Mais si entray je, & n'en vint jamais blasme,
    De nuict & jour.
La nuict je prins d'elle ung fruict savoureux;
Au poinct du jour vy son corps amoureux
Entre deux draps plus odorans que Basme.
Mon Oeil adonc, qui de plaisir se pasme,
Dict à mes Bras: vous estes bien heureux
    De nuict & jour.

A rather different effect is achieved in those *rondeaux* in which Marot, rather as Ronsard was to do later in some of his sonnets in the *Amours de Cassandre,* juxtaposes the preciosity of Petrarchism with a frank expression of erotic desire. This is a conscious juxtaposition in *Rondeau* IV, *De celluy qui incite une jeune Dame à faire Amy,* to which the poet himself draws attention when excusing himself for the unmannerly and outspoken words with which he concludes his poem:

A mon plaisir vous faictes feu et basme;
Parquoy souvent je m'estonne, ma Dame,
Que vous n'avez quelcque Amy par amours.
Au Diable l'ung qui fera ses clamours
Pour vous prier quand vous serez vieille lame.

Or, en effect, je vous jure mon ame
Que si j'estois jeune & gaillarde femme,
J'en auroys un devant qu'il fust trois jours,
    A mon plaisir.
Et pourquoy non? ce seroit grand diffame
Si vous perdiez jeunesse, bruyt & fame,
Sans esbranler Drap, Satin & Velours.
Pardonnez moy si mes motz sont trop lourdz;
Je ne vous veulx qu'aprendre vostre game
    A mon plaisir.

Marot's development of the Petrarchist conceit of the exchange of hearts in *Rondeau* XLIII, *De celluy qui ne pense qu'en s'Amye* is further evidence of the fact that he was no slave to literary modes of expression. He crosses the line between preciosity and eroticism at will although capable of more wit than cynicism in this respect than was ever displayed by Ronsard. Marot's reversal of the conceit gives piquancy to the whole and the *rondeau* ends on an epigrammatic note:

> Toutes les nuyctz je ne pense qu'en celle
> Qui a le Corps plus gent qu'une pucelle
> De quatorze ans sur le poinct d'enrager,
> Et au dedans ung cueur (pour abreger)
> Autant joyeux qu'eut oncque Damoyselle.
>
> Elle a beau tainct, ung parler de bon zelle
> Et le Tetin rond comme une Grozelle.
> N'ay je donc pas bien cause de songer
>   Toutes les nuictz?
> Touchant son cueur, je l'ay en ma cordelle,
> Et son Mary n'a sinon le Corps d'elle.
> Mais toutesfois, quand il vouldra changer,
> Prenne le Cueur, et, pour le soulager,
> J'auray pour moy le gent Corps de la belle
>   Toutes les nuictz.

Marot's *rondeaux*, by their many and diverse qualities, deserve to be better known.

By contrast with the *rondeaux*, Marot's lyrical *épigrammes* have rarely if ever lacked a discerning public to appreciate their considerable charm. It is the *épigrammes* too which have given most encouragement to the frequent and often erroneous attempts of critics to reconstruct what one of them, and not the least distinguished, has termed the poet's *roman d'amour*.[48] To what extent then are the *épigrammes* inspired by the poet's direct personal experience? One may accept, as Monsieur Lefranc has proposed, that the Anne to whom many of these poems are addressed was in fact Anne d'Alençon, the daughter of Charles d'Alençon, the half-brother of Marguerite de Navarre's first husband. The relationship is worthy of note for two reasons. It placed Anne, like Marot, within the circle of Marguerite de Navarre. But if the attachment between them was the result of these circumstances it was also limited by the same to that of a purely sentimental one. Marot himself explains why:

> Je pense en vous & au fallacieux
> Enfant Amour qui par trop sottement
> A fait mon Cueur aymer si haultement;

Si haultement (hélas) que de ma peine
N'ose esperer ung brin d'allegement,
Quelcque doulceur de quoy vous soyez pleine.

(Epigr., CXXIX, vv. 5–10)

Nevertheless, this *alliance,* however restricted it may have been,
was seen to contribute a more personal note to the short poems
which it inspired. Not that this prevented Marot from composing
similar poems for other ladies of the court and including them
within the same grouping of poems. But these were not always or
necessarily written on the poet's own account, and nowhere is this
more certain than in the poem *A la Bouche de Diane.*[49] Love
poetry, in France as in Italy, was a court pastime in which those
unable to turn a verse for themselves might invoke the assistance
of others more practised. Literary inspiration was not absent from
these poems or from the seemingly more personal ones addressed
to Anne. Through the intermediary of the Italian poets, both vernacular and neo-Latin, and the Latin poets Martial and Catullus,
many of Marot's lyrical *épigrammes* rejoin the tradition which
issued from the *Greek Anthology.*[50] In this respect even some of
Marot's earliest compositions, of 1527 for example, are harbingers
of the *Pléiade*'s Anacreontic phase.[51] The element of literary
convention is a particular feature of the publication of Marot's love
epigrams in the *Œuvres* of 1538 of which the French humanist
Estienne Dolet was the publisher. Very probably at the latter's
suggestion, Marot not only gathered together the *petits genres* of
his youth under the title *Epigrammes* and presented them, in the
Classical and neo-Latin tradition, in Books, but he dedicated the
second of the two books to Anne, confirming her predominance by
adding her name to titles from which it had previously been
absent, and even to poems which had formerly borne dedications
to other ladies.[52] In addition to the dedicatory poem there is also
one which serves as an epilogue to the *roman d'amour.* In this the
poet promises Anne immortality through the sequence of poems
she has inspired:

Ilz te feront vivre eternellement;
Demandes tu plus belle recompense?

(Epigr., CLI, vv. 11–12)

This is a convention at least as old as Catullus and one which in

Marot's own age was invoked by Petrarchists and neo-Latin poets alike.

The range of expression given to the theme of love in the *épigrammes* is considerable. The *précieux*, the *galant*, the sensual and the crude, in thought and in language, are all accommodated within the genre. The last register is reserved, as if on social and artistic criteria, for the sexual activities of such characters as Martin, Alix, Robin and Cathon.[53] Their rustic *amours* were later to be celebrated with equal, if not greater realism, by Ronsard's *Folastries*.

The carefully noted incidents of a *roman d'amour*, encounters, departures, obsessive fantasies, the exchange of portraits, presents, kisses, on occasion even a snowball, all are pretexts for poetry in the Classical and Italian tradition. So, too, the exploits of the young Cupid and his mother. These are the starting-points for a form of composition which often resembles that of the miniaturist, but has not its disadvantages. Such, for instance is this evocation of his mistress at the spinet, which not only fixes the object of admiration but also communicates the emotion her presence inspired:

> Lors que je voy en ordre la Brunette
> Jeune, en bon point, de la ligne des Dieux,
> Et que sa Voix, ses Doigtz et l'Espinette
> Meinent ung bruit doulx & melodieux,
> J'ay du plaisir & d'Oreilles & d'Yeux
> Plus que les Sainctz en leur gloire immortelle,
> Et aultant qu'eulx je deviens Glorieux
> Des que je pense estre ung peu aymé d'elle.
>
> (*Epigr.*, CXXII)

Marot sees in nature the reflection of human beauty, a reflection fixed for ever in Petrarchist imagery. Hence the 'Visage... semble à la fresche & vermeillete Rose' (*De la Rose envoyée pour Estreines*), 'ceste gorge d'Albastre' (*Du Ris de ma Damoyselle d'Allebret*), the 'Bouche de coral precieux' (*A la Bouche de Dyane*), the 'doulce, amyable Calandre' (*Il salue Anne*), the 'Fleur de quinze ans' (*Des Cinq Poinctz en Amours*). Fleetingly he approaches in the *épigrammes* that fusion of natural and human beauty which was to be such a conspicuous feature of *Pléiade* poetry.

Art in its execution brings to the *épigrammes*, as indeed to the miniature, a fullness which surpasses expectation, although the means by which it is achieved may be different. Extended comparison is one of the resources of the poet's art which Marot deploys to this effect. This typical conceit establishes a parallel between the lover's condition and that of the earth momentarily deprived of the sun, between the human and the universal which mirrors and magnifies:

> Incontinent que je te vy venue,
> Tu me semblas le cler soleil des cieulx
> Qui sa lumiere a long temps retenue;
> Puis se faict veoir luysant & gracieux.
> Mais ton depart me semble une grand'nue
> Qui se vient mettre au devant de mes yeux.
> Pas n'eusse creu que de joye advenue
> Fust advenu regret si ennuieux.　　　(*Epigr.*, XXXI)

The following conceit is differently employed but with resulting fullness in the poem *Du moys de May & d'Anne*:

> May qui portoit Robe reverdissante
> De fleurs semée, ung jour se mist en place,
> Et quand m'Amye il vit tant florissante,
> De grand despit rougist sa verte Face,
> En me disant: tu cuydes qu'elle efface
> (A mon advis) les fleurs qui de moy yssent.
> Je luy responds: toutes tes fleurs perissent
> Incontinent que Yver les vient toucher,
> Mais en tout temps de Madame florissent
> Les grands vertus que Mort ne peult secher.
> 　　　　　　　　　　　　　　　(*Epigr.*, VIII)

Marot has dramatized the conceit using it as the starting-point for a contest between the month of May and Anne. Cleverly, he has transferred to nature human attributes ('portoit Robe', 'se mist en place', 'de grand despit' etc.) and to his mistress those of nature (m'Amye...tant florissante). It was with just such art and economy that Ronsard was later to dramatize his little masterpiece, 'Mignonne, allons voir si la rose'. Another of Marot's *épigrammes*, *De la Rose envoyée pour Estreines*, receives fullness from the anecdote in which the poet recalled how roses became red before celebrating the beauty of his mistress with the traditional comparison. This anecdote was very popular with the neo-Latin poets who developed many different versions of it:[54]

> La belle Rose à Venus consacrée
> L'Oeil & le Sens de grand plaisir pourvoit;
> Si vous diray Dame qui tant m'agrée
> Raison pourquoy de rouges on en voit.
> Ung jour Venus son Adonis suyvoit
> Parmy Jardins pleins d'Espines & Branches,
> Les Piedz tous nudz & les deux Bras sans manches,
> Dont d'ung Rosier l'Espine luy mesfeit.
> Or estoient lors toutes les Roses blanches,
> Mais de son sang de vermeilles en feit.
>   De ceste Rose ay je faict mon proffit
> Vous estrenant, car, plus qu'à aultre chose
> Vostre Visage en doulceur tout confict
> Semble à la fresche & vermeillette Rose.   (*Epigr.*, XI)

The epigrams which Marot composed for Diane de Poitiers, the dauphin's mistress, were given another dimension by the mythological context which the poet invoked, sometimes comparing, sometimes contrasting the goddess with the royal favourite. The following is probably the most successful of the *Diane* epigrams since it alludes simply to the most celebrated of Diane's activities as goddess of the chase and couples this with an indirect reference to the dauphin's other passion, hunting:

> L'enfant Amour n'a plus son arc estrange,
> Dont il blessoit d'hommes & cueurs & testes;
> Avec celluy de Diane a faict change,
> Dont elle alloit aux champs faire les questes.
> Ilz ont changé; n'en faictes plus d'enquestes!
> Et si on dict: A quoy le congnois tu?
> Je voy qu'Amour chasse souvent aux Bestes,
> Et qu'elle attainct les hommes de vertu.
>   (*Epigr.*, LXIII)

The goddess's legendary coldness and the savage fate which she meted out to those men who chanced across her path inspires this paradoxical desire in the admirer of Diane:

Le cler Phebus donne la vie & l'aise
Par son baiser tant digne & precieux,
Et mort devient ce que Diane baise.
O dur baiser, rude & mal gracieux,
Tu faiz venir ung desir soucieux
De mieulx avoir, dont souvent on desvie.
Mais qui pourroit parvenir à ce mieulx,
Il n'est si mort qui ne revint en vie.   (*Epigr.*, LVI)

Ronsard's allusions to the Trojan war in the *Amours de Cassandre*
and later in the *Sonnets pour Hélène* were likewise inspired by the
need to bring new perspectives to the treatment of love in a short
poem.

The numerous *baisers* among Marot's love epigrams sustain the
interest of the reader without resorting to allusion, anecdote or
dramatic conceits. Doubtless they reflect a current literary fashion
but they also accommodate at first or second hand observation and
experience. Thus what may appear to be the most exiguous of
motifs receives considerable and diverse development. The *baiser*
itself is rarely described. Marot does not repeat his famous
rondeau. He introduces into the motif an element of pyscholo-
gical refinement. *A la Bouche de Dyane* is an attempt on the part
of the admirer to procure the kiss he covets by praise, entreaty
and cajolery:

Bouche de coral precieux,
Qui à baiser semblez semondre;
Bouche qui d'ung cueur gracieux
Savez tant bien dire & respondre;
Respondez moy: doibt mon cueur fondre
Devant vous comme au feu la cire?
Voulez vous bien celluy occire
Qui craint vous estre desplaisant?
Ha, bouche que tant je desire,
Dictes nenny en me baisant.   (*Epigr.*, CII)

Another epigram on this theme (*Du Baiser*) prolongs the memory
of a kiss received and entreats constant mercy from the lady:

Ce franc Baiser, ce Baiser amyable,
Tant bien donné, tant bien receu aussi
Qu'il estoit doulx. O beaulté admirable,
Baisez moy donc cent fois le jour ainsy,

> Me recevant dessoubz vostre mercy
> Pour tout jamais, ou vous pourrez bien dire
> Qu'en me donnant ung Baiser adoulcy,
> M'aurez donné perpetuel martyre. (*Epigr.*, CXXVIII)

The famous epigram *De Ouy & Nenny* instructs the mistress in certain refinements of the art of love:

> Ung doulx Nenny avec ung doulx soubzrire
> Est tant honneste; il le vous fault apprendre.
> Quant est d'Ouy, si veniez à le dire,
> D'avoir trop dit je vouldrois vous reprendre;
> Non que je soys ennuyé d'entreprendre
> D'avoir le fruict dont le desir me poingt;
> Mais je vouldrois qu'en le me laissant prendre
> Vous me dissiez: non, vous l'aurez point!

> (*Epigr.*, LXVII)

The heavy eroticism which attended many of Ronsard's *baisers*, and was a feature of the neo-Latin tradition in particular, is quite absent from Marot's variations on the theme in the *épigrammes*.

To give an impression of fullness to the development of the slightest motifs within the dimensions of the epigram is only one aspect of Marot's art in this genre. His poems may also be judged by the refinement and the ingenuity with which he brought them to a point in the last two lines. This effect is achieved in the epigram *Du Ris de ma Damoyselle D'Allebret* by a striking antithesis:

> Elle a tresbien ceste gorge d'Albastre,
> Ce doulx parler, ce cler tainct, ces beaux yeux;
> Mais en effect ce petit Ris follastre,
> C'est (à mon gré) ce qui luy sied le mieux.
> Elle en pourroit les chemins & les lieux
> Où elle passe à plaisir inciter;
> Et si ennuy me venoit contrister
> Tant que par mort fust ma vie abatue,
> Il ne fauldroit pour me ressusciter
> Que ce Ris là duquel elle me tue.

> (*Epigr.*, LI)

D'Anne qui luy jecta de la Neige ends with the deliberate inversion of a traditional conceit:

Anne, ta seule grace
Estaindre peult le feu que je sens bien,
Non point par Eau, par Neige ne par Glace
Mais par sentir ung feu pareil au mien.

(*Epigr.*, XXIV, vv. 7–10)

Yet another (*A Anne*) ends with the dawning recognition, and
naive acceptance by the lover of his condition:

Quant je te voy, je suis bien d'autre sorte.
Dont vient cela? savoir je ne le puis,
Si n'est d'amour, Anne, que je te porte.

(*Epigr.*, CCIX, vv. 6–8)

Elsewhere the *trait* is used to perfection to crystallize the increasing complexity of the lover's emotions and fears and his own
awareness of them: it is the expression of his dilemma in:

Mais quand je sens son cueur si chaste & hault,
Je l'ayme tant que je ne l'ose aymer.

(*Epigr.*, LXXXVI, vv. 9–10)

and again in:

Et je devroys craindre que cela vienne,
Car j'ayme trop quand on me veult aymer.

(*Epigr.*, CXXXVIII, vv. 9–10)

In both cases the observations would seem to be inspired and
attended by an incipient classicism. Perhaps the most affecting of
all though is the discreet intimation of a past but profound chagrin
which prohibits all further inquiry. Thus, *De Cupido & de sa
dame*:

Amour trouva celle qui m'est amère,
Et je y estois; j'en sçay bien mieulx le compte.
Bon jour (dit il) bon jour, Venus, ma mere.
Puis, tout acoup, il voit qu'il se mescompte,
Dont la couleur au Visage luy monte
D'avoir failly, honteux, Dieu sçait combien.
Non, non, Amour (ce dis je) n'ayez honte,
Plus cler voyans que vous s'y trompent bien.

(*Epigr.*, CVI)

Not the least of the merits of Marot's love epigrams finally, is that
the *trait*, refined and ingenious though it may often be, is

achieved without strain or detriment to the proper development
of a theme. There is no sign here of the practice attributed by Du
Bellay to certain French epigrammatists of accumulating nine
empty verses whose only function was to preface the delivery of a
stinging tenth.[55]

In the celebrated epigram *Du Beau Tetin*, for long retaining its
original nomenclature as a *blason*,[56] Marot allowed himself to
escape from the somewhat exiguous limits of the eight- and ten-
line epigram in order to demonstrate his descriptive facility. The
blason, traditionally enough a poem of praise or blame—and the
Beau Tetin has its counterpart, *Du laid Tetin*—may have been
inspired by such medieval precedents as Villon's *Ballade de la
Belle Heaulmiere*, or equally by such Petrarchist *Capitoli* as
Marot may have encountered at this moment of his stay at
Ferrara.[57] However this may be, its originality lies in the art with
which Marot has achieved a painter's task in this frank expression
of sensual, and almost tactile, delight without the aids reserved for
the painter:

> Tetin refect, plus blanc qu'un oeuf,
> Tetin de satin blanc tout neuf,
> Tetin qui fais honte à la Rose,
> Tetin plus beau que nulle chose,
> Tetin dur, non pas Tetin, voyre,
> Mais petite boule d'Ivoyre
> Au milieu duquel est assise
> Une Fraize ou une Cerise
> Que nul ne voit ne touche aussi,
> Mais je gage qu'il est ainsi;
> Tetin doncq au petit bout rouge,
> Tetin qui jamais ne se bouge,
> Soit pour venir, soit pour aller,
> Soit pour courir, soit pour baller;
> Tetin gaulche, Tetin mignon,
> Tousjours loing de son compaignon;
> Tetin qui portes tesmoignage
> Du demourant du personnage;
> Quant on te voit, il vient à mainctz
> Une envie dedans les mains
> De te taster, de te tenir;
> Mais il se fault bien contenir

D'en approcher, bon gré, ma vie,
Car il viendroit une aultre envie.
O Tetin, ne grand, ne petit,
Tetin meur, Tetin d'appetit,
Tetin qui nuict & jour criez:
Mariez moy tost, mariez!
Tetin qui t'enfles & repoulses
Ton Gorgerin de deux bons poulses,
A bon droict heureux on dira
Celluy qui de laict t'emplira,
Faisant d'ung Tetin de pucelle
Tetin de femme entiere & belle.   (*Epigr.*, LXXVII)

Marot's only aids are comparisons of colour, of texture, of shape and firmness, naive expressions of desire and an indulgent repetition of the noun which lingers like a caress. But they are brilliantly combined and culminate in a wish which brings a certain dignity to eroticism.

It is difficult to find the same enthusiasm for Marot's longer love poems, the elegies. It is not only that they are almost totally impersonal for the same applies without any detriment to the *chansons* and to a lesser extent to the *rondeaux* and *épigrammes* too. It is not only that they develop the themes and situations of medieval lyricism, the *belle dame sans mercy*, the *mal mariée*, the lover rejected and a martyr to his passion, for such themes had not previously inhibited the poet's considerable talent for lyricism. The elegies offend by their prolixity and their sameness. They suffer inevitably as a collection where such defects are not disguised but accentuated.

In many cases Marot's elegies were commissioned pieces of work. This did not prejudice their uniformity. The various women addressed remain as one. Even when described they offer nothing but an idealized 'éternel féminin'.[58] The lovers too are equally indistinct although their social situations may be apparent. Schooled by the *Roman de la Rose* and the *Grands Rhétoriqueurs* the lovers disclose their dreams (*Elégie* VI), personify their fears and emotions in allegorical conflict (*Elégie* I and *passim*), denounce their enemies (*Elégie* XI, *Danger*, *Maubec*, *Jalousie*), indulge in interminable dialogues with their hearts (*Elégie* IV) and eyes (*Elégie* III) and exhibit a remarkable facility for amorous casuistry.

It is with relief that the reader alights upon the occasional Petrarchist conceit:

> Mais je congnois que ton amour de glace
> Pres de mon feu du tout se fond & passe.
>
> (*O.L.*, *Elégie* II, vv. 45–46)

or theme such as the gift of the mirror in *Elégie* XVI. Occasionally too a Classical commonplace is happily illustrated by an image from nature. A reminiscence from Tibullus[59] inspires this development in *Elégie* IV:

> Sçais tu pas bien qu'Amour a de coustume
> D'entremesler ses plaisirs d'amertume,
> Ne plus ne moins comme Espines poignantes
> Sont par Nature au beau Rosier joignantes?
>
> (vv. 43–46)

Protestations of undying love are strongly expressed in this transposition of Ovid, *Heroïdes*, V[60] in *Elégie* XV:

> Commande moy jusques à mon Cueur fendre,
> Mais de t'aymer ne me vien point deffendre.
> Plustost sera Montaigne sous Vallée
> Plustost la Mer on voirra dessalée,
> Et plustost Seine encontremont ira
> Que mon amour de toy se partira.
>
> (vv. 33–38)

But apart from these too rare felicities it is upon developments incidental to the main theme that the reader most willingly lingers, the confident assertion in *Elégie* XXIV of the poet's powers to dispense immortality, the evocation of pastoral delights and the brilliant use of contrasting mood and situation, the impeccable change and control of poetic movement in *Elégie* I:

> Il vault trop mieulx en ung lieu solitaire,
> En Champs ou Boys pleins d'Arbres & de fleurs
> Aller dicter les plaisirs ou les pleurs
> Que l'on reçoit de sa Dame cherie;
> Puis, pour oster hors du cueur fascherie,
> Voller en Plaine, et chasser en Forest,
> Descoupler Chiens, tendre Toilles et Rhetz;
> Aulcunesfois, apres les longues Courses,
> Se venir seoir pres des Ruisseaux & Sources

Et s'endormir au son de l'eau qui bruyt,
Ou escouter la Musique & le bruyt
Des Oyselletz painctz de couleurs estranges,
Comme Mallars, Merles, Mauviz, Mesanges,
Pinsons, Pivers, Passes & Passerons;
En ce plaisir le Temps nous passerons;
Et n'en sera (ce croy je) offensé Dieu,
Puis que la Guerre à l'Amour donne lieu.
    Mais, s'il advient que la Guerre s'esbranle,
Lors conviendra dancer d'un autre branle,
Laisser fauldra Boys, Sources et Ruisseaulx,
Laisser fauldra Chasse, Chiens & Oyseaulx,
Laisser fauldra d'Amours les petitz dons
Pour suyvre aux Champs Estandars & Guydons;
Et lors chascun ses forces reprendra,
Et pour l'amour de s'Amie tendra
A recouvrer Gloire, Honneur & Butins,
Faisant congnoistre aux Espaignolz mutins
Que longuement Fortune variable
En ung lieu seul ne peult estre amyable;   (vv. 110–38)

Significantly again, one welcomes in the second elegy an intercalated development which by its grace and movement, by its
elegant parallelisms could have been fittingly included in the
chansons. In fact its theme takes us back to one of the most
popular songs in the *Jardin de Plaisance*:[61] and the two *sizains*
are verse forms which belong indubitably to the domain of light
popular lyricism rather than to that of elegy:

S'ainsi n'advient, à tel Moys de l'année
Bien me duyra couleur Noire ou Tannée,
A ung tel moys qu'on doibt dancer & rire,
Raison vouldra que d'ennuy je souspire,
Veu qu'en ce temps fut faicte l'alliance
Dont je perdray la totalle fiance.
    Mais, s'il te plaist, à tel Moys de l'Année
Ne me duira couleur Noire & Tannée.
A ung tel Moys qu'on doibt s'esbatre & rire
Raison vouldra que point je ne souspire,
Veu qu'en ce temps fut faicte l'alliance
Dont j'obtiendray la totalle fiance.   (vv. 31–42)

That Marot's talent in popular lyricism should shine through, even in the elegies, and that the reader should welcome this relief, illustrates clearly Marot's limitations as an elegiac love poet while highlighting the vein in which he remained supreme.

GRAND LYRICISM: OFFICIAL POETRY

It is in the domain of *lyrisme grave* that Marot's work has met, until recent years at least, with the most persistent neglect. One has only to think of Jourda's categorical 'de ces poèmes donc, aucun qui vaille d'être relu'[62] to gauge the extent of the prejudice against them, particularly those works inspired by official or political occasions. Where the poet's excursions into *lyrisme grave* were seen to be prompted by his personal circumstances, they escaped such censure. Two such cases spring to mind at once. The *cantiques* which Marot composed on his departure from Lyons, the city which had received him back from exile:

> Adieu, la Saulne et son mignon,
> Le Rhosne qui court de vistesse.
> Tu t'en vas droict en Avignon;
> Vers Paris je prens mon adresse.
> Je diroys: Adieu, ma maistresse,
> Mais le cas viendroit mieulx à point
> Si je disoys: Adieu, jeunesse,
> Car la barbe grise me poingt.
> (*O.L.*, *Cantique* II, vv. 33–40)

and that with which he triumphantly and joyously saluted the French court on his return, *Le Dieu Gard de Marot à la Court de France*:

> Vienne la mort quant bon luy semblera!
> Moins que jamais mon cueur en tremblera,
> Puis que de Dieu je reçoy ceste grace
> De veoir encor de Monseigneur la face.
> (*O.L.*, *Cantique* III, vv. 1–4)

To deduce from this that the initial impulse of these two poems is alone sufficient to set them aesthetically above others in the same vein which have been less favourably reviewed would however be a grotesque over-simplification. And it would be equally unsatisfactory to eliminate from any serious discussion of Marot's poetry his essays in official and political lyricism simply because their originating pretexts seem to place them beyond the immediate appreciation of the majority of readers and critics. Their poetic merits too may be more usefully assessed in terms of themes, inspiration, execution.

However specific the pretext or occasion which the poet is required to serve in his official capacity, his task is not merely to present an inventory of circumstances, a report of a spectacle but to express or interpret the feelings, emotions, reflections which take hold of the spectator or witness directly involved. It is these feelings, emotions or reflections which provide the occasion for lyricism and for the involvement of a much wider public. Marot's *Complainte* III is not simply an account of the execution of Jacques de Beaune, seigneur de Semblançay and treasurer of France, but an expression of the pity which was widely felt for this noble and honoured victim of the machinations and rapacity of Louise de Savoie and Montmorency.[63] It is both macabre and compassionate in its evocation of the vicissitudes of Semblançay's life and death:

> En son gyron jadis me nourrissoit
> Doulce Fortune, & tant me cherissoit
> Qu'a plein soubhaict me faisoit delivrance
> Des haultz Honneurs & grands Tresors de France;
> Mais ce pendant sa main gauche tres orde
> Secretement me filoit une Corde
> Qu'ung de mes Serfz, pour saulver sa jeunesse,
> A mise au col de ma blanche vieillesse.
> Et de ma mort tant laide fut la voye,
> Que mes Enfans, lesquelz (helas) j'avoye
> Hault eslevé en honneur et pouvoir,
> Hault eslevé au Gibet m'ont peu veoir.
>   Ma gloire donc, que j'avoys tant cherie,
> Fut avant moy devant mes yeux perie.
> ....
> Je, qui avoys ferme entente et attente
> D'estre en Sepulchre honnorable estendu,
> Suis tout debout à Montfaulcon pendu.
> Là où le vent (quand est fort & nuysible)
> Mon corps agite, et quand il est paisible,
> Barbe & Cheveulx tous blancs me faict branler
> Ne plus ne moins que fueilles d'arbre en l'Air.

Mes yeux, jadis vigilans de nature,
De vieulx Corbeaux sont devenus pasture;
Mon col, qui eut l'accol de Chevalier,
Est accolé de trop mortel collier;
Mon corps, jadis bien logé, bien vestu,
Est à present de la Gresle battu,
Lavé de pluye, et du Soleil seiché,
Au plus vil lieu qui peulst estre cherché.

(O.L., Complainte III, vv. 1–14, 36–50)

Marot's most celebrated *complainte*, the *Deploration de Florimont Robertet* (IV), goes far beyond the conventional while remaining within the traditional framework of the genre. In the speech of Death the poet transcends his immediate function of commemorating and praising the deceased and enriches his poems with a moving meditation on redemption through death and eternal life in Christ, inspired by the writings of Saint Paul. Thus Marot's own current preoccupation with evangelism,[64] and that of some sections of the French court too, gives an additional dimension to an official exercise. High flown rhetoric, one of the great dangers of official lyricism, gives place to biblical paraphrase whose strength is partly in its sobriety and partly in its movement. This part of the poem is well able to stand comparison with Ronsard's exercise on the same theme in his *Hymne de la Mort*. Marot writes of the virtues of Death:

Celluy ne s'ayme en rien,
Lequel vouldroit tousjours vivre en ce monde,
Pour se frustrer du tant souverain bien
Que luy promet verité pure et monde,
Possedast il mer et terre feconde,
Beaulté, sçavoir, santé sans empirer;
Il ne croit pas qu'il soit vye seconde;
Ou, s'il la croit, il me doibt desirer...

L'ame est le feu, le corps est le tyson;
L'ame est d'en hault, et le corps inutille
N'est autre cas q'une basse prison
En qui languist l'ame noble et gentille.
De tel prison j'ay la clef tressubtille;
C'est le mien dard à l'ame gracieux,
Car il la tire hors de sa prison vile
Pour avec foy la renvoyer es cieulx...

Le Christ, afin que de moy n'eusses crainte,
Premier que toy voulut mort encourir.
Et en mourant ma force a si estraincte
Que quant je tue, on ne sçauroit mourir.
Vaincue m'a pour les siens secourir,
Et plus ne suis q'une porte ou entrée
Qu'on doit passer voulentiers pour courir
De ce vil monde en celeste contrée.

(O.L., Complainte IV, vv. 309–16, 333–40, 389–96)

The same developments may be observed outside the realm of commemorative lyricism, although the means by which they are pursued and attained must obviously vary. Marot's *Dieu Gard à la Court de France* is more than a passing salutation from a returning absentee. It offers, in poetic form, a renewal of his obeisance to the royal family and to the court. This is combined with an expression of the exile's love of his country and the poet's enthusiasm is communicated in a movement of spirited and infectious vitality. How different are these lines from the somewhat sour sonnets of the *Regrets* which Du Bellay composed on his return from Italy:[65]

C'est luy, c'est luy, France, royne sacrée,
C'est luy qui veult que mon oeil se recrée,
Comme souloye, en vostre doulx regart!
Or je vous voy, France, que Dieu vous gard!
Depuis le temps que je ne vous ay veue
Vous me semblez bien amandée et creue.
Que Dieu vous croisse encores plus prospere!
Dieu gard Françoys, vostre cher filz et pere,
Le plus puissant en armes et science
Dont ayez eu encor experience.
Dieu gard la royne Elienor d'Austriche,
D'honneur, de sang et de vertuz tant riche!
Dieu gard du dard mortiffere et hideux
Les filz du roy! Dieu nous les gard tous deulx!
O que mon cueur est plain de dueil et de ire
De ce que plus les troys je ne puis dire!
Dieu gard leur seur, la Margueritte plaine
De dons exquis! Ha, royne Magdelaine,
Vous nous lairrez; bien vous puis, ce me semble,
Dire Dieu gard et adieu tout ensemble.

> Pour abreger, Dieu gard la noble reste
> Du royal sang, origine celeste!
> Dieu gard tous ceulx qui pour la France veillent
> Et pour son bien combattent et conseillent!
> Dieu gard la court des dames, où abonde
> Toute la fleur et l'eslite du monde!
>
> (*O.L.*, *Cantique* III, vv. 11–36)

The *Cantique Sur la venue de l'empereur en France* (VIII) is pregnant with the hope, widely felt and expressed, that François's concession to Charles in allowing him to cross France at the head of his troops on his way to the Low Countries, would result in an era of peace and understanding between the two monarchs. Eschewing prosaic and precise reporting, Marot achieves one of his most successful political poems by nice recourse to historical allusion, political symbolism, personification, all of which remain on a completely accessible level. These figures, in combination with the movement of the poem, create a lasting impression of the nostalgia for peace and the exhortatory mood which accompanied it:

> Or est Caesar, qui tant d'honneur acquit,
> Encor ung coup en ce beau monde né;
> Or est Caesar, qui les Gaules conquit,
> Encor ung coup en Gaule retourné,
>   De legions non point environné
> Pour guerroyer, mais plein d'amour nayve;
> Non point au vent de l'Aigle noir couronné,
> Non point en main le glaive, mais l'Olive.
>   Françoys & luy viennent droict de la rive
> Du Loyre à Seine, affin de Paris veoir,
> Et avec eulx Guerre meinent captive,
> Qui à discord les souloit esmouvoir...
>   Vien donc, Caesar, & une paix apporte
> Perpetuelle entre nous & les tiens.
> Haulse (Paris) haulse bien hault ta porte
> Car entrer veult le plus grand des Chrestiens.
>
> (*O.L.*, *Cantique* VIII, vv. 1–12, 25–28)

Perhaps the most difficult exercise for the court poet is that of anticipatory lyricism in which he must express and provoke enthusiasm for a future event. Here the dangers of empty and

obsequious effusions of sentiment are obvious. Marot faced and
overcame this problem with supreme assurance in the eclogue
which celebrates the forthcoming birth of a child to the duchess
of Ferrara. Marot begins by addressing the unborn child with
solicitous enthusiasm for his future development. Again, the
movement which the poet gives to his verse is important in
communicating mood and emotion:

> Petit enffant, quelque sois, fille ou filz,
> Parfais le temps de tes neuf mois prefix
> Heureusement; puys sors du royal ventre,
> Et de ce monde en la grant lumiere entre!
> Entre sans cry, viens sans peur en lumiere!
> Viens sans donner destresse coustumiere
> A la mere humble en qui dieu t'a fait naistre!
> Puys d'un doulx ris commence à la congnoistre!
> Apres que fait luy auras congnoissance,
> Prens peu à peu nouriture et croissance,
> Tant que à demy tu commence à parler
> Et tout seullet en tripgnant aller
> Sur les carreaulx de ta maison prospere,
> Au passetemps de ta mere et ton pere,
> Qui de te y veoir ung de ces jours pretendent
> Avec ton frere et ta seur qui t'atendent!
> Viens hardiment, car quant grandet seras,
> Et que à entendre ung peu commenceras,
> Tu trouveras ung siecle pour aprendre
> En peu de temps ce que enffant peult comprendre.
>
> (*O.L.*, *Eglogue* II, vv. 1–20)

But the success of the poem lies in the way that Marot has communicated the glories of the present moment to his anticipation
of the child's future. The *pièce de circonstance* becomes a paean of
praise to the Renaissance.[66] This was a subject upon which Marot
could speak, both for himself and others, with unbounded
enthusiasm. The transition is impeccably achieved at the end of
the first section of the poem (vv. 19–20) and the gradual decre-
scendo of the conclusion equally so:

> O siecle d'or le plus fin que l'on treuve,
> Dont la bonté dedans le feu s'espreuve!
> O bien heureulx tous ceulx qui le congnoissent,
> Et encor plus ceulx qui au jourd'huy naissent!...

> Parquoy, enffant, quelque sois, fille ou filz,
> Parfaictz le temps de tes neuf mois prefix
> Heureusement; puis sors du royal ventre,
> Et de ce monde en la grant lumyere entre!
>
> (ibid., vv. 61–64, 71–74)

These are but a few examples of Marot's talent in realizing the possibilities of official lyricism. The list may without difficulty be extended.

Marot's task was facilitated not only by the breadth of his conception of his official mission, by his enthusiasms, his involvement and the vivacity of his own sentiment, but also by the inspiration he gained from the works of other writers. His imitations vary in extent and also in felicity for there are dangers as well as advantages in the practice of creation through imitation. For instance, Marot's imitation of Villon's *Ballade des Pendus* in his *Complainte du riche infortuné Jaques de Beaune, seigneur de Samblançay* (III) suffers in comparison with the sheer force and power of evocation of the original which has been diluted in the process of adaptation. Marot's last eclogue *Sur la Naissance du filz de Monseigneur le Daulphin* (IV) is too close an imitation of Virgil's fourth eclogue and is inadequately transposed to be satisfactory in its new context. In fact Marot's very successful *Avant-naissance* (*Eglogue* II) is inspired by the same Virgilian source and affords an extremely interesting opportunity for comparative study of the two ventures in imitation. Very rare are the detailed borrowings made by Marot from the Latin work in the *Avant-naissance*. On the other hand, he has clearly seen and grasped the poetic possibilities presented by Virgil's use of the Sybil's prophecy of a coming Golden Age[67] which, without any overt reference, he has transposed to accommodate the advent of Renaissance and Reformation in sixteenth-century France. Obviously, he could not repeat this transformation in the later eclogue but one could have wished for some attempt to mitigate the foreignness of these lines:

> Or sommes nous prochains du dernier aage
> Prophetizé par Cumane, la saige;
> Des siecles longs le plus grand & le chef
> Commencer veult à naistre de rechef.
> La vierge Astrée en bref temps reviendra;
> De Saturnus le regne encor viendra;

> Puis que le Ciel, lequel se renouvelle,
> Nous ha pourveuz de lignée nouvelle
>
> (*O.L.*, *Eglogue* IV, vv. 11–18)

and others like them. Later stages of the same poem are more successful, however, partly because Marot makes a positive attempt at adaptation in v. 48, and in v. 64 offers the French Roland in place of Greek heroes, and partly because the passage of Virgil in question is more immediately amenable to the exercise. It offers on the whole general sentiments and images rather than specific allusions:

> At simul heroum laudes et facta parentis
> iam legere et quae sit poteris cognoscere uirtus,
> molli paulatim flauescet campus arista,
> incultisque rubens pendebit sentibus uua,
> et durae quercus sudabunt roscida mella.
> Pauca tamen suberunt priscae uestigia fraudis,
> quae temptare Thetim ratibus, quae cingere muris
> oppida, quae iubeant telluri infindere sulcos.
> Alter erit tum Tiphys, et altera quae uehat Argo
> delectos heroas; erunt etiam altera bella,
> atque iterum ad Troiam magnus mittetur Achilles.[68]

Here is Marot's adaptation of this passage:

> Regarde, Enfant de celeste semence,
> Comment desja ce beau Siecle commence;
> Ja le Laurier te prepare couronne;
> Ja le blanc Liz dedans ton bers fleuronne;
> D'icy à peu, de haultz Princes parfaictz,
> Et du grand Pere aussi les nobles faictz
> Lire pourras, tandis que les louanges
> Du pere tien par nations estranges
> Iront volant; & deslors pourras tu
> Sçavoir combien vault honneur & vertu.
> En celluy temps, steriles Montz & Pleins
> Seront de Bledz & de Vignes tous pleins;
> Et verra l'on les Chesnes plantureux
> Par les Forestz suer miel savoureux.
> Ce neantmoins des fraudes qui sont ores
> Quelque relique on pourra veoir encores.
> La terre encor du Soc on verra fendre,
> Villes & Bourgz de murailles deffendre,

> Conduyre en Mer les navires volans:
> Et aura France encores des Rolands.
>
> (O.L., Eglogue IV, vv. 45–64)

Significantly, in the light of his own pronouncements on the nature of poetic imitation, this was the poem above all others by Marot which Du Bellay signalled out for praise in his *Deffence et Illustration de la françoise* where it is described as '...un des meilleurs petitz ouvrages que fit onques Marot'.[69]

The use of several sources in one poem is a conspicuous feature of Marot's creation through imitation. 'La contamination des sources' was the measure which Du Bellay was later to advocate so strongly and which was effectively to become the impulse for so much of the best *Pléiade* poetry. Marot's first attempt, however, to exploit multiple sources in combination was not entirely successful. *L'Eglogue sur le Trespas de ma Dame Loyse de Savoye* (I) is composed of large-scale borrowings from Greek pastoral poetry and in particular from the *Chant funèbre en honneur de Bion* attributed to Moschus, plus Theocritus's first *Idyll*. Marot was almost equally largely indebted to Jean Lemaire de Belges whose *Temple d'honneur et de Vertu* and *Chansons de Namur* were called into account, not to mention briefer excursions into the *Illustration de Gaule et singularitez de Troye* and the *Seconde Epistre de l'Amant Vert* of the same author. When one adds to the names and works already quoted those of Virgil (*Eclogues* II and V), Ovid (*Metamorphoses*) and Sannazaro (*Arcadia*) one has some idea of Marot's resourceful gleanings. However, on this occasion, resourcefulness has triumphed over art. In one particular and often quoted instance Marot has maladroitly coupled one of the most impressive conventions of Greek funeral poetry with the alliterative style of the *Rhétoriqueurs*. The idea of all the cities connected with the deceased lamenting their illustrious dead had been used with great effect by Moschus.[70] In Marot's work this is considerably diminished, and the successive alliterations produce almost an impression of parody only belied by the recourse to the myth and image of the swan singing at the approach of death:

> Chantez, mes Vers, chantez douleur encore!
> Rien n'est ça bas qui ceste mort ignore;

Coignac s'en coigne en sa poictrine blesme,
Rommorantin la perte rememore,
Anjou faict jou, Angolesme est de mesme,
Amboyse en boyt une amertume extreme,
Le Meine en maine ung lamentable bruyt,
La pauvre Touvre arrousant Angolesme
A son pavé de Truites tout destruict,
Et sur son eau chantent de jour & nuyct
Les Cignes blancs dont toute elle est couverte,
Pronostiquans en leur chant, qui leur nuyt,
Que Mort par mort leur tient sa porte ouverte.

(*O.L.*, *Eglogue* I, vv. 156–68)

In spite of these blemishes however the poem is not without a
certain dignity in its overall conception and movement.

On the whole, Marot's failures in imitation were relative, and
few. His successes, on the other hand, were impressive whether
one thinks of these works like the *Dieu Gard* and the *Avant-
naissance* for which Classical authors provided not a detailed
model but simply a suggestion of style and development, or the
more extensive imitations contained in the two *épithalames* and
the *Eglogue de Marot au Roy, soubz les noms de Pan & Robin*.
These last merit examination in some detail.

The two *épithalames*, for Renée and Magdeleine de France,
were both harshly criticized by Jourda. Without the slightest
regard for the context in which they were conceived, and the
occasion they were meant to enhance he objected that 'la pré-
ciosité l'emporte fâcheusement sur le naturel'.[71] Adverb excepted,
quite true. For in this respect Marot's work does no more than
reflect the spirit and mood of the moment. The festivities which
preceded and followed a royal wedding, ornate, extravagant,
symbolic, were nothing less than *naturel*, nor were they intended
to be otherwise. One can only assume therefore, that in adapting
Catullus to his needs, Marot, however little he may personally
have known of Roman marriage customs and ceremonies, saw
in the invocations, developments and refrains of the Classical
epithalamium something which could be aptly requisitioned to
serve his own milieu, and that he knew his *métier* better than
Jourda ever suspected. In his first *épithalame*, the *Chant Nuptial
du Mariage de Madame Renée, Fille de France, & du Duc de*

Ferrare Marot adopts the antithetical development of Catullus's 'Vesper adest, iuuenes, consurgite; Vesper Olympo'[72] although abandoning its explicit attribution to two alternating choruses, one of young girls and the other of youths. This, in any case, was a reflection of the particular Roman custom in which bands of maidens and youths accompanied the prospective bride and groom. The alternation maintained by Marot allows him to give stylized expression to the contrasting emotions of the prospective partners as they envisage the wedding night. Each strophe culminates in a line embodying the formula 'la bienheureuse nuict' or 'la Nuict tant desirée' which marks a regular cadence throughout the poem. To this extent the formula has the same effect as the Classical refrain 'Hymen o Hymenaee, Hymen ades o Hymenaee!' in Catullus's wedding poem. Had Marot lifted such a line straight from the Latin poet then Jourda could well and with justice have spoken of preciosity and 'souvenirs scolaires'. Instead he has wisely confined himself to the more neutral and adaptable expression in the line:[73]

> Quid datur a diuis felici optatius hora?

It is disconcerting that Jourda should have found it necessary to explain away the repetition of the 'nuict tant desirée, nuict bien-heureuse' by reference to the hoary legend of *gauloiserie*—an obsession to which many French critics remain neurotically faithful. An acquaintance with Catullus provides a more satis-factory account of the genesis of Marot's refrain, as well as evi-dence of the wide currency of wedding-night speculation and pleasantries[74]—should this ever be necessary! Other signs of Marot's desire to avoid a slavish imitation of his model can be seen in his transposition of Catullian imagery. The handing over of the virgin to the young man by her parents is compared by the Roman poet to the cruelty perpetrated by enemies in a captured town:[75]

> Et iuueni ardenti castam donare puellam.
> Quid faciunt hostes capta crudelius urbe?

In the following verse from Marot's poem the comparison involves a specific allusion to the sack of Rome by the troops of the Imperial army just a year previously, an event which had caused

consternation throughout Europe. The effect is one of immediacy
rather than of learned imitation:

> O Nuict, pour vray, si es tu bien cruelle,
> Et tes exces nous sont tous apparens;
> Tu viens ravir la Royalle Pucelle
> Entre les bras de ses propres Parens;
> Et qui plus est, tu la livres et rends
> Entre les mains d'ung ardant & jeune Homme!
> Que feirent pis les Ennemis à Romme,
> N'a pas long temps, par pillage empirée?
> Or, de rechef, cruelle je te nomme;
> Pourquoy es tu doncques Nuict desirée?
>
> (*O.L.*, *Epithalame* I, vv. 11–20)

Two other comparisons Marot took from Erasmus's colloquy *Proci
et Puellae*. While Catullus spoke of the unmarried virgin as a vine
deprived of its elm support, neglected and uncultivated, Marot,
following the example of Erasmus, speaks of a barren apple tree
and unpicked roses.[76] The two sources are therefore not in conflict
but complement each other admirably:

> Fille de Roy, Adieu ton Pucellage;
> Et toutesfoys tu n'en doibs faire pleurs.
> Car le Pommier qui porte bon fructage
> Vault mieulx que cil qui ne porte que Fleurs.
> Roses aussi de diverses couleurs,
> S'on ne les cueult, sans proffiter perissent;
> Et, s'on les cueult, les cueillans les cherissent,
> Prisans l'odeur qui d'elles est tirée.
> Si de toy veulx que fruictz odorans yssent,
> Fuir ne fault la Nuict tant desirée.   (ibid., vv. 31–40)

The second *épithalame* which belongs to a much later period in
Marot's development (1537) is richer in imagery than the first.
Although in conception it is again Catullian there is only one
detailed borrowing from this poet and this time from his 'Collis o
Heliconiei'. The lines

> Quae tuo ueniunt ero,
> Quanta gaudia, quae uaga
> Nocte, quae medio die
> Gaudeat![77]

inspired Marot in this strophe which apostrophizes the future husband:

> Brunette elle est, mais pourtant elle est belle,
> Et te peult suivre en tous lieux où iras
> En chaste Amour. Danger fier & Rebelle
> N'i a que veoir. D'elle tu jouyras;
> Mais, s'il te plaist, demain tu nous diras,
> Lequel des deux t'a le plus grief esté,
> Ou la longueur du Jour que desiras,
> Ou de la Nuict la grande briefveté,
>
> (*O.L.*, *Epithalame* II, vv. 33–40)

On the whole, the poem betrays Marot's principal preoccupation on his return from exile which was his translation of the Psalms. For it is from this source that Marot drew the inspiration for his description of the kingly groom. Psalm 45 sets the style for this verse:[78]

> Tandis les Mains des Nobles gracieuses
> De pied en cap richement l'ont vestu,
> Son Corps luisoit de Pierres precieuses,
> Moins toutesfoys que son Cueur de Vertu.
> De Musq d'eslite avec Ambre batu
> Parfumé ont son vestement propice,
> Puis luy ont ceint son fort Glaive poinctu
> Dont il sçait faire et la Guerre et Justice.
>
> (ibid., vv. 9–16)

Psalm 19 provides the poet with the mere suggestion of a comparison:[79]

Il a mis son tabernacle au soleil; & luy comme ung espoux procedant de sa chambre nuptiale.

to which he has given memorable development at the climax of his portrait in the next strophe:

> Ainsy en poinct de sa Chambre depart
> Pour s'en aller rencontrer Magdelene;
> De beaulté d'homme avoit plus grande part
> Que le Troyen qui fut espris d'Helene;
> Si qu'au sortir sa beaulté souveraine
> Les regardans resjouist tout ainsi
> Que le Soleil, quand à l'Aulbe seraine
> Sont d'Orient pour se monstrer icy.
>
> (ibid., vv. 17–24)

There is here a foretaste of the biblical imagery which was to dignify and raise to an epic level the work of such later poets as D'Aubigné and Du Bartas.

Marot's third eclogue, *De Marot au Roy, soubz les noms de Pan & Robin* is not only remarkable for the discretion and adeptness with which the poet has happily married imitations from three disparate sources in Virgil, Battista Spagnuoli and Jean Lemaire de Belges, it also contains some of his most memorable poetry. The title of the poem heralds the conjunction of Classicism and the old French pastoral tradition. Pan is the name under which the poet addresses his patron while Robin is Marot himself. The analogy round which the whole poem is constructed, the seasons of the year and their correspondence to the main phases of the poet's life, together with the latter's request to the king for protection from hardship in the winter of his life, are most probably derived from the fifth eclogue of the neo-Latin poet Spagnuoli.[80] Within this framework the poet traces a wistful picture of the pleasures and pastimes of a country boyhood. That its source should be a passage of Jean Lemaire's prose work *L'Illustration de Gaule et singularitez de Troye* is immaterial.[81] That Marot, by the discrimination of his adaptation and the lightness of his verse, should have blinded successive generations of critics to this fact, is less so. The apparent spontaneity of this passage seemed for a long time to confer the stamp of autobiography upon it. This is the measure of the poet's art:

> Sur le printemps de ma jeunesse folle,
> Je ressembloys l'arondelle qui volle
> Puis ça, puis là; l'aage me conduisoit,
> Sans peur ne soing, où le cueur me disoit.
> En la forest (sans la craincte des loups)
> Je m'en allois souvent cueillir le houx,
> Pour faire gluz à prendre oyseaulx ramaiges
> Tous differendz de chantz & de plumaiges;
> Ou me souloys (pour les prendre) entremettre
> A faire brics ou caiges pour les mettre;
> Ou transnouoys les rivieres profondes;
> Ou renforçoys sur le genoil les fondes;
> Puis d'en tirer droict & loing j'apprenois,
> Pour chasser loups & abbatre des noix.

O quantes fois aux arbres grimpé j'ay,
Pour desnicher ou la pie ou le geay,
Ou pour gecter des fruictz ja meurs & beaulx
A mes compaings, qui tendoient leurs chappeaulx.
Aucunesfois aux montaignes alloye,
Aucunesfois aux fossés devalloye,
Pour trouver là les gistes des fouynes,
Des herissons ou des blanches hermines;
Ou pas à pas, le long des buissonnetz,
Allois cherchant les nidz des chardonnetz,
Ou des serins, des pinsons ou lynottes.
(O.L., Eglogue III, vv. 15-39)

Not for the first time in Marot's work, poetry of nature is here
linked to the expression of a deep nostalgia. Already in *L'Enfer*
the poet had expressed his love of his native province:

Où le Soleil non trop excessif est;
Parquoy la terre avec honneur s'y vest
De mille fruicts, de maincte fleur & plante;
Bacchus aussi sa bonne vigne y plante
Par art subtil sur montaignes pierreuses
Rendants liqueurs fortes & savoureuses.
Maincte fontaine y murmure & undoye,
En touts temps le Laurier y verdoye
Pres de la vigne...
....
Le fleuve Lot coule son eaue peu claire,
Qui maints rochiers transverse & environne,
Pour s'aller joindre au droict fil de Garonne
(O.S., Enfer, vv. 379-87, 392-4)

long since left behind

...pour venir querre icy
Mille malheurs, ausquelz ma destinée
M'avoit submis   (ibid., vv. 396-8)

and often missed. And his first elegy developed the soldier's longing for a brief respite from war's alarms in a pastoral retreat.

The divinization of François Ier as the great god Pan in a rustic
setting, and the introduction of a pretended speaker, Janot or Jean
Marot himself in pastoral guise, allows a departure from the
normal style of solemn, formal eulogy. Indeed, it makes the varia-

tion in the manner of the compliment necessary, although its substance remains familiar. In the naive and idealized depiction of
François's role as a protector and patron which follows, the details
of rustic life are largely inspired by Virgil:[82]

> Pan (disoit il) c'est le dieu triumphant
> Sur les pasteurs, c'est celluy (mon enfant)
> Qui le premier les roseaulx pertuysa,
> Et d'en former des flustes s'advisa.
> Il daigne bien luy mesme peine prendre
> De user de l'art que je te veulx apprendre.
> Appren le donc, affin que montz & boys,
> Rocz & estangs, appreignent soubz ta voix
> A rechanter le hault nom, apres toy,
> De ce grand dieu que tant je ramentoy;
> Car c'est celluy par qui foisonnera
> Ton champ, ta vigne, & qui te donnera
> Plaisant loge entre sacrez ruisseaulx
> Encourtinez de flairans arbrisseaulx.
> Là, d'ung costé, auras la grand closture
> De saulx espes où, pour prendre pasture,
> Mousches à miel la fleur sucer iront,
> Et d'ung doulx bruit souvent t'endormiront,
> Mesmes alors que ta fluste champestre
> Par trop chanter lasse sentiras estre.
> Puis, tost apres, sur le prochain bosquet,
> T'esveillera aussi la colombelle,
> Pour rechanter encores de plus belle.
> <div align="right">(<i>O.L.</i>, <i>Eglogue</i> III, vv. 79–102)</div>

Marot's evocation of the approaching signs of old age, the
necessary counterpart to his description of boyhood, shows no
detailed imitation of Spagnuoli as far as one can see. But the lines
have a haunting quality which announces the best of Du Bellay's
elegiac vein in the sonnets of the *Regrets*. The Muse is no longer
Marot's to command:

> Mais maintenant que je suis en l'autonne
> Ne sçay quel soing inusité m'estonne
> De tel façon que de chanter la veine
> Devient en moy non point lasse, ne vaine,
> Ains triste & lente. (ibid., vv. 199–203)

Care has put his Muse to flight:

> Voy ma musette, à ung arbre pendue,
> Se plaindre à moy que oysive l'ay rendue;
> Dont tout à coup mon desir se resveille,
> Qui, de chanter voulant faire merveille,
> Trouve ce soing devant ses yeulx planté,
> Lequel le rend morne & espoventé;
> Car tant est soing basanné, laid & pasle,
> Qu'à son regard la muse pastoralle,
> Voyre la muse heroyque & hardie,
> En ung moment se treuve refroidie;
> Et devant luy vont fuyant toutes deux,
> Comme brebis devant ung loup hydeux.
>
> (ibid., vv. 205–16)

This last image is refined and condensed into three lines which remind one of Du Bellay's last tercet[83] in the sonnet, 'Las, où est ce mespris de Fortune'. Marot, however, here foresees happier circumstances:

> Lors à chanter plus soing ne me nuyra,
> Ains devant moy plus viste s'enfuyra
> Que devant luy ne vont fuyant les muses...
>
> (ibid., vv. 239–41)

The poem ends with the most discreet allusion to François Ier's gift of a house to the poet, the original pretext of the poem.

Any conclusion to be reached after an examination of Marot's lyrical poetry must inevitably concentrate on the need for posterity to return to the poet some at least of the praise which it has lately lavished, to Marot's detriment, on Ronsard his successor.

V

SOCIETY VERSE IN THE
MINOR GENRES

To some extent in his *épigrammes* and *épitaphes* but particularly in the *Etrennes aux dames de la Court* Marot fulfilled a function similar to that of a gazeteer. His talents in this respect were as essential to the milieu he served as were in other ways those of a portrait painter. His range of activity though was far greater, covering not only the personalities and pets to which the latter was restricted, but also the various activities such as tournaments and masquerades and the social rites and gallantries of exchanging colours, favours, emblems and devices[1] which were an inseparable part of French court life under François Ier. Since, however, many of the *épigrammes* inspired by such occasions or pretexts duplicate in effect the lighter court epistles,[2] and only in minor respects do the aesthetics of the two genres differ, we may exclude these from the present discussion, as also certain of the *rondeaux*.

The two poems which Marot devoted to the praise of favourite court pets and the epitaph for a horse are particularly worthy of note for their intrinsic literary merit and also have considerable interest from the point of view of literary history. The *Epitaphe du Cheval Vuyart* is the earliest of the three and is quite different in style and origin from the other two. As far as can be determined it has no model of any kind. Marot has simply, and successfully, invoked all the resources of style and metre to bring this horse to life just as he had done in fact with the Lion and the Rat in his fable of 1526. More precisely, his effects are achieved by an adroit use of alliteration and by six-line bursts of short, five-syllabled line verse. The horse's name was Hedart. He belonged to Pierre Vuyart, secretary to the duc de Guise.[2] Both are immortalized in the following lines:

Bucephal en gresse
Eut ung maistre en Grece
Mis entre les Dieux;
Mais mon maistre, qu'est ce?
Plus que luy, sans cesse,
Il est glorieux.
　J'allay, curieux,
En chocs furieux,
Sans craindre astrapade;
Mal rabotez lieux
Passay à cloz yeux,
Sans faire chopade.
　La viste virade,
Pompante pennade,
Le saulx soubzlevant,
La roide ruadde,
Je mis en avant.
　Escumeur bavant,
Au manger sçavant
Au penser tresdoulx,
Relevé devant,
Jusqu'au bout servant,
J'ay esté sur tous.
　Mourant bien secoux,
Senty par deux coups
Mon maistre venir,
Et d'ung foible poulx,
Disant à Dieu vous,
Me prins à hannyr.
　Sur ce souvenir
Voicy advenir
La Mort, sans hucher;
Mon Oeil feit ternir,
Mon ame finir,
Mon corps tresbucher.
　Mais mon Maistre cher
N'a permis seicher
Mon los, bruit & fame;
Car jadis plus cher
M'ayma chevaucher
Que fille ne femme.

(*O.D.*, *Epitaphe* XXXII, vv. 7–48)

The two other poems in question, both *épigrammes*, belong to a genre inspired by the poets of Classical Antiquity, by Catullus and Martial in particular, introduced into French poetry of the sixteenth century by Marot and Mellin de Saint-Gelais, and later much cultivated by the poets of the *Pléiade*.[4] However, Du Bellay's animal epitaphs in the *Divers Jeux Rustiques* which combined something of Marot's earlier manner in *Du Cheval Vuyart* and of his later Classical imitations without ever equalling him in either, were laborious in comparison, and far too long.[5] Ronsard perhaps came nearer to Marot, but never excelled him.[6] Marot's poem *De la Chienne de la Royne Elienor* is a close but clever imitation of Martial's epigram on *Issa*, the pet dog of Publius.[7] Marot has slightly abbreviated his model, omitting some of the initial comparisons with consequent advantage to the limpidity and fluency of his own version. The dominant note of the poem is its sensuality. One might almost say lascivity. Serafino Aquilano had already written a poem in which he, the lover, envied the attentions his mistress paid to her pet dog.[8] Marot writes not as a lover, nor does he necessarily have Serafino's poem in mind, but he too lingers long over the privileges accorded to the animal by its mistress, introducing at the same time a note of Petrarchist preciosity:

> Et dort la petite follastre
> Dessus la gorge d'alebastre
> De sa dame...

This last, together with the impeccable accommodation of style and movement to the subject, a respect in which Marot's art rarely failed him, completes the progression from imitation to invention:

> Mignonne, est trop plus affectée,
> Plus fretillant, moins arrestée
> Que le passeron de Maupas,
> Cinquante pucelles n'ont pas
> La mignardie si friande.
> Mignonne nasquit aussi grande
> Quasi comme vous la voyez;
> Mignonne vault (& m'en croyez)
> Ung petit tresor; aussi est ce
> Le passetemps & la lyesse

De la Royne à qui si fort plaist
Que de sa belle main la paist.
Mignonne est sa petite chienne,
Et la Royne est la dame sienne.
....
La Royne en sa couche parée
Luy a sa place preparée,
Et dort la petite follastre
Dessus la gorge d'alebastre
De sa dame si doucement
Qu'on ne l'oyt souffler nullement.
Et si pisser veult d'aventure,
Ne gaste draps ny couverture,
Mais sa maistresse gratte, gratte
Avecques sa flateuse patte,
L'advertissant qu'on la descende,
Qu'on l'essuye, & puys qu'on la rende
En sa place, tant est honneste
Et nette la petite beste.
Le Jeu d'Amours n'a esprouvé;
Car encores n'avons trouvé
Ung mary digne de se prendre
A une pucelle si tendre.
Or afin que du tout ne meure,
Quand de mourir viendra son heure,
Sa maistresse, en ung beau tableau,
L'a faict paindre à Fontaynebleau,
Plus semblable à elle ce semble,
Qu'elle mesme ne se resemble;
Et qui Mignonne approchera
De sa paincture, il pensera
Que toutes deux vivent sans faincte,
Ou bien que l'une & l'autre est paincte.

(Epigr., CLIV)

The poem has none of the marks of painful imitation which characterizes the version of Marot's contemporary, François Habert.[9]

The epigram *Du Passereau de Maupas*, which owes its inspiration to Catullus's poem on Lesbia's pet sparrow,

Lugete, o Veneres Cupidinesque,
Et quantum est hominum uenustiorum.
Passer mortuus est meae puellae,[10]

receives a development which is not in the Latin poem and may derive from Jean Lemaire's account of the death of L'Amant Vert, Marguerite d'Autriche's parrot.[11] For Marot, like Lemaire, goes on to specify the cause of death. Both pets were killed by another creature. Marot's originality was to make Maupas' sparrow the victim of Cupid who was spurned by the lady:

> Las, il est mort (pleurez le, Damoyselles)
> Le passereau de la jeune Maupas;
> Ung aultre oyseau, qui n'a plumes qu'aux esles,
> L'a devoré; le congnoissez vous pas?
> C'est ce fascheux Amour, qui, sans compas,
> Avecques luy se jectoit au giron
> De la Pucelle & voloyt environ
> Pour l'enflamber & tenir en destresse
> Mais par despit tua le Passeron
> Quand il ne sceut rien faire à la maistresse.   (*Epigr.*, CIX)

One can admire the elegance with which Marot has composed this little masterpiece from literary precedent and allusion to a then intimate reality, even though the details of this reality—perhaps a 'scandale éclatant'[12]—may today elude us.

In the *Etrennes* Marot offered his New Year greetings to the ladies of the court and renewed his social ties with them all—to the number of some forty or more,[13] observing as he did so the strict hierarchy, starting with the queen, and moving in descending order of precedence to the dauphine, Marguerite de Navarre, Jeanne d'Albret, the senior ladies-in-waiting, the royal mistresses and the remaining ladies of the respective entourages. With grace and elegance in form and expression, delicacy of touch and tact in allusion, a Classical limpidity, infinite wit and no less ingenuity Marot diversified all his compliments. This was no mean task.

Sometimes the poem would express a wish which alluded to the personal circumstances of the lady in question. If she was a major figure then the allusion presents no difficulty to the modern reader familiar with the main outlines of the period. Thus the *Etrenne à la Royne* (I) who happened to be both the wife of François Ier and the sister of Charles V delicately alludes to her position between two often irreconcilable parties:

> Au ciel, Madame, je crie,
> Et Dieu prie
> Vous faire veoir au printemps
> Frere & mary si contens
> Que tout rie.   (*O.D.*, *Etrennes*, I)

The *Etrenne A Madame la Daulphine* which follows it expresses Marot's wish that her childless state, after seven years of marriage, will soon be ended. Since the point is made simply, and without insistence, there is no offence against taste in these lines:

> A Madame la Daulphine
> Rien n'assigne.
> Elle a ce qu'il fault avoir;
> Mais je la vouldrois bien veoir
> En gesine.   (*O.D.*, *Etrennes*, II)

Sometimes, however, the allusion may be slightly more difficult to seize even though the particular circumstances involved have been recorded by history. Great tact and discretion accompany Marot's wishes to Madame l'Amiralle, qualities all the more necessary in this case since he refers to the recent fall from favour of her husband, l'Amiral Chabot:

> La doulce beauté bien née
> Estrenée
> Puissions veoir avant l'esté,
> Mieulx qu'elle ne l'a esté
> L'autre année.   (*O.D.*, *Etrennes*, X)

The allusion contained in Marot's *Etrenne à Madame la grand Seneschale* is a very intimate one, but one which would have been perfectly transparent to all members of the court. With finesse and a touch of irony Marot compliments Diane de Poitiers on her good fortune in becoming the mistress of the dauphin Henri:

> Que voulez, Diane bonne,
> Que vous donne?
> Vous n'eustes, comme j'entens,
> Jamais tant d'heur au printemps
> Qu'en Autonne.   (*O.D.*, *Etrennes*, XI)

More commonly, the *Etrennes* offer in miniature a portrait of the recipient in which the poet singles out her most outstanding

attributes, physical or moral, or both. Like this one of Madame
de Nevers which commends itself by its unforced freshness and
simplicity:

> La Duchesse de Nevers
> Aux yeulx vertz,
> Pour l'esprit qui est en elle,
> Aura louenge eternelle
> Par mes vers.   (*O.D.*, *Etrennes*, v)

The poet was not always so direct however. Some of his portraits
were achieved by suggestion and allusion, but again, of the most
transparent kind. One can only stand back and admire the ease
with which Marot retrieves a doubtful homage in the second of
his *Etrennes* to Madame d'Estampes, the king's mistress, by a
simple comparison and turns it into a most audacious compliment:

> Vous reprendrez, je l'affie,
> Sur la vie
> Le tainct que vous a osté
> La Deesse de beaulté
> Par envie.   (*O.D.*, *Etrennes*, VIII)

Mythology again inspires the poet when he writes to Madame de
Canaples:

> Noz yeulx de veoir ne sont las,
> Soubz Athlas,
> Plusieurs Deesses en grace,
> Dont Canaples tient la place
> De Pallas.   (*O.D.*, *Etrennes*, XII)

It was especially useful when referring to the lady's virtue—or
cruelty. The *Etrenne a Chastagneraye* is impeccably discreet on
the conclusion to be reached in this particular case:

> Garde toy de descocher,
> Jeune archer,
> Pour à son cueur faire bresche;
> Car elle feroit la flesche
> Reboucher.   (*O.D.*, *Etrennes*, XXIV)

Imagery provided a means of diversifying the poems when their
recipients shared the same attributes. Like Madame de la

Chastagneraye, Françoise de Brazay showed, although to a less marked degree, signs of a certain *rigueur*:

> En sa doulceur feminine
> Tant benigne
> Rigueur pourroit estre enclose;
> Car tousjours avec la rose
> Croist l'Espine.   (*O.D.*, *Etrennes*, XXIX)

And it is a comparison which distinguishes the pleasing grace of Telligny from that of other ladies in the royal household:

> Montreul monstre clerement,
> Seurement,
> Qu'en beau corps grace rassise,
> C'est la pierre en l'or assise
> Proprement.   (*O.D.*, *Etrennes*, XVII)

Marot's elegance also enabled him to offer personal advice as well as good wishes and compliments. It ensured that there was not the least trace of impertinence in this hint to Madame de Bressuyre that she should remarry as soon as the opportunity presented itself:

> S'on veult changer vostre nom
> De renom
> A un meilleur ou pareil,
> Ne vueillez de mon conseil
> Dire non.   (*O.D.*, *Etrennes*, XIV)

Similar encouragement was offered to Ryeulx shortly before her marriage to a nobleman of the court. Since the lady in question was younger than the widow Madame de Bressuyre, Marot could afford to be more specific in his admonition to *carpe diem*!

> Damoyselle de Ryeulx,
> En maintz lieux
> L'embonpoinct se pert & gaste.
> Je suis d'advis qu'on se haste
> Pour le mieulx.   *O.D.*, *Etrennes*, XVIII)

Certainly, however, Marot's broader vein was not entirely inhibited in these poems. It was masked though by the dimensions of the genre in which the poet was working, for pleasantries of an intimate nature, like other allusions, were executed swiftly and without insistence. This lady's reputation was certainly not harmed by these throw-away lines:

> Voz graces en faict & dict
> Ont credit
> De plaire, Dieu sçait combien.
> Ceux qui s'y congnoissent bien
> Le m'ont dit.   (*O.D.*, *Etrennes*, XXXIII)

The *Etrenne* to Anne d'Alençon, Marot's former friend and now dame de Bernay dicte Sainct Pol, is a compliment which turns upon one of the author's favourite puns:

> Vostre mary a fortune
> Opportune;
> Si de jour ne veult marcher,
> Il aura beau chevaucher
> Sur la brune.   (*O.D.*, *Etrennes*, XLI)

Marot's brilliance in these verses has transformed what might have remained a perfunctory politeness to the society he served, into a record of enduring grace and charm.

VI

MAROT'S SATIRICAL POETRY[1]

It is perhaps a grim reflection on the quality of life in our age that of all Marot's work, it is his satirical poetry which most readily finds an echo today. For Marot fought for the values and the freedoms which, then and now, are constantly assailed and undermined.

Notwithstanding the minor genres, the *rondeaux*, the *épitaphes*, and the *épigrammes* in which Marot indulged—particularly in his early years—in the general satire of types, of monks, theologians, cuckolds and women, deriding irrespectively their hypocrisy, gluttony, ignorance and lewdness, he was no mere facetious observer of society in the tradition of the bourgeois poets of the late fifteenth century, of Baude and of Coquillart.[2] Apart from the fact that such poems represent only a relatively unimportant section of Marot's satire, and that the later epigrams in any case contain felicitous transpositions from the work of Martial, there are two points to be made here. One concerns the character of his satire and the other its inspiration and context. They are interrelated.

Both his circumstances and his nature enjoined Marot to satire. To this extent the poetry which resulted was highly personal. He spoke from close experience of the abuses he condemned. Of many he was himself a victim. Hence the bitterness and poignancy of some of his protests. But he had, too, a ready reaction for the plight of others. And where compassion vied with indignation it was difficult not to write satire. Even more than his lyrical poetry perhaps, Marot's satire reveals a rare emotional depth: which finds poetic expression in verse of lyrical intensity. He was not of course the first satirist to achieve this alliance but by doing so he became a greater one.

In addition, Marot was influenced by the spirit of the age which

manifested itself in a veritable efflorescence of satire. The example
presented by Erasmus, by Hutten, and by other early humanists
whether in their original works or in their translations and
adaptations of the popular Greek satirist Lucian impressed upon
him, as upon Rabelais, Des Périers and many minor writers of
their generation, the efficacity of satire as a weapon with which to
combat the enemies of the Renaissance and Reformation,
obscurantism and medievalism.[3] Marot's satire therefore springs
not only from humanitarian considerations but also from humanist ones which define its particular literary and historical context.

While Marot may have been emboldened and encouraged to
write satire by the precedents afforded, it called for great courage
nonetheless. His satirical poetry is the answer to those critics who
questioned his moral qualities and professed to find them wanting.
Marot was well aware of his mission as a satirical poet but equally
aware of the consequences attendant upon its discharge in a society
overruled by repressive forces. An early satirical poem makes this
point unmistakably clear and the apparent diffidence of the author
merely reinforces his own audacity in the face of the awful
retribution which might end it. The lines in question are from
the second of the *Excuses Aux Dames de Paris* (1529):

> Brief, pour escrire y a bien d'aultres choses
> Dedans Paris trop longuement encloses.
> Tant de Broillis qu'en Justice on tolere,
> Je l'escriroys, mais je crains la colere;
> L'Oysiveté des Prebstres et Cagotz,
> Je la diroys, mais garde les Fagotz!
> Et des abus dont l'Eglise est fourrée,
> J'en parleroys, mais garde la Bourrée!
>
> (*O.S.*, III, vv. 79–86)

Even the most adverse circumstances could not silence his criticisms. There is no finer testimony to his moral courage than the
first epistle he wrote to the king (XXXVI) from exile in Ferrara after
sentence of death had been passed upon him in his absence. This
was no cringing submission for the defence but a firm protestation of innocence reinforced by an outright attack on the king's
justices and law officers, on the Sorbonne, on his enemies high and
low, culminating in an expression of admiration for those who lost

their lives rather than their faith in the persecution authorized by the king himself:

> Puys tost après, Royal chef couronné,
> Sachant plusieurs de vie trop meilleure
> Que je ne suys estre bruslés a l'heure
> Si durement que maincte nation
> En est tombée en admiration,
> J'abandonnay, sans avoir commys crime
> L'ingrate France, ingrate, ingratissime
> A son Poëte...   (*Ep.*, XXXVI, vv. 186–93)

The allusion to the harm which had been done to the king's cause among the Protestant states he courted as allies could scarcely have been lost upon him. And yet Marot's future was very much in the hands of the king.

It is evident from Marot's comment in the *Excuses Aux Dames de Paris* which we quoted earlier in this chapter that personal satire did not occupy a very high place in Marot's programme. Apart from two shorter epistles (XIX, XXVII), some *rondeaux* and *épigrammes* in which Marot defended his work or reputation against the puny attacks of detractors and poetasters he was provoked into a full-scale onslaught on only three occasions in his career. The first, in 1529, was when he indignantly repudiated the authorship of a satire attacking certain Paris prostitutes in his two epistles *Les Excuses de Marot aux Dames de Paris*. The second was in 1536 in his third *coq-à-l'âne*, and the third in the *Epître de Frippelippes* of 1537. On both these occasions Marot heaped scorn and derision on his dangerous but untalented rival, François Sagon. The principal interest of these last two satires lies however in the conscious art with which Marot handled his matter, rather than the matter itself. To this we shall return.

There are comparatively few instances of political satire in Marot's work. One may doubt, for instance, whether the celebrated anti-Italian passage of the epistle to the dauphin[4] (XLV, vv. 54–60) should be included under this heading. Ever since the opening of the French campaigns in Italy at the end of the fifteenth century, expressions of anti-Italian feeling had increasingly occupied French pens.[5] But in the works of some of Marot's predecessors there is, both in intention and effect, a more noticeable element of political propaganda. Although Marot's lines may have been interpreted in this light by some of his contemporaries, their effect is quite different from those of epistle XLII (vv. 13–33) where the physical antagonism displayed by the Ferrarese to the French is expressly emphasized by the poet.[6] To the dauphin Marot sends a character sketch of the Lombards in which he emphasizes their moral shortcomings. His impressions of their deviousness, hypocrisy and hypercautiousness are generalized from particular personal encounters. Similarly, Marot's attack on the Venetians for their lack of charity towards their fellow-men, for their idolatry and ignorance of deeper spirituality which is contained in the contemporaneous epistle from Venice to the duchess of Ferrara (XLIII), must be seen in another context than the political: that of the poet's own transient spirituality and the even more committed attitude of his correspondent.[7]

It is almost equally difficult to classify Marot's protests against the horror and futility of war as political satire, except when these are directed against an aggressor inspired by dreams of territorial aggrandizement and the aggressor is none other than France's enemy Charles V of Spain. But such direct shafts are rare.[8] In this political context, however, Marot early in his career, like Rabelais on another occasion,[9] might more easily countenance France's own military activities off her north-eastern areas where the troops of the Imperial army were threatening. Thus, writing from the campaign headquarters of her husband, the duc d'Alençon, to Marguerite in the summer of 1521 (*Ep.*, III) Marot was able to present an impressionistic, and conventional, account of the brave sights and sounds of the French army as it prepared for future encounters. But the autumn of that year brought home to Marot the awful reality of war, not by camp parades and sporadic brawls, but by the aftermath of battle. His prose epistle to Marguerite, despatched from Hainault where the French troops were then under her brother the king's command, is memorable not for the loyal (yet perfunctory) commendation of the successful French engagement it contains but for the compassion which Marot extends to innocent victims and even to the enemy as he contemplates the scene of utter desolation around him:

Aultre chose (ma souveraine Dame) ne voions nous qui ne soit lamentable, comme pauvres femmes desolées errantes (leurs enfans au col) au travers du pays despouillé de verdure par le froid yvernal, qui ja les commence à poindre; puis s'en vont chauffer en leurs Villes, Villages & Chasteaulx mis à feu, combustion & ruine totale par vengeance reciproque, voire vengeance si confuse et universelle que noz Ennemis propres font passer pitié devant noz yeux. Et en telle miserable façon ceste impitoiable Serpente, la Guerre, a obscurcy l'air pur & nect par pouldre de terre seiche, par salpestre & pouldre artificielle, & par fumée causée de boys mortel ardant en feu (sans eaue de grace) inextinguible. Mais nostre espoir par deça est que les prieres d'entre vous, nobles Princesses, monteront si avant es chambres Celestes que, au moyen d'icelles, la tressacrée fille de Jesuchrist, nommée Paix, descendra trop plus luisante que le Soleil pour illuminer les regions Gallicques. Et lors sera vostre noble sang hors du dangier d'estre espandu sur les mortelles plaines. D'autre part, aux cueurs des jeunes Dames & Damoyselles entrera certaine esperance du retour desiré de leurs Maritz; & vivront pauvres Laboureurs seurement en leurs habitacles, comme Prelatz en chambres bien nattées. (*Ep.*, Appendice I, p. 281)

Increasingly, the broad humanitarian concern which Marot shared with many of the humanists of his day proved a more powerful stimulus to his anti-war satire than the obligation to defend the national cause, and the nation's integrity in a narrow partisan spirit against potential or actual aggressors. Indeed, the conception of a war undertaken in the national interest, on whatever side this might lie, is abhorrent to him:

> Les Françoys crient: vive France,
> Les Espaignolz: vive l'empire,
> Il n'y a pas pour tous à rire.
> Le plus hardy n'est sans terreur.
> N'est ce pas ung trop grant erreur,
> Pour les biens qui ne sont que terre,
> D'exciter si horrible guerre?
> (*O.S., 3ᵉ Coq a l'Asne*, vv. 184–90)

The prizes war offers to the individual combatant, the honour and the glory, he equally unreservedly rejects.

The French legal system was a traditional target for innumerable writers of the fifteenth and sixteenth centuries,[10] who catalogued its iniquities with more assiduity than effect. Few of these authors, however, could claim the experience which allowed Marot to approach this topic with an authority denied to them, and with a compelling directness completely absent from their second-hand editing of popular testimony. None, in fact, seems to have carried his campaign against the judiciary to the notice of the highest authority in the land as Marot did on several occasions. It was the hope of inspiring some reforms which led the poet to read to the king his indictment of French justice which constitutes the greater part of his poem *L'Enfer*. Subsequently the poet was to remind his majesty of the implacable enmity he had incurred thereby:

> Suyvant propos, trop me sont ennemys,
> Pour leur Enfer, que par escript j'ay mys,
> Où quelque peu de leurs tours je descoeuvre:
> Là me veult on grand mal pour petite oeuvre.
> Mais je leur suys encor plus odieux
> Dont je l'osay lire devant les yeulx
> Tant clairvoyants de ta magesté haulte,
> Qui a pouvoir de refformer leur faulte.
>
> *(Ep.*, XXXVI, vv. 21–28)

What Marot had in fact done, repeatedly and fearlessly, was to expose the corruption which permeated the administration of justice in all its stages. To add to the account of the extortion practised by the *sergents* on their prisoners and the venality of his own attorney in *Epître* XI,[11] Marot analysed in his epistle to the king from Ferrara (XXXVI) the various and commonly adopted methods of suborning the king's own judges:

> …je sçay tant de Juges corrumpables
> Dedans Paris, que, par pecune prise,
> Ou par amys, ou par leur entreprise,
> Ou en faveur & charité piteuse
> De quelcque belle humble solliciteuse,
> Ilz saulveront la vie orde & immonde
> Du plus meschant & criminel du monde.
>
> (ibid., vv. 6–12)

Neither did he exempt from his scathing review the litigants themselves who were often motivated by the same greed as the counsel they employed, for a law suit could be, and often was, bought and sold many times over if it showed prospects of a financial return, before it was ever allowed to reach its conclusion:

> Là biens sans cause en causes se despendent,
> Là les causeurs les causes s'entrevendent.
>
> (*O.S.*, *Enfer*, vv. 57–58)

To Marot all the perversions of justice, all the grave abuses of the system were directly attributable to this basic human failing of avarice: the lack of any sense of professional integrity among lawyers as exemplified by

> Ce grand criart qui tant la gueulle tort,
> Pour le grand gaing, tient du riche le tort
>
> (*O.S.*, ibid., vv. 105–6)

and the inordinate length of proceedings often deliberately prolonged:

> Là trouve l'on façon de prolonger
> Ce qui se doibt & se peult abreger
>
> (*O.S.*, ibid., vv. 53–54)

an art in which the *Parlement* of Paris had few, if any, rivals.[12] But great as was Marot's concern to highlight the corrupt practices of the judiciary, his most impassioned protests were those he made against the rigour and inhumanity with which the law pursued the weak and innocent and poor:

> Et au rebours, par faulte de pecune,
> Ou de support, ou par quelcque rancune,
> Aux innocents ilz sont tant inhumains
> Que content suys ne tomber en leurs mains.
>
> (*Ep.*, XXXVI, vv. 13–16)

In the same spirit he recorded the treachery of interrogating judges who offered insidious blandishments to gain the confidence and co-operation of a prisoner who would be cruelly rewarded:

> Si tel' doulceur luy faict rien confesser,
> Rhadamanthus la faict pendre ou fesser;
>
> (*O.S.*, *Enfer*, vv. 271–2)

but from whom in any case a confession could be extracted by more forcible means. Marot was possibly the first French writer before Montaigne to repudiate the frequent recourse to torture as a means of obtaining confessions, not merely from recalcitrant prisoners but, what was worse, from the innocent among them:

Ce nonobstant, si tost qu'il vient à veoir
Que par doulceur il ne la peult avoir,
Aulcunesfoys encontre elle il s'irrite,
Et de ce pas, selon le demerite
Qu'il sent en elle, il vous la faict plonger
Au fonds d'Enfer, où luy faict alonger
Veines & nerfs, & par tourments s'efforce
A esprouver s'elle dira par force
Ce que doulceur n'a sceu d'elle tirer.
....
Parquoy vous pry de plaindre avecques moy
Les Innocents qui en telz lieux damnables
Tiennent souvent la place des coulpables.

(O.S., Enfer, vv. 275–83, 286–8)

Marot discerned among the judges the same perverse delight in invoking against the souls in their charge in this judicial Hell the severest penalty the law allowed:

Et si tant peult en accuser aulcunes
Qu'elles en soyent pendues ou bruslées,
Les infernaulx feront saults & hullées;
Chaines de fer & crochets sonneront,
Et de grand'joye ensemble tonneront,
En faisant feu de flamme sulphurée
Pour la nouvelle ouyr tant malheurée.

(O.S., ibid., vv. 474–80)

If Marot was so strongly moved to protest against the judiciary acting in its civil context, he was even more deeply concerned when the *Parlement* of Paris acted on occasions in concert with the Sorbonne to become an agent of Catholic repression. But this is another topic in itself.

By far the most considerable body of Marot's satire in fact is that directed against the Catholic church both as an entity and in its several institutions, its rites and practices and in certain of its dogmas. Both in extent and implication Marot's satire against the Church goes far beyond the ribald pleasantries which medieval writers had indulged in at the Church's expense or the more abrasive criticisms which the popular peripatetic preachers of the late fifteenth century had hurled at it. While there was increasing awareness, on the most superficial level, of the decadence into which the Church had fallen, there had been little attempt to formulate the fundamental causes of this phenomenon. Nor could there have been before the enlightenment made possible by Renaissance and humanism. Marot's satire on the other hand, and this is where the difference lies, belongs to the period dominated by the critical labours and reformist intentions of Lefèvre, of Erasmus and of Luther.[13]

Marot's attack on the Catholic Church in his long *complainte*, the *Deploration de Florimont Robertet*, is one of his earliest and most sustained. And its violence is scarcely mitigated by the form in which it is couched. The poet personifies the Church accompanying the cortège of the dead man to his grave. She is richly accoutred in a robe decorated with symbolic designs:

>   une fée,
> Fresche, en bon point, et noblement coiffée,
> Sur teste raise ayant triple coronne
> Que mainte perle et rubis environne.
> Sa robe estoit d'un blanc et fin samys
> Où elle avoit en pourtraicture mis,
> Par traict de temps, ung milion de choses,
> Comme chasteaulx, palais et villes closes,
> Villaiges, tours et temples et convents,
> Terres et mers et voilles à tous vents,
> Artillerie, armes, hommes armez,
> Chiens et oiseaulx, plaines et bois ramez;
> Le tout brodé de fine soye exquise,
> Par main d'aultruy torse, taincte et acquise.
> Et pour devise au bort de la besongne
> Estoit escript: Le feu à qui en grongne.
> Ce neantmoins sa robe elle mussoit
> Soubz ung manteau qui humble paroissoit,
> Où plusieurs draps divers furent compris
> De noir, de blanc, d'enfumé et de gris,
> Signiffiant de sectes ung grant nombre
> Qui sans travail vivent dessoubz son umbre.
> Ceste grant dame est l'eglise Romaine
> Qui ce corps mort jusques au tombeau meine,
> La croix davant, en grant ceremonie,
> Chantant mottetz de pyteuse armonye.
>
>   (*O.L.*, VI, vv. 57–82)

The condemnation leaves little to add. It was representative of many made at that time. So too, Erasmus in his *Praise of Folly*, had listed the possessions and great wealth of the Church, her temporal power and her worldliness, her militancy and her repressive intolerance, her hypocrisy in proclaiming poverty and living in parasitism, subsidized and maintained by the labours of the faithful.[14] In his second *coq-à-l'âne*, written in 1535, Marot returned to the charge with a brief and covert attack on the vindictiveness with which the Church (*l'Aasnesse de Jerusalem*) pursued its dissidents for heresy often without formality or reason:

> Mais comment se porte l'Aasnesse
> Que tu sçais, de Jérusalem?
> S'elle veult mordre, garde l'en;
> Elle parle comme de cyre.
>
> (*O.S.*, 2ᵉ *Coq a l'Asne*, vv. 122–5)

Against the Sorbonne Marot felt and expressed an indignation which was scarcely less vehement than that of his elder Erasmus or his contemporary Rabelais to name only two among many.[15] He reviled not only the collective ignorance of this institution, but its attempt to impose this ignorance by formal interdicts, strict censorship and ruthless oppression upon all those bound by its authority. By such obscurantism the Sorbonne sought to remain unchallenged in its custodianship of the sacred text and secure in its dogmatic authority:

> Il est tout manifeste
> Que là dedans, contre ton vueil celeste,
> Est defendu qu'on ne voise allegant
> Hebrieu ny Grec, ne Latin elegant,
> Disant que c'est langaige d'heretiques.
> O pauvres gens, de sçavoir touts ethicques!
> Bien faictes vray ce proverbe courant:
> Science n'a hayneux que l'ignorant.
> Certes, ô Roy, si le profond des cueurs
> On veult sonder de ces Sorboniqueurs,
> Trouvé sera que de toy ilz se deulent.
> Comment, douloir? Mais que grand mal te veulent
> Dont tu as faict les lettres & les artz
> Plus reluysants que du temps des Cesars;
> Car leurs abus voit on en façon telle.
>
> (*Ep.*, XXXVI, vv. 43–57)

Marot is here addressing the king. In his second *coq-à-l'âne*, to Lyon Jamet, Marot had already expressed the opinion shared by humanists and evangelists that the light shed by the study of the three Classical tongues would be sufficient to discredit the teaching and pronouncements of the Sorbonne:

> Ce Grec, cest Hebreu, ce Latin
> Ont descouvert le pot aux roses:
> Mon Dieu, que nous voirrons de choses,
> Si nous vivons l'aage d'ung veau.
>
> (*O.S.*, *2e Coq a l'Asne*, vv. 5–9)

In the same way, the glosses and commentaries by which the *Sorbonistes* set such great store and the humanists so little, are attacked by Marot. The fate of the theologians and of their glosses was intimately connected: the disappearance of the former would inevitably entail the abandonment of the latter, and conversely:

> Laisse mourir ces Sorbonistes.
> Raison: la glose des Legistes
> Lourdement gaste ce beau texte.
>
> (*O.S.*, ibid., vv. 175–7)

In its rigorous defence of orthodoxy, that is, in self-defence, the Sorbonne was aided and abetted by the court of the *Parlement* of Paris:

> Eulx & leur court, en absence & en face
> Par plusieurs foys m'ont usé de menace,
> Dont la plus doulce estoit en criminel
> M'executer.   (*Ep.*, XXXVI, vv. 63–66)

Under such threats it was never wise to tarry:

> Si nous feussions demourez là?
> Tel y estoit qui n'en parla
> Jamais, depuys que j'en partis.
> ....
> Or jamais ne vous laissez prendre,
> S'il est possible de fouyr.
>
> (*O.S.*, *3e Coq a l'Asne*, vv. 165–7, 170–1)

But censorship, and the confiscation and burning of books were almost as much an outrage against the poet's spirit and intellect as judicial murder would have been against his body. This much is

clear from his rigorous protest against the sacrilege committed by
Rhadamanthus.[16]

> En saisyssant de ses mains violentes
> Toutes mes grandz richesses excellentes
> Et beaulx tresors d'avarice delivres,
> C'est assçavoir, mes papiers & mes livres
> Et mes labeurs. O juge sacrilege,
> Qui t'a donné ne loy ne privileige
> D'aller toucher & faire tes massacres
> Au cabinet des sainctes Muses sacres?
> Bien est il vray que livres de deffence
> On y trouva; mais cela n'est offence
> A ung poëte...   (*Ep.*, XXXVI, vv. 127-37)

It seemed to the humanists, and to Marot no less, that the sum
of the iniquities of the Sorbonne was embodied in the person of its
chief syndic, Noel Béda, whose fanatical opposition to the new
learning was equalled only by his uncompromising ignorance. He
was not spared the satirical attentions of Rabelais, of Antoine de
Marcourt and of anonymous writers or the execrations of
Estienne Dolet.[17] Fate too, had been unkind, bestowing upon
him a surname which in its French form (*bédier*) was uncom-
fortably synonymous with *âne* or *ânier* in the sense of idiot or
ignoramus. The fact was noted, and exploited. On this and other
counts Marot consigned him to an uncomfortable immortality,
along with François Sagon, in his third *coq-à-l'âne*, a veritable
rogues' gallery:

> De mon coq à l'asne dernier,
> Lyon, ce malheureulx asnier,
> Fol, foliant, imprudent, indiscrect
> Et moings sçavant q'ung docteur en decrect,
> Ha, ha, dist il, c'est grant oultraige
> De parler de tel personnaige
> Que moy. En est il ung au monde
> En qui tant de sçavoir habonde?
> Et je responds: ouy, ouy vrayement,
> Et n'y fust autre que Clement.
> Les latins, les grecs et hebreuz
> Luy sont langaiges tenebreux.
> Mais en françoys de Heurepoix,
> Et beaulx escuz d'or et de poix,

En quelque latin de marmite—
Par nostre dame, je le quicte—
Pour vray, il est le plus sçavant;
C'est raison qu'il voyse devant.

....

Mais le maquart ne se contente,
Et dit au gendre de sa tente,
S'il nous peult quelque jour avoir,
Il employra tout son povoir
De nous faire brusler tous vifz.
De ma part, je n'en suis d'advis
Et n'y sçauroys prendre plaisir.

(*O.S.*, *3ᵉ Coq a l'Asne*, vv. 1–18, 23–29)

Not only were the attacks which appeared in French literature during the sixteenth century against the Papacy very numerous, they were also diversely inspired. By Gallicanism very often. Such is the bias of certain passages in Jean Lemaire de Belges' *Traité de la Difference des Schismes et des Conciles* (1511) and of many of the attacks against the papacy of Jules II written by Pierre Gringore at the behest of Louis XII.[18] In the middle of the century no less a writer than Rabelais espoused the cause of Henri II in his quarrel with Jules III in the Gallican crisis of 1551, the result being an attack on the *Papimanes* in the *Quart Livre* of 1552.[19] Yet other writers were motivated not by political reasons but by personal ones, French exiles in daily contact with the Papal court who confided their disgust or disenchantment to their verses, as did Du Bellay in the *Regretz* and Olivier de Magny in his *Souspirs*. A third group, in which Marot may be included, attacked the Papacy on religious grounds. But even here there is little or no homogeneity since such a group would number among it evangelists, Lutherans and later Protestant polemicists of the type represented by Pierre Viret and Coignac.

Marot had already implicated the Papacy in his wide-ranging condemnation of the Church in the *Deploration de Florimont Robertet* when he spoke of the

...triple coronne
Que mainte perle et rubis environne.   (vv. 59–60)

But in his subsequent attacks he goes much further, putting into the Pope's mouth, in the second *coq-à-l'âne*, a confession that the basis of his power is financial rather than spiritual and that when financial support is withdrawn from the Papacy its existence is threatened:

> Puis, vous sçavez, Pater sancte,
> Que vostre grand pouvoir s'efface.
> Mais que voulez vous que je y face?
> Mes financiers sont touts perys.
>
> *(O.S., 2ᵉ Coq a l'Asne, vv. 32–35)*

Nor does he refrain from referring to the Pope in the language of the Protestants when he speaks of him as Antichrist and of Rome as Babylon in these lines from the same poem—

> Pour ceste cause je proteste
> Que l'Entechrist succumbera;
> Au moins que de brief tombera
> Sur Babylonne quelcque orage.
>
> *(O.S.*, ibid., vv. 178–81)

The work which contains the most violent of all the attacks against the Papacy is however the epistle to Madame la duchesse de Ferrare written from Venice in the summer of 1536 (XLIII). This poem, if indeed it is by Marot (it is known only from manuscript sources and while its authenticity is presumed it cannot be categorically established) represents his most extreme anti-Catholic position. Taking the terms of his comparison from a biblical source, the *Apocalypse* or *Book of Revelation*[20] he describes the Pope as:

> …la paillarde et grande meretrice,
> Avec qui on[t] faict fornicacion
> Les roys de terre, et dont la potion
> Du vin public de son calice immonde
> A si longtemps enyvré tout le monde.
>
> *(Ep.*, XLIII, vv. 62–66)

Luther too had had recourse to this image, similarly applied, in an illustration which adorned his translation of the New Testament.[21]

Hostility to the monastic orders was endemic in the late fifteenth and early sixteenth centuries in France and elsewhere, particularly in Germany. Their loose-living, ignorance, hypocrisy and parasitism were noted and deplored by persons of all social degrees. Thus, Louise de Savoie expressed her abhorrence of the monastic orders in her private correspondence and her son's comment on

their idleness and debauchery is reported by the writer Brantôme.[22]
The contempt in which Marguerite de Navarre held them is
apparent in many of the stories of her *Heptaméron*. Erasmus was
one of their most implacable opponents. Evidence of this is
provided not only by the well-known passages of the *Praise of
Folly*[23] but also by an *épitaphe* composed in his honour by the
French poet Eustorg de Beaulieu. This short poem records the
unrestrained joy with which the monks

> maintz Loups ravissans
> Blancz, Gris, Noirs et demy Noircys[24]

greeted the news of Erasmus' death in 1536. Rabelais too, like
Erasmus, wrote from his own personal knowledge of the monastic
life and from a similar standpoint in his *Gargantua* and later
again in the *Tiers Livre*.[25] The popular theatre of the period had
a whole repertory of plays satirizing the monks and these were
widely performed.[26] In addition, popular feeling against them
may be gauged from many of the stories in Bonaventure Des
Périers' *Joyeux Devis* where the villains are sometimes bested by
the common working people whom they attempted to tyrannize.

In some respects Marot's own anti-monastic satire belongs to
the long-established tradition. Thus he attacked their loose morals
in his *Ballade de Frere Lubin* (*O.D.*, LXIX), in his epigram
D'un Gros Prieur (CCXXXVI) and in his second *coq-à-l'âne* from
which it appears that the cloisters and the convents of the period,
far from curbing unchaste behaviour actually promoted it and
devotional duties provided an excellent cover for such irregulari-
ties:

> Et puis dictes que les moustiers
> Ne servent point aux Amoureux!
> Bonne macquerelle pour eulx
> Est umbre de devotion.
>
> (*O.S.*, 2ᵉ *Coq a L'Asne*, vv. 52–55)

The same poem also contains a more specific and pointed observation on this topic. While not all nuns suffered the same fate as
Rabelais's *nonnain de Poissy*,[28] many were afflicted with syphilis

> On dict que les Nonnains rendues
> Donnent gentilment la verolle.
>
> (*O.S.*, ibid., vv. 170–1)

Like his contemporaries Marot advanced from such attacks on monastic *mœurs* to a consideration of the social and economic usefulness of monks to the community at large. His conclusions on this aspect of the monastic institution were scarcely more favourable than those of other writers of the period. Economically the institution was indefensible.[29] The first intimation of his thought on this subject occurs naturally enough in the *Deploration de Florimont Robertet* within the framework of the wider attack on the Church as a whole, which concealed its riches:

> Soubz ung manteau qui humble paroissoit,
> Où plusieurs draps divers furent compris
> De noir, de blanc, d'enfumé et de gris,
> Signiffiant de sectes ung grant nombre
> Qui sans travail vivent dessoubz son umbre.
>
> (*O.L.*, VI, vv. 74–78)

A far more violent condemnation of the parasitism of the monastic orders and their members is to be found however in a later poem which is devoted almost entirely to an examination of the fundamental aspects of monasticism. This is the *Second Chant de l'Amour fugitif*, composed before the end of 1533. Its title indicates that Marot envisaged it as a sequel to his translation of a poem by Moschus *Le Chant de l'Amour fugitif*[29] from which he derived the scenario for his own original work. This takes the form of a monologue by Venus who appears in Paris on her search for Cupid who has run away. The rest of the poem consists of the poet's report of the crowd who gathered round her, and their reactions to her dilemma. Prominent among them were a large number of monks, representing most of the orders, in attitudes of ostentatious piety and asceticism:

> ...hommes pieux, ayant la Teste courbe,
> L'oeil vers la Terre en grand Cerimonye,
> Pleins (à les veoir) de dueil & agonie,
> Disant à eulx mondanités adverses,
> Et en habitz monstrans Sectes diverses.
>
> (*O.S.*, IV, vv. 42–46)

This, however, is but the prelude to the attack:

> Que diray plus? Bien loger sans danger,
> Dormir sans peur, sans coust boyre & manger,

Ne faire rien, aulcun mestier n'apprendre,
Riens ne donner, et le bien d'aultruy prendre,
Gras et puissant, bien nourry, bien vestu,
C'est (selon eux) pauvreté et vertu.   (ibid., vv. 53–58)

Such a condemnation is more far reaching than might at first
appear since it is not in any way mitigated by reference to any
pastoral or religious role which the monks might be expected to
fill and which, had they done so, would have provided some
justification for their privileged existence. Indeed, their conduct
is a travesty of any such role:

Aussi (pour vray) il ne sort de leur Bouche
Que motz succrez: quand au Cueur je n'y touche,
Mais c'est ung Peuple à celluy ressemblant
Que Jan de Mehun appelle Faulxsemblant,
Forgeant abus dessoubz Religion.   (ibid., vv. 59–63)

Up to this point in the poem Marot is merely skirmishing. The
real issue is a much more fundamental one, namely, the existence
and observance of the monastic vow of chastity. The monks'
search for Cupid whom they propose to bind and restrain so that
he may never again roam at large is symbolic of their repudiation
of the pleasures of the flesh in taking the vow of chastity. Both
the true nature and the serious import of the poem are stressed by
the author in his concluding lines:

Et sur ce poinct prendra repos ma Muse,
Ne voulant plus qu'à ce propos me amuse;
Ains que je pense à dresser aultre compte,
En concluant que cestuy cy racompte,
A qui aura bien compris mon Traicté,
Dont proceda le Veu de Chasteté. (O.S., IV, vv. 89–94)

The monks are to be condemned in Marot's view for taking a vow
which it lay not within their power to keep:

Incontinent que ceste Legion
(Selon le cry de Venus) sent & voyt
Que Cupido, le Dieu d'Amours, avoit
Prins sa vollée, ainsi que ung vagabond,
Chascun pensa de luy donner le bond.
    Si vont querir Libelles Sophistiques,
Corps enchassez & Bulles Papistiques;

Et là dessus vouerent tous à Dieu
Et au Patron de leur Couvent & Lieu
De Cupido lyer, prendre & estraindre,
Et son pouvoir par leurs Oeuvres contraindre;
Plus pour loyer Celeste en recevoir,
Que pour amour qu'en Dieu puissent avoir.
  Voila comment, par voyes mal directes,
Les presumans, oultrecuydées Sectes
Seures se font d'avoir de Dieu la grace
Et de garder chose que humaine race
Ne peult de soy. Or se sont ilz espars
De Chrestienté aux quatre Coings & Pars;
Tous en propos de Cupido happer.

(O.S., ibid., vv. 64–83)

There are several important points in this passage. Firstly, Marot
is insisting that the degree of continence required to observe the
vow of chastity is not within the bounds of human nature (vv.
80–81). Continence lay only with the power of God's grace to
confer (v. 79). Secondly, and in view of this fact, it was presump-
tuous and pointless for the monks to have recourse to good works
humanly conceived, whether these might take the form of
obedience to the decrees emanating from the Sorbonne (libelles
sophistiques), acceptance of Papal bulls (bulles Papistiques) or the
veneration of holy relics (corps enchassez) as a means of attaining
to this degree of continence (v. 74). On the one hand these are
'voyes mal directes' and on the other it was arrogant and false to
suppose that God's grace could be bought by the performance of
good works (vv. 78–79). Thirdly, Marot attacks the reason behind
the attempted observance of the vow of chastity. Far from being
an expression of true piety or love of God celibacy had come to be
regarded merely as another good work to be performed in order to
improve one's credit in Heaven (vv. 75–76). On the first of these
counts particularly Marot's thought comes very close to that of
Luther as it was expressed in the treatise De Votis Monasticis
(1518) and it is interesting to note that this work was known in the
circles in which Marot moved at this time.[30] And on the third
count Marot's strictures resemble those of Erasmus who denied
that there was any intrinsic merit in celibacy or that it could be
used to accumulate credit.[31] Marot's attitude to monastic celibacy

is therefore very much in line with that of the reformist thinkers of his day.

It was inevitable that his satirical campaign against the abuses of the Catholic Church should include a review of the priesthood and its members. Inevitable since they shared many of the vices of the monastic orders and because they had already attracted the attentions of other writers, Erasmus, the poet Eustorg de Beaulieu and the anonymous authors who wrote for the popular theatre.[32] Marot's earliest complaint against the Catholic priests concerns their ignorance of the basic tenets of Christian charity. Their own pronouncements restrict the concept of charity to one of fund raising for the Church. They themselves, by their constant recourse to litigation, are some of the worse offenders against Christian charity and their example is a most pernicious one. These lines are from *L'Enfer*:

> ...Et si tu quiers raison
> Pourquoy Proces sont si fort en saison,
> Sçaiche que c'est faulte de charité
> Entre Chrestiens. Et, à la verité,
> Comment l'auront dedans leur cueur fichée,
> Quand par tout est si froidement preschée?
> A escouter voz Prescheurs, bien souvent
> Charité n'est que donner au Couvent.
> Pas ne diront combien Proces differe
> Au vray Chrestien, qui de touts se dict frere.
> Pas ne diront qu'impossible leur semble
> D'estre Chrestien & playdeur tout ensemble.
> Ainçois seront eulx mesmes à playder
> Les plus ardantz.   (*O.S.*, *Enfer*, vv. 187–200)

More strongly and precisely in the *Deploration de Florimont Robertet*, Marot attacks them for their rapacious avarice. Their ministrations could be had, but only at a price which their more penurious parishioners could never hope to meet, to the everlasting torment of their souls!

> Messes sans nombre & force anniversaires
> C'est belle chose, et la façon j'en prise;
> Si sont les chants, cloches et luminaires;
> Mais le mal est en l'avare prestrise;

Car, si tu n'as vaillant que ta chemise,
Tiens toy certain, qu'apres le tien trespas,
Il n'y aura convent ny eglise
Qui pour toy sonne ou chante ou face ung pas.

(O.L., VI, vv. 421–8)

This is not the only reference in the speech of Death to priestly avarice. There is another such in the very first stanza of her speech:

Tu me mauldiz quant tes amys assomme,
Mais quant ce vient qu'aux obseques on chante
Le prestre adonc, qui d'argent en a somme,
Ne me dit pas mauldicte ne meschante.

(O.L., ibid., vv. 289–92)

Elsewhere in his poetry Marot fleetingly alludes to their idleness

L'oysiveté des Prebstres et Cagotz   (<i>O.S.</i>, III, v. 83)

Fleetingly, for he is constantly reminded of their powers of retribution

Je la diroys, mais garde les Fagotz!   (<i>O.S.</i>, ibid., v.84)

Significantly perhaps, it was not until six years later, and from the safety or comparative safety of exile that he amplified this last remark. In these lines from the second <i>coq-à-l'âne</i> he attacks them for their menacing and inflammatory pulpit denunciations of heretics:

Ilz escument comme ung Verrat,
En pleine chaiere, ces Cagots,
Et ne preschent que des fagots
Contre ces paouvres Hereticques.

(O.S., 2e Coq a l'Asne, vv. 20–23)

Of the Church's observances and dogmas, and the practices which grew up around them Marot was unsparing. And least surprisingly of all, of the observance of the Lenten abstinence. While many hoped that a long-desired Council of the Church would abolish this commandment, this hope did not manifest itself so fervently among those Roman prelates and clerics practised in the art of circumventing such inconvenient restrictions. And not merely inconvenient, but above all, untimely. For the period of Lent was precisely the season of the year when kid's meat was at its most delectable. It was consumed with devout hypocrisy under a suitably mortifying cover of edible thistles:

> ...adieu le caresme
> Au Concile qui se faira.
> Mais Romme tandis bouffera
> Des chevreaulx à la chardonnette.
>
> (O.S., 2ᵉ Coq a l'Asne, vv. 76–79)

This gibe had become a classic one even at the time at which Marot was writing. It probably had its original publication in the form of a lampoon in Latin verse affixed to the statue of Pasquino in Rome. The clue to this is provided by Rabelais who introduced this shaft against Lenten hypocrisy into his *Pantagruel* (1532). It appears as the title of a book in his burlesque and satirical catalogue of the contents of the library of St. Victor:[33] 'Pasquili, Doctoris marmorei, De Capreolis cum chardoneta comedendis, tempore papali ab Ecclesia interdicto.' In no other poem does Marot seem to have attacked the hypocrisy which surrounded abstinence in Lent.[34] He had, however, repudiated this observance in his personal capacity, and had been imprisoned for his protest.

The belief in a state of Purgatory and the Pope's power over souls in Purgatory is one which Marot calls into question several times in his poetry. In the *Enfer* of 1526 he subjects it to ridicule by informing the mythological judge Rhadamanthus who presides over a Pagan Hell that he has a rival claimant to the souls in his charge, and asking with mock seriousness whether he is not afraid that his own authority might be diminished by this rival, none other than the Pope himself:

> Le crains tu poinct? C'est celluy qui afferme
> Qu'il ouvre Enfer quand il veult & le ferme;
> Celluy qui peult en feu chauld martyrer
> Cent mille esprits, ou les en retirer.
>
> (O.S., Enfer, vv. 355–8)

In Marot's myth, Rhadamanthus had the power either to detain souls indefinitely in his Hell or to allow them to proceed to the Elysian Fields. The parallel with the Pope's supposed power over souls in Purgatory is inescapable, so too Marot's audacity in reducing the Catholic teaching to the level of the Pagan concept: in this sense the poet's sarcasm is even superfluous. But there may be another taunt here too. The form of words in which Marot couches the Pope's affirmation of his power is reminiscent of the ultramontane teaching of the Mendicant orders on this point, namely that: 'Animae in Purgatorio existentes sunt de jurisdictione papae; et si vellet, posset totum Purgatorium evacuare.'[35] This was a proposition which the more gallican-minded Sorbonne had always resisted. Marot, arraigned himself for a breach of the Church's observances, might well delight in hinting at a doctrinal conflict between the bastion of orthodoxy in France and the Pope himself. There seems however insufficient evidence in this passage to justify the suggestion that Marot intended to go even further and to imply the Lutheran objection to the Pope's claim of his power over the souls in Purgatory.[36] That the claim itself was either knowingly false or, if it were true, that the Pope was tyrannically and wickedly abusing his powers when he refused to release the souls except on payment of a certain sum.

Marot appears at first sight to move closer to the Lutheran objection in this second and later passage, taken from the second *coq-à-l'âne* (1535):

> Toutesfoys, Lyon, si les ames
> Ne s'en vont plus en Purgatoire,
> On ne me sçauroit faire à croyre
> Que le Pape y gaigne beaulcoup.
> (*O.S.*, *2ᵉ Coq a l'Asne*, vv. 44–47)

Bold though the passage undoubtedly is however in its dismissive reference to the notion of Purgatory, the force of Marot's attack is concentrated on the sale of indulgences which had become inseparable from the dogma and which consequently made it a highly profitable one for the Church, rather than on the theological weakness of the dogma. Marot had already attacked the sale of indulgences much earlier in his first *coq-à-l'âne* (1530):

> A Romme sont les grands Pardons;
> Il fault bien que nous nous gardons
> De dire qu'on les appetisse;
> (*O.S.*, *Premier Coq a l'Asne*, vv. 11–13)

and Rabelais was to do likewise on several occasions both in his *Pantagruel* and in the *Gargantua*.[37] Marot's words on this subject were later attacked by the Catholic propagandist Artus Désiré as a mockery worthy of a true Lutheran since they were aimed at diminishing the confidence and trust of the people in the Pope's powers and ordinances.[38] It is clear from a further passage in the third *coq-à-l'âne* that Marot intended to question other practices which had arisen as a result of the teaching on Purgatory, and especially the prayers said for the souls of the dead. Imagining that he will be hanged for his sins if Noel Béda can get his hands on him, Marot ironically commissions his friend Lyon Jamet to have a mass said for him and he indulges in a word play on the *de profundis*. The object of this shall be to ensure the passage of his soul from Purgatory into Paradise one might think. But in the lines which follow Marot goes as far as he can to dismiss the notion that such human intervention at that late stage could affect man's salvation or damnation. The passage has a distinctly determinist ring about it. Marot will finally countenance only an epitaph:

> Tu diras, mon amy Lyon,
> Pour moy quelque fidelium
> Ou quelque creux de profundis
> Pour me tirer en paradis.
> Mais, si trouvez qu'il soit ainsi
> Que au partir de ce monde icy
> Nous soyons saulvez ou dampnez
> Ne dictes riens et me donnez
> Ce petit mot en epitaphe...
>
> (*O.S., 3e Coq a l'Asne*, vv. 33–41)

Like Erasmus and Rabelais Marot too condemned in his work the Catholic cult of Saints in many of its aspects. He dismisses the notion that they could in any sense be considered as intermediaries between man and God particularly in the transmission of prayers. His objection is a theological one. In this respect the much-quoted line from the *Deploration de Florimont Robertet*:

> Prie à Dieu seul que par grace te donne
>
> (*O.L.*, VI, v. 325)

is highly significant excluding as it does any reference to the intervention of the Saints. By extension Marot attacked the practice of making vows not solely to God but through the Saints, and the absurd belief of the monks that their vows, by this means, and by the veneration of the relics of holy men, would be more easily implemented:

> Si vont querir Libelles Sophistiques
> Corps enchassez & Bulles Papistiques;
> Et là dessus vouerent tous à Dieu
> Et au Patron de leur Couvent & Lieu,
> De Cupido lyer, prendre & estraindre.
>
> (*O.S.*, IV, vv. 69-73)

The attribution to the Saints of certain powers which they might be prevailed upon to use in man's favour was an element of popular belief which was frequently satirized by Erasmus and Rabelais,[39] much to the fury of certain staunch, not to say bigoted, Catholics of the period. In Marot's first *coq-à-l'âne* he mocked the practice of parading the relics of Saint Marceau in procession through the streets as a means of imploring rain:

> Le Roy va souvent à la chasse,
> Tant qu'il fault descendre la Chasse
> Sainct Marceau pour faire pleuvoir.
>
> (*O.S.*, *Premier Coq a l'Asne*, vv. 117-19)

He too was attacked for undermining popular beliefs. Artus Désiré, the Catholic polemicist, regarded both the passages quoted above as evidence of Calvinistic tendencies in Marot's works.[40] His view-point was, of course, a retrospective one: both the poems he refers to had been written before 1533 and therefore predate the formulation of Calvin's doctrine.

Marot had little time for the vain ceremony, the formalistic observances and general idolatry which he observed in the Catholic cult of his time. Thus he dismisses the ceremonies which accompany the funeral rites, whether they be 'messes sans nombre' or 'chants, cloches et luminaires':

> N'ordonne à toy telles solennitez,
> Ne soubz quel marbre il faudra qu'on t'enterre,
> Car ce ne sont vers Dieu que vanitez.
>
> (*O.L.*, VI, vv. 429-31)

He is even more harshly critical of Venetian excesses in the worship of God. In the epistle he wrote from that city to Renée, the duchess of Ferrara (XLIII) he did not hesitate to describe them as survivals from a pagan past:

> C'est qu'en esprit n'adorent nullement
> Luy [qui] est seul esprit totallement,
> Ains par haulx chantz, par pompes et par mynes,
> Qui est (mon Dieu) ce que tu abhomines.
> Et sont encor les pouvres citoyens
> Pleins de l'erreur de leurs peres payens.
> Temples marbrins y font et y adorent
> Images peinctz qu'à grandz despens ilz dorent...
>
> (Ep., XLIII, vv. 33–40)

Implicit to a greater or lesser degree in many of these passages in which Marot has shown himself hostile to certain aspects of the Catholic cult is a negation of the doctrine of justification by good works. For he has dismissed many of the observances which might be accounted such. This is particularly apparent in the *Deploration de Florimont Robertet* and in *Le Second Chant de l'Amour fugitif*. Reliance on these 'voyes mal directes' is not only misguided when it seeks to achieve

> chose que humaine race
> Ne peult de soy.   (*O.S.*, IV., vv. 80–81)

but also hypocritical. Good works, inspired not by a love of God, but in the hope of striking a favourable bargain with the deity

> Plus pour loyer Celeste en recevoir,
> Que pour amour qu'en Dieu puissent avoir
>
> (O.S., ibid., vv. 75–76)

were similarly condemned by Erasmus, by Lefèvre and by Marguerite de Navarre to name only three people with whose thought Marot may have been acquainted on this subject.[41]

There can be no doubt of the seriousness and boldness of the charges levelled by Marot against the Catholic Church. It remains to be seen whether his anti-Catholic satire was complemented in any degree by a positive expression of current reformist doctrines.[42]

A somewhat overlooked feature of Marot's satirical poetry is the polemical expertise he displayed in his onslaughts. In this respect he yielded nothing to his enemies, whether they were great institutions or small individuals. This expertise which Marot possessed to a very real degree manifests itself in several ways. The first, most essential, and most obvious lay in his ability to diversify his attacks against any one target, both in their substance and more particularly in his method. Thus his attack on the Church in the *Deploration de Florimont Robertet* united in one passage a multiplicity of charges summarily expressed but imposing by their cumulative effect. Subsequently Marot abandoned the all-embracing attack in favour of the specific criticism directed at any one part of the institution and to be found in an enormously wide range of his poems. In this way he avoided the monotony and blunted effect characteristic of much of the satire of his predecessors and which was inevitably attendant upon the repetition of generalized criticisms. Secondly, Marot was adept at associating his patron in the enmity directed principally against himself. Thus in a celebrated passage from the *Epistre au Roy, du temps de son exil à Ferrare* (XXXVI) Marot suggests that the king's wishes and policies are as much at risk from the machinations of the Sorbonne as Marot's own personal safety:

> Aultant comme eulx, sans cause qui soyt bonne,
> Me veult de mal l'ignorante Sorbonne:
> Bien ignorante elle est d'estre ennemye
> De la trilingue & noble Academie
> Qu'as erigée. Il est tout manifeste
> Que là dedans, contre ton vueil celeste,
> Est defendu qu'on ne voise allegant
> Hebrieu ny Grec, ne Latin elegant,
> Disant que c'est langaige d'heretiques.
>
> (*Ep.*, XXXVI, vv. 39–47)

There is added point in these lines when one remembers that the poet is in fact turning against the Sorbonne its own ploy. The syndics of this institution had been quick to point out to François Ier that the alleged heretics were not merely interested in the overthrow of the established Church but had as their ultimate target the overthrow of the monarchy itself. Marot had made allusion to this in his second *coq-à-l'âne*:

> Syre, ce disent ces Capharts,
> Si vous ne bruslez ces mastins,
> Vous serez ung de ces matins
> Sans tribut, taille ne truage.
>
> (*O.S.*, 2ᵉ *Coq a l'Asne*, vv. 60–63)

By extension, Marot's attack on the Sorbonne in the epistle to the
king leads quite naturally to a praise of his patron's support of the
Renaissance of learning. Without detracting from the sincerity of
Marot's enthusiasm for the Renaissance one may still observe the
polemical intent: the praise of the new order allows unfavourable
comment on the old:

> Certes, ô Roy, si le profond des cueurs
> On veult sonder de ces Sorboniqueurs,
> Trouvé sera que de toy ilz se deulent.
> Comment, douloir? Mais grand mal te veulent
> Dont tu as faict les lettres & les artz
> Plus reluysants que du temps des Cesars;
> Car leurs abus voit on en façon telle.
> C'est toy qui as allumé la chandelle
> Par qui mainct oeil voit maincte verité
> Qui soubs espesse & noire obscurité
> A faict tant d'ans icy bas demeurance;
>
> (*Ep.*, XXXVI, vv. 51–61)

Finally, one can only assume that the whole conception of the
Epître de Frippelippes was inspired by Marot's consummate polemical expertise. Directed against his personal rival François Sagon,
this satire purports to come from the pen of Marot's valet after
whom the epistle receives its title. Thus from the outset Marot
evinces his complete disdain for his rival without apparently
compromising his own dignity and superiority in the composition
of a personal attack. He also avoids detailed discussion and rebuttal
of the charges against him. More positively, he conferred upon
himself at the same time a freedom of approach, a freedom of
style and of language which was essential to his purpose of belittling
and indeed trivializing his rival. Marot was ever conscious of
stylistic exigencies. In this poem it is not merely a question of
satisfying them but rather of deliberately invoking them with
deadly satirical intent. In the poet's judgement, only the style of a
valet could fittingly effect the demolition of Sagon. In addition the

adoption of this stratagem by Marot made it impossible for Sagon to reply in his own terms to the valet without considerable loss of face. He was forced to copy Marot's tactics, to fight on ground which was not of his own choosing, and, inevitably, he was completely outgunned.

If the preoccupations betrayed by Marot's satirical poetry situate it in the Renaissance context, so too do the satirical techniques we find there. The delicate interplay of realism and fantasy which in poems such as *L'Enfer*, the three certainly authentic *coqs-à-l'âne* and the *Epitre de Frippelippes* although to a lesser extent in the *Epîtres* properly so called, where it is used more often to delight than to castigate or correct,[43] is carefully fashioned to become Marot's chief weapon of attack. And in this he was no different, except perhaps in matters of degree, from such satirists and humanists as Erasmus and Rabelais.

Realism and fantasy are paramount in the elaboration of the allegory which forms the whole basis of Marot's satire of the Paris judicature in *L'Enfer*. Realism is derived from the poet's own experience and observation of the phenomenon described, fantasy from his reading supplemented by poetic imagination. Thus the poet's *point de départ* for the narrative of his experience is provided by a banal, yet essentially valid comparison between the Châtelet in Paris and Hell:

> Si ne croy pas qu'il y ait chose au monde
> Qui mieulx ressemble ung Enfer tresimmonde:
>
> (*O.S.*, *Enfer*, vv. 13–14)

The initial comparison is not merely justified in reality and by reality, it is also clearly satirical since the *rapprochement* of the two terms is manifestly to the detriment of the Châtelet. What is more the analogy thus established invites, if indeed it does not compel, allegorical extension by the poet. From this moment onwards then the poem proceeds on three levels, the real, the allegorical, the satirical, interwoven and sustained with minimal interruption to the end of the narrative.

Marot's Hell is very much in the tradition of Virgil (*Aeneid*, VI) and Dante (*Divine Comedy*, *Hell*) often transmitted to him through the intermediary of Jean Lemaire de Belges's successful and esteemed *Seconde Epistre De L'Amant Vert*, *A Madame*

Marguerite Auguste, composed five years after the first in 1510.[44] But the intention of the two writers was vastly different, so too their respective starting-points. Jean Lemaire de Belges was merely elaborating a literary fantasy when he imagined and described, as a sequel to the death of Marguerite's pet parrot, l'Amant Vert of the title, its descent into the underworld Hell of Classical tradition, and its subsequent departure to the Elysian Fields after it had been found innocent of all crime during its earthly sojourn by Minos. Jean Lemaire's Hell remains purely mythical and incapable of allegorical interpretation in the strict sense. Marot's is the fictional representation of a real institution. Nevertheless he was aided and abetted in the conception and elaboration of his personal and satirical allegory by certain elements of his predecessor's fantasy.

Physical description of the topography of Hell occupies a very considerable part of Jean Lemaire's poem. It is much reduced in Marot's. This is not surprising when one remembers that Marot can only incorporate into his work details which have a dual relevance, that is, both to Hell and to the Châtelet if it is to be accepted as an allegory. Notions of gloom and darkness, of deep evil-smelling abysses and of constant noise are the most obviously and easily adapted presenting a simplified picture of both places:

> Mais, ains que feusse entré au gouffre noir,
> Je veoy à part ung aultre vieil manoir
> Tout plein de gens, de bruict & de tumulte.
> <div align="right">(<i>O.S., Enfer</i>, vv. 33–35)</div>

Jean Lemaire had written in similar terms:

> Plus aprouchons, plus oyons de tumulte,
> Qui du parfond d'un grand gouffre resulte.[45]

While he imagined the shrieks of the damned and the noise of their chains as they dragged themselves along

> Mais bien ot on des criz espoventables,
> ....
> Bruit de marteaux, chaines et ferremens.[46]

Marot attributes such cacophony to the jubilation of the law's henchmen as they exact full retribution on those the law condemns:

> Et si tant peult en accuser aulcunes
> Qu'elles en soyent pendues ou bruslées,
> Les infernaulx feront saults & hullées;
> Chaines de fer & crochets sonneront,
> Et de grand'joye ensemble tonneront,
> En faisant feu de flamme sulphurée
> Pour la nouvelle ouyr tant malheurée.
>
> <div align="right">(<i>O.S., Enfer</i>, vv. 474–80)</div>

The massive gates of Hell described by both writers are particularly appropriate to a prison sequence and it is through them that the poet is conducted to the various areas of Hell:

> Saiche qu'icy sont d'Enfer les faulxbourgs.
>
> <div align="right">(<i>O.S.</i>, ibid., v. 40)</div>

It is this line which allows Marot to enlarge the compass of his satire to include the proceedings not only of the Châtelet but also of the *Palais de Justice*. There follows naturally within this framework a dramatic sketch of the lawyers at work:

> Prends y esgard & entends leurs propos;
> Tu ne veis onq' si differents suppostz.
> Approche toy pour de plus pres les veoir;
> Regarde bien, je te fais assçavoir
> Que ce mordant que l'on oyt si fort bruyre
> De corps & biens veult son prochain destruire.
> Ce grand criart qui tant la gueulle tort,
> Pour le grand gaing, tient du riche le tort.
> Ce bon vieillart (sans prendre or ou argent)
> Maintient le droict de maincte paouvre gent.
> Celluy qui parle illec sans s'esclatter
> Le Juge assis veult corrompre & flatter.
> Et cestuy là, qui sa teste descoeuvre,
> En playderie a faict ung grand chef d'oeuvre,
> Car il a tout destruict son parentage,
> Dont il est crainct & prisé d'avantage;
> Et bien heureux celluy se peult tenir,
> Duquel il veult la cause soustenir.
>   Amys, voyla quelcque peu des menées,
> Qui aux faulxbourgs d'Enfer sont demenées

Par noz grands loups ravissantz & famys,
Qui ayment plus cent soulz que leurs amys,
Et dont, pour vray, le moyndre & le plus neuf
Trouveroit bien à tondre sur ung oeuf.

(*O.S.*, ibid., vv. 99–122)

A particularly repugnant and noisome feature of the Classical underworld was its serpents. In Virgil's *Aeneid* they are to be found with the fury Tisiphone in the entrance to Tartary. At her bidding these wild-eyed creatures set themselves upon the criminals who entered there. In Dante's Hell hydras hang from the waists of all three Furies whose hair in addition consists of writhing serpents. Jean Lemaire includes serpents in his enumeration of criminal animals encountered among the damned by Marguerite's parrot l'Amant Vert:

> Là sont aussi couleuvres et viperes,
> Aspicz mortelz, serpens tors et obliques,
> Escorpïons, lezardz et basilicques
> Tresvenimeux, et mainte autre vermine,
> Esquelz poison mortiffere domine,
> Et qui ont fait (vivans lassus en terre)
> A maintes gens griefve et mortelle guerre,
> Par quoy ilz sont en paine et en tourment.[47]

Marot's *Enfer* too has its serpents. But the poet has effected a striking transformation of his primary source, the *Seconde Epistre de l'Amant Vert*, in this instance. Marot signals the source of his inspiration at the start of a lengthy development while at the same time rejecting Jean Lemaire's differentiation of various types of venomous creatures:

> Or sçaiches, Amy, doncques,
> Qu'en cestuy parc où ton regard espends
> Une maniere il y a de Serpents,
> Qui de petits viennent grands & felons,
> Non poinct vollantz, mais traynnants & bien longs;
> Et ne sont pas pourtant Couleuvres froiddes,
> Ne verds Lezards, ne Dragons forts & roydes;
> Et ne sont pas Cocodrilles infaicts,
> Ne Scorpions tortuz & contrefaicts;
> Ce ne sont pas Vipereaulx furieux,
> Ne Basilics tuantz les gens des yeulx;

Ce ne sont pas mortiferes Aspics,
Mais ce sont bien Serpents qui vallent pis.

(*O.S.*, ibid., vv. 126-38)

Marot's serpents symbolize the lawsuits which constitute the chief
activity of his judicial *Enfer*. This satirical analogy, sustained at
some length and elaborated by an exuberant poetic imagination
supplemented occasionally by reminiscences from Greek mythology is a secondary detail of the parent allegory. It is singularly
appropriate to the circumstances. The characteristics of the
serpent, its essentially evil connotations, are all reflected in the
lawsuits which Marot abhors: lawsuits intractable, involuted,
venomous in kind and effect, but above all, like the Hydra, self-
generating and self-perpetuating:

> Ce sont Serpents enflés, envenimés,
> Mordantz, mauldicts, ardantz & animés,
> Jettants ung feu qu'à peine on peult estaindre,
> Et en picquant dangereux à l'attaindre.
> Car qui en est picqué ou offensé
> En fin devient chetif ou insensé;
> C'est la nature au Serpent, plein d'exces,
> Qui par son nom est appellé Proces.
> ....
> Celuy qui jecte ainsi feu à planté
> Veult enflammer quelcque grand' parenté;
> Celluy qui tire ainsi hors sa languete
> Destruira brief quelcun, s'il ne s'en guete;
> Celluy qui siffle & a les dents si drues
> Mordra quelcun, qui en courra les rues;
> Et ce froid là, qui lentement se traine,
> Par son venin a bien sceu mettre haine
> Entre la mere & les maulvais enfants,
> Car Serpents froids sont les plus eschauffantz.
> Et de touts ceulx qui en ce parc habitent,
> Les nouveaulx nays qui s'enflent & despitent
> Sont plus subjects à engendrer icy
> Que les plus vieulx. Voyre & qu'il soit ainsi,
> Ce vieil Serpent sera tantost crevé,
> Combien qu'il ait mainct lignage grevé.
> Et cestuy là plus antique qu'ung Roc,
> Pour reposer s'est pendu à ung croc.

Mais ce petit, plus mordant qu'une Loupve,
Dix grands Serpents dessoubs sa pence couve;
....
Car, pour du cas la preuve te donner,
Tu doibs sçavoir qu'yssues sont ces bestes
Du grand Serpent Hydra qui heut sept testes,
Contre lequel Hercules combattoit;
Et quand de luy une teste abbattoit,
Pour une morte en revenoit sept vifves.
    Ainsi est il de ces bestes noysifves;
Ceste nature ilz tiennent de la race
Du grand Hydra, qui au profond de Thrace,
Où il n'y a que guerres & contens,
Les engendra...

    (O.S., ibid., vv. 139–46, 151–70, 176–86)

In conception this satirical analogy is excellent. It may however
be argued that Marot allowed himself too much indulgence in its
execution and that exuberance has given way to prolixity. Critics
who argue thus are invariably the same ones who accuse Marot of
lack of *souffle* and sustained inspiration in his satirical writings.
The analogy has certainly far more dramatic vehemence than that
invoked by Rabelais in the *Tiers Livre*. Here judge Bridoye compared his conduct of a lawsuit to that of a bear licking into shape
its young cub.[48]

Without the traditional underworld figures Marot's allegory
would have been strangely incomplete. It falls to the poet, as
indeed to the parrot in Jean Lemaire's poem and to Dante, to
appear before the judges of Hell. But before doing so he must be
admitted to their presence by a ferocious janitor, Cerberus. Jean
Lemaire had described this mythical personage thus in his *Seconde
Epistre*:

                Si trouvons l'huys de fer,
        Par où on entre ou grant pourpris d'enfer.
        Lors Cerberus, le portier lait et noir,
        En abayant nous ouvrit son manoir.
        Sa voix tonant si fort retombissoit
        Que la valée obscure en gemissoit.
        Si ne fault pas demander se j'euz peur,
        Quand j'apperceuz ung si fier agrippeur.[49]

It is interesting to note how Marot has tailored his source to his own ends. *L'Enfer* continues thus:

> Bien avez leu, sans qu'il s'en faille ung A,
> Comme je fus par l'instinct de Luna
> Mené au lieu plus mal sentant que soulphre
> Par cinq ou six ministres de ce gouffre;
> Dont le plus gros jusques là me transporte.
> Si rencontray Cerberus à la porte,
> Lequel dressa ses troys testes en hault,
> A tout le moins une qui troys en vault.
> Lors de travers me voit ce Chien poussif;
> Puis m'a ouvert ung huys gros & massif,
> Duquel l'entrée est si tres estroicte & basse
> Que pour entrer faillut que me courbasse.
>
> (*O.S.*, ibid., vv. 21–32)

While Lemaire's Cerberus remains purely mythical, Marot's must accommodate two levels of interpretation. Thus his Cerberus is not simply the three-headed dog of Classical tradition but the allegorical representation of a real official. It is with some slight awkwardness that Marot reconciles the two at this point, and almost as an afterthought that he adds the necessary modification to his Cerberus:

> Lequel dressa ses troys testes en hault,
> A tout le moins une qui troys en vault

to preserve credibility on the second level. However, the advantages to the poet who has recourse to such symbols far outweigh any difficulties of adaptation. The character stands before us complete with certain attributes, some of which perhaps more than others may be stressed at the poet's discretion and according to his purpose. The use of the symbol invites the co-operation of the reader, it creates a bond, or a complicity between him and the poet who is merely, in the first instance, invoking part of a common cultural patrimony. The evocative power of the name Cerberus in this case and the myth it represents dispenses the poet from the tiresomely prosaical circumlocutions which marred the satire of certain *Rhétoriqueur* poets as they strove to communicate to their readers the attributes of a personified abstraction which existed only in their own minds. To dignify an abstract quality with a capital letter does not of itself confer plasticity or poetic intensity, still less does it ignite a spark of recognition in the reader's intellect or sensibility. Thus when Octovien de Saint-Gelais wanted to portray an irascible janitor in a satirical section of his poetic autobiography *Le Sejour d'Honneur* he called into being a creature by the name of *Long Aage* whose relevance to the situation would require lengthy elaboration.[50]

The same value attaches in the first instance to Marot's use of the underworld judges Minos and Rhadamanthus, although it would be true to say that these two are subjected to greater modification perhaps than Cerberus. In introducing Minos as the first of the judges of the underworld to be confronted by the prisoner Marot departs slightly from the tradition of his immediate predecessor although, in so doing, he is incidentally closer to the versions of Virgil and Dante. Unlike Lemaire

> Or passons oultre, et verrons se bon semble
> Au roy Minos, le grand juge infernal,
> Que je te maine en ton repos final.
> Je le voy là, qui se siet en son throsne,
> Et Megera, furieuse matrone,
> (O ses cheveulx colubrins, qui lui pendent
> Et grand venin lui distillent et rendent)
> Lui fait lumiere à tout une grand torche,
> Dont bien souvent les umbres bat et torche[51]

Marot dispenses with the attendant Fury who would, in any case, have been difficult to reconcile to his purpose. For his Minos represents Gabriel d'Allegre,[52] *prévôt de Paris*, who combined this office, which he resigned shortly after Marot had been transferred from the Châtelet to the jurisdiction of the Archbishop of Chartres, with those of Chamberlain to the king and Marshal of France. Not only has Marot been selective in his use of the Classical tradition from whomsoever he may have received it, he has also added something to it, a note of human realism which confers upon the portrait a humour which is peculiarly his own:

> Hault devant eulx le grand Minos se sied,
> Qui sur leurs dicts ses sentences assied.
> C'est luy qui juge ou condampne ou deffend,
> Ou taire faict quand la teste luy fend.
>
> (*O.S.*, ibid., vv. 47–50)

Marot's Rhadamanthus is more ferocious, and certainly less
equitable than he would appear to be from Classical sources.
Jean Lemaire does not dwell on this character, mentioning only
briefly that the parrot was taken to see

> le tenebreux convent
> Des infernaulx, où siet Radamanthus,
> Retributeur des vices et vertuz.[53]

He is given far greater importance by Marot in his *Enfer*.
Although Marot preserves the notion of Rhadamanthus's power
to reward the dead as well as to punish them, it is on the discharge
of this latter function that he necessarily insists. Necessarily since
he is attacking under this name Gilles Maillart who held at this
time the office of *lieutenant criminel* of the *Prévôté de Paris* and
who was notorious as a severe and extremely cunning interrogator.[54] A grim portrait is painted of him:

> je trouve en une salle
> Rhadamantus (Juge assis à son aise)
> Plus enflammé qu'une ardante fournaise,
> Les yeulx ouverts, les oreilles bien grandes,
> Fier en parler, cauteleux en demandes,
> Rebarbatif quand son cueur il descharge;
> Brief, digne d'estre aux Enfers en sa charge.
> Là devant luy vient maincte Ame dampnée,
> Et quand il dict: telle me soit menée,
> A ce seul mot ung gros marteau carré
> Frappe tel coup contre ung portal barré
> Qu'il faict crousler les tours du lieu infame.
>
> (*O.S.*, ibid., vv. 220–31)

It is relieved only somewhat by the last line quoted where the
intrusion of concrete reality, to the temporary detriment of the
fantasy, strikes a burlesque note. The 'tours du lieu infame' are
of course the turrets of the Châtelet building. It seems at least
probable that such would have been the interpretation of Marot's
contemporaries of this line. It is the most immediate one, although
more learned commentators might insist on the relevance of this
line to the Dantesque tradition. The Italian poet spoke of the
towers which dominated the city of the god of the underworld,
Pluto. Pluto, however, is no more than a name in Marot's satire.[55]

The dramatic sketch which the poet traces of Rhadamanthus in action must be accounted one of the satirical highlights of the whole poem. As satire it excels by its closeness to reality. It is the psychological insight with which Marot has observed, analysed and presented the techniques of the interrogator intent upon a confession at any price which makes this episode valid, unfortunately, for many centuries and many regimes. One may note the ingratiatingly pseudo-intimate style of speech which the judge adopts towards his suspect, the expression of confidence in his probable innocence which only a little co-operation on his part will suffice to establish beyond doubt, the cynical promises of early release. But here, as elsewhere, Marot's wit has a double edge. The words

> je te jure & promects
> Par le hault Ciel, où je n'iray jamais   (vv. 253–4)

placed in the mouth of Gilles Maillart are a withering, if unconscious self-condemnation. The oath, as it happens, is worthless not only in form but also in effect. The prisoner's docility will win him no respite. And for difficult cases the judge may always call upon his willing assistants the torturers. Here is the interrogation scene in its entirety. The soul stands before the judge of the underworld:

> Des qu'il la voit, il mitigue & pallie
> Son parler aigre, & en faincte doulceur
> Luy dict ainsi: Vien ça, fais moy tout seur,
> Je te supply, d'ung tel crime & forfaict.
> Je croiroys bien que tu ne l'as point faict,
> Car ton maintien n'est que des plus gaillards;
> Mais je veulx bien congnoistre ces paillards
> Qui avec toy feirent si chaulde esmorche.
> Dy hardyment; as tu peur qu'on t'escorche?
> Quand tu diras qui a faict le peché,
> Plus tost seras de noz mains despeché.
> De quoy te sert la bouche tant fermée,
> Fors de tenir ta personne enfermée?
> Si tu dys vray, je te jure & promects
> Par le hault Ciel, où je n'iray jamais,
> Que des Enfers sortiras les brisées
> Pour t'en aller aux beaulx champs Elysées,

Où liberté faict vivre les esprits
Qui de compter verité ont appris.
Vault il pas mieulx doncques que tu la comptes
Que d'endurer mille peines & hontes?
Certes, si faict. Aussi je ne croy mye
Que soys menteur, car ta phizionomie
Ne le dict point, & de maulvais affaire
Seroit celluy qui te vouldroit meffaire.
Dy moy, n'ais peur. Touts ces mots alleschantz
Font souvenir de l'oyselleur des champs
Qui doulcement faict chanter son sublet
Pour prendre au bric l'oyseau nyce & foyblet,
Lequel languist ou meurt à la pippée;
Ainsi en est la paovre Ame grippée;
Si tel' doulceur luy faict rien confesser,
Rhadamanthus la faict pendre ou fesser;
Mais, si la langue elle refraind & mord,
Souventesfoys eschappe peine & mort.
 Ce nonobstant, si tost qu'il vient à veoir
Que par doulceur il ne la peult avoir,
Aulcunesfoys encontre elle il s'irrite,
Et de ce pas, selon le demerite
Qu'il sent en elle, il vous la faict plonger
Au fonds d'Enfer, où luy faict alonger
Veines & nerfs, & par tourments s'efforce
A esprouver s'elle dira par force
Ce que doulceur n'a sceu d'elle tirer.

(O.S., ibid., vv. 240–83)

Shortly, it is Marot's turn to face the judge. The lengthy account
of his life and state which he gives in reply to Rhadamanthus's
questions is justified both by the allegory and by reality. Minos
received such an account of L'Amant Vert.[56] It is the kind of
statement which any detained suspect would have been required
to offer to a judge presiding over the proceedings instituted
against him. Largely lyrical in tone and inspiration, it forms a
delicate contrast artfully executed. Marot continues here to
transpose reality and fantasy, this time by situating the court of
François Ier on the lofty heights of Olympus and conferring
mythological status in the appropriate degree on the monarch and
his suite.[57]

The *ministre d'Enfer* occupies in Marot's allegory a function

similar to that of Mercure in Jean Lemaire's *Seconde Epistre de
l'Amant Vert*, to that of Virgil and Beatrice in Dante's *Inferno*,
and to that of the Sybil of Cumae in the sixth book of the *Aeneid*.
All are guides to visitors to the underworld and provide a commentary on what is seen to their charges. Marot's guide is closest
to Lemaire's Mercure. The latter's description of the vicious
squabbling and lack of charity among the animal souls—

> Brief, tant y a de bestail qui ulule,
> Qui mort l'un l'autre, et regibe et recule,
> Et frappe l'un, et puis escorne l'autre,
> Puis tel survient qui le froisse et espautre,
> Happe la queue ou la patte ou la hure,
> Tout y est plain de si mortelle injure
> Que tu aurois frayeur trop merveilleuse
> De veoir tel tourbe horrible et batailleuse,
> Qui n'a jamais n'amour ne paix ensemble—[58]

is paralleled by the *ministre's* description of vicious human beings
locked in mortal litigation in the judicial Hell. It is one of the
points in Lemaire's epistle which may have prompted Marot to
his adaptation. However, Marot's guide has once again the dis-
tinguishing feature of belonging to reality as well as to fantasy.
On the former level he is presented, although without much
detail, as a member of the legal fraternity. This is essential to
Marot's main purpose. The *ministre d'Enfer* is the inside witness
so useful to every satirist. It is in his mouth that an author places
the most damaging account of the system etc., he wishes to attack, while at the same time appearing himself as an innocent by-
stander free from any suspicion of *parti pris*. Thus Marot's guide
is most forthcoming on the iniquities of the French judicial
system although he sees these as perpetuated by the fatal flaws in
human nature of which the greatest is avarice. It is in this respect
that Marot's commentator differs from those of the three predecessors we have named. This is his analysis of the situation:

> Car s'on vivoit en paix, comme est mestier,
> Rien ne vauldroict de ce lieu le mestier;
> Pource qu'il est de soy si anormal
> Qu'il fault expres qu'il commence par mal,
> Et que quelcun à quelcque autre mefface,
> Avant que nul jamais proffict en face.

Brief en ce lieu ne gaignerions deux pommes,
Si ce n'estoit la maulvaistié des hommes.
Mais, par Pluton, le Dieu que doibs nommer,
Mourir de faim ne sçaurions, ne chommer,
Car tant de gens qui en ce parc s'assaillent
Assés & trop de besongne nous taillent;
Assés pour nous, quand les biens nous en viennent,
Et trop pour eulx, quand paovres en deviennent.
Ce nonobstant, ô nouveau prisonnier,
Il est besoing de pres les manier;
Il est besoing (croy moy), & par leur faulte,
Que dessus eulx on tienne la main haulte;
Ou aultrement les bons bonté fuyroient,
Et les maulvais en empirant iroient.

    Encor (pour vray) mettre on n'y peult tel ordre,
Que tousjours l'ung l'aultre ne vueille mordre;
Dont raison veult qu'ainsi on les embarre,
Et qu'entre deux soit mys distance & barre,
Comme aux Chevaulx en l'estable hargneux.

    Minos, le Juge, est de cela soigneux,
Qui devant luy, pour entendre le cas,
Faict deschiffrer telz noisifz altercas
Par ces crieurs, dont l'ung soustient tout droict
Droict contre tort; l'autre tort contre droict;
Et bien souvent, par cautelle subtille,
Tort bien mené rend bon droict inutile.

(O.S., ibid., vv. 67–98)

Marot's guide has a functional resemblance to some of the Lucianic commentators but his moralizing tendency shows that Marot has not yet liberated himself entirely from the conventions of *Rhétoriqueur* satire.

Marot's personal satire demonstrates the efficacy of fantasy, served by realism in its elaboration, as a means to ridicule. It is precisely this blend of the two elements which rescues this area of satire from the dangers most closely attendant upon it, banality and prosaism. Marot's onslaught on Sagon in the third *coq-à-l'âne* is in the form of an extended simile. It is introduced by a report, accepted as fact, of Sagon's explosive temperament. The report provides the poet with the terms of his comparison, banal in themselves, but frees him from the responsibility of its authorship and from the burden of proof. The unbridled fantasy

with which he imagines Sagon as a cannon to be primed, a
ceremony described with science and precision, and then fired in a
return to fantasy, lifts the attack on to quite a different level:

> On m'a promis qu'il a renom
> De salpestre et pouldre à canon
> Avoir muny tout son cerveau;
> Faictes deux tappons de naveau
> Et les luy mectez en la bouche,
> Et puys apres que l'on le couche
> Tout de son long, et en l'oreille,
> Tout doulcement qu'il ne s'esveille,
> Gectez y pouldre pour l'emorche,
> Et gardez bien qu'on ne l'escorche,
> Car ung homme bien empesché
> Seroit d'un regnard escorché.
> Et cela faict, qu'on le repute
> Pour servir d'une haquebute.
>   Jamais homme n'en parla mieulx;
> Les tappons sortiront des yeulx
> Et feront ung merveilleux bruict;
> Et si la fouldre les conduict,
> Ilz fraperont deux tous d'un coup.
> Cela leur servira beaucoup
> Pour deschasser leurs ennemys;
> Car s'ilz ne sont fort endormyz,
> Tel canon leur donnera craincte.

(O.S., 3^e Coq a l'Asne, vv. 111–33)

In the *Epître de Frippelippes* there is the same blend of fantasy
and realism, albeit differently achieved. Marot's valet feels an
irrepressible urge to administer a good beating to Sagon. The
thought is immediately translated into a reality which his mind
alone experiences. Here the realism derives not from any precision of detail, but from Marot's unique command of stylistic and
metrical resources, from onomatopoeia and from the structure of
the verse which reproduce the sound, the fury and the rhythm
of the onslaught:

> Mais moy, Je ne me puis garder
> De t'en batre & te nazarder;
> Ta meschanceté m' y convye,
> Et m'en fault passer mon envye.

Zon dessus l'oeil, zon sur le groing
Zon sur le dos du Sagouyn,
Zon sur l'asne de Balaan!
Ha! villain, vous petez d'ahan:
Le feu sainct Anthoine vous arde!
Ça, ce nez, que je le nazarde,
Pour t'apprendre avecques deux doitz
A porter honneur où tu doys.
Enflez, villain, que je me joue;
Sus, apres, tournez l'autre joue.
Vous cryez? Je vous feray taire,
Par dieu, monsieur le secretaire
De beurre fraiz. Hou le mastin!
(*O.S.*, *Ep. de Frippelippes*, vv. 207–23)

The end of the flogging is similarly indicated. The last lashes are applied, not frenziedly, but deliberately and heavily as the assailant expends the last of his energy, if not the last of his fury:

Que je donne au dyable la beste!
Il me faict rompre icy la teste
A ses merites collauder,
Et les bras à le pelauder,
Et si ne vault pas le tabut.
Mieulx vault donq icy mettre but,
T'advisant, Sot, t'advisant, Veau,
T'advisant, Valeur d'un naveau,
Que tu ne te vys recevoir
Onques tant d'honneur... (*O.S.*, ibid., vv. 241–50)

Scenarios, similes and dramatic sketches are not the only product of Marot's fantasy in his satirical poetry. Thomas Sebillet held that the greatest charm of the *coq-à-l'âne*, its greatest elegance was 'sa plus grande absurdité'. Others have described the same quality when they have spoken of the incoherence which is of the essence of the genre.[59] This, too, is one of the manifestations of Marot's fantasy, a fantasy which is skilfully deployed, not only as a safeguard in an era of persecution, but also as a weapon of attack in the composition of the *coq-à-l'âne*. Thus the following lines give the impression of a lunatic inconsequentiality:

> Ce Grec, cest Hebreu, ce Latin
> Ont descouvert le pot aux roses:
> Mon Dieu, que nous voirrons de choses,
> Si nous vivons l'aage d'ung veau.
>   Et puis, que dict on de nouveau?
> Quand part le Roy? aurons nous guerre?
> O la belle piece de terre!
> Il la fault joyndre avec la myenne;
> Mais pourtant la Bohemienne
> Porte tousjours ung chapperon.
>   Ne donnez jamais l'esperon
> A cheval qui vouluntiers trotte.
> Dont vient cela, que je me frotte
> Aux coursiers, & suis tousjours rat?
> Ilz escument comme ung Verrat,
> En pleine chaiere, ces Cagots,
> Et ne preschent que des fagots
> Contre ces paouvres Hereticques.
>
> _(O.S., 2ᵉ Coq a l'Asne, vv. 6–23)_

They are not however to be dismissed as lightly as this. Each couplet contains a specific allusion, a satirical shaft in most cases, directed with proper control at a precise target. Thus the first couplet is a reference to the new learning in the three Classical tongues and to the opposition which the Sorbonne showed to its propagation. Before long it would undoubtedly have revealed the untenability of many of its teachings. This indeed is the sense of the second couplet which thus completes the first. The next couplet alludes to the current war fever and the preparations for a renewal of hostilities between France and the Holy Roman Empire. This leads inevitably to a passing attack on the politics of territorial aggrandizement. The fifth couplet with its allusion to the doctoral hood may well be another reference to the Sorbonne although in this case it is difficult to discover its precise import. The sixth is a common proverb embodying the instant wisdom which here introduces a somewhat bitter allusion to the poet's own personal situation: his frequentation with the great of this world has availed him nothing, none of their fortune has rubbed off onto him. The last two are an attack on the fanaticism with which Catholic preachers assailed and threatened the evangelists and reformers from their pulpits.

In other ways too the inconsequentiality of these lines, and others like them, is more apparent than real. There is often a link between two seemingly disparate couplets which may be achieved by an association of ideas in which, once again, the author invites his reader's complicity. The following four lines from later on in the second *coq-à-l'âne* would seem to be largely unrelated:

> Tu ne sçais pas. Thunis est prinse,
> Triboulet a freres & soeurs;
> Les Anglois s'en vont bons danseurs;
> Les Allemants tiennent mesure.   (vv. 140–3)

This is not so. After the capture of Tunis in July 1535 by Charles V a number of Moorish dancers and court entertainers found their way into European courts where they enjoyed a great vogue, possibly to the detriment of the established court jesters represented here by the great Triboulet, the fool of François Ier and probably better known by the name Rigoletto. This is the sense of the second line. Triboulet's 'freres & soeurs' were his Moorish rivals. Their influence extended to England and Germany, as the next couplet informs us, and they gave their name (*mores* or *morisques*) to the grotesque dance performed in fancy costume by the English morris dancers. Sometimes the link between couplets may be made stylistically, as well as by an association of ideas. Thus to return to the earlier passage we quoted, Marot introduced a new topic quite naturally by the rhetorical question, used ostensibly to prompt his own memory:

> Et puis, que dict on de nouveau?

There is a certain degree of ellipsis in what follows, but it is by no means insurmountable. There is in addition something undeniably comical in the way in which Marot answers his own rhetorical question seriously with the reply:

> Quand part le Roy? aurons nous guerre?

which were the questions on everybody's lips at the time. The first line of this couplet provides a stylistic link, and the second the association of ideas, necessary to the understanding of the couplet that follows:

> O la belle piece de terre!
> Il la fault joyndre avec la myenne.

For the author's original question allows him then to present what was in the mind, not of the general public this time, but of the prime mover in any such military enterprise, the prince with territorial ambitions. Hence the monologue form adopted. As for the substance, the connection between *terre* and *guerre* was in fact enshrined in the popular proverb 'qui terre a, guerre a'. The author's satirical intent completes the association. And the process is repeated, with variations, many times in the course of the *coqs-à-l'âne*.

This incoherence is at once the strength and the weakness of the satirical technique forged by Marot and deployed in the *coq-à-l'âne*. On the one hand it could lead by degrees to hermeticism and obscurity, a fault which Marot himself criticized in the poetry of Villon when he attempted to edit his works.[60] This presents a greater obstacle to posterity than to the poet's own contemporaries. Many of Marot's more cryptic allusions were probably less so in his own time. However, this is only one aspect of his apparent incoherence. The most important is his deliberate suppression of transitional phrases or explanatory comment. It should not be forgotten that this type of incoherence in another context was lately held to be a virtue in poetry. It was thus that the *surréalistes* sought to free themselves from the constraints of formal logic in an attempt to explore and exploit the unreal and the irrational. And Marot's incoherence, unlike that of the *surréalistes*, was rescued from the dangers of total impenetrability by his precise satirical intent which serves as guide-line in most cases. The advantages of Marot's technique are easy to perceive. It allows him to make repeated thrusts with speed and elegance. Its very concision imparts added piquancy. Gone for ever are the bluntness and prolixity which disguised or severely incapacitated the satire of many a *Rhétoriqueur* poet. In addition, Marot might achieve a two-fold satire, combining a stinging observation with a deliberately incongruous juxtaposition of ideas. Is it true, he asks, that prostitutes are charging the earth for their services. If this is so, then...

> Et que les jeunes tant pouppines
> Vendent leur chair cher comme cresme?
> S'il est vray, adieu le caresme

Au Concile qui se faira.
Mais Romme tandis bouffera
Des chevreaulx à la chardonnette.

(O.S., 2e Coq a l'Asne, vv. 74–79)

There is no obvious connection between the price charged by prostitutes and the continuance of the Church's ordinances on Lent but the burlesque proposition: *s'il est vray* which hints hypothetically at the dependence of the one upon the other, was well calculated to shock the bigots and to erode the reverence of others. This is not the only example of such a procedure although it is probably the most often quoted being rather less crude than certain others. Casting aside anachronistic sensitivity, since all obscenity is relative, one might also mention Marot's observation that it is

> ...grand'pitié quand beaulté fault
> A cul de bonne voulunté.
>   Puis, vous sçavez, Pater sancte,
> Que vostre grand pouvoir s'efface.

(O.S., ibid., vv. 30–33)

Parody is very much bound up with the fantasy and incoherence of the *coq-à-l'âne*. To begin with, it is possible to describe the genre as a parody of the epistle. The date of composition given in each with a specious precision conferred by fantasy, the charade of giving and receiving news, all these are evidence of the author's intention to parody the serious genre. Marot himself makes this clear at the outset of his second *coq-à-l'âne* when he confesses that his first communication of four years ago still awaits a reply from his friend, with whom, notwithstanding, he had been in more or less constant personal contact since that time. Feigning tolerant resignation at his friend's dilatoriness he proceeds without more ado to compose a reply to himself, like the proverbial *prebstre Martin*:[61]

> Puis que respondre ne me veulx,
> Je ne te prendray aux cheveulx,
> Lyon; mais sans plus te semondre,
> Moy mesmes je me veulx respondre
> Et seray le prebstre Martin.   (*O.S.*, ibid., vv. 1–5)

Secondly, Marot was not adverse to parodying the more platitudi-
nous examples of popular wisdom. He does this by distorting and
inverting the sense of certain adages. Thus he advises Lyon:

> Aprens tandis que tu es vieulx
>
> (*O.S.*, *Premier Coq a l'Asne*, v. 45)

contributing further to the impression of absurdity. It was not
only on this level however that he parodied the laboured and the
self-evident. How pompous he found the conclusions of the
docteurs en Sorbonne is indicated in these lines of the same poem:

> Il n'est pas possible qu'on sorte
> De ces Cloistres aulcunement
> Sans y entrer premierement;
> C'est ung argument de Sophiste.
>
> (*O.S.*, ibid., vv. 64–67)

Similarly when Marot presented propositions and arguments
which were patently inconsequent with every appearance of
logical progression, introducing them scrupulously by *car, aussi,
tellement que, oultre plus, puis, mais pourtant, si* etc., it was with
the intention to parody, on the one hand, the level of conversation,
characterized by the proverb *saulter du coq en l'asne* and the
genre, and on the other perhaps the formal logic of the Schoolmen which could be used to dignify banalities of a more erudite
order. In any event, there is a distinct affinity between Marot's
purpose and procedures here with those of Ionesco in his earliest
comments on language and communication.

Parody is not confined to the *coq-à-l'âne* in Marot's satirical
poetry. If in Marot's treatment of certain popular adages in the
first *coq-à-l'âne* there is too an indication of his willingness to
mock the predilection which his predecessors the *Rhétoriqueurs*
showed for the *cliché* and the instant formula in their poetry, one
finds the same intention to parody their style in the epistle to the
king, *Pour avoir esté desrobé* (XXV) which dates from the same
year (1531). Here (vv. 119–30) with an obvious irony which
distinguishes the true parody from the mere *pastiche*, Marot
commanded his Muse to produce a bombastic eulogy of the king.[62]
Even with this intention however Marot's natural restraint, or
greater art, preserved him from the worst excesses of *Rhétoriqueur* flattery. In the *Epître de Frippelippes* he turned his hand

to the parody of the absurdly pedantic commentaries of the Schoolmen. Thus his valet's epistle appears as:

Le Valet de Marot contre Sagon.
Cum Commento

Rabelais's *Des Pois aux Lards* had been similarly dignified.[63] No serious work, and many others besides, was without it. Likewise Marot's marginal notes with their facetious explanations complete with Latin expressions and specious references:

Huet pour Hueterie, per syncopam
Marmonner, c'est parler en Singe, ou Sagouin, selon Pline
Griffon, id est greffier

mock the glosses of the Schoolmen. From a later period of Marot's career there is an epistle attributed to him which contains a parody of Petrarchist love poetry. This is the epistle *A son amy, en abhorrant folle amour* (LIII).[64] It is not at all unusual for a poet who previously imitated Petrarchism to parody its excesses in his later years. Both Ronsard and Du Bellay did likewise.[65] Here Marot mocks the concept of Petrarchist love, with its emphasis on the unattainable, and its expression by means of antithesis:

Qu'est ce qu'amour? voy qu'en dit Saingelays,
Petrarque aussi & plusieurs hommes lays,
Prebstres & clercs, & gens de tous estophes,
Hebreux & Grecz, Latins & Philosophes.
Ceux là en ont bien dict par leurs sentences
Que de grandz maux petites recompenses.
Je ne ditz pas qu'Amour ne soit bon homme,
Bon filz, bon fol, sage, bon gentilhomme,
Hardy, couard, honteux, audacieux,
Fier, humble, fin, simple, fallacieux,
Malade & sain, aygre & doux, fantastique,
Palle, sanguin, joyeux, melencolique,
Chault, froid & sec, fascheux, plaisant, estrange,
Diable cornu en forme d'un bel Ange,
Amy secret & ennemy publique,
Tresdoux parleur en faincte Rethorique,
Grand & petit, jeune & vieil tout ensemble,
Foible & puissant, à qui nul ne resemble;
C'est un marchant, qui à bon marché preste,
Mais au payer c'est une caulte beste,

Car son credit est d'une telle attente
Qu'il n'est celuy qui ne s'en mescontente.
....
Qu'est ce qu'Amour, sinon doulce amertume,
Tournant bon droict en mauvaise coustume,
Alienant le sens de la raison,
Voysin suspect & certaine prison,
Qui, soubz couleur d'une esperance folle,
Ses favorez mord, destaint & affolle,
En attendant le pretendu plaisir
Dont mal vient tost & le bien à loysir.

(Ep., LIII, vv. 35–56, 75–82)

This epistle is all the more interesting since its estimated date of composition makes it contemporary with the beginning of the polemic known as the *Querelle des Amyes*,[66] in which poets debated the relative merits of two codes of love, the ethereal and chaste or the sensual and earthy.

Although parody must be accompanied by an ironical intention to qualify as such, it is not in the examples quoted above that the full force and range of Marot's irony itself is evident. Of this weapon so indispensable to the satirist Marot had complete mastery. It shows itself in the bitter reflections which accompany his narrative of his own experience of religious intolerance and persecution:

Or jamais ne vous laissez prendre,
S'il est possible de fouyr;
Car tousjours on vous peult ouyr
Tout à loysir et sans collere;
Mais en fureur de telle affaire
Il vault mieulx s'excuser d'absence
Qu'estre bruslé en sa presence.

(O.S., 3e Coq a l'Asne, vv. 170–6)

It shows itself in the almost Voltairian euphemisms with which he characterizes the horrors of mutilation and death in war:

Les gensdarmes sont furieux,
Chocquans au visaige & aux yeulx.
Il ne fault qu'une telle lorgne
Pour faire ung gentilhomme borgne;

> Il ne fault qu'un traict d'arbaleste,
> Passant au travers de la teste,
> Pour estonner ung bon cerveau.
>
> ....
>
> C'est assez d'un petit boullet,
> Qui poingt ung souldart au collet,
> Pour empescher de jamais boire.
>
> (*O.S.*, ibid., vv. 191–7, 201–3)

It is the weapon with which he demolishes his personal enemies as well as the enemies of humanism and the Renaissance. To Sagon, he offers this ironic bouquet, praising only the better to undermine:

> Au reste de tes escriptures
> Il ne fault vint ne cent ratures
> Pour les corriger. Combien donq?
> Seulement une tout du long.
>
> (*O.S.*, *Ep. de Frippelippes*, vv. 65–68)

To Noel Béda he first refuses the reputation of a learned man only to accord him pre-eminence in a field, alas, which will scarcely honour his name or the high position he occupies as chief syndic of the Sorbonne:

> En est il ung au monde
> En qui tant de sçavoir habonde?
> Et je responds: ouy, ouy vrayement,
> Et n'y fust autre que Clement.
> Les latins, les grecs et hebreuz
> Luy sont langaiges tenebreux.
> Mais en françoys de Heurepoix,
> Et beaulx escuz d'or et de poix,
> En quelque latin de marmite—
> Par nostre dame, je le quicte—
> Pour vray, il est le plus sçavant;
> C'est raison qu'il voyse devant.
>
> (*O.S.*, *3ᵉ Coq a l'Asne*, vv. 7–18)

The talents which served Marot so well in the narration of his own or others' misfortunes in the lighter epistles, in particular his quick and observant eye for significant detail, are also appropriate to the satirist's pen. A visual detail will suffice to dramatize a fantasy and to etch indelibly into the reader's mind an aspect of the reality underlying it. Thus, at the 'firing' of Sagon we are told:

> Les tappons sortiront des yeulx
>
> (*O.S.*, ibid., v. 126)

just as, in real life, eyes starting, cod-like, from the forehead of an angry man indicate the mounting pressure of his explosive reaction.

At its most successful Marot's satirical art is characterized by economy. Economy of vision is only one aspect of this art, but it also promotes concentration and economy of expression. These qualities are apparent in his satirical description of the Lombards:

> Car ces Lombars avec qui je chemine
> M'ont fort apris à faire bonne myne,
> A ung seul brin de Dieu ne deviser
> A parler froid, et à poltroniser.
> Dessus ung mot une heure je m'arreste,
> S'on parle à moy, je respondz de la teste.
>
> (*Ep.*, XLV, vv. 55–60)

Here what is in essence a moral commentary on the character of the Lombards as perceived by Marot is condensed into a few lines by the selection of revealing gestures and physical attitudes. Neither Du Bellay nor Ronsard bettered Marot in this art: they were content to copy him.[67] Another example from Marot's work is provided by his portrait of the various monastic orders in the *Second Chant de l'Amour Fugitif*.[68]

The incisiveness which makes satire not only pungent but also durable is dependent in a very large measure on the aptness and economy of its expression. The most remembered lines of Marot's satire demonstrate precisely these qualities. They may be simply aphoristic, like this one from *L'Enfer*:

> Tort bien mené rend bon droict inutile

providing a well-turned *résumé* to a whole indictment. Or they may be pointed by satiric wit and it is this quality which sharpens the incisiveness achieved by aptness and economy. The pun inspired by a definite satirical intention exemplifies best this threefold action. Such is the terrifyingly concise and mordant

tribute Marot pays to the guardians of orthodoxy in their treatment of heretics in the third *coq-à-l'âne*:

> Ilz ont esté si bien rotys
> Qu'ilz sont tous convertiz en cendre.   (vv. 168-9)

As one would expect however it is in the *épigrammes* that these
three qualities are at a premium, not only in the final shaft but
also in the lines which precede and justify its delivery. The
épigramme entitled *D'Un Gros Prieur* is justly famous:

> Un gros prieur son petit filz baisoit,
> Et mignardoit au matin en sa couche,
> Tandis rostir sa Perdrix on faisoit:
> Se leve, crache, esmeutit & se mouche;
> La Perdrix vire; Au sel, de broque en bouche!
> La devora: bien sçavoit la science;
> Puis quand il eut prins sur sa conscience
> Broc de vin blanc, du meilleur qu'on elise;
> Mon Dieu, dit-il, donne moy patience;
> Qu'on a de maulx pour servir saincte Eglise!
>
> (*Epigr.*, CCXXXVI)

The triumph here is not one of invention[69] but of execution.
There is not a word which is superfluous to the poet's intention.
The narrative progresses with a Voltairian rapidity and concision
as verb follows verb. No explicit moral commentary intrudes nor
is any required to complete the satirical sketch or heighten its
relief. Yet there is another element in the success of this epigram
and which ensures that the point strikes home. This is the surprise ending which the author reserves for the reader, the art
with which he introduces the unexpected without detriment to
credibility or realism. The same is true of another famous Marot
epigram, *De Jehan Jehan*, which is one of the group inspired by
Martial.[70] It is in this particular instance a skilful transposition
which Marot has achieved, mainly by substituting for the name
of Martial's victim, the name traditionally reserved in France for
the cuckold:

> Tu as tout seul, Jehan Jehan, vignes & prez;
> Tu as tout seul ton coeur & ta pecune;
> Tu as tout seul deux logis dyaprez,
> Là où vivant ne pretend chose aucune;

Tu as tout seul le fruict de ta fortune;
Tu as tout seul ton boire & ton repas;
Tu as tout seul toutes choses fors une,
C'est que tout seul ta femme tu n'as pas.

(Epigr., CLIX)

It is impossible to say to what extent Marot's imitation of Martial in the *épigrammes* contributed to his expertise in this genre and particularly to the elegance and wit with which he concluded them since these qualities are by no means absent from some earlier poems, *Epître* XI and some of the *épigrammes de circonstance*. Doubtless Marot perceived, or was encouraged to perceive a natural affinity between his own talent and that of Martial and was stimulated to greater efforts by his example.

Not all of Marot's satire depends for its effect on its incisiveness and economy. The emotional protests to which he is inspired in the epistles from exile, in *L'Enfer* and even, though to a lesser extent, in the *coqs-à-l'âne* where elegy occasionally mingles with satire, are accommodated in a very different style. And one which approximates by degrees to the more ample sweep of Classical, declamatory invective, and even at times to epic. Marot's compassion for the innocent victims of judicial torture finds expression in this lyrical apostrophe and moving prayer on their behalf:

O chers Amys, j'en ay veu martirer
Tant que pitié m'en mettoit en esmoy!
Parquoy vous pry de plaindre avecques moy
Les Innocents qui en telz lieux damnables
Tiennent souvent la place des coulpables.

(O.S., Enfer, vv. 284–8)

The Virgilian epic formula 'O terque quaterque beati...' brings to its culminating intensity Marot's protest against the iniquities of the Sorbonne in the *Epistre au Roy, du temps de son exil à Ferrare* (XXXVI):

O quatre foys & cinq foys bien heureuse
La mort, tant soit cruelle & rigoreuse,
Qui feroyt seulle ung million de vies
Soubz telz abus n'estre plus asservyes!

(Ep., XXXVI, vv. 71–74)

Another attack on this institution in the same poem relies stylistically on the epic device of repetition:

> Aultant comme eulx, sans cause qui soyt bonne,
> Me veult de mal l'ignorante Sorbonne:
> Bien ignorante elle est d'estre ennemye
> De la trilingue & noble Academie
> Qu'as erigée.   (ibid., vv. 39–43)

This feature also occurs in the *Epistre envoyée de Venize à Madame
la Duchesse de Ferrare* (XLIII):

> Ce sont, ce sont telles ymaiges vives
> Qui de ces grans despenses excessives
> Estre debvoient aournées et parées,
> Et de nos yeulx les autres separées.
> Car l'Eternel les vives recommande...
>   (*Ep.*, XLIII, vv. 43–47)

But the most sustained example of its use is to be found in the
poem *L'Enfer*:

> Là les plus grands les plus petitz destruisent,
> Là les petitz peu ou poinct aux grands nuisent,
> Là trouve l'on façon de prolonger
> Ce qui se doibt & se peult abreger;
> Là sans argent paovreté n'a raison,
> Là se destruict maincte bonne maison,
> Là biens sans cause en causes se despendent,
> Là les causeurs les causes s'entrevendent,
> Là en public on manifeste & dict
> Là maulvaistié de ce monde mauldict.   (vv. 51–60)

The effect of such repetition is not intended to be simply rhyth-
mical as it was in the *chansons*, but to emphasize or underscore
the main point (the ignorance of the Sorbonne in the first
example, the neglect of God's living creatures in the second), or
points of the poet's indictment. Finally, the metre used by the
poet also reflects a particular mood or intention. The octosyllabic
line is obviously appropriate to the incoherence and humour of
the *coqs-à-l'âne*, or of *Frippelippes*, but for more declamatory
satire, as in *L'Enfer*, the epistles, and the *Second Chant de
L'Amour fugitif* Marot turned to the more ample decasyllabic
line.

For many critics Marot's satirical vein was never ample or sweeping enough. It is on the grounds that he failed to anticipate D'Aubigné that he has most often been found wanting as a satirist worthy of note.[71] While the substance of the criticism may be generally verified, the conclusion drawn from it is not only unfair but also manifestly absurd. By the same token one might reproach any poet with not being more like another. There is in any case, as Marot's own work demonstrates by its variety, more than one way in which to write satire, to flay one's enemies and to serve an ideal, in poetry.

VII

RENAISSANCE AND REFORMATION
ATTITUDES IN MAROT'S POETRY[1]

One may refuse the name of humanist to Marot according to the strictest definitions of the term. But it would be difficult to deny that the poet closely identified with the efforts made by others more learned or more powerful than himself to promote the cause of humanism in the face of obscurantism, and that he voiced the enthusiasm of many besides himself when he celebrated the progress achieved.

The theme of Renaissance is one which provides a link between Marot's satire, his lyrical poems and his epistles. In all three it is expressed with intensity. It was in *L'Enfer* that Marot first commemorated the Renaissance of learning in France, three years before the founding of the Collège des Lecteurs Royaux:

> Le beau verger des lettres plantureux
> Nous reproduict ses fleurs à grands jonchées
> Par cy devant flaistries & seichées
> Par le froid vent d'ignorance & sa tourbe
> Qui hault sçavoir persecute & destourbe,
> Et qui de cueur est si dure ou si tendre
> Que verité ne veult ou peult entendre.
> O Roy heureux, soubs lequel sont entrés
> (Presque periz) les lettres & Lettrés!
>
> (*O.S.*, *Enfer*, vv. 368–76)

The two other passages in which Marot returned to this subject are roughly contemporaneous and both written from exile. In the famous lines from the epistle to the king, *Du temps de son exil à Ferrare* (XXXVI) the poet employs a different metaphor. This time it is that of the 'chandelle' which symbolizes the enlightenment shed by the Renaissance:

> grand mal te veulent
> Dont tu as faict les lettres & les artz
> Plus reluysants que du temps des Cesars;

Car leurs abus voit on en façon telle.
C'est toy qui as allumé la chandelle
Par qui mainct oeil voit mainct everité
Qui soubs espesse & noire obscurité
A faict tant d'ans icy bas demeurance;
Et qu'est il rien plus obscur qu'ignorance.

(*Ep.*, XXXVI, vv. 54–62)

The antithesis between lightness and dark was much favoured by Renaissance writers to distinguish their own era from that of the previous age. Rabelais had employed it in the letter of Gargantua to his son Pantagruel.[2] Marot's third affirmation of confidence in the Renaissance and its progress contained in the *Avant-naissance du troiziesme enffant de madame Renée, duchesse de Ferrare*, is also not without a resemblance to this letter:

Vien hardiment, car ayant plus grant aage
Tu trouveras encores davantage:
Tu trouveras la guerre commencée
Contre ignorance et sa tourbe incensée,
Et au rebours vertu mise en avant,
Qui te rendra personnage sçavant
En tous beaulx artz, tant soient ilz difficiles,
Tant par moyens que par livres faciles!

(*O.L., Eglogue* II, vv. 21–28)

In similar terms Du Bellay and Ronsard too would later rejoice in the defeat of the 'vilain monstre ignorance'.[3]

Marot's involvement in the Renaissance was not merely that of a poet content to record and applaud the victories of others from afar. The whole body of his satire gives the lie to any notion that his was simply a spectator's role. He was a partisan, actively engaged.[4] An important passage of the epistle to the king from Ferrara contains an explicit reference to the poet's mission. It begins as a protest against the censure exercised by the civil and ecclesiastical authorities. It demands a special intellectual freedom for the poet in order that he may fully discharge his duty. Given the specific personal and historical context in which Marot wrote these lines, they contain much more than a simple restatement of a *locus classicus* as some commentators have alleged.[5] For Marot does not envisage himself here as a passive agent. His

protest culminates in a confident assertion of the power to choose
between good and evil, and to reject the latter, which situates it
within the context of Renaissance humanism:

> O juge sacrilege,
> Qui t'a donné ne loy ne privileige
> D'aller toucher & faire tes massacres
> Au cabinet des sainctes Muses sacres?
> Bien est il vray que livres de deffence
> On y trouva; mais cela n'est offence
> A ung poëte, à qui on doibt lascher
> La bride longue, & rien ne luy cacher,
> Soit d'art magicq, nygromance ou caballe;
> Et n'est doctrine escripte ne verballe
> Qu'ung vray Poëte au chef ne deust avoir
> Pour faire bien d'escripre son debvoir.
> Sçavoir le mal est souvent proffitable,
> Mais en user est tousjours evitable.
>
> (*Ep.*, XXXVI, vv. 131–44)

These last two lines have often been overlooked. We shall return
to them later.

Like others of his time Marot celebrated in the Renaissance of
learning an enlightenment which was not confined to the restitution of the Classical disciplines. Like others, Marot questioned
the moral and dogmatic authority of the Sorbonne and the Church.
By the civil and the ecclesiastical authorities he was considered a
dangerous Lutheran for so doing. His anti-Catholic satire was
violently attacked by polemicists on the other side.[6] What does
Marot's religious poetry itself allow us to conclude of his attitude
to the new ideas?

Three times Marot replied to accusations of Lutheranism made
against him. It is of the utmost importance to note the circumstances in which the poet made his replies. The first of these,
which is contained in the epistle sent by the poet in March 1526
while he was held a prisoner in the Châtelet to *Monsieur Bouchart,
Docteur en Theologie* (IX) illustrates the point particularly well.
There are three known versions of the poem which contains a
plea for the poet's release. If, as is supposed, a first version of this
epistle was indeed written by the poet in captivity and, moreover,

anticipating the severest sanctions, then the value of any protestations of orthodoxy it might contain would be severely reduced. There exists in fact a manuscript containing what may have been such a first version. Its authenticity cannot be established beyond doubt but its date would appear to be before 1532. It differs markedly in tone and content from the two later, published versions. It is the only poem under Marot's name which contains a condemnation of Luther:

> Donne responce à mon piteux affaire,
> Docte docteur. Qui ta induict à faire
> Emprisonner depuis six jours en ça
> Ung tien servant qui onc ne t'offensa,
> Et voulloir mectre en luy craincte et terreur
> D'aigre justice, en le chargeant d'erreur
> Lutherienne, en tant de lieux mauldicte,
> Contraire à tous et à tous interdicte?
> Je ne fuz oncq, ne suis et ne seray
> Cynon (*sic*) cristien, et mes jours passeray
> En, par, et pour, et dessouz Jesucrist.[7]

The first published edition of the poem is remarkable, in comparison, for its outspokenness. It was, however, less remarkable in the changed circumstances which made its publication possible.[8] It contains the lines:

> ...Point ne suis Lutheriste
> Ne Zuinglien, encores moins Papiste
> Je ne fuz onq, ne suys et ne seray
> Sinon Chrestien, & mes jours passeray
> S'il plaist à Dieu, soubz son filz JESUSchrist.[9]

These must be set against the definitive version which appeared in 1538 in the complete works. Here the offending lines were again modified (vv. 7–11) although not without some difficulty. This is revealed by the Errata to the addition. The 'Sinon Chrestien' of 1534 appears in the 1538 text as

> Sinon de Dieu par son filz Jesuchrist (v. 9)

which is not an acceptable reading. The Erratum corrected it to 'Je suis de Dieu...'[10] Marot's reply therefore reads thus:

> Donne response à mon present affaire,
> Docte Docteur. Qui t'a induict à faire

Emprisonner, depuis six jours en ça,
Ung tien amy, qui onc ne t'offensa?
Et vouloir mettre en luy crainte & terreur
D'aigre justice, en disant que l'erreur
Tiens de Luther? Point ne suis Lutheriste
Ne Zuinglien, & moins Anabatiste:
Je suis de Dieu par son filz Jesuchrist.
   Je suis celluy qui ay faict maint escript,
Dont ung seul vers on n'en sçauroit extraire
Qui à la Loy divine soit contraire.
Je suis celluy qui prends plaisir & peine
A louer Christ & sa mere tant pleine
De grace infuse; & pour bien l'esprouver,
On le pourra par mes escriptz trouver.
Brief, celluy suis qui croit, honnore & prise
La saincte, vraye & catholique Eglise;

(Ep., IX, vv. 1–18)

This reply represents very much a compromise position. The denial of Lutheranism is not as convincing as it might at first sight appear to be. Coupled with the mention of Zwingle and of Anabaptism, it is merely a rejection of sectarianism such as the reformers themselves often made. In addition, Marot's profession 'Je suis de Dieu etc' would not have precluded his adherence to the doctrines of either Luther, Zwingli or the Anabaptists. Similarly, Marot goes on to state that nowhere in his works has he written anything which is in conflict with the 'loy divine', in other words, the law of God as revealed by the Bible. But the reformists themselves constantly used the expression 'loy divine' as opposed to the 'doctrines humaines', that is to say the dogmas of the Church, which they rejected when they had no foundation in the 'loy divine'. And they were insistent upon the wide divergences which they found between the teachings of the Church and the word of God in the Bible. Again, Marot's allusion to the mother of Christ contains nothing which would make a reformist baulk. There is no suggestion that Marot regarded Mary in any other way than that authorized by the Bible, no hint that he considered her as an intermediary between God and man, no suspicion of Mariolatry. Finally one may note in retrospect that the 'escriptz' (v. 16) on Christian subjects to which the author refers for confirmation of his orthodoxy do not prove much, one

way or the other, since they comprise on the one hand translations
and on the other exercises in a fixed form genre often on a set
subject. This is certainly the case for his first *chant-royal*, *De la
Conception nostre Dame* which was composed as an entry for the
Puy de la Conception de Rouen in 1521.[11] And while Marot's
Ballade de Caresme (XII) which may be another of the works
alluded to would seem to indicate a departure from the purely
formalistic conception of the Lenten observances in favour of a
more fundamentalist one,[12] it is by no means an outright rejection of the traditional abstinence.

It is apparent, even if one only considers the two published
versions of Marot's reply, that its terms were dictated by the
circumstances of the moment as much as by the author's personal
convictions. The definitive version is neither unequivocal in its
condemnation of Luther, nor positive in its profession of orthodoxy. The poet maintains a prudent ambiguity.

The second of Marot's answers to the charge of Lutheranism is
found in *L'Enfer*. It is quite different from the previous one,
except in one respect—it contains no condemnation of Luther or
of his doctrine. The whole tenor of Marot's remarks is one of
derision. There is no attempt on his part at a serious reply:

> Et pour monstrer qu'à grand tort on me triste:
> Clement n'est poinct le nom de Lutheriste;
> Ains est le nom (à bien l'interpreter)
> Du plus contraire ennemy de Luther;
> C'est le sainct nom du Pape, qui accolle
> Les chiens d'Enfer (s'il luy plaist) d'une estolle;
> Le crains tu poinct? C'est celluy qui afferme
> Qu'il ouvre Enfer quand il veult & le ferme;
> Celluy qui peult en feu chauld martyrer
> Cent mille esprits, ou les en retirer.
>
> (*O.S.*, *Enfer*, vv. 349–58)

Apart from the obviously facetious argument that the poet shares
the same first name as the Pope, Luther's arch adversary, and the
burlesque detail of the Pope rounding up the 'chiens d'Enfer'
with his stole which Marot owes to a reminiscence from Villon's
Ballade en vieil langage françoys,[13] the rest of the passage is
highly satirical, at the expense of both the Pope and the Sorbonne.[14] While it is true that this poem circulated widely in

manuscript and that Marot admitted reading it to the king (one must presume at a moment when the latter was not much preoccupied with the claims of current orthodoxies) it is not surprising that it was never published with his consent during his lifetime.

From exile in the summer of 1535 Marot addressed his third reply to accusations against him to the king. Marot starts from the position he had already previously adopted in the epistle to *Monsieur Bouchard* (IX):

> De Lutheriste ilz m'ont donné le nom:
> Qu'à droict ce soit, je leur respondz que non.
> Luther pour moy des cieulx n'est descendu,
> Luther en croix n'a poinct esté pendu
> Pour mes pechés, &, tout bien advisé,
> Au nom de luy ne suys point baptizé:
> Baptizé suys au nom qui tant bien sonne
> Qu'au son de luy le Pere eternel donne
> Ce que l'on quiert: le seul nom soubz les cieulx
> En & par qui ce monde vicieux
> Peult estre sauf; le nom tant fort puissant
> Qu'il a rendu tout genoil fleschissant,
> Soit infernal, soit celeste ou humain;
> Le nom par qui du seigneur Dieu la main
> M'a preservé de ces grandz loups rabis
> Qui m'espioient dessoubz peaulx de brebis.
>
> (*Ep.*, XXXVI, vv. 87–102)

The argumentation of this passage is manifestly casuistical. Marot may well reject the name of Lutheran, may well deny adherence to a sect, but what follows does not in any way constitute a repudiation of Lutheran doctrines for the simple reason that no Lutheran had ever claimed that Luther had come down from heaven, that he had died on the cross to redeem the sins of men, that Christians were baptized in his name. No Lutheran, starting with Luther himself, equated the name of Luther with that of Christ as may well be imagined. Indirectly Marot's arguments are inspired by those which Saint Paul used to warn the Corinthians (I, 10–13) of the dangers of sectarianism. But this passage had attracted the attentions and critical commentaries of many reformists. Of these, it is to Luther and to Erasmus that

Marot is closest here, scarcely a recommendation for an exile under sentence of death for heresy. And Marot's enemies at home in France were not slow to expose the nature of his answer. Jean Leblond's comment on these lines is as follows:

> Je pense bien que fermement tu croys
> Que Luther n'a pour toy pendu en croy,
> Mais j'ay grant peur, le cas bien advisé,
> Qu'au nom de luy tu ne soys atizé,
> Sy ton esprit ne s'adonne & s'aplicque
> De se reduyre à la foy catholicque.[15]

The person writing under the pseudonym of 'le général Chambord' claimed that the reply was contradictory and that its author was in effect imitating Luther in making it, and defending his cause:

> Ta lectre dict que tu n'est lutheriste,
> Et que Luther n'est ton Crist ou Baptiste,
> Qu'il n'est du ciel en terre descendu
> Pour te saulver, ny en la croix pendu.
> Tu as dict vray, car c'est ton traditeur,
> Mais tu apers te estre contradicteur,
> Car tu l'ensuys & sa secte defendz
> Contre divins & souverains deffendz.[16]

As if this were not enough, Marot had gone on to complete his answer to the charges made against him with a ringing declaration of man's redemption in Christ alone, rejecting implicitly at this point, just as Luther and Erasmus did, justification by good works. Marot affirms that Christ's is

> le seul nom soubz les cieulx
> En & par qui ce monde vicieux
> Peult estre sauf.   (*Ep.*, XXXVI, vv. 95–97)

A feast of biblical imagery[17] brings the passage to a triumphant and evangelical conclusion. As a protestation of orthodoxy it could not, and did not, carry conviction. On the contrary, its boldness after the initial casuistry is in perfect conformity with the general tenor of the epistle of which it is part.[18] The boldness of its tone is particularly apparent when it is contrasted with a passage of similar import with which Marot ended another epistle to the king from Ferrara, in November of the same year, *Au Roy nouvellement sorty de maladie* (XXXVII):

> Je ne suis pas si laid comme ilz me font;
> Myré me suis au cler ruysseau profont
> De verité, et à ce qu'il me semble,
> A Turc ne Juif en rien je ne ressemble.
> Je suis chrestien, pour tel me veulz offrir,
> Voire plus prest à peine & mort souffrir
> Pour mon vray Dieu et pour mon Roy, j'en jure,
> Qu'eulx une simple et bien petite injure.
>
> (*Ep.*, XXXVII, vv. 53–60)

One of the problems encountered in assessing Marot's religious convictions is that he wrote so few poems—apart from translations which in themselves prove nothing of his own attitudes—which could be strictly classified as religious poetry.[19] Marot left no complete and systematic profession of faith covering all articles. Nor would his circumstances have allowed it. The literary historian must be content with such evidence as exists in the *Deploration de Florimont Robertet*, in the evangelical passages of the epistles from exile and in the second eclogue, the *Avant-naissance du troiziesme enffant de madame Renée, duchesse de Ferrare* which complements the latter.

Of these it is the speech of Death in the *Deploration de Florimont Robertet* which offers the most cogent and sustained expression of reformist doctrine in Marot's work. The opening lines of the monologue, reminiscent of Saint Paul and Erasmus,[20] proclaim unequivocally the position the poet is about to adopt. It is one of opposition to the teachings of the Catholic Church:

> Peuple seduict, endormy en tenebres
> Tant de longs jours par la doctrine d'homme.
>
> (vv. 285–6)

An attack on the futility of mourning for the dead and all that accompanies it leads the poet into his main theme which is an exposition of the dogma of justification by faith alone:

> Car grant tumbeau, grant dueil, grant luminaire
> Ne peult laver l'ame que peché mord.
> Le sang de Christ, si la foy te remord,
> Lave seul l'ame, ains que le corps devye.   (vv. 295–8)

In the light of this dogma mourning is not only futile, and hyper-critical, it is an offence against God, a relic of paganism:

> Parquoy bien folle est la coustume humaine
> Quant aucun meurt porter & faire dueil.
> Si tu croys bien que Dieu vers luy le maine,
> A quelle fin en gettes larmes d'oeil?
> Le veulx tu vif tirer hors du cercueil,
> Pour à son bien mettre empesche & deffence?
> Qui pour ce pleure est marry dont le vueil
> De Dieu est fait; juge si c'est offence.
>
> Laisse gemyr & brayre les payans
> Qui n'ont espoir d'eternelle demeure.
> Faulte de foy te donne les moyens
> D'ainsi pleurer quant fault que quelq'un meure.
>
> (vv. 405–16)

Throughout Death's monologue Marot insists upon the primacy of faith in man's salvation, a faith which is given to man by the grace of God, a faith which can in no way be earned or constrained although one may beseech it in prayer:

> Prie à Dieu seul que par grace te donne
> La vive foy dont sainct Pol tant escript.
> Ta vye apres du tout luy abandonne
> Qui en peché journellement aigrit. (vv. 325–8)

The soul, described in neo-Platonic terms as imprisoned within the body, can only be released from its prison by death and des-patched to heaven by faith:

> De tel prison j'ay la clef tressubtille;
> C'est le mien dard, à l'ame gracieux,
> Car il la tire hors de sa prison vile
> Pour avec foy la renvoyer es cieulx. (vv. 337–40)

It is for this reason that Death is in no wise to be feared but welcomed:

> Doncques par moy contristé ne seras,
> Ains par fiance et d'un joyeux couraige,
> Pours à Dieu seul obeyr, laisseras
> Tresors, amys, maisons et labourage;

Clair temps de loing est signe que l'orage
Fera de l'air tost separacion;
Ainsi tel foy au mourant personnage
Est signe grant de sa salvacion.   (vv. 381–8)

This idea is reiterated in the next two verses (vv. 389–404), the second of which uses as an illustration the story of Moses and the brass serpent which he was commanded to make and hang from a pole after the Israelites had been plagued by fiery serpents as they journeyed through the desert. All those who had faith in the Lord and looked upon the life-like replica of the reptile were cured. So it is, says Death in an adaptation of Christ's own words, of those who look with faith upon Christ's coming and his crucifixion for they shall enjoy eternal life:

Jadis celluy que Moyse l'on nomme
Ung grant serpent tout d'arain eslevoit,
Qui (pour le veoir) povoit guerir ung homme
Quant ung serpent naturel mors l'avoit.
Ainsi celluy qui par vive foy voit
La mort de Christ guerist de ma blesseure
Et vit ailleurs plus que icy ne vyvoit,
Que dis je plus? mais sans fin, je t'asseure. (vv. 397–404)

The implications of Marot's expression of the dogma of justification by faith are clear. There is insistence upon the fact that all have sinned, that sin is the natural state of man deprived of God's grace. Man is incapable of avoiding sin and good works confer no merit. They are vain:

Et pour autant que l'homme ne peult faire
Qu'il puisse vivre icy bas sans peché,
Jamais ne peult envers Dieu satisfaire;
Et plus luy doibt le plus tard depesché,
Dont, comme le Christ, en la croix attaché
Mourut pour toy, mourir pour luy desire!
Qui pour luy meurt est du tout relaché
D'ennuy, de peine, et peché qui est pire.   (vv. 349–56)

There is more in this passage though, and subsequent ones, than a conviction of the vanity of works. The last two lines in particular rule out completely the Church's teaching on Purgatory, for which in any case there was little biblical justification. The notion of a human soul purified by torments inflicted in this intermediate region is irreconcilable with the statement

> Qui pour luy meurt est du tout relasché
> D'ennuy, de peine, et peché qui est pire.

The same applies to the repeated promises of eternal life for those who have faith. These lines are clear and emphatic:

> J'entens pour Dieu souffrir dueil, maladye,
> Perte et meschef, tant viennent mal à point,
> Et mettre jus par foy, car c'est le point,
> Desirs mondains et lyesses charnelles.
> Ainsi mourant soubz ma darde qui point
> Tu en auras qui seront eternelles.   (vv. 375-80)

Thirdly, Marot's poem also admits the notion of predestination since man is saved by God even before man has knowledge of God:

> S'il t'a tiré d'eternel impropere,
> Durant le temps que ne le congnoissois,
> Que fera il s'en luy ton cueur espere?
> Doubter ne fault que mieulx traicté ne sois.
>
> (vv. 345-8)

The significance of the speech of Death in the *Deploration de Florimont Robertet* is unmistakable. On the one hand it is true that Marot would appear to have simply paraphrased and assimilated into his poem some of the most outstanding and well-known (then and now) passages from New Testament epistles. But the use he has made of these passages to proclaim the dogma of justification by faith is precisely that of the reformists who made this dogma the cornerstone of their theology and of their opposition to the Church's teaching. The Sorbonne, in the person of its chief syndic, Noel Béda, reacted predictably to reformist interpretations of St. Paul when it condemned them, with little concern for any nuances which might distinguish the thought of Luther, Lefèvre, and Erasmus on the subject, as a Lutheran heresy. Marot himself was aware of the boldness of the views he had put forward in the *Deploration* in its original version. This much is indicated by the subsequent modifications he introduced into his text after 1532 at points of capital importance. These modifications all concern the primacy of faith. Thus the lines

> Le sang de Christ, si la foy te remord,
> Lave seul l'ame, ains que le corps devye;   (vv. 297–8)

of the manuscript version and of the first published text of the poem read as follows in the *Adolescence Clementine*:[21]

> Le sang de Christ, quant la loy te remord
> Par foy te lave...

where they have neither the eloquence nor the clarity of the original. Similarly the important line

> Pour avec foy la renvoyer es cieulx   (v. 340)

is uninspiringly rewritten to read

> Pour (d'icy bas) la renvoyer aux cieulx

and the word *foy* is again totally expunged from the line

> Et mettre jus par foy, car c'est le point,   (v. 377)

which becomes

> Et mettre jus par gré, car c'est le point.

It is worth noting that there is no poetic justification for these modifications introduced by Marot, and that the sense and precision of the original lines is either completely lost or considerably reduced.

The poem of 1527 may be regarded as conclusive evidence that Marot's sympathies at this time were with those who advanced the new ideas in religion. It is rather more difficult however to apportion the extent to which the poet was influenced *directly* by the leading thinkers, if at all. The influence of Erasmus's satirical work *Encomium Moriae*, and of his colloquy *Funus* may be discernible in Marot's condemnation of funeral rites[22] while the neo-Platonism of Marot's description of the body as the prison of the soul may well be traced to Marguerite de Navarre and her circle although with this important reservation. The date of composition of her *Miroir de l'Ame Pécheresse* published in 1531 is unknown. Its importance as an influence in the genesis of Marot's *Deploration* of 1527 is impossible to estimate or even to affirm positively. Many critics have doubted that Marot was directly acquainted with Luther's works and so have discounted them as a source of this poem;[23] another has noted concordances between Marot's poem and certain biblical commentaries of Lefèvre d'Etaples.[24] One may feel however that this was inevitable, in view of their common biblical denominator, and not proof of direct influence.

The cogency of Marot's doctrinal exposition in the *Discours de la Mort* which he never quite equalled again in any of his subsequent excursions into religious poetry is explicable and has been explained far more feasibly than in terms of direct literary sources.[25] The *Discours de la Mort* resembles nothing so much as a sermon. This is true of its opening address to the

> Peuple seduict, endormy en tenebres
> Tant de longs jours par la doctrine d'homme

as it is true of the manner of its unfolding prompted ostensibly by an event in real life (the death of Robertet), accompanied by an attack on traditional and superficial observances and earthly values as opposed to spiritual ones, and finally illustrated by copious biblical texts, references and allusions. This resemblance to the form and manner of the sermon is no accident. It is known, for instance, that at the time of writing the *Deploration de Florimont Robertet* Marot was attending the sermons which a Jacobin preacher by the name of Mathieu Malingre was then delivering at Blois. Malingre was later to seek refuge for religious reasons in Neuchâtel from where he was subsequently to exchange poems with Marot in which he recalled the substance of his public sermons and the texts which he had chosen to serve as his lesson. It is of some importance to quote the relevant lines which are dated 2 December 1542:

> Veu qu'il y a desja quinze ans passez
> Que ces abus tu congnoissois assez,
> Et savois bien tout peché et tout vice
> Estre aboly par le seul sacrifice
> Que Jesus-Christ fit pour nous en sa croix,
> Comme tu m'as ouy prescher à Bloys
> En exposant l'epistre des Hebrieux
> Et des Romains et plusieurs autres lieux.[26]

In fact, the substance of the *Discours de la Mort* in the *Deploration* accords closely in many particulars with the substance of Malingre's sermons as described by him in the lines above. Marot's *Discours* draws largely on Romans, in particular on those chapters of Paul's epistle in which he preaches justification by faith, describes the role of God's grace and speaks of the remission of sins by Christ's sacrifice. These chapters and the corresponding passages in Marot are III. 22–27 (vv. 349–56 and *passim*); IV. 16, as also Ephesians II. 8 (vv. 325–6); V. 10 (vv. 347–8); VIII. 4–8 (vv. 331–2) and 14–17 as also Galatians IV. 5–7 and James II. 5 (vv. 341–4). These references also cover a fair number of the 'autres lieux' of which Malingre's poem speaks. A further search in the *Deploration* also reveals the following: Colossians II. 8 (v. 286); St. Mark X. 29 (vv. 383–4); St. John III. 13–15 in conjunction with Numbers XXI. 8–9 (vv. 397–404); the first epistle of John I. 7 (vv. 297–8). This list is not exhaustive but contains the most important concordances.

The evidence which suggests that Marot composed the *Deploration* while he was momentarily under the influence of Malingre's preaching is very impressive.[27] And since Malingre fled the country in 1529 it would also explain why, although Marot's convictions are ardently expressed in later works, he never reproduced again the doctrinal cogency he displayed in the *Deploration de Florimont Robertet*.

A brief return to this vein however occurs in the *Epistre au Roy du temps de son exil à Ferrare* when Marot again advances an argument which appears in retrospect to be of the very essence of Protestantism. This argument is the sequel to the lines quoted earlier in which Marot demanded a special intellectual freedom for the poet, and asserted his ability to choose between good and evil. Then, almost as an afterthought,

> Sçavoir le mal est souvent proffitable,
> Mais en user est tousjours evitable.
> Et d'aultre part, que me nuyst de tout lire?
>
> (vv. 143–5)

Marot backs his humanistic assertion with religious arguments. The intelligence which allows him this facility is God-given. He moves from this to advance the notion of the primacy of the Bible in matters of faith and dogma, and the right of the individual conscience to interpret it:

> Le grand donneur m'a donné sens d'eslire
> En ces livretz tout cela qui accorde
> Aux sainctz escriptz de grace & de concorde,
> Et de jecter tout cela qui differe
> Du sacré sens, quand pres on le confere.
> Car l'escripture est la touche où l'on treuve
> Le plus hault or. Et qui veult faire espreuve
> D'or quel qu'il sòit, il le convient toucher
> A ceste pierre, & bien pres l'approcher
> De l'or exquis, qui tant se faict paroistre
> Que, bas ou hault, tout aultre faict congnoistre.
>
> (vv. 146–56)

This is quite different from the situation which prevailed at that time in the Catholic Church which insisted that it alone had the necessary authority to interpret the Bible, and even forbade the reading of the Bible by its laymen. Marot's claims in this passage are in line with those of the reformists of his day, those of Luther, Erasmus, Lefèvre, but closest to the last two. They are however this much more audacious, that Marot himself was a complete layman, he was neither theologian nor preacher, nor had he the intellectual or theological formation which distinguished the leading figures and prime movers of the Reformation. In this respect he goes further than they in advocating the right of an individual to determine his faith in the light of his God-given intelligence and with the Bible as his touchstone.[28]

In other respects the works composed in exile are distinguished by their fervour and their exaltation rather than their cogency in exposition. To describe them critics no longer speak of the 'précision doctrinale' which they discerned in the *Deploration de Florimont Robertet*. They fall back instead upon vaguer terms such as 'saveur évangélique'.

Marot's fervour in these poems is heightened by the drama of his own persecution and by the spectacle of that endured by others. To this, however, few remained insensible.[29] Moreover,

the correspondences which existed between the fate of his contemporaries martyred in a just cause and that of the faithful as
described in many passages of the Bible, provided a further
stimulus to the poet's exaltation.[30] It is scarcely surprising that
the terms and the tone in which Marot describes the turmoil he
has passed through should have an evangelical character. In the
epistle traditionally addressed to *Deux Soeurs Savoisiennes* (XXXV)
Marot has this to say:

> Les ungs souvant par poyne on persecute,
> D'aultres, helas! par mort on essecute,
> Les ungtz souvant chassés de leur pays,
> Les autres sont ahorrés et hays
> De leurs parens. Pour tout cella, mes dames,
> Flechir ne fault: plustout doit en vos ames
> Croistre la foy, voire à chescun qui l'a,
> Considerant que Jesus pour cella
> Nous aconplit ses parolles escriptes;
> Car tous ses maulx et poynes que j'é dictes
> Promist aux siens par son non precieulx;
> Mais leur loyer certes est grant es cieulx,
> Et pour apprandre aux autres à souffrir,
> Droit à la croix premier se vint offrir.
>
> (*Ep.*, XXXV, vv. 7–20)

For this reason Marot is able to proclaim the triumph of Christ and
the utter futility of all acts of persecution directed against his
followers:

> Certes, mes seurs, ce torment viollent
> Est de Jesus ce triumphe exellent;
> Vous pouvés bien escripre, dire ou chanter,
> Vous pouvés bien hardyment vous vanter
> Qu'avant mourir vous avés veu sur terre
> Crist triumpher, puys qu'on luy fait la guerre.
>
> (ibid., vv. 37–42)

The same theme is repeated in the *Avant-naissance*:

> Viens veoir de Crist le regne commencé,
> Et son honneur par tourmens avancé!
>
> (*O.L.*, *Eglogue* II, vv. 59–60)

Another theme common to both, and expressed in almost identical terms, is the firm belief in eternal life which enables earthly torments to be more easily and gladly borne by the faithful:

> Mais la cher seulle endure ceste poyne,
> Car l'ame franche est de foy toute pleine,
> Et de liesse en se [*sic*] corps tant ravye
> Par ferme espoir de la segonde vie.
>
> (*Ep.*, XXXV, vv. 27–30)

The tone of the corresponding passage of the *Avant-naissance* is more emphatic, and as befits the circumstances, joyful:

> Le vray moyen qui tout ennuy efface
> Et fait que au monde angoisse on ne craint point,
> Ne la mort mesme, alors qu'elle nous point;
> Le vray moien plain de joie feconde
> C'est ferme espoir de la vie seconde,
> Par Jhesus Crist, vaincqueur et tryumphant
> De ceste mort!   (*O.L.*, *Eglogue* II, vv. 44–50)

It seems, so far, that Marot has simply given expression, albeit with force and emotion, to the general but intensely held convictions of the adherents to the new ideas. At the conclusion of the epistle to the *Deux Sœurs Savoisiennes* (XXXV) and especially in the epistle to the king from Ferrara (XXXVI) however, he strikes a much more personal note when he examines his own attitudes and conduct when confronted by actual or possible persecution. Thus in the former he confesses his failure to bear fully the crosses offered to him by God (vv. 49–53) and in the latter he evinces a desire for martyrdom not once, but twice. In fact, there is a distinction to be made between the two passages in question. In the first the poet envisages martyrdom in the cause of all the oppressed who laboured under the tyranny of the Sorbonne. From this evil may his death deliver them:

> Que pleust à l'Eternel,
> Pour le grand bien du peuple desolé,
> Que leur desir de mon sang fust saoulé...
> O quatre foys & cinq foys bien heureuse
> La mort, tant soit cruelle & rigoreuse,
> Qui feroyt seulle ung million de vies
> Soubz telz abus n'estre plus asservyes!
>
> (*Ep.*, XXXVI, vv. 66–68, 71–74)

In the second passage, of even greater intensity and almost visionary exaltation the poet hopes that he may be chosen to serve the glory of God in his lifetime, and also, if this be God's will, by his death. The last lines of the prayer envisage a martyr's end at the stake:

> O seigneur dieu, permettez moy de croire
> Que reservé m'avez à vostre gloire.
> Serpentz tortuz & monstres contrefaictz,
> Certes, sont bien à vostre gloire faictz.
> Puis que n'avez voulu doncq' condescendre
> Que ma chair ville ayt esté mise en cendre,
> Faictes au moins, tant que seray vivant,
> Qu'à vostre honneur soit ma plume escripvant;
> Et si ce corps avez predestiné
> A estre ung jour par flamme terminé,
> Que ce ne soit au moins pour cause folle,
> Ainçoys pour vous & pour vostre parolle;
> Et vous supply, pere, que le tourment
> Ne luy soit pas donné si vehement
> Que l'ame vienne à mettre en oubliance
> Vous, en qui seul gist toute sa fiance;
> Si que je puysse, avant que d'assoupir,
> Vous invocquer jusque au dernier souspir.
>
> (*Ep.*, XXXVI, vv. 103–20)

The poet is lost in his own exalted contemplation and reminds himself with difficulty of the object and destination of his letter in the next two lines.

Marot did not regain this intensity, outside of the realm of polemic, in the remaining religious poetry from exile. One notes a certain exaltation, although on a lower and possibly rhetorical and self-conscious level, in the evangelical language with which Marot presented the story of his enforced departure from Ferrara. This is an epistle written almost certainly after the event, and extant only in the manuscript collection offered to the orthodox Montmorency.[31] This almost dual dedication explains Marot's need to speak with two voices, but his dexterity in so doing throws doubt on the value of the poem as evidence of his own true convictions. Is the evangelical tone, such as it is, anything more than a style appropriate to the duchess Marot purports to address? This poem highlights the problems facing those who attempt to interpret the intimate convictions of a writer of this period through his works, particularly when they are written within the aesthetic conventions of court poetry. To the duchess then, Marot speaks of God's hand in his departure: to Montmorency he offers an account of Italian hostility to the French:

> L'esprit de Dieu me conseille et enhorte
> Que hors d'icy plustost que tard je sorte.
> Ne voys tu pas comment Dieu eternel
> Par ung courroux de zelle paternel
> M'en veult chasser? Penses tu que l'oultraige
> Que Ferraroys mal nobles de couraige
> M'ont fait de nuyct, armez couardement,
> Ne soit à moy ung admonestement
> Du seigneur Dieu pour desloger d'icy?
> Certes, encor quant ne seroit ainsy,
> Mon cueur qui ayme estre franc & delivre
> Ne pourroit parmy telles gens vivre.
>
> (*Ep.*, XLII, vv. 9–20)

This passage, and in particular the last three lines, is consummate in its ambiguity. But Marot does not stop here. He continues to weave together the two threads of his story:

> Si n'ay je nerf qui à se venger tende,
> Mais je veulx bien que la Ferrare entende
> Que ses manans à leur grant vitupere
> Se sont ruez dessus l'enfant d'un pere
> Qui des meschans fait vengeance condigne
> Jusqu'à la tierce et la quarte origine.
> Donques à luy j'en laisse le venger,
> Et seullement loing d'eulx me veulx renger.
> Parquoy, Princesse, ouvre moy de ta grace
> De mon congé le chemin et la trace,
> Affin que voyse en ville ou en pays
> Où les Françoys ne sont ainsy hays...
>
> (ibid., vv. 21–32)

God will take vengeance upon his enemies while Marot himself will take practical steps to secure his departure from Ferrara.

On his return from exile, and after the composition of this poem,[32] the evangelical tone and language of these earlier works is conspicuously absent from Marot's poetry. One can only guess at the reasons for this. But he was doubtless counselled by the prudence in religious matters which he jocularly confessed to having learnt from the Lombards.[33] And also by a more just appreciation of the climate of opinion in France of which he was largely unaware during his exile. At any rate, he diverted his attentions to his Psalm translations, temporarily sanctioned by the king.

Two further observations remain to be made. Marot's religious poetry from exile reveals a commitment to the new ideas which, more than ever before, is concerned not so much with their positive aspects as with the threat which they posed to the established forces of Catholicism. Marot's emotional and moral revulsion for the Catholic Church, constantly apparent in his satire, led him to champion the new ideas against the old and against the agents of the old. The triumph of the former he presented as the defeat of the latter. Thus, in the epistle to the *Deux Sœurs Savoisiennes* (XXXV), it is the 'bruleurs' (v. 31) and those who are 'Jaloux des loix dont il[s] sont inventeurs' (v. 46) who are destined to encounter futility and despair, not those whom they persecute. In the *Avant-naissance*, the obscurantism of the 'caphards' is seen to be overwhelmed by the revelations of the new teaching, and the downfall of the Papacy is pronounced imminent. Such lines as this are clearly Protestant:

> Viens escouter verité revellée,
> Qui tant de jours nous a esté cellée!
> Viens escouter, pour ames resjoir,
> Ce que caphards veullent garder d'oyr!
> Viens veoir, viens voir la beste sans raison,
> Grand ennemy de ta noble maison!
> Viens tost la veoir à tout sa triple creste,
> Non cheute encor, mais de tomber bien preste!
> Viens veoir de Crist le regne commencé...
>
> (*O.L.*, *Eglogue* II, vv. 51–59)

In a later poem to Renée de Ferrare, the epistle from Venice (XLIII) the same sentiments are given their most powerful expression anywhere in Marot's work. The conversion of a large part of the 'monde caphardant' is welcomed as a reality, the fate of the remainder deplored:

De ceste erreur tant creue et foisonnée
La ch[r]estienté est toute empoisonnée.
Non toute, non, le Seigneur, regardant
D'oeil de pitié ce monde caphardant,
S'est faict congnoistre à une grand partie,
Qui à luy seul est ores convertie.
O Seigneur Dieu, faictz que le demourant
Ne voyse pas les pierres adorant.
C'est ung abbus d'ydollastres sorty,
Entre ch[r]estiens plusieurs foys amorty,
Et remys sus tousjours pour l'avarice
De la paillarde et grande meretrice,
Avec qui on[t] faict fornicacion
Les roys de terre, et dont la potion
Du vin public de son calice immonde[34]
A si longtemps envyré tout le monde.

(*Ep.*, XLIII, vv. 51–66)

The same epistle reveals not only the polemical emphasis of
Marot's support for the new ideas but also the importance he
attached to the humanitarianism they allowed and even demanded
of those who espoused them. Again the contrast between the old
idolatry and the new concern for the living is tellingly made:

Temples marbrins y font et y adorent
Images peinctz qu'à grandz despens ilz dorent;
Et à leurs piedz, helas, sont gemissans
Les pouvres nudz, palles et languissans.
Ce sont, ce sont telles ymaiges vives
Qui de ces grans despenses excessives
Estre debvoient aournées et parées,
Et de nos yeulx les autres separées.
Car l'Eternel les vives recommande,
Et de fuir les mortes nous commande.

(ibid., vv. 39–48)

Something in the nature of a postscript to the evolution of
Marot's sympathies, and a most interesting one, is provided by the
two epistles which accompanied his Psalm translations.[35]

The first epistle, to the king, is notable for two reasons. It combines an insistence upon the neo-Platonic theory of poetic
inspiration with the divine inspiration of David's Psalms. Marot

envisages the poet, seized by the poetic *furor*, as the passive interpreter of the heavenly intelligence:

> O doncques roy, prens l'oeuvre de David,
> Oeuvre plustost de Dieu qui le ravit,
> D'autant que Dieu son Apollo estoit,
> Qui luy en train et sa Harpe mettoit.
> Le sainct esprit estoit sa Caliope:
> Son Parnasus montaigne à double croppe
> Fut le sommet du hault ciel cristalin:
> Finablement, son ruisseau Cabalin
> De grace fut la fontaine profonde,
> Où à grans traictz il beut de la claire unde,
> Dont il devint Poete en ung moment,
> Le plus profond de soubz le firmament.
> Car le subject qui la plume en la main
> Prendre luy feit, est bien autre qu'humain.
> ....
> Icy oyt on l'esprit de Dieu, qui crye
> Dedans David, alors que David prye.[36]

The neo-Platonism inherent in these lines reminds us of the preoccupations of the circle of Marguerite de Navarre, and to the French translation of Plato's *Io* which was to be published in 1546.[37] The translator's preface to this work affords interesting comparisons with Marot's epistle. A short quotation will suffice to present them:

en l'exaltation de poesie peult estre valable (non pas esgallement) l'authorité de Platon, philosophe divin, lequel enquerant diligemment des choses humaines et divines, prouve par subtiles raisons en ce present dialogue intitulé Io, que poesie est ung don de Dieu...une fureur procedant de Dieu, qui est une inspiration divine...Et tout ce que les poetes excellentz, soient Grecz, Latins ou Françoys, ont faict, dict, et composé, il procede de la grace divine...Et véritablement, jouxte notre philosophie evangelique, nous croyons fidelement que nul bon oeuvre peult estre faict sans le Sainct Esprit, qui est la grace de Dieu.[38]

Secondly, towards the conclusion of his epistle, Marot pays generous tribute to the humanist scholars, and the Hebrew specialists particularly, for their part in facilitating the restitution of the sacred texts which made his own enterprise possible:

> Mais tout ainsi qu'avecques diligence,
> Sont esclarcis, par bons espritz rusez,
> Les escripteaulx, des vieulx fragmentz usez,
> Ainsi (ô roy) par les divins espritz
> Qui ont soubz toy Hebrieu langaige appris,
> Nous sont jectez les Pseaulmes en lumiere,
> Clairs, et au sens de la forme premiere.[39]

In spite of Calvin's concern to avail himself of Marot's translations for the Protestant liturgy, these lines clearly show that the poet himself envisaged his translation as a contribution to the broad humanist task of vulgarization. There are no echoes here of the Calvinistic design[40] for a French Psalter.

The second epistle places Marot's Psalm translations in a context even further removed from that of Calvinism. In fact, Marot would appear to place himself within the category of those secular practitioners of the Gospel whom the reformer so emphatically condemned:

Il y a puis apres une seconde secte...Ce sont les prothonotaires delicatz, qui sont bien contens d'avoir l'Evangile, et d'en deviser joyeusement et par esbat avec les Dames, moyennant que cela ne les empesche point de vivre à leur plaisir.[41]

Marot proposes in his epistle *Aux Dames de France* that these ladies who formerly sang of earthly and physical love should broadcast through their singing of his Psalms the message of divine love, at the same time attaining to a spiritual satisfaction for themselves:

> L'amour que je veulx que chantez
> Ne rendra vos cueurs tormentez
> Ainsi que l'autre; mais sans doute
> Il vous remplira l'ame toute
> De ce plaisir solatieux
> Que sentent les anges des cieulx:
> Car son esprit vous fera grace
> De venir prendre en vos cueurs place,
> Et les convertir et muer
> Faisant voz levres remuer,
> Et vos doigtz sur les espinettes,
> Pour dire sainctes chansonnettes.[42]

Again the poet returns to the Platonic theory of poetic transmission and the antithesis between the torments of earthly love and the joyful plenitude bestowed by the divine. He is closer to Marguerite de Navarre and her circle than to Calvin. For the latter, love of God was inseparable from the fear of God. Of this influence there is no trace in Marot's Geneva epistle.

Far from having succumbed to the spiritual domination of Calvin and his theology Marot, at the close of his life, looks back perhaps with nostalgia to the influences which formed him before his first exile.[43]

There is no easy formula which allows one to sum up Marot's personal convictions in a few words although there is abundant evidence of his support for and adherence to the new ideas. The facts of his life, and notably his abjuration in 1536, together with his flight from Calvin's Geneva in 1543 show, however, that this support was in no way tinged with fanaticism. This much is confirmed by his own condemnation, in his epistle to the king from Ferrara (XXXVI) of 'certains folz' who were responsible for the disastrous *affaire des Placards* in 1534.[44] And after his return from exile he was able at last to maintain a discreet prudence in the face of adverse shifts in the climate of religious opinion.

The strength and nature of Marot's sympathies varied also with the personal influences he encountered. That of Marguerite de Navarre may be the most constant and long-standing, but is also the most difficult to assess directly or in any precise detail. Our ignorance of the dates of composition of many of her works and the most relevant of those of Marot makes any inference drawn from resemblances between them interesting rather than conclusive.[45] The case of Marot's passing acquaintance with Malingre however is quite conclusive and explains the most doctrinal of all Marot's works, the *Deploration de Florimont de Robertet*. Similarly, the religious poetry from exile may owe much of its tenor and conviction to influences within the Lutheran enclave at Ferrara and doubtless particularly to the personality of Renée herself[46] whose sympathies were broadcast with an audacity denied, or alien to Marguerite de Navarre in France.

The relevance of particular stresses to Marot's religious state is not to be lightly dismissed either. The unusual degree of exaltation developed by Marot in the poems recalling his flight into exile and the atrocities perpetrated against those who remained, is quite in keeping with the state of mind of a man who had recently escaped death for his known opposition to the 'humaines doctrines'.[47]

Marot's interest in the new ideas was rarely, and then only briefly, doctrinal, unless it was to argue the rejection of opposing Catholic doctrine as he did for instance in such a poem as the *Second Chant de l'Amour fugitif*.[48] But it is worth noting briefly in this context that Marot never explicitly rejected the Mass, although condemning its exploitation by the 'avare pretrise' and including it with certain other rites accompanying the burial of the dead in the description 'telles solennitez'. He did not express any view on the doctrine of transubstantiation. His satire of many aspects of Catholicism was, however, constant and motivated at least as much by the moral decrepitude of the faith and its institutions as by its dubious theology, each of which buttressed the other and was in turn defended by authoritarianism, intolerance and repression. In this context evangelism was for Marot, and for many others, merely an extension of the secular Renaissance, promoting and safeguarding the same values, offering an advance towards enlightenment, a humanization and, in the best sense of the word, a vulgarization of the faith and the texts upon which it reposed. It was for this reason that he celebrated with such eloquence the end of the abusive monopoly and control asserted by the Church over the sacred texts, for this reason that he welcomed the possibility of an individualistic or personal faith and acknowledged only the authority of God, directly accessible to the individual through prayer

Vous, en qui seul gist toute sa fiance.

Marot's beliefs, like those of Erasmus, conceded to man the intelligence and dignity which repressive Catholicism everywhere denied him. They allowed for love rather than fear. It is in the context of the humanism of the early 1530s, open to so many currents of thought, hostile only to rigid dogmatism,[49] that they may best be understood.

VIII

CONCLUSION: MAROT AND THE *PLÉIADE*[1]

However great or understandable their reluctance to admit it, the poets of the *Pléiade* received a considerable legacy from Marot. His innovations went far to realize the poetic 'reforms' which Ronsard was later to claim as his own. Far from being the first to break with the traditions of the *Rhétoriqueurs* and with everything that was medieval in the poetry of their predecessors, the *Pléiade* poets were themselves denied this role by one of these same predecessors.

They recommended the cultivation in French poetry of the genres of Classical Antiquity and of Italy when Marot had already written the first French elegies, had introduced the epithalamium, the eclogue and the sonnet, had established the epigram and composed in his *chansons* and *cantiques* poems which differed only in name from those which Ronsard was later to call *Odes*.

They demanded the imitation of Classical and Italian models as a step towards the rehabilitation of French poetry. Although Marot had no recourse to Pindar (whom Ronsard himself later abandoned), Horace or Juvenal, he learned to give both depth and universality to his treatment of personal and official poetry by his adaptations of the developments, images, symbols, periphrases of Greek and Latin models. His was the first direct French imitation of Theocritus and of Ovid's poetry of exile; his the first extensive imitation of Catullus and Martial. And long before the *Pléiade*'s Petrarchist and Anacreontic phases, Marot's poetry introduced into French the conceits of the Italian love poets and, indirectly, those of the *Greek Anthology*.

It is in the domain of versification that the *Pléiade* was most indebted to Marot as an innovator. Partly from his familiarity with the vitality and diversity of verse forms in the popular tradition Marot was led to experiment with verse structures in the *chansons* of his youth, and to a lesser extent in the *cantiques* of his maturity. The result was to confer upon French poetry a rich variety of strophic structures which Marot himself put to use in his Psalm translations. It is ironic that Ronsard's most strident protestations of independence from the earlier native tradition should have concerned his Pindaric odes, the metrical and strophic arrangement of every one of which was taken from Marot's translations of the Hebrew Psalms![2]

It is of course far more difficult to prove that the poets of the *Pléiade* owed anything to Marot in the treatment of themes or topics which they commonly pursued. But it is not unreasonable to suggest that the personal vein cultivated by Marot in *Epîtres* and *Epigrammes* finds an echo in some of Ronsard's *Elégies*, and that the mixture of satire and elegy in the epistles from exile and the *coqs-à-l'âne* of the same period is an admirable foretaste of Du Bellay's *Regrets*, not to mention the similarities of detail which we have already indicated elsewhere. It is in their nature poetry that the poets of the *Pléiade* are generally held to be superior to Marot. In the extent to which they turned to nature and the felicity with which they most often did so, this is probably true. But it should not be forgotten that Marot, on fewer occasions admittedly, had already associated nature with the expression of nostalgia for youth, for peace and solitude, for his native province; with the expression of the haunting fear of old age, with the depiction of human beauty; and that he, too, on such occasions, had been most happily inspired. In one respect, Marot's poetry demonstrates an awareness of the possibilities attendant upon natural imagery which is completely, or almost completely, absent from the poetry of Ronsard and Du Bellay. That is its usefulness in satirical comparisons, a usefulness fully exploited later on by D'Aubigné.

As far as satire generally is concerned, the *Pléiade* poets have on the whole little in common with Marot, preferring instead the somewhat suave style of the Classical satirists. But Marot's art of suggesting moral defects through the selection and description of physical gestures is one which Du Bellay remembered and relied heavily upon in the *Regrets*.

It has often been asserted by critics that Marot lacked the dignified conception of the poet and of his mission which the

Pléiade, and Ronsard in particular, constantly proclaimed. Evidence for this is usually drawn from the epistle to the king (XII) in which Marot represented the advice of his dying father to the son who aspired to poetic fame. As such, the poem is a conscious archaism. The views on poetry which are there expressed are necessarily those of the generation of *Rhétoriqueurs* to which his father belonged, and for whom poetry was most often equated with propaganda. It would be impossible to limit Marot's conception of poetry to this. In common with certain poets of the fourteenth and fifteenth centuries, not excluding some of the more cultured *Rhétoriqueurs*, Marot, like the *Pléiade*, was confident of the poet's power to bestow immortality. Like the *Pléiade* too, he claimed for poetry consolatory and therapeutic powers. Furthermore, towards the end of his career, influenced not merely by Ovid but also by neo-Platonism, Marot, like the *Pléiade* subscribed to the theory of the poet divinely inspired. He felt, and expressed, a legitimate pride in his work. Well might he, not only as a poet but also as a man of the Renaissance concerned to assert, often in the most moving terms, man's right to dignity and hope even when these were all but extinguished by intolerance and repression, boast:[3]

> Et tant qu'ouy & nenny se dira
> Par l'univers, le monde me lira.

NOTES

PREFACE

1. The most recent edition of P. Jourda's *Marot, l'homme et l'œuvre*, Paris, 1967, is brought up to date in its bibliography but the text of the work remains substantially unchanged.

I. THE CONTEXT OF MAROT'S POETRY

THE CRITICAL PERSPECTIVE

1. Charles d'Héricault, *Œuvres de Clément Marot, annotées, revues et précédées de la vie de Clément Marot*, Paris, Garnier, 1867.
D'Héricault's plea and Arnold's reply appear in Arnold's essay on 'The Study of Poetry' in *Essays in Criticism, Second Series*, London, Macmillan, 1960, pp. 5–7.
2. Arnold, op. cit., *Gray*, p. 57.

THE MAN: 1496?–1544

3. See *Epîtres* XII, *passim*, XL, vv. 18–20; *Œuvres Satiriques, L'Enfer*, v. 402; *Œuvres Lyriques, Eglogue* III, v. 49 ff.
4. See *Œuvres Satiriques*, I, notes.
5. See *Epîtres, Notice Biographique*, p. 6.
6. See below, ch. IV, p. 179.
7. Mayer, *La Religion de Marot*, p. 7, 'Marot...ne bénéficia pas d'une instruction poussée!'
8. Rabelais, *Gargantua*, XIV–XV.
9. The *coq-à-l'âne* was written in the summer or autumn of the year 1535 (cf. *Œuvres Satiriques*, p. 120) and the epistle in November (cf. *Epîtres*, p. 208).
10. See Guy, *Clément Marot et son école*, para. 132.
11. Cf. Guy, ibid., n. 132.
12. Guy, ibid. Du Bellay, in the *Deffence et Illustration* writes of: 'quelques-uns des nostres, qui sans doctrine, à tout le moins non autre que mediocre, ont acquis grand bruyt en nostre vulgaire...' *éd.* Chamard, p. 105. Pasquier's verdict in the *Recherches de la France*, VII. 5, is that Marot was not 'accompagné de bonnes lettres'.
13. Guy, ibid., para 132.
14. Jonson, *To the Memory of Shakespeare*. Cf. T. W. Baldwin, *William Shakespere's Small Latine & Lesse Greeke*, University of Illinois, 1944.
15. For Shakespeare's use of Ovid's *Metamorphoses* see Baldwin, op. cit., vol. II, p. 427; for Marot's latinity see P. Villey, *Marot et Rabelais*, op. cit., p. 17.
16. See *Epîtres, Notice Biographique*, p. 6 n. 1.
17. Cf. Mayer, *Bibliographie*, vol. II, no. 1 and *Œuvres Lyriques*, p. 87.
18. See *Œuvres Diverses, Ballade* IV, *De soy mesme du temps qu'il apprenoit à escrire au Palais à Paris*, v. 9:

> Adieu vous dy, mon Maistre Jehan Grisson!

Nothing at all is known of Jehan Grisson.

19. See *Epîtres*, p. 140 n. 1.

20. Excepting, of course, the intermittent writing of poetry, which does not seem, at this moment, to have been a gainful employment. See the *Petite Epistre au Roy*, I, vv. 21–26.

21. See *Œuvres Lyriques*, *Eglogue* III, p. 346 n. 1. The evidence is contained in two poems of Jean Marot addressed to *Mgr d'Angolesme par avant son advenement à la couronne de France, c'est assavoir l'an mil cinq cens et quatorze à Paris*.

22. *Le Jugement de Minos*, a verse transcription of a French prose translation by Jean Miélot of the twelfth of Lucian's *Mortuorum Dialogi*. It is alleged by Guy, op. cit., para. 139 and by Villey, op. cit., p. 5, that the poem was composed before François's accession, in 1514.

23. An event described in the *Epistre du despourveu à ma Dame la Duchesse d'Alençon & de Berry, soeur unique du roy*, III, vv. 107–9. The epistle also contains Marot's formal request to Marguerite, vv. 171–4.

24. See *Epîtres*, *Notice Biographique*, p. 6.

25. See below, pp. 11, 14, 19, 20, 27, 31, 33, 50 and ch. VII, p. 271.

26. *Epîtres*, *Appendice* I, pp. 280–2.

27. The exception being an entry in the accounts of the household of Marguerite d'Angoulême for the year 1524. Here Marot is listed as 'pensionnaire' with a salary of 85 *livres*. See *Epîtres*, *Notice Biographique*, p. 7 n. 3.

28. In *Œuvres Lyriques*, LII, *Elégie* I, *La premiere Elegie en forme d'Epistre*. Title variant *e*.

29. See Villey, op. cit., p. 16 and Mayer, *Epîtres*, *Notice Biographique*, p. 7; *Œuvres Lyriques*, *Introduction*, p. 20 and p. 211 n. 1.

30. This last in *Œuvres Diverses*, LXXX, *Ballade* XIV.

31. The identity of 'Monsieur Bouchard, Docteur en Theologie' and his role in this affair is discussed in *Epîtres*, p. 124 n. 1 and in Mayer's article, *Clément Marot et le Docteur Bouchart*, in BHR, 1959, pp. 98–102. Bouchard was probably not a doctor of the Sorbonne at all, since such a person had no powers to issue warrants for the arrest of others etc. It seems that Marot thought of Jean Bouchard, the legal adviser to the Sorbonne, as a member of the institution he was merely acting for in a legal capacity.

32. *Œuvres Satiriques*, *L'Enfer*, vv. 344–58. See below, ch. VII, p. 252.

33. *Œuvres Diverses*, LXIII. On the denunciation and the poems relating to it see Mayer, *Marot et 'Celle qui fut s'Amye'*, in BHR, 1966, pp. 369–76.

34. See, apart from *La Religion de Marot*, p. 11 ff., *Œuvres Diverses*, p. 163 n. 1, and the article *Marot et 'Celle qui fut s'Amye'*, p. 371 n. 2.

35. Quoted by Mayer, *La Religion de Marot*, p. 11 n. 2.

36. See *La Religion de Marot*, pp. 15–19.

37. The *Parlement* of Paris was the highest judicial authority in France, the supreme court. It had also certain administrative functions.

38. Quoted by Mayer, *La Religion de Marot*, p. 15.

39. 'Jeusner ainsi que l'on nous fait faire, ne manger chair le vendredy, vivre en continence, sont d'elles-mêmes de très belles choses. Mais qui nous les commande sur peine d'éternelle damnation (d'autre commandement ne veux-je parler) nous oste la liberté que J.C nous a donnée et nous met en intolérante servitude.' Text quoted by Mayer, op. cit., p. 19.

On Meigret see also Hauser, *Etudes sur la réforme française*, Paris, 1909, pp. 71 ff.

40. Texts in Mayer, op. cit., *Appendice* 1, nos. 1 and 2, p. 139.

41. Mayer, ibid., p. 142, no. 6. Cf. also nos. 3, 4, 5.

42. Mayer, ibid., pp. 145–8, no. 10.

43. The interpretation of 'il a mangé le lard' proposed by M. A. Screech in BHR, 1964, pp. 363–4, can only be sustained in defiance of the particular historical and religious context. It will be noted that all of the examples of the expression which Screech alleges in support of his interpretation are from quite different contexts. Screech has recently returned to this question in *L'Evangélisme de Marot* but without advancing the argument at all.

44. See S. G. Nichols, *Marot, Villon and the Roman de la Rose*, in SP., LXIII, 2, 1966, pp. 135–43, and M. Pelan, *The Influence of Villon on Clément Marot*, in *Mélanges Rita Lejeune*, Gembloux, 1969, II, pp. 1469–79.

45. Mayer, *Marot et 'Celle qui fut s'Amye'*, art. cit., pp. 369–76.

46. Mayer, ibid., and *Œuvres Diverses*, p. 132 n. 1. See also *La Religion de Marot*, p. 13.

47. The *Prévôté* was the seat and court of the *prévôt*, 'the ordinarie judge of differences between the citizens and all others that reside within the jurisdiction of the Châtelet in Paris; the governor general of the Police of that town...'. Cotgrave, *Dictionary of the French and English Tongues*, London, 1611 (and many times thereafter).

48. *Œuvres Satiriques, L'Enfer*, vv. 7–9:

Les passetemps & consolations
Que je reçoy par visitations
En la prison claire & nette de Chartres...

49. On Jamet's and Guillard's roles in the affair see Mayer, *La Religion de Marot*, p. 23 and *Epîtres*, p. 130 n. 1.

50. *Œuvres Diverses*, LXIV, *Rondeau* LXIV.

51. *Epîtres*, p. 132 n. 1.

52. See epistles XII, XIII, XIV, XV.

53. *Œuvres Lyriques*, LXXXV, *Epithalame* I.

54. *Œuvres Diverses*, LVII, *Rondeau* LVII.

55. *Œuvres Diverses*, LXXXII, *Ballade* XVI.

56. See *La Religion de Marot*, p. 16 and *Epîtres*, p. 197 n. 1.

57. See Guy, *Clément Marot et son école*, para. 264.

58. Charles de Sainte-Marthe quoted by Guy, loc. cit.

59. See *Œuvres Satiriques, Introduction*, p. 14 and *Appendice* II, pp. 185 ff.

60. Cf. *Epîtres, Notice Biographique*, p. 9. For details of the two pirated editions see Mayer, *Bibliographie*, II, 6 and 6 bis.

61. On these editions see Mayer, *Bibliographie*, II, 9 ff.

62. Cf. *Bibliographie*, II, 15.

63. *Bibliographie*, II, 18. See also *Epîtres*, XXII, *Epistre à Monseigneur de Lorraine nouvellement venu à Paris, par laquelle Marot luy presente le premier Livre translaté de la Metamorphose d'Ovide*.

64. *Bibliographie*, II, 21. These poems appear in a section entitled *Certaines Œuvres qu'il feit en la prison*. Cf. Mayer, *Marot et 'Celle qui fut a'Amye'*, art. cit., pp. 369–70.

65. For the emendation and a discussion of it see below, ch. VII, p. 249–52. On the question of textual emendations in Marot's work see Mayer, *Le Texte de Marot*, in BHR, 1952, XIV, pp. 314–28 and 1953, XV, pp. 71–91. This particular case is discussed on pp. 72–74. Cf. also *La Religion de Marot*, pp. 97–100.

66. *La Religion de Marot*. pp. 71–73.

67. For details of this affair and its consequences for Marot see *La Religion de Marot*, pp. 23–26. On the text of the sacramentarian placards see *Aspects de la Propagande Religieuse*, Geneva, Droz, 1957, p. 116.

68. See the passage quoted in *Epîtres*, p. 202 n. 3 and also *La Religion de Marot*, pp. 73 ff.

69. On this person see *La Religion de Marot*, pp. 81–85 and Mayer, *Clément Marot et le général de Caen*, in BHR, 1958, XX, pp. 277–95. B.N., ms. fr. 2202, fo. 44r° contains a *chant-royal*, 'Pensant en toy, mere miseratrice', which is signed Le General de Caen. He was probably one of the Palinodz poets.

70. Quoted in *Epîtres*, p. 202 n. 3.

71. Cf. Jourda, *Marot, l'homme et l'œuvre*, 1956, p. 25; Mayer, *Bibliographie*, II, 240. There may have appeared an earlier edition of *Le sixième psaume*, s.l.n.d. *Bibliographie*, II, 8.

72. Text quoted by Mayer, *La Religion*, p. 25.

73. See *La Religion*, p. 26.

74. Text ibid., *Appendice* I, 19.

75. See Mayer, ibid., p. 27.

76. Mayer, ibid., pp. 27–31.

77. *Epîtres*, XL, vv. 18–20. See above, ch. I, p. 3. For further details on Michelle de Saubonne see *La Religion*, p. 51.

78. *Epîtres*, XXXIV, vv. 39–46.

79. See *Epîtres, Notice Biographique*, p. 13 n. 1.

80. On this *concours* see *Epîtres*, XXXIX, and p. 213 n. 2 and p. 217 n. 1.

81. On all the points relating to Marot's stay in, and departure from, Ferrara see, in addition to *La Religion de Marot*, pp. 27–34, Mayer, *Le Départ de Marot de Ferrare*, in BHR, 1956, XVIII, pp. 197–221.

82 Text quoted in art. cit., p. 199 and op. cit., p. 29.

83. Art. cit., p. 199 n. 2 and op. cit., p. 29.

84. Text in art. cit., p. 204 and op. cit., p. 29.

85. Art. cit., p. 205.

86. See *La Religion*, p. 32 n. 107.

87. Text in art. cit., p. 212.

88. See below, ch. VII, pp. 265-6.

89. Cf. *Epîtres*, p. 222 n. 1; *Le départ de Marot de Ferrare*, art. cit., pp. 214–17; *Bibliographie*, t. I, pp. 12–18.

90. Cf. *La Religion*, p. 34 n. 121.

91. *Epîtres*, XLV, vv. 49–52:

> ...mais si le Roy vouloit
> Me retenir ainsi comme il souloit,
> Je ne dy pas qu'en gré je ne le prinse,
> Et puis il fault obeyr à son prince.

92. On this and the following points see *La Religion de Marot*, pp. 35–39.

93. Text ibid., *Appendice* I, no. 20, pp. 153–4. The last clause of the edict specifically excluded sacramentarians and recidivists and prohibited freedom of examination and expression in religious matters. Marot's protest against such censorship in epistle XXXVI would preclude his acceptance of the terms of this particular edict.

94. Text ibid., *Appendice* I, no. 21, pp. 154–5.

95. Jourda, *Marot, l'homme et l'œuvre*, p. 35.

96. Jourda, ibid., suggests October; Mayer, *La Religion*, p. 35, late November, although this seems rather late, especially if, as Mayer suggests, he stopped in Geneva on the way.

97. See *La Religion*, pp. 38–39.

98. *Epîtres*, p. 253 n. 1.

99. Quoted by Mayer, *La Religion*, p. 38.

100. *Epîtres*, p. 253 n. 1.

101. Cf. *La Religion*, p. 37: 'François Ier semble avoir permis à Marot de rentrer en France, non pour six mois seulement, mais pour de bon, et de reprendre sa place de valet de chambre...'

102. *Œuvres Lyriques*, LXXVII, *Cantique* II.

103. Guy, op. cit., paras. 350–1.

104. See *La Religion*, p. 42: 'Malgré l'abjuration, bon nombre de 'rappelés ont persévéré dans leur hérésie.'

105. Guy, *Clément Marot et son école*, p. 27: 'Je n'ignore pas, lui dit Calvin, que ton coeur est maintenant "destourné et aliéné de nous, j'adjouste même enflambé: toutefois je pense que nous pourrons regaigner sa grâce".'

106. *Œuvres Lyriques*, LXXVII, *Cantique* II, v. 36.

107. Guy, op. cit., para. 354 and Mayer, *La Religion*, pp. 61–62.

108. *Œuvres Lyriques*, p. 284 n. 2.

109. Ibid., LXXVIII, *Cantique* III.

110. Guy, op. cit., para. 356.

111. Guy, ibid., para. 355.

112. Cf. *La Religion de Marot*, pp. 76–77.

113. Ibid., pp. 77–85.

114. *Œuvres Satiriques*, IX, *Du coq à l'asne faict à Venise par ledict Marot le dernier jour de juillet MVCXXXVI.*

115. See *Œuvres Satiriques*, pp. 93 ff. n. 1, and *La Religion*, p. 63.

116. Although some of the poems had appeared in the *Adolescence* etc., under the title of *huitains*, *dizains* etc. See below, ch. II, pp. 78, 86–7, and ch. IV, p. 155. On the Chantilly manuscript, offered to Montmorency, see Mayer, *Bibliographie*, I, pp. 10–18.

117. *Bibliographie*, II, 70.

118. See *Le Texte de Marot*, art. cit., t. XV, pp. 80–84 and *Epîtres*, *Notice Biographique*, p. 16.

119. *Œuvres Lyriques*, LXXXIX, *Eglogue* III, p. 353 n. 3.

120. See *La Religion de Marot*, pp. 105–7; M. Jeanneret, *Marot traducteur des Psaumes entre le néo-platonisme et la réforme*, in BHR, 1965, XXVII, pp. 630, 636; and below, p. 43.

121. Cf. Villey, op. cit., pp. 126–7; Guy, op. cit., para. 430.

122. See Mayer *Bibliographie*, II, 74, 82, 93; Guy, op. cit., pp. 95–99, D.-*Les Psaumes de David*, and Jeanneret, art. cit., p. 630 on the question of the author's part in these editions.

123. *Bibliographie*, II, 101. On the epistle to the king see Jeanneret, art. cit., pp. 632–7 and below, ch. VII, pp. 268–70.

124. On the following points see *La Religion*, pp. 40–47.

125. Text in *La Religion*, *Appendice* I, nos. 22, 23, 24, 25, pp. 156–62.

126. Ibid., *Appendice* I, nos. 26, 27, pp. 163–4.

127. See Mayer, *The Problem of Dolet's Evangelical Publications*, in BHR, 1952, XIV, pp. 405–14.

128. See *La Religion*, p. 45.

129. Herminjard, *Correspondance des Réformateurs dans les pays de langue française*, Geneva, 1866–97, vol. VIII, p. 218. The same letter also contains the story of the warrant issued for Marot's arrest: 'Marotium cum videro, salutabo tuis verbis. Haec causa adventus: quod cum ex aula domum se conferret, audierit decretum fuisse a curia Parisiensi, ut captus illuc quam primum adducerentur. Flexit iter alio, ut diligentius inquireret. Re bene comperta, huc

recta concessit. Nunc penitus habere in animo se dicit, hic manere,' op. cit., p. 218.

130. See Jeanneret, art. cit., p. 629.
131. Jeanneret, ibid., pp. 642–3.
132. Quoted by Jeanneret, loc. cit.
133. See also below, ch. VII, p.27 0-1.
134. *Œuvres Lyriques*, XC, *Eglogue* IV.
135. *Epîtres, Notice Biographique*, p. 19.
136. Ibid.
137. Ibid., pp. 19–21.
138. Quoted by Mayer, *La Religion*, p. 9.
139. See Abel Lefranc, *Le Roman d'amour de Clément Marot*, in *Grands Ecrivains français de la Renaissance*, Paris, Champion, 1914, pp. 1–61. Although accepting the Anne d'Alençon hypothesis V. L. Saulnier introduced some modifications in his *Les Elégies de Clément Marot*, Paris, 1952.

THE MOMENT: RENAISSANCE AND REFORMATION

140. The bibliography of this subject is enormous. For English readers Tilley's book, *The Dawn of the French Renaissance*, Cambridge, 1919, has never been bettered. Short introductions to the subject in French are provided by Guy, *Clément Marot et son école*, ch. 1; J. Plattard, *La Renaissance des lettres en France*, Paris, A. Colin, 1962; V. L. Saulnier, *La Littérature française de la Renaissance*, Paris, PUF, 1962. For more detailed study Renaudet, *Préréforme et humanisme à Paris, 1494–1517*, Paris, 1953, is indispensable. See also Imbart de la Tour, *Les Origines de la Réforme*, Paris, 1905–35, 4 vols. L. Febvre, *Les Origines de la Réforme française et le problème des causes de la Réforme*, in *Au cœur Religieux du XVIe siècle*, Paris, 1957. For the historiography of the subject, and related problems, see F. Simone, *Il Rinascimento Francese*, Turin, 1961.

141. France itself, and the French court, had never, except at rare moments such as the reign of Charles V, enjoyed the splendour of the Burgundian courts in the fifteenth century.

142. Jean Bouchet, *Panegyric du Chevallier sans reproche* quoted by P. M. Smith, *The Anti-Courtier Trend in Sixteenth Century French Literature*, Geneva, Droz, 1966, p. 87.

143. See P. M. Smith, op. cit., pp. 58–61.

144. See C. A. Mayer and D. Bentley-Cranch, *Le premier pétrarquiste français Jean Marot*, in BHR, 1965, XXVII, and Marguerita White, *Petrarchism in the French Rondeau before 1527*, in *French Studies*, 1968, XXII, pp. 287–95.

145. For details of visits by individual scholars see Tilley, op. cit., and Renaudet, op. cit., *passim*.

146. *Œuvres Diverses*, XCI, *Epitaphe* II, *De Longueil, homme docte*.

147. On these developments see Renaudet, op. cit., pp. 79–89 and pp. 114–17.

148. Renaudet, ibid., p. 401.

149. Renaudet, ibid., pp. 501–3, 509, 510.

150. Renaudet, ibid., p. 501.

151. Renaudet, op. cit., *passim*.

152. Erasmus on the proverb *Illotis Manibus* in *Adagia*, 1515, translated and quoted by M. M. Phillips in *The 'Adages' of Erasmus: a study with translations*. Cambridge, 1964, pp. 266–7.

153. Erasmus, *Ne Bos quidem pereat*, in *Adagia*, 1526, in M. M. Phillips, op. cit., p. 377.

154. Erasmus, loc. cit.

155. See Guy, op. cit., p. 30 f.

156. Rabelais, *Pantagruel*, Paris, Les Belles Lettres, 1959, ch. VIII, pp. 41–42.

157. Renaudet, op. cit., pp. 628–9: 'Ne placez votre confiance ni dans la foi, ni dans les œuvres, mais en Dieu.'

158. Renaudet, ibid., p. 629: 'Le Christ n'ordonne rien de tel; il nous enseigne de n'attendre notre salut que de la grâce divine, et non de nous fier à des pratiques plus superstitieuses peut-être que religieuses.'
For Lefevre then, 'Les observances n'ont donc nul mérite par elles-mêmes et ne valent que par l'esprit dans lesquelles nous nous y soumettons', ibid., p. 630.

159. In the colloquies *Naufragium* and *Peregrinatio*. Cf. Mayer, *La Religion de Marot*, p. 119.

160. See Guy, op. cit., paras. 37–40.

161. See Renaudet, op. cit., pp. 626–7.

162. The respective positions of Erasmus and Luther are expressed in the former's *De Libero Arbitrio* and the latter's *De Servo Arbitrio*. See P. Mesnard, *Erasme de Rotterdam, Essai sur le Libre Arbitre*, Algiers, 1945, pp. 24–73, for an analysis of this quarrel.

163. Imbart de La Tour, vol. IV, pp. 69–84.

164. See H. Busson, *Les Sources et le développement du rationalisme dans la littérature française de la Renaissance*, Paris, Vrin, 1957.

THE MILIEU: THE FRENCH COURT

165. On the court of François Ier as a literary milieu see Guy, op. cit., chs. II and III. On the influence exerted by Marguerite de Navarre see A. Lefranc, *Le Platonisme et la littérature française*, in *Grands Ecrivains de la Renaissance*, Paris, 1914, vol. II, and P. Jourda, *Marguerite d'Angoulême*, Paris, Champion, 1930, vol. I.

166. See P. M. Smith, op. cit., p. 93 and n. 4 where Castiglione's remark 'Se la buona sorte vuole, che Monsignor d'Angolen (come si spera), succede alla corona, estimo, che si come la gloria dell'arme fiorisce, e risplende in Francia; cosi vi debba ancor con supremo ornamento fiorir quelle delle lettere...' is quoted.

167. Guy, op. cit., para. 60.

168. Guy, ibid., para. 29. Lefranc's view in *Le Platonisme et la littérature française*, op. cit., p. 88, is that this policy owed far more to his sister Marguerite de Navarre. He quotes Héroet's dedication of his translation of the *Androgyne* to the king:

> Sur ce propos ma langue ne peult taire
> Ce que vous doibt nostre langue vulgaire,
> Laquelle avez en telz termes reduicte
> Que par elle est la plus grand part traduicte
> De ce qu'on lit de toute discipline,
> En langue grecque, hebraicque et latine,
> Et a acquis telle perfection...

and adds that it was 'formulée à l'instigation (de Marguerite) qui préférait reporter sur son frère le mérite des entreprises qu'elle avait inspirées. Il en arriva de même...à propos des deux traductions de Dolet et de celle du *Criton* par Pierre du Val'.

169. See Guy, op. cit., paras. 116–21.

170. See Jourda, *Marguerite d'Angoulême*, vol. I, and Lefranc, op. cit., for Marguerite's relations with the humanists and reformers of her day.

171. See above, n. 168.

172. See W. G. Moore, *La Réforme allemande et la littérature française: Recherches sur la notoriété de Luther en France*, Strasburg, 1930, p. 102 f.

173. Lefranc, op. cit., *passim*.

174. Condemned to death and burnt at the stake in 1546 for having supposedly mistranslated Plato, or at least, to have translated him in such a way as to lay himself open to the charge of atheism. See R. Copley Christie, *E. Dolet, The Martyr of the Renaissance*, London, 1899, pp. 458–77, and Lefranc, op. cit., pp. 112–13.

175. Claude Chappuys, *Discours de la Court*, 1543, quoted by Guiffrey, *Œuvres Complètes de Marot*, vol. IV, p. 147 n. 3.

176. See Charles de Sainte-Marthe, quoted by Lefranc in *Marguerite de Navarre et le Platonisme de la Renaissance* in op. cit., p. 236, 'Tantost elle parloit des histoires ou des préceptes de philosophie avec d'aultres très érudits personnages dont sa maison n'estoit jamais desgarnie.'

CONDITIONS OF CREATIVITY: POETRY FOR PATRONAGE

177. An attitude which probably owes much to Dr Johnson's definition of the word *patron* in his *Dictionary of the English Language* as 'commonly a wretch who supports with insolence, and is paid with flattery'.

178. See Guy, *L'Ecole des Rhétoriqueurs*, Paris, 1910, paras. 64–67 and H. Weber, *La Création Poétique au XVIe Siècle*, en France, Paris, 1956, vol. I, p. 63 f.

179. On each of these poets, and their conditions, see Guy, op. cit.

180. Guy, op. cit., pp. 174–206.

181. See P. M. Smith, op. cit., ch. III, pp. 110–16, ch. IV, pp. 180–4.

II. FORMATION AND EVOLUTION

THE ELEMENTS OF THE PROBLEM

1. On these poets of the fifteenth and early sixteenth centuries who take their name from the fact that poetry was often described as the 'art de seconde rhétorique' see Guy, *L'Ecole des Rhétoriqueurs*, Paris, 1910.

2. A discussion of these problems is to be found in Mayer's article *Le Texte de Marot*, art. cit., in his *Bibliographie*, I, pp. 10–18, and in the prolegomena to individual volumes of the critical edition.

3. In *Les Epigrammes de Clement Marot*, Poitiers, E. and J. Marnef, 1547, (*Bibliographie*, II, 154). The case of the various versions of the *Avant-naissance* is discussed in *Œuvres Lyriques*, pp. 64–67.

4. All the epistles listed above were first published from the Chantilly manuscript by G. Mâcon, *Poésies inédites de Clément Marot*, in BdB, 1898, pp. 158–70 and pp. 233–48. The first *cantique* and the fourth *coq-à-l'âne* were first published from manuscript versions by the eighteenth-century editor Lenglet-Dufresnoy.

5. This work was started by P. Villey's *Tableau chronologique des publications de Clément Marot*, vols. VII–VIII, RSS, 1920–21 and Champion, Paris, 1921 (also in his *Marot et Rabelais*, Champion, 1923) and his *Recherches sur la chronologie des*

œuvres de Marot, BdB, 1920–23. It has been continued by Mayer in his *Bibliographie* and in the five volumes of the critical edition so far published.

6. T. Sebillet, *Art Poétique françoys*, éd. F. Gaiffe, Paris, STFM, 1910; J. Peletier, *Art Poétique* (1955), éd. A. Boulenger, Publications de la Faculté des Lettres de l'Université de Strasbourg, fasc. 53, Paris, 1930. See also Mayer, *Marot et l'Archaisme* in Cahiers de l'Association Internationale des Etudes Françaises, 1967, pp. 28–29.

It is worth noting that Sebillet did not despise all the forms of *Rhétoriqueur* poetry. His verdict is therefore not coloured by any *parti pris* against them, although he did appreciate the contribution which the Classical literatures could, and had already made, to French literature.

7. See Villey, *Marot et Rabelais*, op. cit., p. 145: 'Pour lui (Brunetière), le rôle de Marot a consisté à interrompre ou à retarder le mouvement de la Renaissance.'

8. Jourda, *Marot, l'homme et l'œuvre*, p. 80, 'Cependant, jusqu'à sa fin, qu'il s'agisse de pleurer G. Preudhomme ou de juger des événements, il se souviendra de ses maîtres: ses derniers vers, sur plus d'un point, rappellent ses premiers essais…Il reste, à plus d'un égard…le dernier représentant de la poésie du Moyen Age.' Plattard, in *Marot, sa carrière poétique, son œuvre*, pp. 110–11, speaks with the same voice on the subject of this *complainte*. He says: 'Voilà donc par quels liens Marot demeure attaché à cette école des Rhétoriqueurs. A quarante-sept, il éprouve le besoin de dire quelle admiration il éprouve pour la plupart d'entre eux. Et il reste leur disciple.'

For the eclogue see *Œuvres Lyriques*, LXXXVII, *Eglogue* I; for the *complainte*, ibid., IX, *Complainte* VII.

9. See below, ch. IV, pp. 174–5.

10. Similar examples of the introduction of the pretended speaker in an identical setting, namely, the arrival at the Elysian Fields (after *Aeneid*, VI) in the works of Molinet and Cretin are given in the notes to this poem, *Œuvres Lyriques*, p. 166 n. 1.

11. *Epîtres*, XIII, vv. 37–62:

> Puis qu'en ce donc tous aultres precellez,
> Je vous supply (tresnoble Pré) seellez
> Le mien Acquit; pour quoy n'est il seellé?
> Le Parchemin a long et assez Lé.
> Dictes (sans plus): il fault que le seellons,
> Seellé sera sans faire proces longs.
>   S'on ne le veult d'adventure seeller,
> Je puis bien dire (en effect) que c'est l'Aer,
> L'Eau, Terre et Feu qui tout bon heur me celent,
> Consideré que tant d'aultres se seellent.
> Mais si je touche argent par la seellure,
> Je beniray des fois plus de sept l'Heure,
> Le Chancellier, le Seau et le Seelleur
> Qui de ce bien m'auront pourchassé l'heur.
>   C'est pour Marot, vous le congnoissez ly;
> Plus legier est, que *Volucres Coeli*,
> Et a suivy long temps Chancellerie,
> Sans proffiter rien touchant seellerie.
> Brief, Monseigneur, je pense que c'est là
> Qu'il fault seeller, si jamais on seella.
> Car vous sçavez que tout Acquit sans seel

Sert beaucoup moins qu'ung Potage sans sel,
Qu'ung Arc sans corde, ou qu'ung Cheval sans selle.
 Si prie à Dieu et sa tresdoulce Ancelle
Que dans cent ans, en santé excellent,
Vous puisse veoir de mes deux yeux seellant.

12. On Louise de Savoie see Guy, *Clément Marot et son école*, paras. 76–79. On Du Prat and Preudhomme see ibid., paras. 208–9. Also, on the former, *Epîtres*, p. 140 n. 1, on the latter, ibid., p. 143 n. 2 and *Œuvres Lyriques*, p. 165 n. 1, p. 168 nn. 1, 2 and 3. Preudhonne's exact date of birth is difficult to establish but he died in 1543 at an advanced age. He had resigned his official function as *Trésorier* in 1540 on the grounds of old age and ill-health. See B.N., ms. fr. 25722, no. 780.

13. See Mayer, *Marot et l'archaisme*, art. cit., pp. 33–35. Mayer does not include the eclogue for Louise de Savoie, however, under the same heading. Cf. p. 32.

14. See Mayer, ibid., p. 35.

15. See below, ch. IV, n. 15.

16. See Mayer, art. cit., pp. 35–37.

17. Villey, *Marot et Rabelais*, p. 37. Villey, however, reconciles this statement with the opinion, expressed at the end of his study, that 'Marot est au contraire un artisan de notre Renaissance poétique', p. 145.

18. Plattard, op. cit., pp. 90–91.

19. Alan Boase, *The Poetry of France*, London, Methuen, 1964, vol. I, p. xxxvi.

20. See on this point Chamard's edition of Du Bellay's *Deffence et Illustration*, Paris, 1948 and his *Histoire de la Pléiade*, Paris, Didier, 1939; Laumonier, *Ronsard, Poète Lyrique*, Paris, 1909; Vianey, *Les Odes de Ronsard*, Paris, SFELT, 1946.

21. Mayer, *Marot et l'archaisme*, p. 28.

MAROT'S EARLY YEARS

22. Described in pastoral terms in Marot's *Eglogue au Roy soubz les noms de Pan & Robin (Eglogue III)*.

23. See Guy, *L'Ecole des Rhétoriqueurs*, pp. 174–206.

24. *Epîtres*, p. 96.

25. *Œuvres Diverses, Epitaphe* xxv. Note the *rimes équivoquées* (v. 12) etc.

26. *Epîtres*, p. 96.

27. *Epîtres*, p. 8.

28. See Guy, op. cit., pp. 9–135.

29. *Œuvres Lyriques*, I. See also *Introduction*, pp. 6–7.

30. *Œuvres Lyriques*, II. See *Introduction*, pp. 6–8.

31. In a similar situation Ovid made Penelope send several messengers in pursuit of Ulysses. Leander sent a letter by sailor because the sea was too rough for swimming. The limits of realism in Ovid's *Heroides* are discussed by L. P. Wilkinson in ch. V of *Ovid Surveyed*, Cambridge, 1962.

32. See below, pp. 74–5.

33. Text in *Œuvres Lyriques*, III, *Complainte* I.

34. See *Œuvres Lyriques*, IV, *Complainte* II.

35. Examples of these figures of speech in *rhétoriqueur* poetry are given in the notes accompanying these poems in the critical edition. See *Œuvres Lyriques*, p. 128 n. 2 and p. 129 n. 1.

36. See *Œuvres Lyriques, Introduction*, pp. 12–16.

37. On these genres in the Middle Ages see D. Poirion, *Le Poète et le Prince. L'Evolution du lyrisme courtois de Guillaume de Machaut à Charles d'Orléans*, Paris, PUF, 1965, ch. VIII and IX. On their use by the *Rhétoriqueurs* see Guy, *L'Ecole des Rhétoriqueurs*, paras. 213–21; by Marot, *Œuvres Diverses, Introduction*, pp. 6–11, 32–35. There is in a sense something misleading about the term 'fixed form' although it is constantly used. This is particularly so when applied to the *rondeau*, in view of its development through the Middle Ages. See N. Wilkins, *The Structure of Ballades, Rondeaux and Virelais in Froissart and in Christine de Pisan*, in *French Studies*, 1969, XXIII, pp. 337–48.

38. Sebillet, ed. cit., p. 131.

39. See Guy, *L'Ecole des Rhétoriqueurs*, ch. 1.

40. See below, ch. IV, pp. 127, 150–2.

41. See below, ch. IV, pp. 141–53.

42. See below, ch. IV, p. 155 and n. 50.

43. On this work see Guy, op. cit., para. 24.

44. This point was first made by Guy, ibid., para. 113.

45. Cf. Guy, ibid., paras. 114–15. The *Epistre du Despourveu* is by no means the only example of false humility in Marot's work at this stage. The *Epistre du Camp d'Atigny*, III, offers an equally good specimen.

46. On this poem see Guy, ibid., paras. 508–12.

47. *Œuvres Lyriques*, I, vv. 117–19:

> I souspiroit le doulx vent Zephirus
> Et y chantoit le gaillard Tityrus;
> Le grant Dieu Pan avec ses pastoureaux...

Tityrus is a character from Virgil's first eclogue.

48. *Œuvres Lyriques*, I. Apollo and Daphne are mentioned in vv. 161–2, Dido, Biblis and Helen in vv. 235–6.

49. A list of Molinet's latinisms is given by N. Dupire in *Jean Molinet, sa vie, les Œuvres*, Paris, Droz, 1932, pp. 258–88. Robertet's latinisms are particularly prominent in his prose, but some idea of their extent in his verse can be obtained from the edition of his poetry by C. M. Douglas, *A Critical Edition of the Works of Jean and François Robertet*, University of London thesis' M.A., 1962.

50. *Bibliographie* II, 1. Variants from this *plaquette* are given in *Œuvres Lyriques*, I.

51. Numerous examples are given by Guy, *L'Ecole des Rhétoriqueurs*, paras. 143–8.

52. See *Œuvres Lyriques*, p. 132 n. 2, for examples of this particular play on words in the work of Jean Robertet and Jean Molinet.

53. See Guy, op. cit., paras. 126–40.

54. Quoted by Guy, ibid., para. 133.

55. Quoted by Mayer, *Œuvres Lyriques, Introduction*, p. 11.

56. See *Epîtres, Introduction*, p. 48 n. 4.

57. See Guy, op. cit., p. 101 n. 138.

58. See above ch. I, p. 16 and n. 64.

59. See *Œuvres Satiriques, L'Enfer*, vv. 348–58. For a discussion of this passage see below, ch. VII, p. 252.

60. Ibid., vv. 359–76:

> Quant au surnom, aussi vray qu'Evangille,
> Il tire à cil du Poete Vergille,
> Jadis chery de Mecenas à Romme:
> Maro s'appelle, & Marot je me nomme,

Marot je suis, & Maro ne suis pas;
Il n'en fut oncq' depuis le sien trespas;
Mais puis qu'avons ung vray Mecenas ores,
Quelcque Maro nous pourrons veoir encores.
Et d'aultre part (dont noz jours sont heureux)
Le beau berger des lettres plantureux
Nous reproduict ses fleurs à grands jonchées...

The praise of the Renaissance is quoted in full and discussed in ch. VII, p. 247.

61. See below, ch. III, p. 101.

62. Quoted by Vianey, *Les Epttres de Marot*, Paris, Nizet, 1962, p. 27. The lines are by Guillaume Cretin whose friend Honorat de la Jaille (v. 1) asked him to write to a mutual friend, François Charbonnier (v. 3).

63. Quoted by Vianey, ibid., p. 28.

64. See below, ch. III, pp. 99, 101, 103 and ch. VI, pp. 219–31.

65. On this question see Villey, *Recherches sur la chronologie des œuvres de Marot*, in BdB, 1920, pp. 189–209 and 238–49.

66. *Dixain audict Seigneur* (Du Prat). Since this poem follows the epistle to the chancellor it is included by Mayer in *Epitres*, XIV.

The *huictain* was addressed to Jacques Colin, abbé de Saint-Ambroise; it follows *Ep.* XXV in *Epitres*.

67. *Ballade sans refrain, responsive a l'epistre de celluy qui blasma Marot, touchant ce qu'il escrivit au Roy, quant son valet le desroba.* Text in *Epitres*, XXVII.

68. *Chant Royal Chrestien* and the *Chant Royal dont le Roy bailla le refrain.* See *Œuvres Diverses*, LXXXVII, LXXXVIII.

POST-'ADOLESCENCE' AND MATURITY

69. Text in Guiffrey, *Les Œuvres de Clement Marot*, vol. II, p. 266.

70. *Epttres*, XLV, v. 34. See also *Œuvres Lyriques*, LXXVIII, *Cantique* III, v. 38, where the court is described as
Lyme et rabot des hommes mal polys.

71. A. Boase, *The Poetry of France*, vol. I, p. xli, 'Humanist and Italian influence on him was quite negligible. If he translated the third *Canzone* and some six of Petrarch's Sonnets (and thus ranks with Mellin as the first to use the form in France) it was at the King's express invitation.'

72. Vianey, *Le Pétrarquisme en France au XVIe siècle*, Montpellier, 1909, pp. 45–49. Villey, *Marot et Rabelais*, p. 412, thinks that Vianey exaggerated the amount of Italian influence on the epigram.

73. See Mayer and Bentley-Cranch, *Clément Marot, poète pétrarquiste*, in BHR, 1966, XXVIII, pp. 32–51. See especially p. 44.

74. Ibid., p. 51.

75. See below, ch. III, pp. 114–17, 120 and ch. IV, pp. 176–8, 181–2.

76. See below, ch. VII, pp. 260–1.

77. See below, ibid., pp. 267–8, 271.

78. See below, ch. IV, pp. 141–56.

79. It is worth noting that the elegies are probably the most consistently medieval (in treatment, if not in genre) of all Marot's poems. Their composition is spread mainly over the years 1525–33, so that they overlap from the period of the *Adolescence* to that of post-*Adolescence*. There are only four elegies composed after 1533. See below, ch. IV, p. 163–6.

80. See below, ch. IV, pp. 178–82 and *Œuvres Lyriques*, pp. 344, n. 1, 345 n. 1.

81. Cf. Du Bellay, *Deffence et Illustration*, ed. cit., livre II, ch. II, pp. 93–94:

'Bien diray-je que Jan le Maire de Belges me semble avoir premier illustré & les Gaules & la Langue Francoyse, luy donnant beaucoup de motz & manieres de parler poètiques, qui ont bien servy mesmes aux plus excellens de notre tens.'

Jean Lemaire was also recognized as a precursor by Peletier, Ronsard and Pasquier. On this point see Chamard, *Histoire de la Pléiade*, I, pp. 136–8, and III, 125–7.

82. It is true that there are one or two possible reminiscences of the *Metamorphoses* in the *Temple de Cupido*, and the *Epistre de Maguelonne* prior to this period. See the notes accompanying these two poems in *Œuvres Lyriques*.

83. See below, ch. III, pp. 120–4 and ch. IV, pp. 175–82.

84. Cf. *ed. princeps*   *Œuvres*, 1538 (reproduced in *Œuvres Lyriques*)

  v. 15, Et qui plus est les   Brief il congneut que toute nation...
    altitonens dieux,   Et qui plus est, les plus souverains Dieux

  vv. 96–97,
    Par ung matin que Aurora Par ung matin lors qu'Aurora separe
    la tresgente   D'avec le jour la tenebreuse nuict.
    Vient esclarer l'essence
    diuturne.

85. With the exception of the continuing appearance in the elegies especially of certain allegorical personages from the *Rose*, such as *Faulx Dangier* etc. See below, ch. IV, p. 163.

86. The mythological setting is used, for example, in the *Second Chant de l'Amour fugitif*, published in 1533 but date of composition unknown. The extended simile replacing the allegorical description of the state of mind of the poet can be seen at its best in epistle XLVI. See below, ch. III, p. 115 and for the *Second Chant*, ch. VI, pp. 207–8.

87. See, for instance, the epistle written by Marot on behalf of Pierre Vuyart to Madame de Lorraine (XXIII) in order to obtain a new horse. *Rhétoriqueur* rhymes are used to suggest the broken down condition of the horse which needs replacing:

  Car le Cheval que je pourmaine & maine
  Est malheureux, & brunche en pleine Plaine: (vv. 19–20)

88. See *Œuvres Diverses*, *Introduction*, pp. 6–8 and 19–29 and Mayer and Bentley-Cranch, *Clément Marot, poète pétrarquiste*, art. cit.

89. Sebillet, *Art Poétique françoys*, ed. cit., p. 120.

90. *Œuvres Diverses*, *Introduction*, pp. 8–10.

91. See *Œuvres Lyriques*, *Introduction*, pp. 8–12.

92. See ibid., pp. 12–16.

93. It seems to me that there is a distinct tendency in Marot's later *chansons* for him to assimilate this genre into that of the epigram. Epigrammatic characteristics are discernible in some of them, and in one case at least, Marot seems to take his inspiration from themes common among the neo-Latin Italian epigrammatists. See below, ch. IV, p. 135 and n. 27.

94. See *Œuvres Diverses*, *Introduction*, p. 15 and Mayer, *Marot et l'Archaisme*, art. cit., p. 33.

95. A. Boase, *The Poetry of France*, vol. I, p. xxxviii, 'The *Epîtres* have, no doubt, their historical importance. In them the purely *colloquial* poem comes near to being achieved, and this in itself is enough to reveal where Marot represents a real reaction from the pedantry of the then existing tradition.'

96. Quoted from *Les Œuvres de Clement Marot*, Paris, 1544. See the *Preface au Roy touchant la Metamorphose*, p. 32.

97. The information about the reading of the translation to the king at Amboise, which incidentally helps to date the work, is contained in the above preface, p. 33. For the rest see Guy, *Clément Marot et son école*, para. 203.

98. The sixth volume of Mayer's critical edition containing the translations is still awaited. In the meantime they may be consulted in Guiffrey's edition. With the exception of the *Psaumes* (vol. v) they are all to be found in the second volume.

99. See below, ch. VII, pp. 270–1.

100. Cf. *Œuvres Lyriques, Introduction*, pp. 28–30.

101. On this subject see Saulnier, *Les Elégies de Clément Marot*, Paris, SEDES, 1952, p. 6: 'L'elégie, c'est Clément Marot qui l'a créée en France,' and p. 105: 'Dans toute la mesure où un genre se laisse "créer", il y avait bien création d'un genre.' Cf. also *Œuvres Lyriques, Introduction*, pp. 16–21 and C. M. Scollen, *The Birth of the Elegy in France*, Geneva, Droz, 1967, ch. II.

102. Sebillet, *Art Poétique*, ed. cit., p. 156.

103. See *Œuvres Lyriques, Introduction*, pp. 24–25.

104. For a discussion of these two poems see below, ch. IV, pp. 175–9.

105. See *Œuvres Lyriques, Introduction*, pp. 25–28.

106. See ibid., pp. 21–23.

107. *Les Cantiques de la Paix par Clement Marot*, Paris, E. Roffet, s.d., (January 1540). *Bibliographie*, II, 86. For its value see *Œuvres Lyriques, Introduction*, p. 42.

108. See *Œuvres Lyriques, Introduction*, p. 22 n. 7 and p. 51.

109. The problem of the classification of these three poems is considered in more detail in Mayer's article *Les Œuvres de Clement Marot: L'Economie de l'édition critique*, in BHR, 1967, XXIX, pp. 357–72.

110. In the *Cantique à la Deesse Santé, pour le Roy malade* (IV) Marot imitated, in the first seven verses, Flaminio's *Hymnus in bonam valetudinam*. See *Œuvres Lyriques*, p. 289.

111. On this work see J. Hutton, *The Greek Anthology in France*, Cornell, 1946, p. 304.

112. Hutton, ibid., mentions this fact but supplies no details. Angeriano's *Erotopaegnion* seems to have been a very popular collection of neo-Latin epigrams. There were editions in 1520, 1525 (probably Paris) and 1530 prior to Amboise's translations.

113. See Mayer, *Le premier sonnet français*, in RHLF, 1967, pp. 481–93.

114. See Mayer and Bentley-Cranch, *Clément Marot, poète pétrarquiste*, art. cit., p. 47 f.

115. Sebillet, *Art Poétique*, ed. cit., p. 120.

116. See *Œuvres Diverses, Introduction*, pp. 17–19 and Mayer, *Le premier sonnet français*, art. cit.

117. See ibid., p. 492.

118. *Les estreines de Clement marot*, Paris, J. Dupré, 1541. *Bibliographie*, II, 91.

119. See below, ch. V, pp. 187–91.

120. See Poirion, *Le Poète et le Prince*, op. cit., p. 117 nn. 56, 58.

121. See *Œuvres Diverses, Introduction*, pp. 15–16.

122. See O. Trtnik-Rossettini, *Les Influences Anciennes et Italiennes sur la Satire en France au XVIe siècle*, Florence, 1958, 1st series, no. 13; P. M. Smith, *The Anti-Courtier Trend in Sixteenth Century French Literature*, Geneva, Droz, 1966, pp. 14–17.

123. See *Œuvres Satiriques, Introduction*, pp. 6–7 and Mayer, *Les Œuvres de Clément Marot*, art. cit., p. 361.

124. See *Œuvres Satiriques, Introduction*, pp. 8–14 and Mayer, *Coq-à-l'Ane Définition-Invention-Attributions*, in *French Studies*, 1962, XVI, pp. 1–13.

125. See below, ch. VI, p. 237.

126. On the *sottie*, and its importance for the *coq-à-l'âne*, see E. Droz, *Le Recueil Trepperel*, Paris, 1938, vol. I, pp. lxv–lxvi; Mayer, art. cit.

127. Theoreticians were not unanimous in their praise for the genre. Du Bellay condemned its title as inept. Cf. *Deffence*, ed. cit., pp. 118–19. He was not pleased either by Sebillet's likening it to Classical satire.

128. Sebillet, *Art Poétique*, ed. cit., p. 168.

129. Peletier, *Art Poétique*, ed. cit., p. 184.

III. MAROT IN THE EPISTLES

1. See on this point J. Vianey, *Les Epître de Marot*, Paris, Nizet, 1962, ch. X, *L'épître après Marot et la fortune des Epîtres marotiques*.

2. See *Epîtres, Introduction*, p. 49.

THE LIGHTER EPISTLES

3. Madame de Stael, *De la Littérature considérée dans ses rapports avec les Institutions sociales*, 1800. *Discours Préliminaire* and *passim*.

4. *Gargantua*, XI, XII.

5. The dauphin died on 10 August 1536 at the age of nineteen after taking part in a game of tennis. His page was arrested and executed on suspicion of having poisoned him. See V. L. Saulnier, *La Mort du Dauphin François et son tombeau poétique*, in BHR, 1945, VI, pp. 50 ff.

6. This process was analysed by Bergson in *Le Rire*, Paris, PUF, 1967, pp. 146–7, with an example from the work of Twain. His observations are also relevant for Marot.

7. Epistle XXI, *A la Royne Elienor nouvellement arrivée d'Espaigne avec les deux Enfans du Roy, delivrez des mains de l'Empereur*, is lyrical in tone and movement but belongs more to the category of official lyricism and is a foretaste of some of Marot's considerable achievements in the domain of *lyrisme grave*.

8. The image appears notably in a sonnet by Pamphilo Sasso, *Opere*, Venice, 1519, fo. 14r., 'Come el timido agnel del gregge foro'. It is worth noting that these lines of Marot are echoed by sonnet IX, vv. 12–14 of Du Bellay's *Regrets*, although whether directly or merely through a common source is impossible to say.

9. *Epîtres*, XLV, vv. 74–78:

> J'ay entrepris faire pour recompense
> Ung œuvre exquis, si ma Muse s'enflamme,
> Qui maulgré temps, maulgré flamme,
> Et maulgré mort fera vivre sans fin
> Le Roy Françoys et son noble Daulphin.

These lines were composed only shortly before the dauphin's death.

10. Villey, *Marot et Rabelais*, p. 42, 'Avec un dosage différent des deux éléments, avec moins de lyrisme et plus d'esprit, c'est en somme l'inspiration de Villon et de ses disciples que nous retrouvons ici.'

11. Rabelais in his *Quart Livre*, XII–XV, on the subject of 'Les Chicanoux' and Racine in his comedy, *Les Plaideurs*.

12. See P. M. Smith, *The Anti-Courtier Trend*, ch. II, pp. 90–91.

13. See Boase, *The Poetry of France*, vol. I, pp. xxxviii-xxxix.

14. Sainte-Beuve: 'Si la versification n'a dû à Marot aucune réforme matérielle d'importance, personne mieux que lui alors n'en a possédé l'esprit et entendu le mécanisme.' Quoted in *Epîtres, Introduction*, p. 45. See also J. Vianey, *L'art du vers chez Cl. Marot*, in *Mélanges Lefranc*, Paris, 1936, pp. 44–57 and C. Camproux, *Langue et métrique…* in FM, 1964, pp. 194–205.

THE ELEGIAC EPISTLES FROM EXILE

15. See above, ch. II, p. 57.

16. See above, p. 93.

17. The combination of satire and lyricism in the same poem is by no means unusual. One has only to think of the fierce invective etc., to which Catullus was sometimes moved in his lyricism.

18. See below, ch. VI, pp. 201, 217–18, 244–5 and ch. VII, pp. 247–9.

19. Notably in his epilogue to the first three books of the *Pontic Epistles*, III, 9, 39–56. Here is part of the passage in English, quoted by L. P. Wilkinson, *Ovid Surveyed*, Cambridge, 1962, p. 174: 'Should I, lest the reader twice find the same matter, petition you alone, Brutus, of all my friends?... My purpose and care was that each friend should receive his letter, not that a book should result. Do not imagine that this work is a selection: I simply collected the letters afterwards and put them together unarranged. So be indulgent to my writings…'

20. For the image of the stag pursued by hounds see the famous simile in Virgil, *Aeneid*, XII, 749–53:

> inclusum ueluti si quando flumine nactus
> ceruom aut puniceae saeptum formidine pinnae
> uenator cursu canis et latratibus instat,
> ille autem insidiis et ripa territus alta
> mille fugit refugitque uias.

21. The selection is discreet, as can be gauged from a comparison of the French with its source in *Pontics*, ed. Owen, Oxford, 1951, II, 7: 5–16:

> nec dubito quin sit: sed me timor ipse malorum
> saepe supervacuos cogit habere metus.
> da veniam, quaeso, nimioque ignosce timori.
> tranquillas etiam naufragus horret aquas.
> qui semel est laesus fallaci piscis ab hamo,
> omnibus unca cibis aera subesse putat.
> saepe canem longe visum fugit agna lupumque
> credit, et ipsa suam nescia vitat opem.
> membra reformidant mollem quoque saucia tactum,
> vanaque sollicitis incutit umbra metum.
> sic ego Fortunae telis confixus iniquis
> pectore concipio nil nisi triste meo.

22. Cf. Ovid, *Tristia*, III, 8: 8–9, 11–12:

> aspicerem patriae dulce repente solum,
> desertaeque domus vultus…
>   …
> stulte, quid haec frustra votis puerilibus optas,
> quae non ulla tibi fertque feretque dies?

23. An imitation of *Pontics*, I, 3: 33–34

> non dubia est Ithaci prudentia, sed tamen optat
> fumum de patriis posse videri focis.

Cf. Du Bellay, *Regrets*, XXXI, (éd. crit. de Chamard, vol. II), v. I, vv. 5–6:

> Heureux qui, comme Ulysse, a fait un beau voyage
> ....
> Quand revoiray-je, helas, de mon petit village
> Fumer la cheminee.

Marot's allusion to Ulysses has the disadvantage of being more recondite in its reference to one particular episode of the *Odyssey* than either Ovid's or Du Bellay's.

24. The precise source is *Tristia*, II, 142–4

> nube solet pulsa candidus ire dies
> vidi ego pampineis oneratam vitibus ulmum,
> quae fuerat saevi fulmine tacta Iovis.

25. This image occurs in the same elegy to Augustus, *Tristia*, II: 83–88

> cum coepit quassata domus subsidere, partes
> in proclinatas omne recumbit onus,
> cunctaque fortuna rimam faciente dehiscunt,
> ipsa suoque eadem pondere tracta ruunt.
> ergo hominum quaesitum odium mihi carmine, quosque
> debuit, est vultus turba secuta tuos.

26. See Du Bellay, *Deffence et Illustration*, ed. cit., II, ΙV, pp. 115–16: 'Quand aux epistres, ce n'est un poeme qui puisse grandement enrichir nostre vulgaire, pource qu'elles sont volontiers de choses familieres & domestiques.'

27. Boase, *The Poetry of France*, vol. I, p. xxxviii.

28. Ronsard, *Odes*, ed. Laumonier, STFM, I, p. 82.

29. Du Bellay, op. cit., pp. 116–17: 'si tu ne les voulois faire à l'immitation d'elegies, comme Ovide...'

30. See *Epîtres*, XLVI, vv. 13, 37, 38, 135—invocation; XLVII, vv. 53, 55, 56, 57, 68—salutation; XLVI, vv. 142, 143, 145, 146, 148—negation.

31. These are indicated in full in the footnotes to *Epîtres*. They are in many cases too lengthy to quote here.

32. Implying above all *creativeness* and not, as in the more recent acceptation, *inventiveness*. *Creation not invention* was a byword in sixteenth-century poetics. See H. Weber, *La Création Poétique au XVIe siècle en France* and G. Castor, *Pléiade Poetics*, Cambridge, 1964.

33. See *Epîtres*, XLIV, v. 134 and n.

34. Marot attacked the solecisms committed by courtiers in his second *coq-à-l'âne* (*Œuvres Satiriques*, VIII, vv. 156–60). In one of his epigrams, *A ses disciples* (LXXVI), he laid down the rules for the agreement of the past participle.

IV. MAROT'S LYRICAL POETRY

1. See above, ch. I, Conditions of Creativity, pp. 52–6.

2. See above, ch. II, pp. 57–61.

3. Villey, *Marot et Rabelais*, p. 146, speaks of Marot as having, almost involuntarily 'forgé dans ses *Psaumes* l'instrument du lyrisme'. Plattard, in *Marot, sa carrière poétique, son œuvre*, Paris, 1938, p. 169, concentrates likewise

on this aspect and concludes his chapter: 'Il a orienté notre poésie lyrique vers des formes qui sont encore celles du lyrisme moderne.' Jourda, *Marot, l'homme et l'œuvre*, p. 136, says: 'Marot auteur de *Chansons* et traducteur des *Psaumes* fait figure de devancier de la Pléiade, sinon de créateur,' and, on p. 138: 'Aussi ce qu'il faut voir surtout dans les chansons, c'est un exercice de métrique.'

One earlier critic, the eighteenth-century author La Harpe, distinguishes himself by his refusal to limit Marot's skill to that of clever versification: 'Le nom de Marot est la première époque vraiment remarquable dans l'histoire de notre poésie, bien plus par le talent dans ses ouvrages, et qui lui est particulier, que par les progrès qu'il fit faire à notre versification...' quoted by Mayer in *Clément Marot*, Paris, Seghers, p. 68. Laumonier too, in his *Ronsard, poète lyrique*, p. 615, sees much more in Marot's *chansons* than their versification.

4. One has only to think of La Bruyère's judgement on the two poets in *Les Caractères*: 'Marot, par son tour et par son style, semble avoir écrit depuis Ronsard: il n'y a guère, entre ce premier et nous, que la différence de quelques mots...' and Boileau's position in *L'Art Poétique* to appreciate this. But the opposition to Ronsard started much earlier, with Malherbe in fact, and continues through Balzac, Sorel, Sarrasin. Those who attempted to redress the balance of critical opinion were few. Their testimony is recorded by Vianey, *Les Odes de Ronsard*, ch. x.

5. See Vianey, ibid., p. 162 f. He notes that, until the advent of Sainte-Beuve, Ronsard was known to the public at large in France by only fifteen odes.

6. In 1828 with the publication of his two volumes *Tableau de la Poésie française au XVIe siècle*, and *Œuvres choisies de Pierre de Ronsard*. See Vianey, ibid., p. 170 f.

7. The worst and most recent offenders in this respect are Plattard and Jourda. Thus the former writes, op. cit., p. 168: 'Il se dit lui-même plus léger que *volucres coeli*. Il est mobile, muable. Il a des émotions brèves et fugaces, mais il est trop inconstant pour avoir de profondes passions et trop spirituel aussi pour ne pas s'aviser de ce que peut avoir de ridicule chez le poète l'affectation ou le complaisant étalage de certains sentiments intimes.' The latter, in *Marot, l'homme et l'œuvre*, p. 139, speaks of Marot lacking 'l'âme d'un vrai lyrique' whatever that may be, and in his concluding chapter he sums up thus, p. 157: 'Esprit léger...il ne pouvait s'élever à la grande poésie...Alors même que la vie l'éprouve, et qu'il souffre son tempérament l'emporte sur sa peine: il est incapable de s'élever au grand lyrisme...La poésie n'est pour lui qu'un amusement.'

8. In discussing the epistles as a genre in the previous chapter, rather than dividing them, or trying to divide them up, into categories by their tone or inspiration—satirical, lyrical etc., we follow the principles established by Mayer for the economy of his critical edition of Marot.

9. See Plattard, op. cit., p. 176: 'la chanson populaire mettait Marot sur la voie d'une poésie toute différente de celle que recommandaient les Rhétoriqueurs, une poésie vraiment lyrique, parce qu'elle était destinée à être chantée.' See also Françon, *Lyrisme et Technique Poétique*, in French Studies, 1968, XXII, p. 101: 'toutes ces poésies—qu'elles aient une forme fixe ou non-sont lyriques, en ce sens qu'elles sont composées en vue d'un accompagnement musical, ou qu'elles peuvent s'y adapter.'

10. This point is well brought out by Barthélemy Aneau in his *Quintil Horatian*, published in Lyon in 1550 as a reply and counter to Du Bellay's *Deffence et Illustration*. Aneau says: 'Car il n'est pas en usage (ce que tu dis

autrepart) que les poetes composans chansons se assujectissent à suivre la musique: ains au contraire les musiciens suyvent la lettre & le subject (qu'ils appellent) à eux baillé par les poetes. Et qu'ainsi soit, j'en demande à Claudin, Certon, Sandrin, Villiers & autres renommez musiciens...' quoted by Chamard in his edition of the *Deffence*, p. 112 n. 4. An interesting article by F. Lesure, *Autour de Clément Marot et ses Musiciens*, in the RdM, 1951, pp. 109–19, supports Aneau's contention and adds further light to the way in which a poet lost all jurisdiction over his work once the musicians got to work on it. See art. cit., p. 113: 'Ils retranchaient à leur guise telle strophe qui ne leur plaisait pas, n'hésitaient pas à prendre une élégie au quinzième vers.'

11. These are *Chansons* XXIV and XXV (*Œuvres Lyriques*, pp. 194–5). See Mayer, ibid., *Introduction*, p. 15.

12. Lesure's article lists the poems set to music on p. 114. They include 44 *chansons*, 48 *épigrammes*, 12 *rondeaux*, 2 *ballades*, 3 *élégies*, 2 *étrennes*, 1 *épître* (fragment only), 1 *épitaphe*, 2 *sonnets* and the *Psaumes*. See Mayer, *Œuvres Lyriques*, *Introduction*, p. 15.

LIGHT LYRICISM: LOVE POETRY

13. The theme of the vine and the *serpe*, the tool with which it was pruned etc., was a traditional one. See *Œuvres Lyriques*, p. 201 n. 1.

14. *Le Jardin de Plaisance et Fleur de Rethorique*, ed. E. Droz and A. Piaget, Paris, SATF, vol. I, Text (facsimile of the first Paris edition of 1501 by A. Vérard); 1910; vol. II, *Introduction et Notes*, 1925.

For the composition of this anthology see ed. cit., vol. II. The poems which the editors have attributed to the courtly love poets of the fourteenth and fifteenth centuries are those which were originally composed in literary milieux, 'les cours littéraires', for a corresponding public. By the time they reach the sixteenth century in this anthology, however, they have become part of a popular tradition, their original authorship largely unknown, and the original texts often reshaped, are cannibalized in an extraordinary way. There is for instance a *Balade faicte de plusieurs chançons* (no. 18, fo. lxij) which consists of the incipits of 32 other poems and is considered to be an imitation of a poem by Charles d'Orléans, 'Mon seul amy, mon bien, ma joye'.

The poems of this anthology are popular in another sense too. That is, that they are the very antithesis of the pedantic, pseudo-erudite poetry at this moment being produced by the *Rhétoriqueurs*. Their own representation in the anthology is minimal as far as it has been possible to establish authorship.

15. There are eight poems attributed to Machaut in the *Jardin de Plaisance*. See vol. II, nos. 40, 42, 45, 46, 48, 72, 77, 80. Chartier's tally is sixteen: nos. 460, 620 and 621—this last being in fact a sequence of fourteen poems under one heading. Jean de Garancières has five (76, 403, 463, 466, 470); Othon de Grandson two (74, 446); Charles d'Orléans eight (184, 215, 219, 303, 505, 559, 648, 649) in addition to a number of alleged imitations. It seems however that in most cases only his incipits have been used.

The poetry of Charles d'Orléans was extensively plagiarized by Blaise d'Auriol, the compiler of the anthology prefaced by Octovien de Saint-Gelais's *Chasse et depart damours*, Paris, Vérard, 1509. No fewer than 253 of his *rondeaux* and *ballades* are used, without acknowledgement, by d'Auriol.

The importance of these anthologies in the transmission of medieval love poetry to the sixteenth century is great. With the exception of Chartier's *Belle*

Dame Sans Mercy, and one or two only of his shorter love poems, none of the work of these poets was printed elsewhere. They remained in manuscript until the nineteenth and twentieth centuries when complete editions were prepared, that of Garancières, for instance, as late as 1953.

16. It was extremely popular judging from the number of editions it went into. Droz and Piaget, ed. cit., vol. II, cite eight between 1501–1527, so that it is not an unexpected influence. See Poirion, *Le Poète et le Prince*, op. cit., p. 620: 'Quant à la tradition courtoise, toujours vivante dans les anthologies comme le *Jardin de Plaisance*, elle n'est pas sans avoir influencé directement deux poètes que respectent la Pléiade: Clément Marot et Jean Lemaire de Belges.' Marot's second *complainte* contains the incipits (cf. vv. 44, 55, 66) of three poems appearing in the *Jardin de Plaisance*. Other resemblances will be noted in passing.

17. An indication of this is provided not only by the vast number of manuscripts in which they appear, but also by the printed editions issued in the early years of the sixteenth century. A bibliography of this subject is provided by J. Rollin, *Les Chansons de Clément Marot*, Paris, Fischbacher, 1951, who also indicates the influence of these anonymous popular songs on those of Marot, pp. 79–82. On this subject see also Ph. A. Becker, *Clément Marot, sein Leben und seine Dichtung*, Munich, 1926, pp. 226–7, and M. Françon, *Clément Marot and Popular Songs*, in *Speculum*, 1950, XXV, pp. 247–8.

On the introduction of literary motifs into these compositions see D. Poirion, op. cit., p. 256, who comments: 'Une chose semble certaine: l'extrême popularité de tous les motifs poétiques attribuables à Alain Chartier, à la fois dans les chansonniers anonymes et dans les cours littéraires.'

18. See *Œuvres Lyriques*, Chanson III, n. 1; *Chanson* VIII, n. 2; *Chanson* IX, n. 3; *Chanson* XVIII, n. 1; *Chanson* XXVIII, n. 1; *Chanson* XXXI, n. 1.

19. See *Œuvres Lyriques*, Introduction, pp. 13, 15, 34 and Rollin, op. cit.

20. See Poirion, op. cit., ch. XV.

21. In the tradition of Chartier's *Belle Dame Sans Mercy*.

22. Cf. Garancières, in *Jardin de Plaisance*, no. 76 and its variant no. 403:

Las! pourquoy vis de mes yeulx
Vostre belle plaisant beaulté... (ed. cit., vol. I, fo. lxix)

and Machaut, no. 80, v. 2

Dame, mal vis vo doulx regard riant (ibid.)

23. One of the most frequent conceits encountered in the love poetry of the fifteenth century. Cf. Blosseville, a contemporary of Charles d'Orléans, 'Le cueur qui souloit estre mien,' (ed. G. Raynaud in *Rondeaux et autres poésies du XVe siècle*, Paris, SATF, 1889, no. CX); anon, 'Je m'en vois et mon cueur demeure', in *Jardin de Plaisance*, fo. lxxxviii; anon, 'Le cueur la suyt et mon oeil la regrete,' *Chasse et Depart Damours*, fo. B v; anon, 'Le corps s'en va et le cueur vous demeure/Lequel fera avec vous sa demeure,' ibid., fo. P ii; anon, 'Le cueur qui aultrefois fut mien, ibid. These last two may simply be variants of the first two.

24. The *Roman de la Rose* of course, and then through the works of Chartier, Charles d'Orléans etc. See Poirion, op. cit., for the use of allegory in the works of these poets.

25. Cf. Chartier,

Traistre plaisir et amoureuse joye,
Aspre doulceur, desconfort envieux...

in *Jardin de Plaisance*, no. 621, *Rondeau* v. Plagiarized by the mid fifteenth-century poet Jean Regnier. The version reproduced by Piaget in his edition of

Chartier's poems, Geneva, Droz, TLF, 1949, differs somewhat from the text presented by the *Jardin de Plaisance*. Cf. Chartier, ed. cit. p. 52, VI. *Chançon nouvele*:

> Triste plaisir et doulereuse joie,
> Aspre doulceur, reconfort ennuyeux...

26. Cf. G. Paris, *Chansons du XVe siècle*, Paris, SATF, 1875, no. LXXIV, v. 9:

> Qui bien actend bien luy en viendra

quoted in *Œuvres Lyriques*, p. 178 n. 1). Marot was later to mock this practice in his *coqs-à-l'âne*: See below, ch. VI, p. 238.

27. This *chanson* echoes a motif of the *Greek Anthology* (*A.P.*, 5.36) popular with many of the neo-Latin poets. It is therefore extremely difficult to say with certainty from which intermediary Marot received it. Mellin de Saint-Gelais composed a short poem on this theme which it is interesting to compare with Marot's. Here it is:

> Amour me fit, auquel je suis tenu
> Offre de trois, et me donna loisir
> De les cognoistre avant que les choisir.
> Puis, quand je suis au jugement venu,
> Toutes les trois ay prins et retenu
> Secrettement en egale fortune.
> Comme Paris, je n'en eusse aimé qu'une
> Mais trop de mal luy en est advenu.

(Quoted by Hutton, *The Greek Anthology in France*, op. cit., p. 319.)

28. The Psalm translations are unfortunately outside the scope of this book and we must forgo any detailed discussion of them, but on the versification of the *chansons* see *Œuvres Lyriques*, Introduction, pp. 36–40.

29. Cf. *Jardin de Plaisance*, no. 363, fo. xcv v°:

> Adieu, ma tres belle maistresse,
> Adieu, celle que j'ayme tant,
> Adieu vous dy, tout mon vivant
> Adieu, l'espoir de ma liesse.

See also, ibid., no. 473. There are scores of similar verses in the anthologies of fifteenth-century poetry.

30. See Poirion, op. cit., ch. VIII, and G. Raynaud, *Rondeaux et autres poésies du XVe siècle*, Paris, SATF, 1889, pp. xxxv-lv.

31. See *Œuvres Diverses*, Introduction, pp. 19–29 and Mayer and Bentley-Cranch, *Clément Marot, poète pétrarquiste*, art. cit.

32. On this subject see Poirion, op. cit., p. 618: 'Il reste beaucoup à faire pour établir clairement les rapports spirituels de la France et de l'Italie à partir du XIVe siècle. On sait déjà que nos poètes courtois connaissaient Pétrarque et Boccace. Mais leur intérêt n'allait pas aux mêmes aspects de l'œuvre qu'au temps de la Pléiade. On n'a pas l'impression qu'ils aient voulu imiter la poésie italienne. Si nous retrouvons chez eux des motifs pétrarquistes: le dialogue avec les yeux, la prison d'amour, l'allégorie de la nef, etc., n'oublions pas la source commune de cette littérature, l'art des trouvères!...on peut constater, chez nos poètes, une réaction de défense devant le goût italien, qu'ils associent à une mode outrée, répandue dans leur entourage par des gens d'ailleurs suspects d'intrigues et de cupidité. On n'admet pas encore facilement la superiorité esthétique de l'Italie.'

This is obviously a subject on which much remains to be done. There is perhaps something rather too easy about the *trouvère* argument and we have already seen the earliest date for the introduction of Petrarchism into French literature considerably pushed back by the recent articles of Mayer and Bentley-Cranch, and M. White. See also below, nn. 35, 40, 44, 46.

33. See below, pp. 156–7.

34. See Mayer and Bentley-Cranch, art. cit., pp. 37, 43. The text of the poem of Serafino is as follows:

> El cor te dedi, non chel tormentasti,
> Ma che fusse da te ben conservato;
> Servo ti fui, non che me abandonasti,
> Ma che fusse da te remeritato:
> Contento fui che schiavo m'acatasti,
> Ma non de tal moneta esser pagato:
> Or poi che regna in te poca pietade
> Non ti spiacia s'io torni in libertade.

(*Opere*, Venise, 1508)

For Bembo see *Prose e Rime di Pietro Bembo*, ed. Dionisotti, Turin, 1960, pp. 397–8.

35. Compare vv. 6–8 here with Sassoferrato's lines:

> Mi parto con sospir, come tu vede,
> E nel partir ti lasso il cuore in pegno
> Per farte universal mia erede

(*Capitolo di partenza ala sua signora*, vv. 16–18, in *Gloria d'Amore*, s.d.) But see also above, n. 23 for the same conceit in fifteenth-century French love poetry.

36. See below pp. 153–4.

37. Quoted in *Œuvres Diverses*, p. 123 n. 1, and by Mayer and Bentley-Cranch, art cit., pp. 43–44.

38. Quoted in *Œuvres Diverses*, ibid.

39. Christine de Pisan, *Œuvres Poétiques*, ed. M. Roy, Paris, SATF, 1886, vol. III, p. 249, vv. 28–31.

40. Since the *ballade* of Charles d'Orléans in which this phrase occurs was one of those published in the *Chasse et depart Damours*, Paris, 1509, fo. Riii + 2 v°, there can be no doubt that the source is a feasible one. Here is the first stanza as it appears in the *Chasse et depart Damours*:

> Si dieu plaist, briefvement l'année (sic)
> De ma tristesse passera
> Belle tres loyaument amée
> Et le beau temps se moustrera.
> Mais sçavez vous quant ce sera?
> Quant le doulx soleil gracieux
> De vostre beaulté entrera
> Par les fenestres de mes yeulx.

Champion, in his edition, *Charles d'Orléans*, *Poésies*, Paris, CFMA, 1923, vol. I, p. 67, reads 'la nuée' for 'l'année' in v. 1.

41. See Mayer and Bentley-Cranch, art. cit., p. 45. Suggested, apart from Latin sources, are Tebaldeo ('Non serano i capei sempre dor fino' and 'Gia de la vita mia breve e mortale'), Serafino ('Risguarda donna come el tempo vola'), and Chariteo ('Voi, che mi state sempre in mezo al core'). However, it is not at all certain that possible neo-Latin sources for this poem can be ruled out as the authors indicate (ibid., n. 5) on grounds of dating, and specifically, that neo-Latin influence is unlikely before 1527. This does not take into account the influence of the neo-Latin poets on the strambottistes themselves, and hence, indirectly, their influence on Marot.

42. Examples from Petrarch, the two sonnets by Chariteo, and the lines of

Sassoferrato, are quoted in full in *Œuvres Diverses*, pp. 93–94 and in art. cit., pp. 41–42.

43. From the *Capitolo di testamento che fa l'amante partendosi dalla sua diva*, vv. 13–18, in *Gloria d'Amore*, quoted in *Œuvres Diverses*, p. 77 n. 2 and art. cit., pp. 44–45.

44. See Chartier, *La Belle Dame Sans Mercy et les Poésies Lyriques*, ed. Piaget, Geneva, Droz, 1949, p. 56 no. 13. This poem is one of the sequence of fourteen in the *Jardin de Plaisance*, no. 621, *La Complainte du prisonnier d'amours faicte au jardin de plaisance*, XIV. There is a variant in the incipit:

Au feu! Au feu! qui trestout mon cueur ard...

This poem has not so far been indicated as a source for Marot. Mellin de Saint-Gelais composed a *Chanson* and a *Responce* on the same theme. See *Œuvres*, 1547, no. 83:

Au feu, au feu, venez moy secourir.

45. Quoted in *Œuvres Diverses*, p. 71 n. 1.

46. Quoted by Poirion, op. cit., p. 460 from B.N, ms. fr. 1727, fo. 21, this poem, which has as much chance of belonging to Grandson as to Chartier, appears in the Paris, G. Du Pré, 1526 edition of Chartier's works, fo. cvi vº, under the title *Complainte de gransson de maistre Alain Chartier*. It is obvious from this that the editor had no idea of who, or what, *gransson* was. The poem had also appeared in the Paris, Verard, 1492 edition. See also, on the same theme, *La Complaincte de Sainct Valentin gransson compilee par maistre Alain Charretier*, ed. 1526, fo. ci vº.:

Je voy le temps estre joyeulx
Je voy le temps renouveller
Je voy chanter, rire, dancer
Mais je me voy seul en tristesse
Pource que j'ay perdu mon per...   (vv. 3–7).

47. See *Œuvres Diverses*, p. 114 n. 1.

48. Abel Lefranc, *Le Roman d'Amour de Clément Marot* in *Grands Ecrivains français de la Renaissance*, Paris, Champion, 1914, pp. 1–61.

49. See *Epigrammes*, CII. The Diane of the title is Diane de Poitiers, mistress of the dauphin, the future Henri II.

50. Cf. Hutton, *The Greek Anthology in France*, op. cit., pp. 34–35: 'More easily measured but equally indirect, is its (The Anthology's) influence as a source of poetical ideas...Marot, who has a number of motives reminiscent of our epigrams...was also undoubtedly dependent on the Latin poets...Seldom, we notice, do the French poets draw these, or indeed any other subjects, from the Latin poets of their own country...but together looked towards Italy and the Ancients.'

51. For instance, *De la Rose envoyee pour Estreines*. See below, pp. 157–8 and n. 54.

52. See *Epigrammes*, where variants to the poems provide full details.

53. See *Epigrammes*, XXXV (*De Martin & Alix*); CLXXX (*De Martin & de Catin*); CCXXXVII (*De Alix & de Martin*); CCLXV (*De Robin & Catin*).

54. See, for instance, Pontano's *De Venere et Rosis*, in *Eridanus*, XXXIX (ed. B. Soldati, Florence, 1902, vol. II, pp. 369–70).

55. *Deffence et Illustration*, ed. cit., p. 110. An attack on Sebillet, whose *Art Poétique* had praised the wit of Marot's and Saint-Gelais's epigrams, and in particular, their *trait*.

56. On this genre see D. Wilson, *Descriptive Poetry in France from blason to baroque*, Manchester University Press, 1967.

57. On this subject see Mayer and Bentley-Cranch, art. cit., p. 33.

58. See V. L. Saulnier, *Les Elégies de Clément Marot*, op. cit.; *Œuvres Lyriques, Introduction*, pp. 16–21, 33–34.

59. Tibullus, III, IV. 73 (ed. Les Belles Lettres, Paris, 1955)
Nescis quid sit amor, iuuenis.

60. Ovid, *Heroides*, v, vv. 29–30 (ed. Les Belles Lettres, Paris, 1928)
Cum Paris Oenone poterit spirare relicta,
Ad fontem Xanthi uersa recurret aqua.

61. *Jardin de Plaisance*, no. 237, fo. cxvij v°. *Autre Rondel.*
Noir et tanné sont mes couleurs
De gris ne vueil plus porter
Car je ne puis plus supporter
Mes tres graves douleurs.

J'ay en amours tant de douleurs
Que contraint suis de porter
Noir et tanné.

Le noir est signe que je meurs
Pour ma loyaulté comporter
Et puis pour me reconforter
Le tanné si sera de pleurs.
Noir et tanné.

Marot himself wrote a *rondeau* (XLI) on this theme. Rabelais quoted the song in *Le Cinquième Livre*, XXIII.

GRAND LYRICISM: OFFICIAL POETRY

62. Jourda, op. cit., p. 89.

63. See *Œuvres Lyriques*, p. 134 n. 1.

64. See below, ch. VII, pp. 255–61.

65. Only Du Bellay's sonnet on the town of Lyons, *Regrets*, CXXXVII, has anything of the enthusiasm of Marot's two *Cantiques*. His sonnet on Paris, *Regrets*, CXXXVIII, vv. 12–14, and the subsequent ones, are bitter.

66. See below, ch. VII, p. 248.

67. Virgil, *Bucolics, Eclogue* IV, vv. 4–6 (ed. Les Belles Lettres, Paris, 1942),
Vltima Cumaei uenit iam carminis aetas;
magnus ab integro saeclorum nascitur ordo.
Iam redit et Virgo, redeunt Saturnia regna.

68. Virgil, ibid., vv. 26–36.

69. Du Bellay, *Deffence et Illustration*, ed. cit., p. 124.

70. See *Œuvres Lyriques*, p. 331 n. 2.

71. Jourda, op. cit., p. 87.

72. Catullus, ed. Les Belles Lettres, Paris, 1966, no. 62, v. 1.

73. Catullus, ibid., v. 30.

74. Cf. Catullus, ibid., no. 61, vv. 121–2, and editor's note (4) on them:
Ne diu taceat procax
Fescennina iocatio.

75. Catullus, ibid., no. 62, vv. 23–24.

76. See *Œuvres Lyriques*, p. 311 n. 1: '...dic mihi, si tibi esset elegam pomarium, optares illic nihil unquam gigni praeter flores: an malles, delapsis floribus, videre arbores maturis pomis gravidas?...
Ego rosam existimo feliciorem, quae marcescit in hominis manu, delectans

interim et oculos et nares, quam quae senescit in frutice: name et illic futurum erat, ut marcesseret.'

77. Catullus, ed. cit., no. 61, vv. 116–19.

78. Psalm 45, verses 3–8. See *Œuvres Lyriques*, p. 315 n. 1.

79. Psalm 19, verse 5, quoted in *Œuvres Lyriques*, ibid., n. 2. This same source is exploited again later in the poem. Cf. *Œuvres Lyriques*, p. 317 n. 1. Screech, *Marot Evangélique*, p. 120 n. 7, is mistaken when he asserts categorically that the source is in St Matthew, xx: 5–6. There is nothing remotely resembling these verses in Marot's poem.

80. See *Œuvres Lyriques*, p. 351 n. 1, p. 352 n. 1.

81. See ibid., pp. 344–5 n. 1. The passage is unfortunately too long to quote here.

82. Virgil, *Bucolics*, ed. cit., *Eclogue* I, vv. 53–58:

> Hinc tibi, quae semper, uicino, ab limite saepes
> Hyblaeis apibus florem depasta salicti
> saepe leui somnum suadebit inire susurro;
> hinc alta sub rupe canet frondator ad auras;
> nec tamen interea raucae, tua cura, palumbes,
> nec gemere aeria cessabit turtur ab ulmo.

83. *Regrets*, ed. Chamard, vol. II, p. 57:

> De la posterité je n'ay plus de souci,
> Ceste divine ardeur, je ne l'ay plus aussi,
> Et les Muses de moy, comme estranges, s'enfuyent.

V. SOCIETY VERSE IN THE MINOR GENRES

1. See *Epigrammes*, XXX, LXXXVII, XCII, CXCVII, CCXII, CCXIII, CCXIV, CCXV, CCXVI, CCXVII, CCXXIV.

2. See above, ch. III, pp. 92f.

3. See *Œuvres Diverses*, p. 225 n. 1 and 2. Marot had mentioned Hedart's demise when petitioning the duchesse de Lorraine on Vuyart's behalf for another horse in *Epitres*, XXIII.

4. On this genre and its cultivation in the Renaissance see Laumonier, *Ronsard, Poète Lyrique*, p. 265 n. 5 and H. Nais, *Les Animaux dans la poésie française de la Renaissance*, Paris, Didier, 1961.

5. These poems are the *Epitaphe d'un Chien*, XI; *Epitaphe d'un Petit Chien*, XXVII; *Epitaphe d'un Chat*, XXVIII. See Chamard, ed. crit., t. V.

6. See Laumonier, op. cit., p. 265.

7. Martial, *Epigrammes*, I. CIX (ed. Les Belles Lettres, Paris, 1961).

8. See Laumonier, ibid., n. 5.

9. Reproduced by Guiffrey, ed. cit., t. IV, p. 180.

10. Catullus, *Poésies*, ed. Les Belles Lettres, Paris, 1966, no. 3, vv. 1–3.

11. In the *Premiere Epistre de l'Amant Vert*, Lemaire imagined a situation in which the parrot, 'martyr amoureux' allowed himself to be eaten by a dog so great was its distress at its mistress's departure. See Frappier, éd. cit., p. 15, vv. 304 ff.

12. See *Œuvres Diverses*, p. 249 n. 1. Marot later composed an *Etrenne* (XVI) for Barbe de Maupas.

13. The *Etrennes* were originally forty-one in number. Later two more were published whose authenticity is probable but not certain beyond all doubt. See *Œuvres Diverses*, pp. 16 and 47.

VI. MAROT'S SATIRICAL POETRY

1. There is one study of this subject: C. Kinch, *La Poésie satirique de Clément Marot*, Paris, Boivin, 1940. It has in many respects been superseded though, by more recent research. On his religious satire see *La Religion de Marot*, op. cit.

2. On Henri Baude (1430?–1496) see Guy, *L'Ecole des Rhétoriqueurs*, paras. 26–30, and P. Champion, *Histoire Poétique du Quinzième Siècle*, Paris, Champion, 1923, vol. II, pp. 239–307. On Coquillart (?–1510) see the edition of his poetry by Charles d'Héricault, Paris, 1857.

3. Erasmus's *Praise of Folly*, his *Colloquies*, Ulrich von Hutten's *Epistulae Obscurorum Virorum*, Rabelais's *Pantagruel* and *Gargantua* and Des Périers's *Cymbalum Mundi* are of course the landmarks of this literature.

4. See below, p. 242.

5. See P. M. Smith, *The Anti-Courtier Trend*, op. cit., ch. II, p. 94 f.

6. See above, ch. I, p. 25, and below, ch. VII, p. 266.

7. See below, ch. VII, p. 268.

8. See *Œuvres Satiriques*, *Premier Coq a l'Asne*, v. 18:
    L'empereur est grand terrien.

9. See *Tiers Livre*, *Prologue de l'Auteur*. For an account of Rabelais's activities as a royal propagandist see A. Lefranc, *Etudes sur le Gargantua, le Pantagruel, et le Tiers Livre*, Paris, 1953, p. 361 f.

10. See Kinch, op. cit., pp. 49–68 for a list of such writers and a *résumé* of their criticisms. In Rabelais note *Pantagruel*, X; *Gargantua*, XX; *Tiers Livre*, XLII.

11. See above, ch. III, p. 110.

12. See *Œuvres Satiriques*, *2e Coq a l'Asne*, vv. 36–57:
    Et n'est bourreau que de Paris,
    Ny long proces que dudict lieu.

13. Mayer, *La Religion de Marot*, op. cit., pp. 107–8, makes this point forcefully and well.

14. See Erasmus, op. cit., para. LIX. I shall quote from the French translation, *Eloge de la Folie*, by Pierre de Nolhac, Paris, Garnier, 1964, pp. 76–78: 'Si les Souverains Pontifes, qui sont à la place du Christ, s'efforçaient de l'imiter dans sa pauvreté, ses travaux, sa sagesse, sa croix et son mépris de la vie...ne seraient-ils pas les plus malheureux des hommes? Celui qui emploie toutes ses ressources à acheter cette dignité ne doit-il pas la deffendre ensuite par le fer, le poison et la violence?...Tant de richesses, d'honneurs, de trophées, d'offices, dispenses, impôts, indulgences, tant de cnevaux, de mules, de gardes, et tant de plaisirs, vous voyez quel trafic, quelle moisson, quel océan de biens j'ai fait tenir en peu de mots!...ils sont fort enclins à prodiguer...les interdits, suspensions, aggravations, anathèmes, peintures vengeresses, et cette foudre terrible qui leur fait d'un seul geste précipiter les âmes au-dessous même du Tartare...

    L'Eglise chrétienne ayant été fondée par le sang, confirmée par le sang, accrue par le sang, ils continuent à en verser, comme si le Christ ne saurait pas défendre les siens à sa manière. La guerre est chose si féroce qu'elle est faite pour les bêtes et non pour les hommes...Les Papes, cependant, négligent tout pour en faire leur occupation principale.'

15. See Erasmus, ed. cit., *Lettre d'Erasme à Dorpius*, para. XVII, p. 108: 'Ce sont eux qui se moquent du grec, de l'hébreu et même du latin; et, bien qu'ils soient plus stupides qu'un cochon, et n'aient même pas le sens commun, qui

croient détenir l'arsenal de la sagesse. Ils tranchent, condamnent, prononcent, ne doutent de rien, n'ignorent rien. Et pourtant ces deux ou trois individus suscitent souvent de grandes tragédies. Qu'y a-t-il en effect de plus impudent, ou de plus obstiné que l'ignorance? Ils conspirent avec un grand zèle contre les belles-lettres...et ils craignent que, si les belles lettres renaissaient et que le monde se ressaisît, tels passent pour ne rien savoir qui jusqu'alors passaient communément pour ne rien ignorer. De là leurs clameurs, de là leur soulèvement, de là leur conjuration contre les hommes qui ont le culte des belles-lettres.'

Rabelais attacked the ignorance of the theologians in *Pantagruel*, VII, and caricatured them in *Gargantua* in the persons of Jobelin Bridé, Thubal Holoferne and Janotus de Bragmardo.

On the stage they were pilloried in the anonymous *Farce des Théologastres*, s.d., and in Marguerite de Navarre's *Farce de l'Inquisiteur*. See V. L. Saulnier, *Marguerite Navarre, Théâtre Profane*, Droz, 1946 and Jonker, *Le Protestantisme et le théâtre de langue française au XVIe siècle*, Groningen, 1939.

16. See below, ch. VII, p. 249.

17. See *Œuvres Satiriques*, p. 136 n. 2.

18. See Guy, *L'Ecole des Rhétoriqueurs*, paras. 342 and 557–8, on the anti-papal writings of these two authors.

19. *Quart Livre*, XLVIII–LIV.

20. *Apocalypse*, XVII.1–2: 'Alors un des sept anges qui avaient les sept coupes vint me parler, et me dit: Venez, et je vous montrerai la condamnation de la grande prostituée, qui est assise sur les grandes eaues;

'avec laquelle les rois de la terre se sont corrompus, et qui a enivré du vin de sa prostitution les habitants de la terre.' Quoted in *Epîtres*, p. 228 n. 4.

21. Ph. Schmidt, *Die Illustration der Lutherbibel*, Basle, 1962, p. 111.

22. See *Œuvres Satiriques*, p. 88 n. 8, for both these comments.

23. Erasmus, op. cit., LIV, pp. 68–69: 'Leur espèce est universellement exécrée, au point que leur rencontre fortuite passe pour porter malheur, et pourtant ils ont d'eux-mêmes une opinion magnifique. Ils estiment que la plus haute piété est de ne rien savoir, pas même lire. Quand ils braient comme des ânes dans les églises, en chantant leurs psaumes qu'ils numérotent sans les comprendre, ils croient réjouir les oreilles des personnes célestes. De leur crasse et de leur mendicité beaucoup se font gloire...' Erasmus goes on to mock their formalism and their 'petites traditions tout humaines'.

24. Eustorg de Beaulieu, *Les Divers Rapportz*, Lyons, 1537, *Le Septiesme Epitaphe*, fo. cxlij r°, vv. 10–11.

25. Rabelais, *Gargantua*, XL; *Tiers Livre*, XV, XIX, XXI–XXIII, XLVII.

26. Cf. Jonker, op. cit., p. 17: 'Les pièces écrites contre la vie luxurieuse et l'indignité des moines et des prêtres pullulent.'

27. Rabelais, *Pantagruel*, ed. cit., VII, p. 33: 'L'apparition de saincte Geltrude à une nonain de Poissy estant en mal d'enfant.'

28. Cf. Rabelais, *Gargantua*, ed. cit., XL, p. 139: 'un moyne (j'entends de ces ocieux moynes) ne laboure comme le paisant, ne guarde le pays comme l'homme de guerre, ne guerist les malades comme le medicin, ne presche ny endoctrine le monde comme le bon docteur evangelicque et pedagogue, ne porte les commoditez et choses necessaires à la republicque comme le marchant. Ce est la cause pourquoy de tous sont huez at abhorrys.'

29. Text in Guiffrey, *Les Œuvres de Clément Marot*, Paris, 1875–1931, vol. II, pp. 129–34.

30. See above, ch. I, p. 50. The relevant passage of Luther's treatise is quoted by Mayer in *Œuvres Satiriques*, p. 89 n. 2, as also the judgement of the

contemporary writer Jean Leblond that Marot's poem contained 'propos conformes à Luther'.

31. On Erasmus's position ('coelibatus ex se nullus habet laudem') see E. V. Telle, *Erasme de Rotterdam et le septième sacrement*, Geneva, Droz, 1954.

32. Cf. Erasmus, op. cit., LX, p. 79: 'Le commun des prêtres, dans la grande crainte de ne pas égaler en sainteté leurs prélats, combattent en véritables soldats pour la défense de leurs dîmes...

'Ils ont cela de commun avec les laiques qu'ils sont également âpres à la récolte de l'argent et habiles à imposer la reconnaissance de leurs droits.' Eustorg de Beaulieu's *Divers Rapportz* contains a *ballade, La Troisiesme Ballade*, fo. lij v°, which accuses them of laziness, avariciousness, loose morals, lack of faith and luxurious living. On the plays see Jonker, op. cit., pp. 18–25.

33. Rabelais, *Pantagruel*, VII.

34. Such an attack is perhaps implicit in the *envoy* to *Ballade* XII, *De Caresme*:

> Prince Chrestien, sans que nul te confonde,
> Presche chascun qu'à jeusner il se fonde,
> Non seulement de mectz bien delectables,
> Mais de peché et vice trop immunde
> En ces sainctz jours piteux et lamentables!
>
> (O.D., *Ballade* XII, vv. 31–35)

35. See *Œuvres Satiriques*, p. 68 n. 3.

36. See Screech, *Marot Evangélique*, Geneva, Droz, 1967, p. 37.

37. See *Pantagruel*, VII, p. 34: 'La Profiterolle des indulgences'; *Gargantua*, XIX, p. 66: 'Vultis etiam pardonos? Per diem, vos habebitis et nihil payabitis!'

38. See Mayer, *La Religion de Marot*, pp. 89 and 119, and *Œuvres Satiriques*, p. 111 n. 3.

39. Erasme, op. cit., XL and *Colloquies, Naufragium* and *Peregrinatio*; Rabelais, *Gargantua*, XXVII, p. 100; XLV, pp. 155–6.

40. See *La Religion de Marot*, p. 89.

41. On the problem of possible influences on Marot in this poem see *La Religion de Marot*, p. 122.

42. See below, ch. VII.

43. See above, ch. III, p. 99 and p. 111 for examples of realism and fantasy in the *Epîtres*.

44. Jean Lemaire de Belges, *Les Epîtres de l'Amant Vert*, ed. J. Frappier, Geneva, Droz, 1948 and Frappier, *Sur quelques emprunts de Clément Marot à Jean Lemaire de Belges*, in *Mélanges Huguet*, Paris, 1940, p. 170 f.

45. Jean Lemaire, ed. cit., p. 22, vv. 115–16.

46. Ibid., p. 21, vv. 91, 94. Compare also *Aeneid*, VI, vv. 557–8.

47. Ibid., p. 24, vv. 190–7. Compare *Aeneid*, VI, 554–5, 570–2, and Dante, *Hell*, IX, 34–60.

48. *Tiers Livre*, XLII.

49. Jean Lemaire, ed. cit., p. 20, vv. 73–80. See *Aeneid*, VI, 552–4.

50. On this work see Guy, *L'Ecole des Rhétoriqueurs*, paras. 235–56.

51. Jean Lemaire, ed. cit., p. 25, vv. 234–42. For Virgil's placing of Minos see *Aeneid*, VI, 431–3, and for Dante's, *Hell*, V, 4–24.

52. See *Œuvres Satiriques*, p. 56 n. 3, and Mayer, *Clément Marot et le Grand Minos*, in BHR, 1957, XIX, pp. 482–4.

53. Jean Lemaire, ed. cit., p. 20, vv. 62–64.

54. See *Œuvres Satiriques*, p. 63 n. 1 and p. 64 n. 3.

55. *Œuvres Satiriques*, *L'Enfer*, vv. 75, 435.

56. Jean Lemaire, ed. cit., p. 26. In fact it is Mercure who makes the state-

ment of the parrot's past life to Minos, vv. 249–58, but the parrot is brought before the judge for his inspection.

57. Œuvres Satiriques, L'Enfer, vv. 318–38.

58. Jean Lemaire, ed. cit., p. 25, vv. 225–33.

59. See Œuvres Satiriques, Introduction, pp. 8–14, 19–25, and Mayer, Coq-à-l'Ane, in French Studies, 1962, XVI, pp. 1–13.

60. Guiffrey, Les Œuvres de Clement Marot, vol. II, p. 267: 'Pour ceste cause, qui vouldra faire une œuvre de longue durée ne preigne son subiect sur telles choses basses & particulieres.'

61. See Œuvres Satiriques, p. 120 n. 3. Prêtre Martin chanted and made his own responses.

62. See above, ch. I, p. 55.

63. Pantagruel, VII. Des Pois aux Lards, cum commento is one of the titles in the Librairie de Sainct Victor.

64. Note, however, the reservations expressed on the authenticity of this poem and its attribution in Epitres, pp. 60–61.

65. Du Bellay, ed. cit., vol. V, Divers Jeux Rustiques, XX, Contre les Pétrarquistes; Ronsard, Meslanges and Bocage, of 1554, where the same reaction appears in many poems.

66. On the Querelle des Amyes see A. Lefranc, Le Tiers Livre de Rabelais et la Querelle des Femmes, in Grands Ecrivains de la Renaissance, Paris, 1914; E. V. Telle, Marguerite de Navarre et la Querelle des Femmes, Paris, Droz, 1937.

67. Du Bellay in Regrets LXXXV and LXXXVI and Ronsard in his Elegie en forme d'invective. On these poems see P. M. Smith, The Anti-Courtier Trend, op. cit., p. 177.

68. Œuvres Satiriques, IV, vv. 42–44.

69. The subject is a traditional one. However, Marot's last two lines are a textual borrowing from Henri Baude's Les Lamentations Bourrien. But Baude took 120 lines to cover the ground which is encompassed by Marot's art in 10. For Baude's poem see the edition of his work by Quicherat, Paris, 1856, pp. 28–35.

70. Martial, Epigrammes, ed. cit., III, XXVI:

> Praedia solus habes et solus, Candide, nummos,
> aurea solus habes, murrina solus habes,
> Massica solus habes, et Opimi Caecuba solus,
> et cor solus habes, solus et ingenium.
> Omnia solus habes-nec me puta uelle negare—
> uxorem sed habes, Candide, cum populo.

71. Jourda, op. cit., p. 128. Cf. Kinch, op. cit., p. 259. Lefranc, in contrast, when describing L'Enfer, spoke of its 'éloquence si saisissante', in Grands Ecrivains Français de la Renaissance, p. 4.

VII. RENAISSANCE AND REFORMATION ATTITUDES IN MAROT'S POETRY

1. There are two recent studies on this subject: C. A. Mayer, La Religion de Marot, Geneva, Droz, 1960 and M. A. Screech, Marot Evangélique, Geneva, Droz, 1967.

The former is the more comprehensive of the two. It gives the relevant biographical and historical background to the question together with a wealth of documentary evidence of contemporary reaction to the reformists, and of judicial and other proceedings instituted against them. It also examines Marot's satire of the Catholic Church and finally his religious poetry itself. While accepting the attraction Marot felt for the new ideas, it stresses the humanistic and humanitarian basis of Marot's evangelism.

Screech's essay sets out to supplement the third part of Mayer's book by studying the scriptural allusions in Marot's poetry. It reduces to insignificant proportions the underlying humanism of Marot's evangelism. Shifts of perspective and other inconsistencies make this a work to be used with great caution. Thus, while insisting that the problem can only be studied *à la lumière de l'époque*, the author more often than not rejects contemporary charges and indictments of Lutheranism on the grounds that what was meant then by Lutheranism is not what is meant now by Lutheranism, and does not correspond to modern ideas of what Lutheranism *should* have been. To what perspective does the statement, p. 18—'Luther n'est pas luthérien' belong, and how far does it advance us? Neither does the author accept the Pope and the Sorbonne as the norms of current orthodoxy (p. 55, p. 76—'Pour admettre que Luther soit schismatique, il faut accepter sans réserves les autorités qui le condamnent. Or, ces autorités sont le pape et la Sorbonne') for a minority of Gallicans and evangelists challenged the one or the other. One would like to know what other norms of orthodoxy there were at the time, and why it was, if the Pope and the Sorbonne were not widely considered to be so, that the evangelists and reformers should have disputed their orthodoxy! There are many other instances of this kind in the work.

2. Rabelais, *Pantagruel*, VIII.

3. Du Bellay, *La Musagnoeomachie* in *Œuvres*, ed. Chamard, vol. IV, p. 6, v. 56 and Ronsard, *Ode à Madame Marguerite*, in *Œuvres*, ed. Laumonier, STFM, t. 1, p. 72. See also Laumonier, *Ronsard, poète lyrique*, p. 19 n. 6 and p. 64 n. 3.

4. This is why it seems impossible to reach a sound conclusion on Marot's attitudes to humanism and religion if one resolutely ignores his satire and its humanistic emphasis. See above, ch. VI.

5. Screech, op. cit., p. 96.

6. See Mayer, *La Religion*, p. 48, and pp. 71–92.

7. Quoted and discussed by Mayer, op. cit., pp. 98–100. We have given vv. 1–11 of the epistle which is there reproduced in its entirety.

8. See above, ch. I, p. 16.

9. Quoted by Mayer, *La Religion de Marot*, p. 98, vv. 7–11. See also *Epîtres*, IX, p. 125, variants.

10. See Mayer, *La Religion*, ibid., and *Epîtres*, IX, p. 125 n. 2.

11. See *Œuvres Diverses*, LXXXVI, *Chant-Royal* I, pp. 175–8.

12. See above, ch. VI, n. 34.

13. Here is the text of the Villon passage:

> Car, ou soit ly sains apostolles,
> D'aubes vestus, d'amys coeffez,
> Qui ne saint fors saintes estolles
> Dont par le col prent ly mauffez.
>
> (*Le Testament*, ed. Foulet, CFMA, vv. 385–8)

14. See above, ch. VI, pp. 212–13.

15. Quoted by Mayer, *La Religion*, p. 102. Vv. 139–44.

16. Mayer, *La Religion*, p. 103. Vv. 117–24. See also *Epîtres*, XXXVI, p. 201 n. 1.

17. Philippians II. 10 and Matthew VII.15. (Unless otherwise stated, and for the convenience of the general reader, verse numbers are those of the Authorized Version).

18. One would nevertheless not go as far as Screech when he says, op. cit., p. 18: 'Cette confession de foi n'est point ambigue...Au contraire, avec une étonnante hardiesse, Marot s'avoue luthérien.' Even less would one endorse the following statement: 'il (Marot) nie être "luthérien" précisément pour montrer qu'il l'est au sens moderne du mot.' This attributes to the poet a prescience little short of miraculous and is difficult, to say the least, to reconcile with the author's declared intention to eschew anachronism! See above, n. 1.

19. We exclude from this discussion all those poems which have been classed by the latest editor as of doubtful authenticity. See Mayer, La Religion, p. 104.

20. Colossians, II.8 and Erasmus, Adnotationes, 3rd ed. on St Matthew, II.3: 'doctrina Christi...nunc impedita, spinosa, ne dicam tenebricosa facta, partim admixtu legum, ac disciplinarum humanarum.' Quoted by Mayer, Œuvres Lyriques, p. 152 n. 2.

21. All the following variants from this edition are given by Mayer in La Religion de Marot, p. 127.

22. See above, ch. VI, p. 215 and Mayer, La Religion, p. 124.

23. See W. G. Moore, La Réforme Allemande et la Littérature Française: Recherches sur la notoriété de Luther en France, Strasbourg, 1930, p. 180–1: 'Il se peut que Marot, dans l'entourage de la Reine de Navarre ait lu des traductions de Luther. Il est certain qu'elles n'ont pas fait impression sur lui au point de l'inciter à des développements poétiques du même genre. Il a reflété les idées que l'on débattait autour de lui; la vraie source de son inspiration poétique était ailleurs. On le voit bien aux mentions mêmes du nom de Luther, qui ne sont pas rares dans son œuvre. Aucune n'indique un commerce suivi avec l'œuvre du réformateur.'
See also Mayer, La Religion, p. 127: 'En ce qui concerne Luther, il est fort douteux que Marot l'ait lu.'

24. Screech, op. cit., p. 61.

25. Mayer, op. cit., pp. 66–68 and pp. 127–9.

26. Mayer, ibid., pp. 127–8. Marot's reply confirms what Malingre has said in his letter. Cf. Mayer, ibid., p. 128 n. 110:
> ...car tu es l'excellence
> Et le premier des Jacobins de Bloys
> Qui tous estats à Jesus assemblois
> Par tes sermons et ta vie angelique:
> En quoi faisant à saint Paul ressemblois
> Cent mille fois plus qu'à Saint Dominique.

27. Screech, op. cit., p. 68 n. 39 dismisses it without examination.

28. The same idea was also to be expressed, at an unknown date, by Marguerite de Navarre in those poems grouped together under the heading Dernières Poésies and published by A. Lefranc, Paris, 1896. Cf. p. 227:
> Mais pour juger des mauvais et des bons
> Ce qui en est, fault que nous regardons
> Qui le plus près de l'Escripture touche,
> Car l'Evangile est la pierre de touche
> Ou de bon or se congnoist la valeur
> Et du plus bas la foiblesse et paleur...

The same sentiment finds expression in the Heptaméron, Paris, Garnier, 1964,

p. 304: 'depuis l'heure que l'entendis, ne vouluz croire en parolle de prescheur, si je ne la trouve conforme à celle de Dieu, qui est la vraye touche pour sçavoir les parolles vraies ou mensongeres.'

29. See above, ch. VI, p. 146 and *Epitres*, XXXVI, p. 206 n. 1.

30. Indicated by Screech, op. cit., pp. 84–92. Not all of these correspondences are equally convincing as *sources*.

31. See above, ch. I, p. 26.

32. Or its revision, not later than March 1538. See above, loc. cit.

33. *Epitres*, XLV, vv. 55–57. See above, ch. VI, p. 242.

34. See above, ch. VI, p. 205 and n. 21 for the relevance of this image.

35. See M. Jeanneret, *Marot traducteur des Psaumes entre le Néo-Platonisme et la Réforme*, in BHR, 1965, pp. 629–43.

36. Vv. 39–52, vv. 79–80. Text in Jeanneret, art. cit., pp. 633 and 634.

37. See above, ch. I, p. 51.

38. Quoted by A. Lefranc, *Le Platonisme et la littérature en France*, in *Grands Ecrivains Français de la Renaissance*, pp. 125–6.

39. See Jeanneret, art. cit., p. 636. Vv. 158–65.

40. It will be remembered that Calvin had already obtained, in what circumstances is unknown, the text of thirteen of Marot's Psalm translations which he published in Strasburg, 1539 under the title *Aulcuns pseaulmes et cantiques mys en chant*. Cf. Jeanneret, art. cit., p. 629.

41. From Calvin's *Excuse...à Messieurs les Nicodemites*, quoted by Jeanneret, art. cit., p. 639.

42. Text in Jeanneret, art. cit., p. 640. Vv. 29–40.

43. Cf. Mayer, *La Religion de Marot*, p. 137 and Jeanneret, art. cit., p. 640: 'il (Marot) envisage sa traduction dans la perspective de l'Evangélisme pratiqué largement dans les années 1530 et, après 1540, dans quelques groupes restés attachés à un passé révolu.'

44. *Epitres*, XXXVI, vv. 160–2:

> Où certains folz feirent choses trop viles
> Et de scandalle, helas, au grand ennuy,
> Au detriment & à la mort d'aultruy.

45. Such is the influence of her *Miroir de l'Ame Pécheresse* alleged by Screech, op. cit., p. 78, to have been important in the composition of Marot's *Second Chant de l'Amour fugitif*.

46. Cf. Guy, *Clément Marot et son école*, para. 297.

47. *Epitres*, XXXV, v. 56.

48. See above, ch. VI, pp. 208–10.

49. See above, ch. I, pp. 43–8.

VIII. CONCLUSION: MAROT AND THE *PLÉIADE*

1. For the main details of the programme of the *Pléiade* see Du Bellay, *Deffence et Illustration de la Langue francoyse*, especially the second book, and Ronsard's *Preface aux Odes de 1550* which is to be found in any edition of the complete works.

2. See Laumonier, *Ronsard, Poète Lyrique*, p. 638 f.

3. *Epitres*, LVI, vv. 83–84.

ABBREVIATIONS

All references to the text of Marot's Poems, unless otherwise stated, are to the *Œuvres Complètes de Clément Marot*, ed. C. A. Mayer, University of London, The Athlone Press, 5 vols., 1958–. The following abbreviations are used in connection with this edition:

Ep.	*Les Epîtres*, 1958	*O.D.*	*Oeuvres Diverses*, 1966
O.S.	*Oeuvres Satiriques*, 1962	*Epigr.*	*Les Epigrammes*, 1970
O.L.	*Oeuvres Lyriques*, 1964	*var.*	*variante(s)*

Abbreviations used in the Notes (*Journals, Series, etc.*)

A.P.	*Anthologia Palatina*
BdB	*Bulletin du Bibliophile et du Bibliothécaire*
BHR	*Bibliothèque d'Humanisme et Renaissance*
Bibliographie	C. A. Mayer, *Bibliographie des Oeuvres de Clément Marot*, I: *Les Manuscrits*; II: *Les Editions*.
CFMA	*Classiques Français du Moyen Age*
FM	*Français Moderne*
PUF	*Presses Universitaires de France*
RdM	*Revue de Musicologie*
RHLF	*Revue d'Histoire Littéraire de la France*
RSS	*Revue du Seizième Siècle*
SATF	*Société des Anciens Textes Français*
SEDES	*Société d'Edition d'Enseignement Supérieur*
SFELT	*Société française d'éditions littéraires et techniques*
SP	*Studies in Philology*
STFM	*Société des Textes Français Modernes*
TLF	*Textes Littéraires Français*

SELECT BIBLIOGRAPHY OF WORKS CONSULTED

Classification

I. MODERN EDITIONS OF MAROT'S WORKS

II. RELATED FRENCH TEXTS

III. CRITICAL WORKS ON MAROT

   (a) *Complete Studies*
   (b) *Bibliography*
   (c) *Biography*
   (d) *Genres*
   (e) *Inspiration, Influences*
   (f) *Versification*
   (g) *Iconography*

IV. CRITICAL WORKS ON RELATED TEXTS

I. MODERN EDITIONS OF MAROT'S WORKS

GUIFFREY, G., *Œuvres de Clément Marot*, Paris, 1875–1931, 5 vols. In no way a critical edition, but still useful for those works which have not yet appeared in Professor Mayer's edition.

MAYER, C. A., *Œuvres Complètes de Clément Marot*, University of London, The Athlone Press, 1958–.
1. *Les Epîtres.*
2. *Œuvres Satiriques.*
3. *Œuvres Lyriques*
4. *Œuvres Diverses.*
5. *Les Epigrammes.*
6. *Traductions* (awaited).

—, *Clément Marot* (choix de textes), Paris, Pierre Seghers, Ecrivains d'hier et d'aujourd'hui, 16, 1964. Second edition 1969.

II. RELATED FRENCH TEXTS

CHARLES D'ORLEANS, *Poésies*, ed. P. Champion, Paris, CFMA, 1923, 1927.

CHARTIER, ALAIN, *Les Faictz et Dictz*, Paris, G. du Pré, 1526.

—, *La Belle Dame Sans Mercy et les Poésies Lyriques*, ed. A. Piaget, Geneva, Droz, TLF, 1949.

La Chasse et Depart Damours, Paris, Vérard, 1509.

DU BELLAY, JOACHIM, *Œuvres*, ed. H. Chamard, Paris, STFM, 1908–1931.

—, *La Deffence et Illustration de la Langue Francoyse*, ed. Chamard, Paris, STFM, 1948.

Le Jardin de Plaisance et Fleur de Rethorique, ed. E. Droz and A. Piaget, Paris, SATF, 1910, 1925.

LEMAIRE DE BELGES, JEAN, *Les Epîtres de l'Amant Vert*, ed. J. Frappier, Geneva, Droz, TLF, 1948.

MARGUERITE DE NAVARRE, *Dernières Poésies*, ed. A. Lefranc, Paris, 1896.

—, *Théâtre Profane*, ed. V. L. Saulnier, Paris, 1946.

—, *L'Heptaméron*, ed. M. François, Paris, Garnier, 1964.

PELETIER, JACQUES, *Art Poétique*, ed. A. Boulenger, Paris, 1930.

RABELAIS, *Œuvres*, ed. Plattard, Paris, Les Belles Lettres, 1946–48.

Recueil Trepperel, ed. E. Droz, Paris, 1938 (vol. I); Geneva, 1961 (vol. II).

RONSARD, PIERRE DE, *Œuvres Complètes*, ed. Laumonier, Paris, STFM, 1924–.

SEBILLET, THOMAS, *Art Poétique françoys*, ed. F. Gaiffe, Paris, STFM, 1910.

VILLON, FRANÇOIS, *Œuvres*, ed. L. Foulet, Paris, CFMA, 1932.

III. CRITICAL WORKS ON MAROT

(a) *Complete Studies*

GUY, H., *Clément Marot et son école* (vol. II of the *Histoire de la poésie française au XVIe siècle*), Paris, Champion, 1926.

VILLEY, P., *Marot et Rabelais*, Paris, Champion, 1923.

(b) *Bibliography*

MAYER, C. A., *Le Texte de Marot*, in BHR, 1952–1953, vols XIV, XV.

—, *Bibliographie des Œuvres de Clément Marot*, Geneva, Droz, 1954, 2 vols.

—, *Les Œuvres de Clément Marot; L'Economie de l'édition critique*, in BHR, 1967, vol. XXIX.

(c) *Biography*

MAYER, C. A., *Le Départ de Marot de Ferrare*, in BHR, 1956, vol. XVIII.

MAYER, C. A., *Clément Marot et le grand Minos*, in BHR, 1957, vol. XIX.

—, *Clément Marot et le général de Caen*, in BHR, 1958, vol. XX.

—, *Clément Marot et le docteur Bouchart*, in BHR, 1959, vol. XXI.

—, *Marot et 'Celle Qui Fut S'Amye'*, in BHR, 1966, vol. XXVIII.

(d) *Genres*

JEANNERET, M., *Marot traducteur des Psaumes entre le néo-platonisme et la Réforme*, in BHR, 1965, vol. XXVII.

LESURE, F., *Autour de Clément Marot et ses Musiciens*, in RdM, 1951, pp. 109–19.

MAYER, C. A., *Coq-à-l'âne: Définition-Invention-Attributions*, in *French Studies*, 1962, vol. XVI.

—, *Le Premier Sonnet Français: Marot, Mellin de Saint-Gelais et Jean Bouchet*, in RHLF, 1967, no. 3.

SAULNIER, V. L., *Les Elégies de Clément Marot*, Paris, SEDES, 1952.

VIANEY, J., *Les Epîtres de Marot*, Paris, Nizet, 1962.

(e) *Inspiration, Influences*

FRAPPIER, J., *Sur quelques emprunts de Clément Marot à Jean Lemaire de Belges*, in *Mélanges Huguet*, Paris, 1940.

MAYER, C. A., *La Religion de Marot*, Geneva, Droz, 1960.

—, *Clément Marot et l'archaisme*, in Cahiers de l'Association Internationale des Etudes Françaises, 1967, no. 19.

MAYER, C. A., and BENTLEY-CRANCH, D., *Clément Marot, poète pétrarquiste*, in BHR, 1966, vol. XXVIII.

NICHOLS, S. G., *Marot, Villon and the Roman de la Rose*, in *SP*, 1966, LXII, 2, pp. 135–43; 1967, LXIV, 1, pp. 25–43.

(f) *Versification*

CAMPROUX, C., *Langue et métrique. A propos du décasyllabe des Epîtres de Marot*, in FM, 1964, pp. 194–205.

VIANEY, J., *L'Art du vers chez Cl. Marot*, in *Mélanges Lefranc*, Paris, 1936, pp. 44–57.

(g) *Iconography*

BENTLEY-CRANCH, D., *A Portrait of Clément Marot by Corneille de Lyon*, in BHR, 1963, t. 25, pp. 174–7.

—, *Further additions to the iconography of Clément Marot*, in BHR, 1964, t. 26, pp. 418–23.

IV. CRITICAL WORKS ON RELATED FRENCH TEXTS

GUY, H., *L'Ecole des Rhétoriqueurs* (vol. I of the *Histoire de la poésie française au XVIe siècle*), Paris, 1910.

LAUMONIER, P., *Ronsard, Poète Lyrique*, Paris, 1923.

LEFRANC, A., *Grands Ecrivains Français de la Renaissance*, Paris, 1914.

MAYER, C. A., and BENTLEY-CRANCH, D., *Le Premier Pétrarquiste Français—Jean Marot*, in BHR, 1965, vol. XXVII.

POIRION, D., *Le Poète et le Prince. L'Evolution du lyrisme courtois de Guillaume de Machaut à Charles d'Orléans*, Paris, PUF, 1965.

SCOLLEN, C. M., *The Birth of the Elegy in France*, Geneva, Droz, 1967.

SMITH, P. M., *The Anti-Courtier Trend in Sixteenth Century French Literature*, Geneva, Droz, 1966.

VIANEY, J., *Le Pétrarquisme en France au XVIe siècle*, Montpellier, 1909.

—, *Les Odes de Ronsard*, Paris, SFELT, 1946.

WEBER, H., *La Création Poétique au XVIe siècle en France*, Paris, 1956.

WHITE, M., *Petrarchism in the French Rondeau before 1527*, in *French Studies*, 1968, vol. XXII.

INDEX

Excluded from this index are personifications, place names, names occurring in minor references in the notes and Clément Marot himself.